THE **COMPLETE WORKS** OF **SWAMI VIVEKANANDA**

VOLUME VII

Discovery Publisher

2019, Discovery Publisher

No part of this book may be reproduced in any form or by any electronic or mechanical means including information storage and retrieval systems, without permission in writing from the publisher.

Author: Swami Vivekananda

616 Corporate Way, Suite 2-4933
Valley Cottage, New York, 10989
www.discoverypublisher.com
edition@discoverypublisher.com
facebook.com/discoverypublisher
twitter.com/discoverypb

New York • Paris • Dublin • Tokyo • Hong Kong

TABLE OF CONTENTS

Inspired Talks — 3

I	4	XXI	24
II	5	XXII	25
III	6	XXIII	26
IV	7	XXIV	26
V	9	XXIV	27
VI	10	XXV	28
VII	11	XXVI	29
VIII	11	XXVII	30
IX	12	XXVIII	31
X	13	XXIX	32
XI	14	XXX	33
XII	15	XXXI	34
XIII	17	XXXII	35
XIV	17	XXXIII	35
XV	18	XXXIV	36
XVI	19	XXXV	37
XVII	20	XXXVI	39
XVIII	21	XXXVII	40
XIX	22	XXXVIII	42
XX	23	XXXIX	43

XL	44	XLII	47
XLI	45	XLIII	49

Conversations And Dialogues — 52

FROM THE DIARY OF A DISCIPLE (SHRI SHARAT CHANDRA CHAKRAVARTY, B.A.) — 54

I	54	XXII	110
II	56	XXIII	111
III	60	XXIV	113
IV	63	XXV	114
V	65	XXVI	116
VI	67	XXVII	118
VII	70	XXVIII	119
VIII	73	XXIX	122
IX	75	SHRI PRIYA NATH SINHA	124
X	80	XXX	124
XI	82	XXXI	125
XII	84	MISCELLANEOUS	128
XIII	87	Vengeance Of History (Mrs. Wright) XXXII	128
XIV	88		
XV	89	Religion, Civilisation, And Miracles (The Appeal-Avalanche) XXXIII	129
XVI	94		
XVII	96	Religious Harmony (The Detroit Free Press, February 14, 1894) XXXIV	133
XVIII	99		
XIX	104	Fallen Women (The Detroit Tribune, March 17, 1894) XXXV	134
XX	105		
XXI	107		

Translation of writings — 138

MEMOIRS OF EUROPEAN TRAVEL	140
I	140
II	173
ADDENDA	184

Notes Of Class Talks And Lectures — 190

ON ART	192
ON MUSIC	192
ON MANTRA AND MANTRA-CHAITANYA	192
ON CONCEPTIONS OF GODHEAD	192
ON FOOD	192
ON SANNYASA AND FAMILY LIFE	193
ON QUESTIONING THE COMPETENCY OF THE GURU	193
SHRI RAMAKRISHNA: THE SIGNIFICANCE OF HIS LIFE AND TEACHINGS	193
ON SHRI RAMAKRISHNA AND HIS VIEWS	194
SHRI RAMAKRISHNA: THE NATION'S IDEAL	195
NOTES OF LECTURES MERCENARIES IN RELIGION	195
THE DESTINY OF MAN	197
REINCARNATION	198
COMPARATIVE THEOLOGY	199
THE SCIENCE OF YOGA	201

Epistles-Third Series — 206

I — SHRI BALARAM BOSE	208
II — SHRI BALARAM BOSE	208
III — SHRI BALARAM BOSE	209
IV — SHRI BALARAM BOSE	209
V — GUPTA	210
VI — SHRI BALARAM BOSE	211
VII — ATUL BABU	211
VIII — ADHYAPAKJI	211
IX — ADHYAPAKJI	212
X — ADHYAPAKJI	213
XI — MRS. TANNATT WOODS	215
XII — ADHYAPAKJI	215
XIII — MRS. WOODS	216
XIV — SISTER	216
XV — BROTHER	216
XVI — PROFESSOR	217
XVII — SISTER	217
XVIII — SISTER	218
XIX — ADHYAPAKJI	219
XX — ADHYAPAKJI	219
XXI — ADHYAPAKJI	220
XXII — ADHYAPAKJI	221
XXIII — MR. BHATTACHARYA	221

XXIV — KALI	224
XXV — BROTHER SHIVANANDA	226
XXVI — BRAHMANANDA	228
XXVII — ALASINGA	228
XXVIII — BROTHER	229
XXIX — DEAR__	229
XXX — RAKHAL	229
XXXI — ALASINGA	230
XXXII — DEAR	230
XXXIII — SISTER	233
XXXIV — SHASHI	234
XXXV — ADHYAPAKJI	234
XXXVI — MISS NOBLE	234
XXXVII — FRIEND AND BROTHER	235
XXXVIII — SHARAT CHANDRA CHAKRAVARTI	235
XXXIX — MRS. BULL	236
XL — SHUDDHANANDA	237
XLI — MISS NOBLE	238
XLII — MISS NOBLE	239
XLIII — MADAM	240
XLIV — STURDY	240
XLV — MRS. LEGGETT	242
XLVI — MOTHER	243
XLVII — MARGOT	243
XLVIII — MOTHER	243

IL — MOTHER	244
L — MOTHER	244
LI — MR. LEGGETT	245
LII — AUNT ROXY	245
LIII — ALBERTA	245

THE **COMPLETE WORKS** OF SWAMI VIVEKANANDA

VOLUME VII

INSPIRED TALKS

I

RECORDED BY MISS S. E. WALDO, A DISCIPLE

This day marks the beginning of the regular teaching given daily by Swami Vivekananda to his disciples at Thousand Island Park. We had not yet all assembled there, but the Master's heart was always in his work, so he commenced at once to teach the three or four who were with him. He came on this first morning with the Bible in his hand and opened to the Book of John, saying that since we were all Christians, it was proper that he should begin with the Christian scriptures.

WEDNESDAY, June 19, 1895.

"In the beginning was the Word, and the Word was with God, and the Word was God." The Hindu calls this Mâyâ, the manifestation of God, because it is the power of God. The Absolute reflecting through the universe is what we call nature. The Word has two manifestations — the general one of nature, and the special one of the great Incarnations of God — Krishna, Buddha, Jesus, and Ramakrishna. Christ, the special manifestation of the Absolute, is known and knowable. The absolute cannot be known: we cannot know the Father, only the Son. We can only see the Absolute through the "tint of humanity", through Christ.

In the first five verses of John is the whole essence of Christianity: each verse is full of the profoundest philosophy.

The Perfect never becomes imperfect. It is in the darkness, but is not affected by the darkness. God's mercy goes to all, but is not affected by their wickedness. The sun is not affected by any disease of our eyes which may make us see it distorted. In the twenty-ninth verse, "taketh away the sin of the world" means that Christ would show us the way to become perfect. God became Christ to show man his true nature, that we too are God. We are human coverings over the Divine; but as the divine Man, Christ and we are one.

The Trinitarian Christ is elevated above us; the Unitarian Christ is merely a moral man; neither can help us. The Christ who is the Incarnation of God, who has not forgotten His divinity, that Christ can help us, in Him there is no imperfection. These Incarnations are always conscious of their own divinity; they know it from their birth. They are like the actors whose play is over, but who, after their work is done, return to please others. These great Ones are untouched by aught of earth; they assume our form and our limitations for a time in order to teach us; but in reality they are never limited, they are ever free....

Good is near Truth, but is not yet Truth. After learning not to be disturbed by evil, we have to learn not to be made happy by good. We must find that we are beyond both evil and good; we must study their adjustment and see that they are both necessary.

The idea of dualism is from the ancient Persians. [6]* Really good and evil are one (Because they are both chains and products of Maya.) and are in our own mind. When the mind is self-poised, neither good nor bad affects it. Be perfectly free; then neither can affect it, and we enjoy freedom and bliss. Evil is the iron chain, good is the gold one; both are chains. Be free, and know once for all that there is no chain for you. Lay hold of the golden chain to loosen the hold of the iron one, then throw both away. The thorn of evil is in our flesh; take another thorn from the same bush and extract the first thorn; then throw away both and be free....

In the world take always the position of the giver. Give everything and look for no return. Give love, give help, give service, give any little thing you can, but keep out barter. Make no conditions, and none will be imposed. Let us give out of our own bounty, just as God gives to us.

The Lord is the only Giver, all the men in the world are only shopkeepers. Get His cheque, and it must be honoured everywhere.

"God is the inexplicable, inexpressible essence of love", to be known, but never defined.

***

In our miseries and struggles the world seems to

us a very dreadful place. But just as when we watch two puppies playing and biting we do not concern ourselves at all, realising that it is only fun and that even a sharp nip now and then will do no actual harm, so all our struggles are but play in God's eyes. This world is all for play and only amuses God; nothing in it can make God angry.

***

"Mother! In the sea of life my bark is sinking. The whirlwind of illusion, the storm of attachment is growing every moment.

My five oarsmen (senses) are foolish, and the helmsman (mind) is weak.

My bearings are lost, my boat is sinking. O Mother! Save me!"

"Mother, Thy light stops not for the saint or the sinner; it animates the lover and the murderer." Mother is ever manifesting through all. The light is not polluted by what it shines on, nor benefited by it. The light is ever pure, ever changeless. Behind every creature is the "Mother", pure, lovely, never changing. "Mother, manifested as light in all beings, we bow down to Thee!" She is equally in suffering, hunger, pleasure, sublimity. "When the bee sucks honey, the Lord is eating." Knowing that the Lord is everywhere, the sages give up praising and blaming. Know that nothing can hurt you. How? Are you not free? Are you not Âtman? He is the Life of our lives, the hearing of our ears, the sight of our eyes.

We go through the world like a man pursued by a policeman and see the barest glimpses of the beauty of it. All this fear that pursues us comes from believing in matter. Matter gets its whole existence from the presence of mind behind it. What we see is God percolating through nature. (Here "nature" means matter and mind.)

II

RECORDED BY MISS S. E. WALDO, A DISCIPLE

SUNDAY, *June 23, 1895.*

Be brave and be sincere; then follow any path with devotion, and you must reach the Whole. Once lay hold of one link of the chain, and the whole chain must come by degrees. Water the roots of the tree (that is, reach the Lord), and the whole tree is watered; getting the Lord, we get all.

One-sidedness is the bane of the world. The more sides you can develop the more souls you have, and you can see the universe through all souls — through the Bhakta (devotee) and the Jnâni (philosopher). Determine your own nature and stick to it. Nishthâ (devotion to one ideal) is the only method for the beginner; but with devotion and sincerity it will lead to all. Churches, doctrines, forms, are the hedges to protect the tender plant, but they must later be broken down that the plant may become a tree. So the various religions, Bibles, Vedas, dogmas — all are just tubs for the little plant; but it must get out of the tub. Nishthâ is, in a manner, placing the plant in the tub, shielding the struggling soul in its path. . . .

Look at the "ocean" and not at the "wave"; see no difference between ant and angel. Every worm is the brother of the Nazarene. How say one is greater and one less? Each is great in his own place. We are in the sun and in the stars as much as here. Spirit is beyond space and time and is everywhere. Every mouth praising the Lord is my mouth, every eye seeing is my eye. We are confined nowhere; we are not body, the universe is our body. We are magicians waving magic wands and creating scenes before us at will. We are the spider in his huge web, who can go on the varied strands wheresoever he desires. The spider is now only conscious of the spot where he is, but he will in time become conscious of the whole web. We are now conscious only where the body is, we can use only one brain; but when we reach ultraconsciousness, we know all, we can use all brains. Even now we can "give the push" in consciousness, and it goes beyond and acts in the superconscious.

We are striving "to be" and nothing more, no "I" ever — just pure crystal, reflecting all, but ever the same, When that state is reached, there is no more doing; the body becomes a mere mechanism, pure without care for it; it cannot become impure.

Know you are the Infinite, then fear must die. Say ever, "I and my Father are one."

* * *

In time to come Christs will be in numbers like bunches of grapes on a vine; then the play will be over and will pass out — as water in a kettle beginning to boil shows first one bubble, then another then more and more, until all is in ebullition and passes out as steam. Buddha and Christ are the two biggest "bubbles" the world has yet produced. Moses was a tiny bubble, greater and greater ones came. Sometime, however, all will be bubbles and escape; but creation, ever new, will bring new water to go through the process all over again.

III

RECORDED BY MISS S. E. WALDO, A DISCIPLE

MONDAY, June 24, 1895.

The reading today was from the Bhakti-Sutras by Nârada.

"Extreme love to God is Bhakti, and this love is the real immortality, getting which a man becomes perfectly satisfied, sorrows for no loss, and is never jealous; knowing which man becomes mad."

My Master used to say, "This world is a huge lunatic asylum where all men are mad, some after money, some after women, some after name or fame, and a few after God. I prefer to be mad after God. God is the philosophers' stone that turns us to gold in an instant; the form remains, but the nature is changed — the human form remains, but no more can we hurt or sin."

"Thinking of God, some weep, some sing, some laugh, some dance, some say wonderful things, but all speak of nothing but God."

Prophets preach, but the Incarnations like Jesus, Buddha, Ramakrishna, can give religion; one glance, one touch is enough. That is the power of the Holy Ghost, the "laying on of hands"; the power was actually transmitted to the disciples by the Master — the "chain of Guru-power". That, the real baptism, has been handed down for untold ages.

"Bhakti cannot be used to fulfil any desires, itself being the check to all desires." Narada gives these as the signs of love: "When all thoughts, all words, and all deeds are given up unto the Lord, and the least forgetfulness of God makes one intensely miserable, then love has begun."

"This is the highest form of love because therein is no desire for reciprocity, which desire is in all human love."

"A man who has gone beyond social and scriptural usage, he is a Sannyâsin. When the whole soul goes to God, when we take refuge only in God, then we know that we are about to get this love."

Obey the scriptures until you are strong enough to do without them; then go beyond them. Books are not an end-all. Verification is the only proof of religious truth. Each must verify for himself; and no teacher who says, "I have seen, but you cannot", is to be trusted, only that one who says, "You can see too". All scriptures, all truths are Vedas in all times, in all countries; because these truths are to be seen, and any one may discover them.

"When the sun of Love begins to break on the horizon, we want to give up all our actions unto God; and when we forget Him for a moment, it grieves us greatly."

Let nothing stand between God and your love for Him. Love Him, love Him, love Him; and let the world say what it will. Love is of three sorts — one demands, but gives nothing; the second is exchange; and the third is love without thought of return — love like that of the moth for the light.

"Love is higher than work, than Yoga, than knowledge."

Work is merely a schooling for the doer; it can do no good to others. We must work out our own problem; the prophets only show us how to work. "What you think, you become", so if you throw your burden on Jesus, you will have to think of Him and thus become like Him — you love Him.

"Extreme love and highest knowledge are one."

But theorising about God will not do; we must love and work. Give up the world and all worldly things, especially while the "plant" is tender. Day and night think of God and think of nothing else as far as possible. The daily necessary thoughts can all be thought through God. Eat to Him, drink to Him, sleep to Him, see Him in all. Talk of God to others; this is most beneficial.

Get the mercy of God and of His greatest children: these are the two chief ways to God. The company of these children of light is very hard to get; five minutes in their company will change a whole life; and if you really want it enough, one will come to you. The presence of those who love God makes a place holy, "such is the glory of the children of the Lord". They are He; and when they speak, their words are scriptures. The place where they have been becomes filled with their vibrations, and those going there feel them and have a tendency to become holy also.

"To such lovers there is no distinction of caste, learning, beauty, birth, wealth, or occupation; because all are His."

Give up all evil company, especially at the beginning. Avoid worldly company, that will distract your mind. Give up all "me and mine". To him who has nothing in the universe the Lord comes. Cut the bondage of all worldly affections; go beyond laziness and all care as to what becomes of you. Never turn back to see the result of what you have done. Give all to the Lord and go on and think not of it. The whole soul pours in a continuous current to God; there is no time to seek money, or name, or fame, no time to think of anything but God; then will come into our hearts that infinite, wonderful bliss of Love. All desires are but beads of glass. Love of God increases every moment and is ever new, to be known only by feeling it. Love is the easiest of all, it waits for no logic, it is natural. We need no demonstration, no proof. Reasoning is limiting something by our own minds. We throw a net and catch something, and then say that we have demonstrated it; but never, never can we catch God in a net.

Love should be unrelated. Even when we love wrongly, it is of the true love, of the true bliss; the power is the same, use it as we may. Its very nature is peace and bliss. The murderer when he kisses his baby forgets for an instant all but love. Give up all self, all egotisms get out of anger, lust, give all to God. "I am not, but Thou art; the old man is all gone, only Thou remainest." "I am Thou." Blame none; if evil comes, know the Lord is playing with you and be exceeding glad.

Love is beyond time and space, it is absolute.

IV

RECORDED BY MISS S. E. WALDO, A DISCIPLE

TUESDAY, June 25, 1895.

After every happiness comes misery; they may be far apart or near. The more advanced the soul, the more quickly does one follow the other. What we want is neither happiness nor misery. Both make us forget our true nature; both are chains — one iron, one gold; behind both is the Atman, who knows neither happiness nor misery. These are states and states must ever change; but the nature of the Soul is bliss, peace, unchanging. We have not to get it, we have it; only wash away the dross and see it.

Stand upon the Self, then only can we truly love the world. Take a very, very high stand; knowing out universal nature, we must look with perfect calmness upon all the panorama of the world. It is but baby's play, and we know that, so cannot be disturbed by it. If the mind is pleased with praise, it will be displeased with blame. All pleasures of the senses or even of the mind are evanescent but within ourselves is the one true unrelated pleasure, dependent upon nothing. It is perfectly free, it is bliss. The more our bliss is within, the more spiritual we are. The pleasure of the Self is what the world calls religion.

The internal universe, the real, is infinitely greater

than the external, which is only a shadowy projection of the true one. This world is neither true nor untrue, it is the shadow of truth. "Imagination is the gilded shadow of truth", says the poet.

We enter into creation, and then for us it becomes living. Things are dead in themselves; only we give them life, and then, like fools, we turn around and are afraid of them, or enjoy them. But be not like certain fisher-women, who, caught in a storm on their way home from market, took refuge in the house of a florist. They were lodged for the night in a room next to the garden where the air was full of the fragrance of flowers. In vain did they try to rest, until one of their number suggested that they wet their fishy baskets and place them near their heads. Then they all fell into a sound sleep.

The world is our fish basket, we must not depend upon it for enjoyment. Those who do are the Tâmasas or the bound. Then there are the Râjasas or the egotistical, who talk always about "I", "I". They do good work sometimes and may become spiritual. But the highest are the Sâttvikas, the introspective, those who live only in the Self. These three qualities, Tamas, Rajas, and Sattva (idleness, activity, and illumination), are in everyone, and different ones predominate at different times.

Creation is not a "making" of something, it is the struggle to regain the equilibrium, as when atoms of cork are thrown to the bottom of a pail of water and rush to rise to the top, singly or in clusters. Life is and must be accompanied by evil. A little evil is the source of life; the little wickedness that is in the world is very good; for when the balance is regained, the world will end, because sameness and destruction are one. When this world goes, good and evil go with it; but when we can transcend this world, we get rid of both good and evil and have bliss.

There is no possibility of ever having pleasure without pain, good without evil; for living itself is just the lost equilibrium. What we want is freedom, not life, nor pleasure, nor good. Creation is infinite, without beginning and without end — the ever-moving ripple in an infinite lake. There are yet unreached depths and others where the equilibrium has been regained; but the ripple is always progressing, the struggle to regain the balance is eternal. Life and death are only different names for the same fact, the two sides of the one coin. Both are Maya, the inexplicable state of striving at one time to live, and a moment later to die. Beyond this is the true nature, the Atman. While we recognise a God, it is really only the Self which we have separated ourselves from and worship as outside of us; but it is our true Self all the time — the one and only God.

To regain the balance we must counteract Tamas by Rajas; then conquer Rajas by Sattva, the calm beautiful state that will grow and grow until all else is gone. Give up bondage; become a son, be free, and then you can "see the Father", as did Jesus. Infinite strength is religion and God. Avoid weakness and slavery. You are only a soul, if you are free; there is immortality for you, if you are free; there is God, if He is free....

The world for me, not I for the world. Good and evil are our slaves, not we theirs. It is the nature of the brute to remain where he is (not to progress); it is the nature of man to seek good and avoid evil; it is the nature of God to seek neither, but just to be eternally blissful. Let us be God! Make the heart like an ocean, go beyond all the trifles of the world, be mad with joy even at evil; see the world as a picture and then enjoy its beauty, knowing that nothing affects you. Children finding glass beads in a mud puddle, that is the good of the world. Look at it with calm complacency; see good and evil as the same — both are merely "God's play"; enjoy all.

***

My Master used to say, "All is God; but tiger-God is to be shunned. All water is water; but we avoid dirty water for drinking."

The whole sky is the censer of God, and sun and moon are the lamps. What temple is needed? All eyes are Thine, yet Thou hast not an eye; all hands are Thine; yet Thou hast not a hand.

Neither seek nor avoid, take what comes. It is liberty to be affected by nothing; do not merely endure, be unattached. Remember the story of the bull. A mosquito sat long on the horn of a certain bull. Then his conscience troubled him, and he said, "Mr. Bull, I have been sitting here a long time, perhaps I annoy you. I am sorry, I will go away." But the bull replied, "Oh no, not at all! Bring your whole family and live on my horn; what can you do to me?"

V

RECORDED BY MISS S. E. WALDO, A DISCIPLE

WEDNESDAY, June 26, 1895.

Our best work is done, our greatest influence is exerted, when we are without thought of self. All great geniuses know this. Let us open ourselves to the one Divine Actor, and let Him act, and do nothing ourselves. "O Arjuna! I have no duty in the whole world", says Krishna. Be perfectly resigned, perfectly unconcerned; then alone can you do any true work. No eyes can see the real forces, we can only see the results. Put out self, lose it, forget it; just let God work, it is His business. We have nothing to do but stand aside and let God work. The more we go away, the more God comes in. Get rid of the little "I", and let only the great "I" live.

We are what our thoughts have made us; so take care of what you think. Words are secondary. Thoughts live, they travel far. Each thought we think is tinged with our own character, so that for the pure and holy man, even his jests or abuse will have the twist of his own love and purity and do good.

Desire nothing; think of God and look for no return. It is the desireless who bring results. The begging monks carry religion to every man's door; but they think that they do nothing, they claim nothing, their work is unconsciously done. If they should eat of the tree of knowledge, they would become egoists, and all the good they do would fly away. As soon as we say "I", we are humbugged all the time; and we call it "knowable", but it is only going round and round like a bullock tied to a tree. The Lord has hidden Himself best, and His work is best; so he who hides himself best, accomplishes most. Conquer yourself, and the whole universe is yours.

In the state of Sattva we see the very nature of things, we go beyond the senses and beyond reason. The adamantine wall that shuts us in is egoism; we refer everything to ourselves, thinking. "I do this, that, and the other." Get rid of this puny "I"; kill this diabolism in us; "Not I, but Thou" — say it, feel it, live it. Until we give up the world manufactured by the ego, never can we enter the kingdom of heaven. None ever did, none ever will. To give up the world is to forget the ego, to know it not at all — living in the body, but not of it. This rascal ego must be obliterated. Bless men when they revile you. Think how much good they are doing you; they can only hurt themselves. Go where people hate you, let them thrash the ego out of you, and you will get nearer to the Lord. Like the mother-monkey, we hug our "baby", the world, as long as we can, but at last when we are driven to put it under our feet and step on it[6]* then we are ready to come to God. Blessed it is to be persecuted for the sake of righteousness. Blessed are we if we cannot read, we have less to take us away from God.

Enjoyment is the million-headed serpent that we must tread under foot. We renounce and go on, then find nothing and despair; but hold on, hold on. The world is a demon. It is a kingdom of which the puny ego is king. Put it away and stand firm. Give up lust and gold and fame and hold fast to the Lord, and at last we shall reach a state of perfect indifference. The idea that the gratification of the senses constitutes enjoyment is purely materialistic. There is not one spark of real enjoyment there; all the joy there is, is a mere reflection of the true bliss.

Those who give themselves up to the Lord do more for the world than all the so-called workers. One man who has purified himself thoroughly accomplishes more than a regiment of preachers. Out of purity and silence comes the word of power.

"Be like a lily — stay in one place and expand your petals; and the bees will come of themselves." There was a great contrast between Keshab Chandra Sen and Shri Ramakrishna. The second never recognised any sin or misery in the world, no evil to fight against. The first was a great ethical reformer, leader, and founder of the Brahmo-Samaj. After twelve years the quiet prophet of Dakshineswar had worked a revolution not only in India, but in the world. The power is with the silent ones, who only live and love and then withdraw their personality. They never say "me" and "mine"; they are only blessed in being instruments. Such men are the makers of Christs and Buddhas, ever living fully identified with God, ideal existences, asking nothing, and not consciously doing anything. They are the real movers, the Jivanmuktas, (Literally, free even while living.) absolutely selfless, the little personality entirely blown away, ambition non-existent. They are all principle, no personality.

VI

RECORDED BY MISS S. E. WALDO, A DISCIPLE

THURSDAY, June 27, 1895.

The Swami brought the New Testament this morning and talked again on the book of John.)

Mohammed claimed to be the "Comforter" that Christ promised to send. He considered it unnecessary to claim a supernatural birth for Jesus. Such claims have been common in all ages and in all countries. All great men have claimed gods for their fathers.

Knowing is only relative; we can be God, but never know Him. Knowledge is a lower state; Adam's fall was when he came to "know". Before that he was God, he was truth, he was purity. We are our own faces, but can see only a reflection, never the real thing. We are love, but when we think of it, we have to use a phantasm, which proves that matter is only externalised thought.

Nivritti is turning aside from the world. Hindu mythology says that the four first-created (The four first-created were Sanaka, Sanandana, Sanâtana, and Sanatkumâra.) were warned by a Swan (God Himself) that manifestation was only secondary; so they remained without creating. The meaning of this is that expression is degeneration, because Spirit can only be expressed by the letter and then the "letter killeth" (Bible, 2 Cor. III. 6.); yet principle is bound to be clothed in matter, though we know that later we shall lose sight of the real in the covering. Every great teacher understands this, and that is why a continual succession of prophets has to come to show us the principle and give it a new covering suited to the times. My Master taught that religion is one; all prophets teach the same; but they can only present the principle in a form; so they take it out of the old form and put it before us in a new one. When we free ourselves from name and form, especially from a body — when we need no body, good or bad — then only do we escape from bondage. Eternal progression is eternal bondage; annihilation of form is to be preferred. We must get free from any body, even a "god-body". God is the only real existence, there cannot be two. There is but One Soul, and I am That.

Good works are only valuable as a means of escape; they do good to the doer, never to any other.

Knowledge is mere classification. When we find many things of the same kind we call the sum of them by a certain name and are satisfied; we discover "facts", never "why". We take a circuit in a wider field of darkness and think we know something! No "why" can be answered in this world; for that we must go to God. The Knower can never be expressed; it is as when a grain of salt drops into the ocean, it is at once merged in the ocean.

Differentiation creates; homogeneity or sameness is God. Get beyond differentiation; then you conquer life and death and reach eternal sameness and are in God, are God. Get freedom, even at the cost of life. All lives belong to us as leaves to a book; but we are unchanged, the Witness, the Soul, upon whom the impression is made, as when the impression of a circle is made upon the eyes when a firebrand is rapidly whirled round and round. The Soul is the unity of all personalities, and because It is at rest, eternal, unchangeable. It is God, Atman. It is not life, but It is coined into life. It is not pleasure, but It is manufactured into pleasure....

Today God is being abandoned by the world because He does not seem to be doing enough for the world. So they say, "Of what good is He?" Shall we look upon God as a mere municipal authority?

All we can do is to put down all desires, hates, differences; put down the lower self, commit mental suicide, as it were; keep the body and mind pure and healthy, but only as instruments to help us to God; that is their only true use. Seek truth for truth's sake alone, look not for bliss. It may come, but do not let that be your incentives. Have no motive except God. Dare to come to Truth even through hell.

VII

RECORDED BY MISS S. E. WALDO, A DISCIPLE

FRIDAY, June 28, 1895.

The entire party went on a picnic for the day, and although the Swami taught constantly, as he did wherever he was, no notes were taken and no record, therefore, of what he said remains. As he began his breakfast before setting out, however, he remarked:

Be thankful for all food, it is Brahman. His universal energy is transmuted into our individual energy and helps us in all that we do.

VIII

RECORDED BY MISS S. E. WALDO, A DISCIPLE

SATURDAY, June 29, 1895.

The Swami came this morning with a Gita in his hand.

Krishna, the "Lord of souls", talks to Arjuna or Gudâkesha, "lord of sleep" (he who has conquered sleep). The "field of virtue" (the battlefield) is this world; the five brothers (representing righteousness) fight the hundred other brothers (all that we love and have to contend against); the most heroic brother, Arjuna (the awakened soul), is the general. We have to fight all sense-delights, the things to which we are most attached, to kill them. We have to stand alone; we are Brahman, all other ideas must be merged in this one.

Krishna did everything but without any attachment; he was in the world, but not of it. "Do all work but without attachment; work for work's sake, never for yourself."

Freedom can never be true of name and form; it is the clay out of which we (the pots) are made; then it is limited and not free, so that freedom can never be true of the related. One pot can never say "I am free" as a pot; only as it loses all ideas of form does it become free. The whole universe is only the Self with variations, the one tune made bearable by variation; sometimes there are discords, but they only make the subsequent harmony more perfect. In the universal melody three ideas stand out — freedom, strength, and sameness.

If your freedom hurts others, you are not free there. You must not hurt others.

"To be weak is to be miserable", says Milton. Doing and suffering are inseparably joined. (Often, too, the man who laughs most is the one who suffers most.) "To work you have the right, not to the fruits thereof."

* * *

Evil thoughts, looked at materially, are the disease bacilli.

Each thought is a little hammer blow on the lump of iron which our bodies are, manufacturing out of it what we want it to be.

We are heirs to all the good thoughts of the universe, if we open ourselves to them.

The book is all in us. Fool, hearest not thou? In thine own heart day and night is singing that Eternal Music — Sachchidânanda, soham, soham — Existence-Knowledge-Bliss Absolute, I am He, I am He.

The fountain of all knowledge is in every one of us, in the ant as in the highest angel. Real religion is one, but we quarrel with the forms, the symbols, the illustrations. The millennium exists already for those who find it; we have lost ourselves and then think the world is lost.

Perfect strength will have no activity in this world; it only is, it does not act.

While real perfection is only one, relative perfections must be many.

IX

RECORDED BY MISS S. E. WALDO, A DISCIPLE

SUNDAY, June 30, 1895.

To try to think without a phantasm is to try to make the impossible possible. We cannot think "mammalia" without a concrete example. So with the idea of God.

The great abstraction of ideas in the world is what we call God.

Each thought has two parts — the thinking and the word; and we must have both. Neither idealists nor materialists are right; we must take both idea and expression.

All knowledge is of the reflected, as we can only see our face in a mirror. No one will ever know his own Self or God; but we are that own Self, we are God.

In Nirvana you are when you are not. Buddha said, "You are best, you are real, when you are not" — when the little self is gone.

The Light Divine within is obscured in most people. It is like a lamp in a cask of iron, no gleam of light can shine through. Gradually, by purity and unselfishness we can make the obscuring medium less and less dense, until at last it becomes as transparent as glass. Shri Ramakrishna was like the iron cask transformed into a glass cask through which can be seen the inner light as it is. We are all on the way to become the cask of glass and even higher and higher reflections. As long as there is a "cask" at all, we must think through material means. No impatient one can ever succeed.

* * *

Great saints are the object-lessons of the Principle. But the disciples make the saint the Principle, and then they forget the Principle in the person.

The result of Buddha's constant inveighing against a personal God was the introduction of idols into India. In the Vedas they knew them not, because they saw God everywhere, but the reaction against the loss of God as Creator and Friend was to make idols, and Buddha became an idol — so too with Jesus. The range of idols is from wood and stone to Jesus and Buddha, but we must have idols.

* * *

Violent attempts at reform always end by retarding reform. Do not say, "You are bad"; say only, "You are good, but be better."

Priests are an evil in every country, because they denounce and criticise, pulling at one string to mend it until two or three others are out of place. Love never denounces, only ambition does that. There is no such thing as "righteous" anger or justifiable killing.

If you do not allow one to become a lion, he will become a fox. Women are a power, only now it is more for evil because man oppresses woman; she is the fox, but when she is not longer oppressed, she will become the lion.

Ordinarily speaking, spiritual aspiration ought to be balanced through the intellect; otherwise it may degenerate into mere sentimentality....

All theists agree that behind the changeable there is an Unchangeable, though they vary in their conception of the Ultimate. Buddha denied this in toto. "There is no Brahman, no Atman, no soul," he said.

As a character Buddha was the greatest the world has ever seen; next to him Christ. But the teachings of Krishna as taught by the Gita are the grandest the world has ever known. He who wrote that wonderful poem was one of those rare souls whose lives sent a wave of regeneration through the world. The human race will never again see such a brain as his who wrote the Gita.

* * *

There is only one Power, whether manifesting as evil or good. God and the devil are the same river with the water flowing in opposite directions.

X

RECORDED BY MISS S. E. WALDO, A DISCIPLE

MONDAY, July 1, 1895. (Shri Ramakrishna Deva)

Shri Ramakrishna was the son of a very orthodox Brahmin, who would refuse even a gift from any but a special caste of Brahmins; neither might he work, nor even be a priest in a temple, nor sell books, nor serve anyone. He could only have "what fell from the skies" (alms), and even then it must not come through a "fallen" Brahmin. Temples have no hold on the Hindu religion; if they were all destroyed, religion would not be affected a grain. A man must only build a house for "God and guests", to build for himself would be selfish; therefore he erects temples as dwelling places for God.

Owing to the extreme poverty of his family, Shri Ramakrishna was obliged to become in his boyhood a priest in a temple dedicated to the Divine Mother, also called Prakriti, or Kâli, represented by a female figure standing with feet on a male figure, indicating that until Maya lifts, we can know nothing. Brahman is neuter, unknown and unknowable, but to be objectified He covers Himself with a veil of Maya, becomes the Mother of the Universe, and so brings forth the creation. The prostrate figure (Shiva or God) has become Shava (dead or lifeless) by being covered by Maya. The Jnâni says, "I will uncover God by force" (Advaitism); but the dualist says, "I will uncover God by praying to Mother, begging Her to open the door to which She alone has the key."

The daily service of the Mother Kali gradually awakened such intense devotion in the heart of the young priest that he could no longer carry on the regular temple worship. So he abandoned his duties and retired to a small woodland in the temple compound, where he gave himself up entirely to meditation. These woods were on the bank of the river Ganga; and one day the swift current bore to his very feet just the necessary materials to build him a little enclosure. In this enclosure he stayed and wept and prayed, taking no thought for the care of his body or for aught except his Divine Mother. A relative fed him once a day and watched over him. Later came a Sannyasini or lady ascetic, to help him find his "Mother". Whatever teachers he needed came to him unsought; from every sect some holy saint would come and offer to teach him and to each he listened eagerly. But he worshipped only Mother; all to him was Mother.

Shri Ramakrishna never spoke a harsh word against anyone. So beautifully tolerant was he that every sect thought that he belonged to them. He loved everyone. To him all religions were true. He found a place for each one. He was free, but free in love, not in "thunder". The mild type creates, the thundering type spreads. Paul was the thundering type to spread the light. (And it has been said by many that Swami Vivekananda himself was a kind of St. Paul to Shri Ramakrishna.)

The age of St. Paul, however, is gone; we are to be the new lights for this day. A self-adjusting organisation is the great need of our time. When we can get one, that will be the last religion of the world. The wheel must turn, and we should help it, not hinder. The waves of religious thought rise and fall, and on the topmost one stands the "prophet of the period". Ramakrishna came to teach the religion of today, constructive, not destructive. He had to go afresh to Nature to ask for facts, and he got scientific religion which never says "believe", but "see"; "I see, and you too can see." Use the same means and you will reach the same vision. God will come to everyone, harmony is within the reach of all. Shri Ramakrishna's teachings are "the gist of Hinduism"; they were not peculiar to him. Nor did he claim that they were; he cared naught for name or fame.

He began to preach when he was about forty; but he never went out to do it. He waited for those who wanted his teachings to come to him. In accordance with Hindu custom, he was married by his parents in early youth to a little girl of five, who remained at home with her family in a distant village, unconscious of the great struggle through which her young husband was passing. When she reached maturity, he was already deeply absorbed in religious devotion. She travelled on foot from her home to the temple at Dakshineswar where he was then living; and as soon as she saw him, she recognised what he was, for she herself was a great soul, pure and holy, who only desired to help his work, never to drag him down to the level of the Grihastha (householder).

Shri Ramakrishna is worshipped in India as one of the great Incarnations, and his birthday is celebrated there as a religious festival. . . .

A curious round stone is the emblem of Vishnu, the omnipresent. Each morning a priest comes in, offers sacrifice to the idol, waves incense before it, then puts it to bed and apologises to God for worshipping Him in that way, because he can only conceive of Him through an image or by means of some material object. He bathes the idol, clothes it, and puts his divine self into the idol "to make it alive".

* * *

There is a sect which says, "It is weakness to worship only the good and beautiful, we ought also to love and worship the hideous and the evil." This sect prevails all over Tibet, and they have no marriage. In India proper they cannot exist openly, but organise secret societies. No decent men will belong to them except sub rosa. Thrice communism was tried in Tibet, and thrice it failed. They use Tapas and with immense success as far as power is concerned.

Tapas means literally "to burn". It is a kind of penance to "heat" the higher nature. It is sometimes in the form of a sunrise to sunset vow, such as repeating Om all day incessantly. These actions will produce a certain power that you can convert into any form you wish, spiritual or material. This idea of Tapas penetrates the whole of Hindu religion. The Hindus even say that God made Tapas to create the world. It is a mental instrument with which to do everything. "Everything in the three worlds can be caught by Tapas." . . .

People who report about sects with which they are not in sympathy are both conscious and unconscious liars. A believer in one sect can rarely see truth in others.

* * *

A great Bhakta (Hanuman) once said when asked what day of the month it was, "God is my eternal date, no other date I care for."

XI

RECORDED BY MISS S. E. WALDO, A DISCIPLE

TUESDAY, July 2, 1895. (The Divine Mother.)

Shâktas worship the Universal Energy as Mother, the sweetest name they know; for the mother is the highest ideal of womanhood in India. When God is worshipped as "Mother", as Love, the Hindus call it the "right-handed" way, and it leads to spirituality but never to material prosperity. When God is worshipped on His terrible side, that is, in the "left-handed" way, it leads usually to great material prosperity, but rarely to spirituality; and eventually it leads to degeneration and the obliteration of the race that practices it.

Mother is the first manifestation of power and is considered a higher idea than father. With the name of Mother comes the idea of Shakti, Divine Energy and Omnipotence, just as the baby believes its mother to be all-powerful, able to do anything. The Divine Mother is the Kundalini ("coiled up" power) sleeping in us; without worshipping Her we can never know ourselves. All-merciful, all-powerful, omnipresent are attributes of Divine Mother. She is the sum total of the energy in the universe. Every manifestation of power in the universe is "Mother". She is life, She is intelligence, She is Love. She is in the universe yet separate from it. She is a person and can be seen and known (as Shri Ramakrishna saw and knew Her). Established in the idea of Mother, we can do anything. She quickly answers prayer.

She can show; Herself to us in any form at any moment. Divine Mother can have form (Rupa) and name (Nâma) or name without form; and as we worship Her in these various aspects we can rise to pure Being, having neither form nor name.

The sum total of all the cells in an organism is one person; so each soul is like one cell and the sum of them is God, and beyond that is the Absolute. The sea calm is the Absolute; the same sea in waves is Divine Mother. She is time, space, and causation. God is Mother and has two natures, the conditioned and the unconditioned. As the former, She is God, nature, and soul (man). As the latter, She is unknown and unknowable. Out of the Unconditioned came the trinity — God, nature, and soul, the triangle of existence. This is the Vishishtâdvaitist idea.

A bit of Mother, a drop, was Krishna, another was Buddha, another was Christ. The worship of even one spark of Mother in our earthly mother leads to greatness. Worship Her if you want love and wisdom.

XII

RECORDED BY MISS S. E. WALDO, A DISCIPLE

WEDNESDAY, July 3, 1895.

Generally speaking, human religion begins with fear. "The fear of the Lord is the beginning of wisdom." But later comes the higher idea. "Perfect love casteth out fear." Traces of fear will remain with us until we get knowledge, know what God is. Christ, being man, had to see impurity and denounced it; but God, infinitely higher, does not see iniquity and cannot be angry. Denunciation is never the highest. David's hands were smeared with blood; he could not build the temple. (Bible, Samuel, Chap. XVII — end.)

The more we grow in love and virtue and holiness, the more we see love and virtue and holiness outside. All condemnation of others really condemns ourselves. Adjust the microcosm (which is in your power to do) and the macrocosm will adjust itself for you. It is like the hydrostatic paradox, one drop of water can balance the universe. We cannot see outside what we are not inside. The universe is to us what the huge engine is to the miniature engine; and indication of any error in the tiny engine leads us to imagine trouble in the huge one.

Every step that has been really gained in the world has been gained by love; criticising can never do any good, it has been tried for thousand of years. Condemnation accomplishes nothing.

A real Vedantist must sympathise with all. Monism, or absolute oneness is the very soul of Vedanta. Dualists naturally tend to become intolerant, to think theirs as the only way. The Vaishnavas in India, who are dualists, are a most intolerant sect. Among the Shaivas, another dualistic sect, the story is told of a devotee by the name of Ghantâkarna or the Bell-eared, who was so devout a worshipper of Shiva that he did not wish even to hear the name of any other deity; so he wore two bells tied to his ears in order to drown the sound of any voice uttering other Divine names. On account of his intense devotion to Shiva, the latter wanted to teach him that there was no difference between Shiva and Vishnu, so He appeared before him as half Vishnu and half Shiva. At that moment the devotee was waving incense before Him, but so great was the bigotry of Ghantakarna that when he saw the fragrance of the incense entering the nostril of Vishnu, he thrust his finger into it to prevent the god from enjoying the sweet smell....

The meat-eating animal, like the lion, gives one blow and subsides, but the patient bullock goes on all day, eating and sleeping as it walks. The "live Yankee" cannot compete with the rice-eating Chinese coolie. While military power dominates, meat-eating still prevail; but with the advance of science, fighting will grow less, and then the vegetarians will come in.

***

We divide ourselves into two to love God, myself loving my Self. God has created me and I have created God. We create God in our image; it is we who create Him to be our master, it is not God who makes us His servants. When we know that we are one with God, that we and He are friends, then come equality and freedom. So long as you hold yourself separated by a hair's breadth from this Eternal One, fear cannot go.

Never ask that foolish question, what good will it do to the world? Let the world go. Love and ask nothing; love and look for nothing further. Love and forget all the "isms". Drink the cup of love and become mad. Say "Thine, O Thine for ever O Lord!" and plunge in, forgetting all else. The very idea of God is love. Seeing a cat loving her kittens stand and pray. God has become manifest there; literally believe this. Repeat "I am Thine, I am Thine", for we can see God everywhere. Do not seek for Him, just see Him.

"May the Lord ever keep you alive, Light of the world, Soul of the universe!"...

The Absolute cannot be worshipped, so we must worship a manifestation, such a one as has our nature. Jesus had our nature; he became the Christ; so can we, and so must we. Christ and Buddha were the names of a state to be attained; Jesus and Gautama were the persons to manifest it. "Mother" is the first and highest manifestation, next the Christs and Buddhas. We make our own environment, and we strike the fetters off. The Atman is the fearless. When we pray to a God outside, it is good, only we do not know what we do. When we know the Self, we understand. The highest expression of love is unification.

"There was a time when I was a woman and he was a man. Still love grew until there was neither he nor I; Only I remember faintly there was a time when there were two. But love came between and made them one." — Persian Sufi Poem

Knowledge exists eternally and is co-existent with God. The man who discovers a spiritual law is inspired, and what he brings is revelation; but revelation too is eternal, not to be crystallised as final and then blindly followed. The Hindus have been criticised so many years by their conquerors that they (the Hindus) dare to criticise their religion themselves, and this makes them free. Their foreign rulers struck off their fetters without knowing it. The most religious people on earth, the Hindus have actually no sense of blasphemy; to speak of holy things in any way is to them in itself a sanctification. Nor have they any artificial respect for prophets or books, or for hypocritical piety.

The Church tries to fit Christ into it, not the Church into Christ; so only those writings were preserved that suited the purpose in hand. Thus the books are not to be depended upon and book-worship is the worst kind of idolatry to bind our feet. All has to conform to the book — science, religion, philosophy; it is the most horrible tyranny, this tyranny of the Protestant Bible. Every man in Christian countries has a huge cathedral on his head and on top of that a book, and yet man lives and grows! Does not this prove that man is God?

Man is the highest being that exists, and this is the greatest world. We can have no conception of God higher than man, so our God is man, and man is God. When we rise and go beyond and find something higher, we have to jump out of the mind, out of body and the imagination and leave this world; when we rise to be the Absolute, we are no longer in this world. Man is the apex of the only world we can ever know. All we know of animals is only by analogy, we judge them by what we do and feel ourselves.

The sum total of knowledge is ever the same, only sometimes it is more manifested and sometimes less. The only source of it is within, and there only is it found.

***

All poetry, painting, and music is feeling expressed through words, through colour, through sound....

Blessed are those upon whom their sins are quickly visited, their account is the sooner balanced! Woe to those whose punishment is deferred, it is the greater!

Those who have attained sameness are said to be living in God. All hatred is killing the "Self by the self", therefore love is the law of life. To rise to this is to be perfect; but the more perfect we are, less work (so-called) can we do. The Sâttvika see and know that all is mere child's play and do not trouble themselves about anything.

It is easy to strike a blow, but tremendously hard to stay the hand, stand still, and say, "In Thee, O Lord, I take refuge", and then wait for Him to act.

XIII

RECORDED BY MISS S. E. WALDO, A DISCIPLE

FRIDAY, July 5, 1895.

Until you are ready to change any minute, you can never see the truth; but you must hold fast and be steady in the search for truth....

Chârvâkas, a very ancient sect in India, were rank materialists. They have died out now, and most of their books are lost. They claimed that the soul, being the product of the body and its forces, died with it; that there was no proof of its further existence. They denied inferential knowledge accepting only perception by the senses.

* * *

Samâdhi is when the Divine and human are in one, or it is "bringing sameness"....

Materialism says, the voice of freedom is a delusion. Idealism says, the voice that tells of bondage is delusion. Vedanta says, you are free and not free at the same time — never free on the earthly plane, but ever free on the spiritual.

Be beyond both freedom and bondage.

We are Shiva, we are immortal knowledge beyond the senses.

Infinite power is back of everyone; pray to Mother, and it will come to you.

"O Mother, giver of Vâk (eloquence), Thou self-existent, come as the Vak upon my-lips," (Hindu invocation).

"That Mother whose voice is in the thunder, come Thou in me! Kali, Thou time eternal, Thou force irresistible, Shakti, Power!"

XIV

RECORDED BY MISS S. E. WALDO, A DISCIPLE

SATURDAY, July 6, 1895.

Today we had Shankaracharya's commentary on Vyâsa's Vedânta Sutras.

Om tat sat! According to Shankara, there are two phases of the universe, one is I and the other thou; and they are as contrary as light and darkness, so it goes without saying that neither can be derived from the other. On the subject, the object has been superimposed; the subject is the only reality, the other a mere appearance. The opposite view is untenable. Matter and the external world are but the soul in a certain state; in reality there is only one.

All our world comes from truth and untruth coupled together. Samsâra (life) is the result of the contradictory forces acting upon us, like the diagonal motion of a ball in a parallelogram of forces. The world is God and is real, but that is not the world we see; just as we see silver in the mother-of-pearl where it is not. This is what is known as Adhyâsa or superimposition, that is, a relative existence dependent upon a real one, as when we recall a scene we have seen; for the time it exists for us, but that existence is not real. Or some say, it is as when we imagine heat in water, which does not belong to it; so really it is something which has been put where it does not belong, "taking the thing for what it is not". We see reality, but distorted by the medium through which we see it.

You can never know yourself except as objectified. When we mistake one thing for another, we always take the thing before us as the real, never the unseen; thus we mistake the object for the subject. The Atman never becomes the object. Mind is the internal sense, the outer senses are its instruments. In the subject is a trifle of the objectifying power that enables him to know "I am"; but the subject is the object of its own Self, never of the mind or the senses. You can, however, superimpose one idea on another idea, as when we say, "The sky is blue", the sky itself being only an idea. Science and nescience there are, but the Self is never affected by any nescience. Relative knowledge is good, because it leads to absolute knowledge; but neither the knowledge of the senses, nor of the mind, nor even of the Vedas is true, since they are all within the realm of relative knowledge. First get rid of the delusion, "I am the body", then only can we want real knowledge. Man's knowledge is only a higher degree of brute knowledge.

* * *

One part of the Vedas deals with Karma — form and ceremonies. The other part deals with the knowledge of Brahman and discusses religion. The Vedas in this part teach of the Self; and because they do, their knowledge is approaching real knowledge. Knowledge of the Absolute depends upon no book, nor upon anything; it is absolute in itself. No amount of study will give this knowledge; is not theory, it is realization. Cleanse the dust from the mirror, purify your own mind, and in a flash you know that you are Brahman.

God exists, not birth nor death, not pain nor misery, nor murder, nor change, nor good nor evil; all is Brahman. We take the "rope for the serpent", the error is ours. . . . We can only do good when we love God and He reflects our love. The murderer is God, and the "clothing of murderer" is only superimposed upon him. Take him by the hand and tell him the truth.

Soul has no caste, and to think it has is a delusion; so are life and death, or any motion or quality. The Atman never changes, never goes nor comes. It is the eternal Witness of all Its own manifestations, but we take It for the manifestation; an eternal illusion, without beginning or end, ever going on. The Vedas, however, have to come down to our level, for if they told us the highest truth in the highest way, we could not understand it.

Heaven is a mere superstition arising from desire, and desire is ever a yoke, a degeneration. Never approach any thing except as God; for if we do, we see evil, because we throw a veil of delusion over what we look at, and then we see evil. Get free from these illusions; be blessed. Freedom is to lose all illusions.

In one sense Brahman is known to every human being; he knows, "I am"; but man does not know himself as he is. We all know we are, but not how we are. All lower explanations are partial truths; but the flower, the essence of the Vedas, is that the Self in each of us is Brahman. Every phenomenon is included in birth, growth, and death — appearance, continuance and disappearance. Our own realisation is beyond the Vedas, because even they depend upon that. The highest Vedanta is the philosophy of the Beyond.

To say that creation has any beginning is to lay the axe at the root of all philosophy.

Maya is the energy of the universe, potential and kinetic. Until Mother releases us, we cannot get free.

The universe is ours to enjoy. But want nothing. To want is weakness. Want makes us beggars, and we are sons of the king, not beggars.

XV

RECORDED BY MISS S. E. WALDO, A DISCIPLE

SUNDAY MORNING, July 7, 1895.

Infinite manifestation dividing itself in portion still remains infinite, and each portion is infinite.

Brahman is the same in two forms — changeable and unchangeable, expressed and unexpressed. Know that the Knower and the known are one. The Trinity — the Knower, the known, and knowing —

is manifesting as this universe. That God the Yogi sees in meditation, he sees through the power of his own Self.

What we call nature, fate, is simply God's will.

So long as enjoyment is sought, bondage remains. Only imperfection can enjoy, because enjoyment is the fulfilling of desire. The human soul enjoys nature. The underlying reality of nature, soul, and God is Brahman; but It (Brahman) is unseen, until we bring It out. It may be brought out by Pramantha or friction, just as we can produce fire by friction. The body is the lower piece of wood, Om is the pointed piece and Dhâna (meditation) is the friction. When this is used, that light which is the knowledge of Brahman will burst forth in the soul. Seek it through Tapas. Holding the body upright, sacrifice the organs of sense in the mind. The sense-centres are within, and their organs without; drive them into the mind and through Dhârana (concentration) fix the mind in Dhyana. Brahman is omnipresent in the universe as is butter in milk, but friction makes It manifest in one place. As churning brings out the butter in the milk, so Dhyana brings the realisation of Brahman in the soul.

All Hindu philosophy declares that there is a sixth sense, the superconscious, and through it comes inspiration.

***

The universe is motion, and friction will eventually bring everything to an end; then comes a rest; and after that all begins again....

So long as the "skin sky" surrounds man, that is, so long as he identifies himself with his body, he cannot see God.

SUNDAY AFTERNOON

There are six schools of philosophy in India that are regarded as orthodox, because they believe in the Vedas.

Vyasa's philosophy is par excellence that of the Upanishads. He wrote in Sutra form, that is, in brief algebraical symbols without nominative or verb. This caused so much ambiguity that out of the Sutras came dualism, mono-dualism, and monism or "roaring Vedanta"; and all the great commentators in these different schools were at times "conscious liars" in order to make the texts suit their philosophy.

The Upanishads contain very little history of the doings of any man, but nearly all other scriptures are largely personal histories. The Vedas deal almost entirely with philosophy. Religion without philosophy runs into superstition; philosophy without religion becomes dry atheism.

Vishishta-advaita is qualified Advaita (monism). Its expounder was Râmânuja. He says, "Out of the ocean of milk of the Vedas, Vyasa has churned this butter of philosophy, the better to help mankind." He says again, "All virtues and all qualities belong to Brahman, Lord of the universe. He is the greatest Purusha. Madhva is a through-going dualist or Dvaitist. He claims that even women might study the Vedas. He quotes chiefly from the Purânas. He says that Brahman means Vishnu, not Shiva at all, because there is no salvation except through Vishnu.

XVI

RECORDED BY MISS S. E. WALDO, A DISCIPLE

MONDAY, July 8, 1895.

There is no place for reasoning in Madhva's explanation, it is all taken from the revelation in the Vedas.

Ramanuja says, the Vedas are the holiest study. Let the sons of the three upper castes get the Sutra (The holy thread.) and at eight, ten, or eleven years of age begin the study, which means going to a Guru and learning the Vedas word for word, with perfect intonation and pronunciation.

Japa is repeating the Holy Name; through this the devotee rises to the Infinite. This boat of sacrifice and ceremonies is very frail, we need more than that to know Brahman, which alone is freedom. Liberty is nothing more than destruction of ignorance, and that can only go when we know Brahman. It is not necessary to go through all these ceremonials to reach the meaning of the Vedanta. Repeating Om is enough.

Seeing difference is the cause of all misery, and ignorance is the cause of seeing difference. That is why ceremonials are not needed, because they increase the idea of inequality; you practice them to get rid of something or to obtain something.

Brahman is without action, Atman is Brahman, and we are Atman; knowledge like this takes off all error. It must be heard, apprehended intellectually, and lastly realised. Cogitating is applying reason and establishing this knowledge in ourselves by reason. Realising is making it a part of our lives by constant thinking of it. This constant thought or Dhyana is as oil that pours in one unbroken line from vessel to vessel; Dhyana rolls the mind in this thought day and night and so helps us to attain to liberation. Think always "Soham, Soham"; this is almost as good as liberation. Say it day and night; realisation will come as the result of this continuous cogitation. This absolute and continuous remembrance of the Lord is what is meant by Bhakti.

This Bhakti is indirectly helped by all good works. Good thoughts and good works create less differentiation than bad ones; so indirectly they lead to freedom. Work, but give up the results to the Lord. Knowledge alone can make us perfect. He who follows the God of Truth with devotion, to him the God of Truth reveals Himself. . . . We are lamps, and our burning is what we call "life". When the supply of oxygen gives out, then the lamp must go out. All we can do is to keep the lamp clean. Life is a product, a compound, and as such must resolve itself into its elements.

XVII

RECORDED BY MISS S. E. WALDO, A DISCIPLE

TUESDAY, July 9, 1895.

Man as Atman is really free; as man he is bound, changed by every physical condition. As man, he is a machine with an idea of freedom; but this human body is the best and the human mind the highest mind there is. When a man attains to the Atman state, he can take a body, making it to suit himself; he is above law. This is a statement and must be proved. Each one must prove it for himself; we may satisfy ourselves, but we cannot satisfy another. Râja-Yoga is the only science of religion that can be demonstrated; and only what I myself have proved by experience, do I teach. The full ripeness of reason is intuition, but intuition cannot antagonise reason.

Work purifies the heart and so leads to Vidyâ (wisdom). The Buddhists said, doing good to men and to animals were the only works; the Brahmins said that worship and all ceremonials were equally "work" and purified the mind. Shankara declares that "all works, good and bad, are against knowledge". Actions tending to ignorance are sins, not directly, but as causes, because they tend to increase Tamas and Rajas. With Sattva only, comes wisdom. Virtuous deeds take off the veil from knowledge, and knowledge alone can make us see God.

Knowledge can never be created, it can only be discovered; and every man who makes a great discovery is inspired. Only, when it is a spiritual truth he brings, we call him a prophet; and when it is on the physical plane, we call him a scientific man, and we attribute more importance to the former, although the source of all truth is one.

Shankara says, Brahman is the essence, the reality of all knowledge, and that all manifestations as knower, knowing, and known are mere imaginings in Brahman. Ramanuja attributes consciousness to God; the real monists attribute nothing, not even existence in any meaning that we can attach to it. Ramanuja declares that God is the essence of conscious knowledge. Undifferentiated consciousness, when differentiated, becomes the world. . . .

Buddhism, one of the most philosophical religions in the world, spread all through the populace, the common people of India. What a wonderful culture there must have been among the Aryans twenty-five hundred years ago, to be able to grasp ideas!

Buddha was the only great Indian philosopher who would not recognise caste, and not one of his followers remains in India. All the other philosophers pandered more or less to social prejudices; no matter how high they soared, still a bit of the vulture remained in them. As my Master used to say, "The vulture soars high out of sight in the sky, but his eye is ever on a bit of carrion on the earth."

* * *

The ancient Hindus were wonderful scholars, veritable living encyclopaedias. They said, "Knowledge in books and money in other people's hands is like no knowledge and no money at all."

Shankara was regarded by many as an incarnation of Shiva.

XVIII

RECORDED BY MISS S. E. WALDO, A DISCIPLE

WEDNESDAY, July 10, 1895.

There are sixty-five million Mohammedans in India, some of them Sufis.[6]* Sufis identify man with God, and through them this idea came into Europe. They say, "I am that Truth"; but they have an esoteric as well as an exoteric doctrine, although Mohammed himself did not hold it.

"Hashshashin" has become our word "assassin", because an old sect of Mohammedanism killed nonbelievers as a part of its creed.

A pitcher of water has to be present in the Mohammedan worship as a symbol of God filling the universe.

The Hindus believe that there will be ten Divine Incarnations. Nine have been and the tenth is still to come.

* * *

Shankara sometimes resorts to sophistry in order to prove that the ideas in the books go to uphold his philosophy. Buddha was more brave and sincere than any teacher. He said: "Believe no book; the Vedas are all humbug. If they agree with me, so much the better for the books. I am the greatest book; sacrifice and prayer are useless." Buddha was the first human being to give to the world a complete system of morality. He was good for good's sake, he loved for love's sake.

Shankara says: God is to be reasoned on, because the Vedas say so. Reason helps inspiration; books and realised reason — or individualized perception — both are proofs of God. The Vedas are, according to him, a sort of incarnation of universal knowledge. The proof of God is that He brought forth the Vedas, and the proof of the Vedas is that such wonderful books could only have been given out by Brahman. They are the mine of all knowledge, and they have come out of Him as a man breathes out air; therefore we know that He is infinite in power and knowledge. He may or may not have created the world, that is a trifle; to have produced the Vedas is more important! The world has come to know God through the Vedas; no other way there is.

And so universal is this belief, held by Shankara, in the all-inclusiveness of the Vedas that there is even a Hindu proverb that if a man loses his cow, he goes to look for her in the Vedas!

Shankara further affirms that obedience to ceremonial is not knowledge. Knowledge of God is independent of moral duties, or sacrifice or ceremonial, or what we think or do not think, just as the stump is not affected when one man takes it for a ghost and another sees it as it is.

Vedanta is necessary because neither reasoning nor books can show us God. He is only to be realised by superconscious perception, and Vedanta teaches how to attain that. You must get beyond personal God (Ishvara) and reach the Absolute Brahman. God is the perception of every being: He is all there is to he perceived. That which says "I" is Brahman, but although we, day and night, perceive Him; we do not know that we are perceiving Him. As soon as we become aware of this truth, all misery goes; so we must get knowledge of the truth. Reach unity; no more duality will come. But knowledge does not come by sacrifice, but by seeking, worshipping, knowing the Atman.

Brahmavidyâ is the highest knowledge, knowing the Brahman; lower knowledge is science. This is the teaching of the Mundakopanishad or the Upanishad for Sannyâsins. There are two sorts of knowledge — principal and secondary. The unessential is that part of the Vedas dealing with worship and ceremonial, also all secular knowledge. The essential is that by which we reach the Absolute. It (the Absolute) creates all from Its own nature; there is nothing to cause, nothing outside. It is all energy, It is all there is. He who makes all sacrifices to himself, the Atman, he alone knows Brahman. Fools think outside worship the highest; fools think works can give us God. Only those who go through the Sushumnâ (the "path" of the Yogis) reach the Atman. They must go to a Guru to learn. Each part has the same nature as the whole; all springs from the Atman. Meditation is the arrow, the whole soul going out to God is the bow, which speeds the arrow to its mark, the Atman. As finite, we can never express the Infinite, but we are the Infinite. Knowing this we argue with no one.

Divine wisdom is to be got by devotion, meditation, and chastity. "Truth alone triumphs, and not untruth. Through truth alone the way is spread to Brahman" — where alone love and truth are.

XIX

RECORDED BY MISS S. E. WALDO, A DISCIPLE

THURSDAY, July 11, 1895.

Without mother-love no creation could continue. Nothing is entirely physical, nor yet entirely metaphysical; one presupposes the other and explains the other. All Theists agree that there is a background to this visible universe, they differ as to the nature or character of that background. Materialists say there is no background.

In all religions the superconscious state is identical. Hindus, Christians, Mohammedans, Buddhists, and even those of no creed, all have the very same experience when they transcend the body....

The purest Christians in the world were established in India by the Apostle Thomas about twenty-five years after the death of Jesus. This was while the Anglo-Saxons were still savages, painting their bodies and living in caves. The Christians in India once numbered about three millions, but now there are about one million.

Christianity is always propagated by the sword. How wonderful that the disciples of such a gentle soul should kill so much! The three missionary religions are the Buddhist, Mohammedan, and Christian. The three older ones, Hinduism, Judaism and Zoroastrianism, never sought to make converts. Buddhists never killed, but converted three-quarters of the world at one time by pure gentleness.

The Buddhists were the most logical agnostics. You can really stop nowhere between nihilism and absolutism. The Buddhists were intellectually all-destroyers, carrying their theory to its ultimate logical issue. The Advaitists also worked out their theory to its logical conclusion and reached the Absolute — one identified Unit Substance out of which all phenomena are being manifested. Both Buddhists and Advaitists have a feeling of identity and non-identity at the same time; one of these feelings must be false, and the other true. The nihilist puts the reality in non-identity, the realist puts the reality in identity; and this is the fight which occupies the whole world. This is the "tug-of-war".

The realist asks, "How does the nihilist get any idea of identity?" How does the revolving light appear a circle? A point of rest alone explains motion. The nihilist can never explain the genesis of the delusion that there is a background; neither can the idealist explain how the One becomes the many. The only explanation must come from beyond the sense-plane; we must rise to the superconscious, to a state entirely beyond sense-perception. That metaphysical power is the further instrument that the idealist alone can use. He can experience the Absolute; the man Vivekananda can resolve himself into the Absolute and then come back to the man again.

For him, then the problem is solved and secondarily for others, for he can show the way to others. Thus religion begins where philosophy ends. The "good of the world" will be that what is now superconscious for us will in ages to come be the conscious for all. Religion is therefore the highest work the world has; and because man has unconsciously felt this, he has clung through all the ages to the idea of religion.

Religion, the great milch cow, has given many kicks, but never mind, it gives a great deal of milk. The milkman does not mind the kick of the cow which gives much milk. Religion is the greatest child to be born, the great "moon of realisation"; let us feed it and help it grow, and it will become a giant. King Desire and King Knowledge fought, and just as the latter was about to be defeated, he was reconciled to Queen Upanishad and a child was born to him, Realisation, who saved the victory to him.(From the Prabodha-chandrodaya, a Vedantic Sanskrit masque.)

Love concentrates all the power of the will without effort, as when a man falls in love with a woman.

The path of devotion is natural and pleasant. Philosophy is taking the mountain stream back to its force. It is a quicker method but very hard. Philospophy says, "Check everything." Devotion says, "Give the stream, have eternal self-surrender." It is a longer way, but easier and happier.

"Thine am I for ever; henceforth whatever I do, it is Thou doing it. No more is there any me or mine."

"Having no money to give, no brains to learn, no time to practice Yoga, to Thee, O sweet One, I give myself, to Thee my body and mind."

No amount of ignorance or wrong ideas can put a barrier between the soul and God. Even if there be no God, still hold fast to love. It is better to die seeking a God than as a dog seeking only carrion. Choose the highest ideal, and give your life up to that. "Death being so certain, it is the highest thing to give up life for a great purpose."

Love will painlessly attain to philosophy; then after knowledge comes Parâbhakti (supreme devotion).

Knowledge is critical and makes a great fuss over everything; but Love says, "God will show His real nature to me" and accepts all.

RABBIA

Rabbia, sick upon her bed,
By two saints was visited —
Holy Malik, Hassan wise —
Men of mark in Moslem eyes.

Hassan said, "Whose prayer is pure
Will God's chastisements endure."
Malik, from a deeper sense
Uttered his experience:
"He who loves his master's choice
Will in chastisement rejoice."

Rabbia saw some selfish will
In their maxims lingering still,
And replied "O men of grace,
He who sees his Master's face,
Will not in his prayers recall
That he is chastised at all !"

— Persian Poem

XX

RECORDED BY MISS S. E. WALDO, A DISCIPLE

FRIDAY, July 12, 1895. (Shankara's Commentary.)

Fourth Vyasa Sutra. "Âtman (is) the aim of all."

Ishvara is to be known from the Vedanta; all Vedas point to Him (Who is the Cause; the Creator, Preserver and Destroyer). Ishvara is the unification of the Trinity, known as Brahmâ, Vishnu, and Shiva, which stand at the head of the Hindu Pantheon. "Thou art our Father who takest us to the other shore of the dark ocean" (Disciple's words to the

Master).

The Vedas cannot show you Brahman, you are That already; they can only help to take away the veil that hides the truth from our eyes. The first veil to vanish is ignorance; and when that is gone, sin goes; next desire ceases, selfishness ends, and all misery disappears. This cessation of ignorance can only come when I know that God and I are one; in other words, identify yourself with Atman, not with human limitations. Dis-identify yourself with the body, and all pain will cease. This is the secret of healing. The universe is a case of hypnotisation; de-hypnotise yourself and cease to suffer.

In order to be free we have to pass through vice to virtue, and then get rid of both. Tamas is to be conquered by Rajas, both are to be submerged in Sattva; then go beyond the three qualities. Reach a state where your very breathing is a prayer.

Whenever you learn (gain anything) from another man's words, know that you had the experience in a previous existence, because experience is the only teacher.

With all powers comes further misery, so kill desire. Getting any desire is like putting a stick into a nest of hornets. Vairâgya is finding, out that desires are but gilded balls of poison.

"Mind is not God" (Shankara). "Tat tvam asi" "Aham Brahmâsmi" ("That thou art", "I am Brahman"). When a man realises this, all the knots of his heart are cut asunder, all his doubts vanish". Fearlessness is not possible as long as we have even God over us; we must be God. What is disjoined will be for ever disjoined; if you are separate from God, then you can never be one with Him, and vice versa. If by virtue you are joined to God, when that ceases, disjunction will come. The junction is eternal, and virtue only helps to remove the veil. We are âzâd (free), we must realise it. "Whom the Self chooses" means we are the Self and choose ourselves.

Does seeing depend upon our own efforts or does it depend upon something outside? It depends upon ourselves; our efforts take off the dust, the mirror does not change. There is neither knower, knowing, nor known. "He who knows that he does not know, knows It." He who has a theory knows nothing.

The idea that we are bound is only an illusion.

Religion is not of this world; it is "heart-cleansing", and its effect on this world is secondary. Freedom is inseparable from the nature of the Atman. This is ever pure, ever perfect, ever unchangeable. This Atman you can never know. We can say nothing about the Atman but "not this, not this".

"Brahman is that which we can never drive out by any power of mind or imagination." (Shankara).

* * *

The universe is thought, and the Vedas are the words of this thought. We can create and uncreate this whole universe. Repeating the words, the unseen thought is aroused, and as a result a seen effect is produced. This is the claim of a certain sect of Karmis. They think that each one of us is a creator. Pronounce the words, the thought which corresponds will arise, and the result will become visible. "Thought is the power of the word, the word is the expression of the thought," say Mimâmsakas, a Hindu philosophical sect.

XXI

RECORDED BY MISS S. E. WALDO, A DISCIPLE

SATURDAY, July 13th, 1895.

Everything we know is a compound, and all sense-knowledge comes through analysis. To think that mind is a simple, single, or independent is dualism. Philosophy is not got by studying books; the more you read books, the more muddled becomes the mind. The idea of unthinking philosophers was that the mind was a simple, and this led them to believe in free-will. Psychology, the analysis of the mind, shows the mind to be a compound, and every compound must be held together by some outside force; so the will is bound by the combination of outside forces. Man cannot even will to eat unless he is hungry. Will is subject to desire. But we are free; everyone feels it.

The agnostic says this idea is a delusion. Then, how do you prove the world? Its only proof is that we all see it and feel it; so just as much we all feel freedom. If universal consensus affirms this world, then it must be accepted as affirming freedom; but freedom is not of the will as it is. The constitutional belief of man in freedom is the basis of all reasoning. Freedom is of the will as it was before it became bound. The very idea of free-will shows every moment man's struggle against bondage. The free can be only one, the Unconditioned, the Infinite, the Unlimited. Freedom in man is now a memory, an attempt towards freedom.

Everything in the universe is struggling to complete a circle, to return to its source, to return to its only real Source, Atman. The search for happiness is a struggle to find the balance, to restore the equilibrium. Morality is the struggle of the bound will to get free and is the proof that we have come from perfection. . . .

The idea of duty is the midday sun of misery scorching the very soul. "O king, drink this one drop of nectar and be happy." ("I am not the doer", this is the nectar.)

Let there be action without reaction; action is pleasant, all misery is reaction. The child puts its hand in the flame, that is pleasure; but when its system reacts, then comes the pain of burning. When we can stop that reaction, then we have nothing to fear. Control the brain and do not let it read the record; be the witness and do not react, only thus can you be happy. The happiest moments we ever know are when we entirely forget ourselves. Work of your own free will, not from duty. We have no duty. This world is just a gymnasium in which we play; our life is an eternal holiday.

The whole secret of existence is to have no fear. Never fear what will become of you, depend on no one. Only the moment you reject all help are you free. The full sponge can absorb no more.

* * *

Even fighting in self-defence is wrong, though it is higher than fighting in aggression. There is no "righteous" indignation, because indignation comes from not recognising sameness in all things.

XXII

RECORDED BY MISS S. E. WALDO, A DISCIPLE

SUNDAY, July 14, 1895.

Philosophy in India means that through which we see God, the rationale of religion; so no Hindu could ever ask for a link between religion and philosophy.

Concrete, generalised, abstract are the three stages in the process of philosophy. The highest abstraction in which all things agree is the One. In religion we have first, symbols and forms; next, mythologies; and last, philosophy. The first two are for the time being; philosophy is the underlying basis of all, and the others are only stepping stones in the struggle to reach the Ultimate.

In Western religion the idea is that without the New Testament and Christ there could be no religion. A similar belief exists in Judaism with regard to Moses and the Prophets, because these religions are dependent upon mythology only. Real religion, the highest, rises above mythology; it can never rest upon that. Modern science has really made the foundations of religion strong. That the whole universe is one, is scientifically demonstrable. What the metaphysicians call "being", the physicist calls "matter", but there is no real fight between the two, for both are one. Though an atom is invisible, unthinkable, yet in it are the whole power and potency of the universe. That is exactly what the Vedantist says of Atman. All sects are really saying the same thing in different words.

Vedanta and modern science both posit a self-evolving Cause. In Itself are all the causes. Take for example the potter shaping a pot. The potter is the primal cause, the clay the material cause, and the wheel the instrumental cause; but the Atman is all three. Atman is cause and manifestation too.

The Vedantist says the universe is not real, it is only apparent. Nature is God seen through nescience. The Pantheists say, God has become nature or this world; the Advaitists affirm that God is appearing as this world, but He is not this world.

We can only know experience as a mental process, a fact in the mind as well as a mark in the brain. We cannot push the brain back or forward, but we can the mind; it can stretch over all time — past, present, and future; and so facts in the mind are eternally preserved. All facts are already generalised in mind, which is omnipresent.[6]*

Kant's great achievement was the discovery that "time, space, and causation are modes of thought," but Vedanta taught this ages ago and called it "Maya." Schopenhauer stands on reason only and rationalises the Vedas. . . . Shankara maintained the orthodoxy of the Vedas.

***

"Treeness" or the idea of "tree", found out among trees is knowledge, and the highest knowledge is One. . . .

Personal God is the last generalization of the universe, only hazy, not clear-cut and philosophic. . . .

Unity is self-evolving, out of which everything comes.

Physical science is to find out facts, metaphysics is the thread to bind the flowers into a bouquet. Every abstraction is metaphysical; even putting manure at the root of a tree involves a process of abstraction. . . .

Religion includes the concrete, the more generalized and the ultimate unity. Do not stick to particularisations. Get to the principle, to the One. . . .

Devils are machines of darkness, angels are machines of light; but both are machines. Man alone is alive. Break the machine, strike the balance[7]* and then man can become free. This is the only world where man can work out his salvation.

"Whom the Self chooses" is true. Election is true, but put it within. As an external and fatalistic doctrine, it is horrible.

XXIII

RECORDED BY MISS S. E. WALDO, A DISCIPLE

MONDAY, July 15, 1895.

Where there is polyandry, as in Tibet, women are physically stronger than the men. When the English go there, these women carry large men up the mountains.

In Malabar, although of course polyandry does not obtain there, the women lead in everything. Exceptional cleanliness is apparent everywhere and there is the greatest impetus to learning. When I myself was in that country, I met many women who spoke good Sanskrit, while in the rest of India not one woman in a million can speak it. Mastery elevates, and servitude debases. Malabar has never been conquered either by the Portuguese or by the Mussulmans.

The Dravidians were a non-Aryan race of Central Asia who preceded the Aryans, and those of Southern India were the most civilised. Women with them stood higher than men. They subsequently divided, some going to Egypt, others to Babylonia, and the rest remaining in India.

XXIV

RECORDED BY MISS S. E. WALDO, A DISCIPLE

TUESDAY, July 16, 1895. (Shankara)

The "unseen cause" (Or mass of subtle impressions.) leads us to sacrifice and worship, which in turn produce seen results; but to attain liberation we must first hear, then think or reason, and then meditate upon Brahman.

The result of works and the result of knowledge are two different things. "Do" and "Do not do" are the background of all morality, but they really belong only to the body and the mind. All happiness and misery are inextricably connected with the senses, and body is necessary to experience them.

The higher the body, the higher the standard of virtue, even up to Brahma; but all have bodies. As long as there is a body, there must be pleasure and pain; only when one has got rid of the body can one escape them. The Atman is bodiless, says Shankara.

No law can make you free, you are free. Nothing can give you freedom, if you have it not already. The Atman is self-illumined. Cause and effect do not reach there, and this disembodiedness is freedom. Beyond what was, or is, or is to be, is Brahman. As an effect, freedom would have no value; it would be a compound, and as such would contain the seeds of bondage. It is the one real factor. Not to be attained, hut the real nature of the soul.

Work and worship, however, are necessary to take away the veil, to lift oh the bondage and illusion. They do not give us freedom; but all the same, without effort on our own part we do not open our eyes and see what we are. Shankara says further that Advaita-Vedanta is the crowning glory of the Vedas; hut the lower Vedas are also necessary, because they teach work and worship, and through these many come to the Lord. Others may come without any help but Advaita. Work and worship lead to the same result as Advaita.

Books cannot teach God, but they can destroy ignorance; their action is negative. To hold to the books and at the same time open the way to freedom is Shankara's great achievement. But after all, it is a kind of hair-splitting. Give man first the concrete, then raise him to the highest by slow degrees. This is the effort of the various religions and explains their existence and why each is suited to some stage of development. The very books are a part of the ignorance they help to dispel. Their duty is to drive out the ignorance that has come upon knowledge. "Truth shall drive out untruth." You are free and cannot he made so. So long as you have a creed, you have no God. "He who knows he knows, knows nothing." Who can know the Knower? There are two eternal facts in existence, God and the universe, the former unchangeable, the latter changeable. The world exists eternally. Where your mind cannot grasp the amount of change, you call it eternally.... You see the stone or the bas-relief on it, but not both at once; yet both are one.

* * *

Can you make yourself at rest even for a second? All Yogis say you can....

The greatest sin is to think yourself weak. No one is greater: realise you are Brahman. Nothing has power except what you give it. We are beyond the sun, the stars, the universe. Teach the Godhood of man. Deny evil, create none. Stand up and say, I am the master, the master of all. We forge the chain, and we alone can break it.

No action can give you freedom; only knowledge can make you free, Knowledge is irresistible; the mind cannot take it or reject it. When it comes the mind has to accept it; so it is not a work of the mind; only, its expression comes in the mind.

Work or worship is to bring you back to your own nature. It is an entire illusion that the Self is the body; so even while living here in the body, we can be free. The body has nothing in common with the Self. Illusion is taking the real for the unreal — not "nothing at all".

XXIV

RECORDED BY MISS S. E. WALDO, A DISCIPLE

WEDNESDAY, July 17, 1895.

Râmânuja divides the universe into Chit, Achit, and Ishvara — man, nature, and God; conscious, subconscious, and superconscious. Shankara, on the contrary, says that Chit, the soul, is the same as God. God is truth, is knowledge, is infinity; these are not qualities. Any thought of God is a qualification, and all that can be said of Him is "Om tat sat".

Shankara further asks, can you see existence separate from everything else? Where is the differentiation between two objects? Not in sense-perception, else all would be one in it. We have to perceive in sequence. In getting knowledge of what a thing is, we get also something which it is not. The differentiae are in the memory and are got by comparison with what is stored there. Difference is not in the nature of a thing, it is in the brain. Homogeneous one is outside, differentiae are inside (in the mind); so the idea of "many" is the creation of the mind.

Differentiae become qualities when they are separate but joined in one object. We cannot say positively what differentiation is. All that we see and feel about things is pure and simple existence, "isness". All else is in us. Being is the only positive proof we have of anything. All differentiation is really "secondary reality", as the snake in the rope, because the serpent, too, had a certain reality, in that something was seen although misapprehended. When the knowledge of the rope becomes negative, the knowledge of the snake becomes positive, and vice versa; but the fact that you see only one does not prove that the other is non-existent. The idea of the world is an obstruction covering the idea of God and is to be removed, but it does have an existence.

Shankara says again, perception is the last proof of existence. It is self-effulgent and self-conscious, because to go beyond the senses we should still need perception. Perception is independent of the senses, of all instruments, unconditioned. There can be no perception without consciousness; perception has self-luminosity, which in a lesser degree is called consciousness. Not one act of perception can be unconscious; in fact, consciousness is the nature of perception. Existence and perception are one thing, not two things joined together. That which is infinite; so, as perception is the last it is eternal. It is always subjective; is its own perceiver. Perception is not: perception brings mind. It is absolute, the only knower, so perception is really the Atman. Perception itself perceives, but the Atman cannot be a knower, because a "knower" becomes such by the action of knowledge; but, Shankara says, "This Atman is not I", because the consciousness "I am" (Aham) is not in the Atman. We are but the reflections of that Atman; and Atman and Brahman are one.

When you talk and think of the Absolute, you have to do it in the relative; so all these logical arguments apply. In Yoga, perception and realisation are one. Vishishtâdvaita, of which Ramanuja is the exponent, is seeing partial unity and is a step toward Advaita. Vishishta means differentiation. Prakriti is the nature of the world, and change comes upon it. Changeful thoughts expressed in changeful words can never prove the Absolute. You reach only something that is minus certain qualities, not Brahman Itself; only a verbal unification, the highest abstraction, but not the nonexistence of the relative.

XXV

RECORDED BY MISS S. E. WALDO, A DISCIPLE

THURSDAY, July 18, 1895.

The lesson today was mainly Shankara's argument against the conclusion of the Sânkhya philosophy.

The Sankhyas say that consciousness is a compound, and beyond that, the last analysis gives us the Purusha, Witness, but that there are many Purushas — each of us is one. Advaita, on the contrary, affirms that Purushas can be only One, that Purusha cannot be conscious, unconscious, or have any qualification, for either these qualities would bind, or they would eventually cease; so the One must be without any qualities, even knowledge, and It cannot be the cause of the universe or of anything. "In the beginning, existence only, One without a second", says the Vedas.

***

The presence of Sattva with knowledge does not prove that Sattva is the cause of knowledge; on the contrary, Sattva calls out what was already existing in man, as the fire heats an iron ball placed near it by arousing the heat latent in it, not by entering into the ball.

Shankara says, knowledge is not a bondage, because it is the nature of God. The world ever is, whether manifested or unmanifested; so an eternal object exists.

Jnâna-bala-kriyâ (knowledge, power, activity) is

God. Nor does He need form, because the finite only needs form to interpose as an obstruction to catch and hold infinite knowledge; but God really needs no such help. There is no "moving soul", there is only one Atman. Jiva (individual soul) is the conscious ruler of this body, in whom the five life principles come into unity, and yet that very Jiva is the Atman, because all is Atman. What you think about it is your delusion and not in the Jiva. You are God, and whatever else you may think is wrong. You must worship the Self in Krishna, not Krishna as Krishna. Only by worshipping the Self can freedom be won. Even personal God is but the Self objectified. "Intense search after my own reality is Bhakti", says Shankara.

All the means we take to reach God are true; it is only like trying to find the pole-star by locating it through the stars that are around it.

* * *

The Bhagavad-Gita is the best authority on Vedanta.

XXVI

RECORDED BY MISS S. E. WALDO, A DISCIPLE

FRIDAY, July 19, 1895.

So long as I say "you", I have the right to speak of God protecting us. When I see another, I must take all the consequences and put in the third, the ideal, which stands between us; that is the apex of the triangle. The vapour becomes snow, then water, then Ganga; but when it is vapour, there is no Ganga, and when it is water, we think of no vapour in it. The idea of creation or change is inseparably connected with will. So long as we perceive this world in motion, we have to conceive will behind it. Physics proves the utter delusion of the senses; nothing really is as ever see, hear, feel, smell, taste it. Certain vibrations producing certain results affect our senses; we know only relative truth.

The Sanskrit word for truth is "isness" (Sat). From our present standpoint, this world appears to us as will and consciousness. Personal God is as much an entity for Himself as we are for ourselves, and no more. God can also be seen as a form, just as we are seen. As men, we must have a God; as God, we need none. This is why Shri Ramakrishna constantly saw the Divine Mother ever present with him, more real than any other thing around him; but in Samâdhi all went but the Self. Personal God comes nearer and nearer until He melts away, and there is no more Personal God and no more "I", all is merged in Self.

Consciousness is a bondage. The argument from design claims that intelligence precedes form; but if intelligence is the cause of anything, it itself is in its turn an effect. It is Maya. God creates us, and we create God, and this is Maya. The circle is unbroken; mind creates body, and body creates mind; the egg brings the chicken, the chicken the egg; the tree the seed, the seed the tree. The world is neither entirely differentiated nor yet entirely homogeneous. Man is free and must rise above both sides. Both are right in their place; but to reach truth, "isness", we must transcend all that we now know of existence, will, consciousness, doing, going, knowing. There is no real individuality of the Jiva (separate soul); eventually it, as a compound, will go to pieces. Only that which is beyond further analysis is "simple", and that alone is truth, freedom, immortality, bliss. All struggles for the preservation of this illusive individuality are really vices. All struggles to lose this individuality are virtues. Everything in the universe is trying to break down this individuality, either consciously or unconsciously. All morality is based upon the destruction of separateness or false individuality, because that is the cause of all sin. Morality exists first; later, religion codifies it. Customs come first, and then mythology follows to explain them. While things are happening, they come by a higher law than reasoning; that arises later in the attempt to understand them. Reasoning is not the motive power, it is "chewing the cud" afterwards. Reason is the historian of the actions of the human beings.

* * *

Buddha was a great Vedantist (for Buddhism was really only an offshoot of Vedanta), and Shankara is often called a "hidden Buddhist". Buddha made the analysis, Shankara made the synthesis out of it. Buddha never bowed down to anything — neither Veda, nor caste, nor priest, nor custom. He fearlessly reasoned so far as reason could take him. Such a fearless search for truth and such love for every living thing the world has never seen. Buddha was the Washington of the religious world; he conquered a throne only to give it to the world, as Washington did to the American people. He sought nothing for himself.

XXVII

RECORDED BY MISS S. E. WALDO, A DISCIPLE

SATURDAY, July 20, 1895.

Perception is our only real knowledge or religion. Talking about it for ages will never make us know our soul. There is no difference between theories and atheism. In fact, the atheist is the truer man. Every step I take in the light is mine for ever. When you go to a country and see it, then it is yours. We have each to see for ourselves; teachers can only "bring the food", we must eat it to be nourished. Argument can never prove God save as a logical conclusion.

It is impossible to find God outside of ourselves. Our own souls contribute all the divinity that is outside of us. We are the greatest temple. The objectification is only a faint imitation of what we see within ourselves.

Concentration of the powers of the mind is our only instrument to help us see God. If you know one soul (your own), you know all souls, past, present, and to come. The will concentrates the mind, certain things excite and control this will, such as reason, love, devotion, breathing. The concentrated mind is a lamp that shows us every corner of the soul.

No one method can suit all. These different methods are not steps necessary to be taken one after another. Ceremonials are the lowest form; next God external, and after that God internal. In some cases gradation may be needed, but in many only one way is required. It would be the height of folly to say to everyone, "You must pass through Karma and Bhakti before you can reach Jnana."

Stick to your reason until you reach something higher; and you will know it to be higher, because it will not jar with reason. The stage beyond consciousness is inspiration (Samâdhi); but never mistake hysterical trances for the real thing. It is a terrible thing to claim this inspiration falsely, to mistake instinct for inspiration. There is no external test for inspiration, we know it ourselves; our guardian against mistake is negative — the voice of reason. All religion is going beyond reason, but reason is the only guide to get there. Instinct is like ice, reason is the water, and inspiration is the subtlest form or vapour; one follows the other. Everywhere is this eternal sequence — unconsciousness, consciousness, intelligence — matter, body, mind — and to us it seems as if the chain began with the particular link we first lay hold of. Arguments on both sides are of equal weight, and both are true. We must reach beyond both, to where there is neither the one nor the other. These successions are all Maya.

Religion is above reason, supernatural. Faith is not belief, it is the grasp on the Ultimate, an illumination. First hear, then reason and find out all that reason can give about the Atman; let the flood of reason flow over It, then take what remains. If nothing remains, thank God you have escaped a superstition. When you have determined that nothing can take away the Atman, that It stands every test, hold fast to this and teach it to all. Truth cannot be partial; it is for the good of all. Finally, in perfect rest and peace meditate upon It, concentrate your mind upon It, make yourself one with It. Then no speech is needed; silence will carry the truth. Do not spend your energy in talking, but meditate in silence; and do not let the rush of the outside world disturb you. When your mind is in the highest state, you are unconscious of it. Accumulate power in silence and become a dynamo of spirituality. What can a beggar give? Only a king can give, and he only when he wants nothing himself.

Hold your money merely as custodian for what is God's. Have no attachment for it. Let name and fame and money go; they are a terrible bondage. Feel the wonderful atmosphere of freedom. You are free, free, free! Oh, blessed am I! Freedom am I! I am the Infinite! In my soul I can find no beginning and no end. All is my Self. Say this unceasingly.

XXVIII

RECORDED BY MISS S. E. WALDO, A DISCIPLE

SUNDAY, *July 21, 1895. (Patanjali's Yoga Aphorisms)*

Yoga is the science of restraining the Chitta (mind) from breaking into Vrittis (modifications). Mind is a mixture of sensation and feelings, or action and reaction; so it cannot be permanent. The mind has a fine body and through this it works on the gross body. Vedanta says that behind the mind is the real Self. It accepts the other two, but posits a third, the Eternal, the Ultimate, the last analysis, the unit, where there is no further compound. Birth is re-composition, death is de-composition, and the final analysis is where Atman is found; there being no further division possible, the perdurable is reached.

The whole ocean is present at the back of each wave, and all manifestations are waves, some very big, some small; yet all are the ocean in their essence, the whole ocean; but as waves each is a part. When the waves are stilled, then all is one; "a spectator without a spectacle", says Patanjali. When the mind is active, the Atman is mixed up with it. The repetition of old forms in quick succession is memory.

Be unattached. Knowledge is power, and getting one you get the other. By knowledge you can even banish the material world. When you can mentally get rid of one quality after another from any object until all are gone, you can at will make the object itself disappear from your consciousness.

Those who are ready, advance very quickly and can become Yogis in six months. The less developed may take several years; and anyone by faithful work and by giving up everything else and devoting himself solely to practice can reach the goal in twelve years. Bhakti will bring you there without any of these mental gymnastics, but it is a slower way.

Ishvara is the Atman as seen or grasped by mind. His highest name is Om; so repeat it, meditate on it, and think of all its wonderful nature and attributes. Repeating the Om continually is the only true worship. It is not a word, it is God Himself.

Religion gives you nothing new; it only takes off obstacles and lets you see your Self. Sickness is the first great obstacle; a healthy body is the best instrument. Melancholy is an almost insuperable barrier. If you have once known Brahman, never after can you be melancholy. Doubt, want of perseverance, mistaken ideas are other obstacles.

***

Prânas are subtle energies, sources of motion. There are ten in all, five inward and five outward. One great current flows upwards, and the other downwards. Prânâyâma is controlling the Pranas through breathing. Breath is the fuel, Prana is the steam, and the body is the engine. Pranayama has three parts, Puraka (in-breathing), Kumbhaka (holding the breath), Rechaka (out-breathing)....

The Guru is the conveyance in which the spiritual influence is brought to you. Anyone can teach, but the spirit must be passed on by the Guru to the Shishya (disciple), and that will fructify. The relation between Shishyas is that of brotherhood, and this is actually accepted by law in India. The Guru passes the thought power, the Mantra, that he has received from those before him; and nothing can be done without a Guru. In fact, great danger ensues. Usually without a Guru, these Yoga practices lead to lust; but with one, this seldom happens. Each Ishta has a Mantra. The Ishta is the ideal peculiar to the particular worshipper; the Mantra is the external word to express it. Constant repetition of the word helps to fix the ideal firmly in the mind. This method of worship prevails among religious devotees all over India.

XXIX

RECORDED BY MISS S. E. WALDO, A DISCIPLE

TUESDAY, July 23, 1895. (Bhagavad-Gita, Karma-Yoga)

To attain liberation through work, join yourself to work but without desire, looking for no result. Such work leads to knowledge, which in turn brings emancipation. To give up work before you know, leads to misery. Work done for the Self gives no bondage. Neither desire pleasure nor fear pain from work. It is the mind and body that work, not I. Tell yourself this unceasingly and realise it. Try not to know that you work.

Do all as a sacrifice or offering to the Lord. Be in the world, but not of it, like the lotus leaf whose roots are in the mud but which remains always pure. Let your love go to all, whatever they do to you. A blind man cannot see colour, so how can we see evil unless it is in us? We compare what we see outside with what we find in ourselves and pronounce judgment accordingly. If we are pure, we cannot see impurity. It may exist, but not for us. See only God in every man, woman and child; see it by the antarjyotis, "inner light", and seeing that, we can see naught else. Do not want this world, because what you desire you get. Seek the Lord and the Lord only. The more power there is, the more bondage, the more fear. How much more afraid and miserable are we than the ant! Get out of it all and come to the Lord. Seek the science of the maker and not that of the made.

"I am the doer and the deed." "He who can stem the tide of lust and anger is a great Yogi."

"Only by practice and non-attachment can we conquer mind." . . .

Our Hindu ancestors sat down and thought on God and morality, and so have we brains to use for the same ends; but in the rush of trying to get gain, we are likely to lose them again.

***

The body has in itself a certain power of curing itself and many things can rouse this curative power into action, such as mental conditions, or medicine, or exercise, etc. As long as we are disturbed by physical conditions, so long we need the help of physical agencies. Not until we have got rid of bondage to the nerves, can we disregard them.

There is the unconscious mind, but it is below consciousness, which is just one part of the human organism. Philosophy is guess-work about the mind. Religion is based upon sense contact, upon seeing, the only basis of knowledge. What comes in contact with the superconscious mind is fact. Âptas are those who have "sensed" religion. The proof is that if you follow their method, you too will see. Each science requires its own particular method and instruments. An astronomer cannot show you the rings of Saturn by the aid of all the pots and pans in the kitchen. He needs a telescope. So, to see the great facts of religion, the methods of those who have already seen must be followed. The greater the science the more varied the means of studying it. Before we came into the world, God provided the means to get out; so all we have to do is to find the means. But do not fight over methods. Look only for realisation and choose the best method you can find to suit you. Eat the mangoes and let the rest quarrel over the basket. See Christ, then you will be a Christian. All else is talk; the less talking the better.

The message makes the messenger. The Lord makes the temple; not vice versa.

Learn until "the glory of the Lord shines through your face", as it shone through the face of Shvetaketu.

Guess against guess makes fight; but talk of what you have been, and no human heart can resist it. Paul was converted against his will by realisation.

TUESDAY AFTERNOON

After dinner there was a short conversation in the

course of which the Swami said:

Delusion creates delusion. Delusion creates itself and destroys itself, such is Maya. All knowledge (so-called), being based on Maya, is a vicious circle, and in time that very knowledge destroys itself. "Let go the rope", delusion cannot touch the Atman. When we lay hold of the rope — identify ourselves with Maya — she has power over us. Let go of it, be the Witness only, then you can admire the picture of the universe undisturbed.

XXX

RECORDED BY MISS S. E. WALDO, A DISCIPLE

WEDNESDAY, *July 24, 1895.*

The powers acquired by the practice of Yoga are not obstacles for the Yogi who is perfect, but are apt to be so for the beginner, through the wonder and pleasure excited by their exercise. Siddhis are the powers which mark success in the practice; and they may be produced by various means, such as the repetition of a Mantra, by Yoga practice, meditation, fasting, or even by the use of herbs and drugs. The Yogi, who has conquered all interest in the powers acquired and who renounces all virtue arising from his actions, comes into the "cloud of virtue" (name of one of the states of Samadhi) and radiates holiness as a cloud rains water.

Meditation is on a series of objects, concentration is on one object.

Mind is cognised by the Atman, but it is not self-illuminated. The Atman cannot be the cause of anything. How can it be? How can the Purusha join itself to Prakriti (nature)? It does not; it is only illusively thought to do so. . . .

Learn to help without pitying or feeling that there is any misery. Learn to be the same to enemy and to friend; then when you can do that and no longer have any desire, the goal is attained.

Cut down the banyan tree of desire with the axe of non-attachment, and it will vanish utterly. It is all illusion. "He from whom blight and delusion have fallen, he who has conquered the evils of association, he alone is âzâd (free)."

To love anyone personally is bondage. Love all alike, then all desires fall off.

Time, the "eater of everything", comes, and all has to go. Why try to improve the earth, to paint the butterfly? It all has to go at last. Do not be mere white mice in a treadmill, working always and never accomplishing anything. Every desire is fraught with evil, whether the desire itself be good or evil. It is like a dog jumping for a piece of meat which is ever receding from his reach, and dying a dog's death at last. Do not be like that. Cut off all desire.

* * *

Paramâtman as ruling Maya is Ishvara; Paramâtman as under Maya is Jivâtman. Maya is the sum total of manifestation and will utterly vanish.

Tree-nature is Maya, it is really God-nature which we see under the veil of Maya. The "why" of anything is in Maya. To ask why Maya came is a useless question, because the answer can never be given in Maya, and beyond Maya who will ask it? Evil creates "why", not "why" the evil, and it is evil that asks "why". Illusion destroys illusion. Reason itself, being based upon contradiction, is a circle and has to kill itself. Sense-perception is an inference, and yet all inference comes from perception.

Ignorance reflecting the light of God is seen; but by itself it is zero. The cloud would not appear except as the sunlight falls on it.

There were four travellers who came to a high wall. The first one climbed with difficulty to the top and without looking back, jumped over. The second clambered up the wall, looked over, and with a shout of delight disappeared. The third in his turn climbed to the top, looked where his companions had gone, laughed with joy, and followed them. But the fourth one came back to tell what had happened to his fellow-travellers. The sign to us that there is something beyond is the laugh that rings back from those great ones who have plunged from Maya's wall.

***

Separating ourselves from the Absolute and attributing certain qualities to It give us Ishvara. It is the Reality of the universe as seen through our mind. Personal devil is the misery of the world seen through the minds of the superstitious.

XXXI

RECORDED BY MISS S. E. WALDO, A DISCIPLE

THURSDAY, July 25, 1895. (Patanjali's Yoga Aphorisms)

"Things may be done, caused to be done, or approved of", and the effect upon us is nearly equal.

Complete continence gives great intellectual and spiritual power. The Brahmachârin must be sexually pure in thought, word, and deed. Lose regard for the body; get rid of the consciousness of it so far as possible.

Âsana (posture) must be steady and pleasant; and constant practice, identifying the mind with the Infinite, will bring this about.

Continual attention to one object is contemplation.

When a stone is thrown into still water, many circles are made, each distinct but all interacting; so with our minds; only in us the action is unconscious, while with the Yogi it is conscious. We are spiders in a web, and Yoga practice will enable us like the spider to pass along any strand of the web we please. Non-Yogis are bound to the particular spot where they are.

***

To injure another creates bondage and hides the truth. Negative virtues are not enough; we have to conquer Maya, and then she will follow us. We only deserve things when they cease to bind us. When the bondage ceases, really and truly, all things come to us. Only those who want nothing are masters of nature.

Take refuge in some soul who has already broken his bondage, and in time he will free you through his mercy. Higher still is to take refuge in the Lord (Ishvara), but it is the most difficult; only once in a century can one be found who has really done it. Feel nothing, know nothing, do nothing, have nothing, give up all to God, and say utterly, "Thy will be done". We only dream this bondage. Wake up and let it go. Take refuge in God, only so can we cross the desert of Maya. "Let go thy hold, Sannyasin bold, say, Om tat sat, Om!"

It is our privilege to be allowed to be charitable, for only so can we grow. The poor man suffers that we may be helped; let the giver kneel down and give thanks, let the receiver stand up and permit. See the Lord back of every being and give to Him. When we cease to see evil, the world must end for us, since to rid us of that mistake is its only object. To think there is any imperfection creates it. Thoughts of strength and perfection alone can cure it. Do what good you can, some evil will inhere in it; but do all without regard to personal result, give up all results to the Lord, then neither good nor evil will affect you.

Doing work is not religion, but work done rightly leads to freedom. In reality all pity is darkness, because whom to pity? Can you pity God? And is there anything else? Thank God for giving you this world as a moral gymnasium to help your development, but never imagine you can help the world. Be grateful to him who curses you, for he gives you a mirror to show what cursing is, also a chance to practise self-restraint; so bless him and be glad. Without exercise, power cannot come out; without the mirror, we cannot see ourselves.

Unchaste imagination is as bad as unchaste action. Controlled desire leads to the highest result. Transform the sexual energy into spiritual energy, but do not emasculate, because that is throwing away the power. The stronger this force, the more can be done with it. Only a powerful current of water can do hydraulic mining.

What we need today is to know there is a God and that we can see and feel Him here and now.

A Chicago professor says, "Take care of this world, God will take care of the next." What nonsense! If we can take care of this world, what need of a gratuitous Lord to take care of the other!

XXXII

RECORDED BY MISS S. E. WALDO, A DISCIPLE

FRIDAY, July 26, 1895. (Brihadâranyakopanishad.)

Love all things only through and for the Self. Yâjnavalkya said to Maitreyi, his wife, "Through the Atman we know all things." The Atman can never be the object of knowledge, nor can the Knower be known. He who knows he is the Atman, he is law unto himself. He knows he is the universe and its creator. . . .

Perpetuating old myths in the form of allegories and giving them undue importance fosters superstition and is really weakness. Truth must have no compromise. Teach truth and make no apology for any superstition; neither drag truth to the level of the listener.

XXXIII

RECORDED BY MISS S. E. WALDO, A DISCIPLE

SATURDAY, July 27, 1895. (Kathopanishad)

Learn not the truth of the Self save from one who has realised it; in all others it is mere talk. Realisation is beyond virtue and vice, beyond future and past; beyond all the pairs of opposites. "The stainless one sees the Self, and an eternal calm comes in the Soul." Talking, arguing, and reading books, the highest flights of the intellect, the Vedas themselves, all these cannot give knowledge of the Self.

In us are two — The God-soul and the man-soul. The sages know that the latter is but the shadow, that the former is the only real Sun.

Unless we join the mind with the senses, we get no report from eyes, nose, ears, etc. The external organs are used by the power of the mind. Do not let the senses go outside, and then you can get rid of body and the external world.

This very "x" which we see here as an external world, the departed see as heaven or hell according to their own mental states. Here and hereafter are two dreams, the latter modelled on the former; get rid of both, all is omnipresent, all is now. Nature, body, and mind go to death, not we; we never go nor come. The man Swami Vivekananda is in nature, is born, and dies; but the self which we see as Swami Vivekananda is never born and never dies. It is the eternal and unchangeable Reality.

The power of the mind is the same whether we divide it into five senses or whether we see only one. A blind man says, "Everything has a distinct echo, so I clap my hands and get that echo, and then I can tell everything that is around me." So in a fog the blind man can safely lead the seeing man. Fog or darkness makes no difference to him.

Control the mind, cut off the senses, then you are a Yogi; after that, all the rest will come. Refuse to hear, to see, to smell, to taste; take away the mental power from the external organs. You continually do it unconsciously as when your mind is absorbed; so you can learn to do it consciously. The mind can put the senses where it pleases. Get rid of the fundamental superstition that we are obliged to act through the body. We are not. Go into your own room and get the Upanishads out of your own Self. You are the greatest book that ever was or ever will be, the infinite depository of all that is. Until the inner teacher opens, all outside teaching is in vain. It must lead to the opening of the book of the heart to have any value.

The will is the "still small voice", the real Ruler who says "do" and "do not". It has done all that binds us. The ignorant will leads to bondage, the knowing will can free us. The will can be made strong in thousands of ways; every way is a kind of Yoga, but the systematised Yoga accomplishes the work more quickly. Bhakti, Karma, Raja, and Jnana-Yoga get over the ground more effectively. Put on all powers, philosophy, work, prayer, meditation — crowd all sail, put on all head of steam — reach the goal. The sooner, the better....

Baptism is external purification symbolising the internal. It is of Buddhist origin.

The Eucharist is a survival of a very ancient custom of savage tribes. They sometimes killed their great chiefs and ate their flesh in order to obtain in themselves the qualities that made their leaders great. They believed that in such a way the characteristics that made the chief brave and wise would become theirs and make the whole tribe brave and wise, instead of only one man. Human sacrifice was also a Jewish idea and one that clung to them despite many chastisements from Jehovah. Jesus was gentle and loving, but to fit him into Jewish beliefs, the idea of human sacrifice, in the form of atonement or as a human scapegoat, had to come in. This cruel idea made Christianity depart from the teachings of Jesus himself and develop a spirit of persecution and bloodshed....

Say, "it is my nature", never say, "It is my duty" — to do anything whatever.

"Truth alone triumphs, not untruth." Stand upon Truth, and you have got God.

* * *

From the earliest times in India the Brahmin caste have held themselves beyond all law; they claim to be gods. They are poor, but their weakness is that they seek power. Here are about sixty millions of people who are good and moral and hold no property, and they are what they are because from their birth they are taught that they are above law, above punishment. They feel themselves to be "twice-born", to be sons of God.

XXXIV

RECORDED BY MISS S. E. WALDO, A DISCIPLE

SUNDAY, July 28, 1895.

Avadhuta Gita or "Song of the Purified" by Dattâtreya (Dattatreya, the son of Atri and Anasuyâ, was an incarnation of Brahmâ, Vishnu and Shiva.)

"All knowledge depends upon calmness of mind."

"He who has filled the universe, He who is Self in self, how shall I salute Him!"

To know the Atman as my nature is both knowledge and realisation. "I am He, there is not the least doubt of it."

"No thought, no word, no deed, creates a bondage for me. I am beyond the senses, I am knowledge and bliss."

There is neither existence nor non-existence, all is Atman. Shake off all ideas of relativity; shake off all superstitions; let caste and birth and Devas and all else vanish. Why talk of being and becoming? Give up talking of dualism and Advaitism! When were you two, that you talk of two or one? The universe is this Holy One and He alone. Talk not of Yoga to make you pure; you are pure by your very nature. None can teach you.

Men like him who wrote this song are what keep religion alive. They have actually realised; they care for nothing, feel nothing done to the body, care not for heat and cold or danger or anything. They sit still and enjoy the bliss of Atman, while red-hot coals burn their body, and they feel them not.

"When the threefold bondage of knower, knowledge, and known ceases, there is the Atman."

"Where the delusion of bondage and freedom ceases, there the Atman is."

"What if you have controlled the mind, what if you have not? What if you have money, what if you have not? You are the Atman ever pure. Say, 'I am the Atman. No bondage ever came near me. I am the changeless sky; clouds of belief may pass over me, but they do not touch me.'"

"Burn virtue, burn vice. Freedom is baby talk. I am that immortal Knowledge. I am that purity."

"No one was ever bound, none was ever free. There is none but me. I am the Infinite, the Ever-free. Talk not to me! What can change me, the essence of knowledge! Who can teach, who can be taught?"

Throw argument, throw philosophy into the ditch.

"Only a slave sees slaves, the deluded delusion, the impure impurity."

Place, time causation are all delusions. It is your disease that you think you are bound and will be free. You are the Unchangeable. Talk not. Sit down and let all things melt away, they are but dreams. There is no differentiation, no distinction, it is all superstition; therefore be silent and know what you are.

"I am the essence of bliss." Follow no ideal, you are all there is. Fear naught, you are the essence of existence. Be at peace. Do not disturb yourself. You never were in bondage, you never were virtuous or sinful. Get rid of all these delusions and be at peace. Whom to worship? Who worships? All is the Atman. To speak, to think is superstition. Repeat over and over, "I am Atman", "I am Atman". Let everything else go.

XXXV

RECORDED BY MISS S. E. WALDO, A DISCIPLE

MONDAY, July 29, 1895.

We sometimes indicate a thing by describing its surroundings. When we say "Sachchidananda" (Existence-Knowledge-Bliss), we are merely indicating the shores of an indescribable Beyond. Not even can we say "is" about it, for that too is relative. Any imagination, any concept is in vain. Neti, neti ("Not this, not this") is all that can be said, for even to think is to limit and so to lose.

The senses cheat you day and night. Vedanta found that out ages ago; modern science is just discovering the same fact. A picture has only length and breadth, and the painter copies nature in her cheating by artificially giving the appearance of depth. No two people see the same world. The highest knowledge will show you that there is no motion, no change in anything; that the very idea of it is all Maya. Study nature as a whole, that is, study motion. Mind and body are not our real self; both belong to nature, but eventually we can know the ding an sich. Then mind and body being transcended, all that they conceive goes. When you cease utterly to know and see the world, then you realise Atman. The superseding of relative knowledge is what we want. There is no infinite mind or infinite knowledge, because both mind and knowledge are limited. We are now seeing through a veil; then we reach the "x", which is the Reality of all our knowing.

If we look at a picture through a pin-hole in a cardboard, we get an utterly mistaken notion; yet what we see is really the picture. As we enlarge the hole, we get a clearer and clearer idea. Out of the reality we manufacture the different views in conformity with our mistaken perceptions of name and form. When we throw away the cardboard, we see the same picture, but we see it as it is. We put in all the attributes, all the errors; the picture itself is unaltered thereby. That is because Atman is the reality of all; all we see is Atman, but not as we see it, as name and form; they are all in our veil, in Maya.

They are like spots in the object-glass of a telescope, yet it is the light of the sun that shows us the spots; we could not even see the illusion save for the background of reality which is Brahman. Swami Vivekananda is just the speck on the object-glass; I am Atman, real, unchangeable, and that reality alone enables me to see Swami Vivekananda. Atman is the essence of every hallucination; but the sun is never identified with the spots on the glass, it only shows them to us. Our actions, as they are evil or good, increase or decrease the "spots"; but they never affect the God within us. Perfectly cleanse the mind of spots and instantly we see, "I and my father are one".

We first perceive, then reason later. We must have this perception as a fact, and it is called religion, realisation. No matter if one never heard of creed or prophet or book. Let him get this realisation, and he needs no more. Cleanse the mind, this is all of religion; and until we ourselves clear off the spots, we cannot see the Reality as it is. The baby sees no sun; he has not yet the measure of it in himself. Get rid of the defects within yourself, and you will not be able to see any without. A baby sees robbery done, and it means nothing to him. Once you find the hidden object in a puzzle picture, you see it ever more; so when once you are free and stainless, you see only freedom and purity in the world around. That moment all the knots of the heart are cut asunder, all crooked places are made straight, and this world vanishes as a dream. And when we awake, we wonder how we ever came to dream such trash!

"Getting whom, misery mountain high has no power to move the soul."

With the axe of knowledge cut the wheels asunder, and the Atman stands free, even though the old momentum carries on the wheel of mind and body. The wheel can now only go straight, can only do good. If that body does anything bad, know that the man is not Jivanmukta; he lies if he makes that claim. But it is only when the wheels have got a good straight motion (from cleansing the mind) that the axe can be applied. All purifying action deals conscious or unconscious blows on delusion. To call another a sinner is the worst thing you can do. Good action done ignorantly produces the same result and helps to break the bondage.

To identify the sun with the spots on the object-glass is the fundamental error. Know the sun, the "I", to be ever unaffected by anything, and devote yourself to cleansing the spots. Man is the greatest being that ever can be. The highest worship there is, is to worship man as Krishna, Buddha, Christ. What you want, you create. Get rid of desire....

The angels and the departed are all here, seeing this world as heaven. The same "x" is seen by all according to their mental attitude. The best vision to be had of the "x" is here on this earth. Never want to go to heaven, that is the worst delusion. Even here, too much wealth and grinding poverty are both bondages and hold us back from religion. Three great gifts we have: first, a human body. (The human mind is the nearest reflection of God, we are "His own image".) Second, the desire to be free. Third, the help of a noble soul, who has crossed the ocean of delusion, as a teacher. When you have these three, bless the Lord; you are sure to be free.

What you only grasp intellectually may be overthrown by a new argument; but what you realise is yours for ever. Talking, talking religion is but little good. Put God behind everything — man, animal, food, work; make this a habit.

Ingersoll once said to me: "I believe in making the most out of this world, in squeezing the orange dry, because this world is all we are sure of." I replied: "I know a better way to squeeze the orange of this world than you do, and I get more out of it. I know I cannot die, so I am not in a hurry; I know there is no fear, so I enjoy the squeezing. I have no duty, no bondage of wife and children and property; I can love all men and women. Everyone is God to me. Think of the joy of loving man as God! Squeeze your orange this way and get ten thousandfold more out of it. Get every single drop."

That which seems to be the will is the Atman behind, it is really free.

MONDAY AFTERNOON

Jesus was imperfect because he did not live up fully to his own ideal, and above all because he did not give woman a place equal to man. Women did everything for him, and yet he was so bound by the Jewish custom that not one was made an apostle. Still he was the greatest character next to Buddha, who in his turn was not fully perfect. Buddha, however, recognised woman's right to an equal place in religion, and his first and one of his greatest disciples was his own wife, who became the head of the whole Buddhistic movement among the women of India. But we ought not to criticise these great ones, we should only look upon them as far above ourselves. Nonetheless we must not pin our faith to any man, however great; we too must become Buddhas and Christs.

No man should be judged by his defects. The great virtues a man has are his especially, his errors are the common weaknesses of humanity and should never be counted in estimating his character.

***

Vira, the Sanskrit word for "heroic", is the origin of our word "virtue", because in ancient times the best fighter was regarded as the most virtuous man.

XXXVI

RECORDED BY MISS S. E. WALDO, A DISCIPLE

TUESDAY, July 30, 1895.

Christs and Buddhas are simply occasions upon which to objectify our own inner powers. We really answer our own prayers.

It is blasphemy to think that if Jesus had never been born, humanity would not have been saved. It is horrible to forget thus the divinity in human nature, a divinity that must come out. Never forget the glory of human nature. We are the greatest God that ever was or ever will be. Christs and Buddhas are but waves on the boundless ocean which I am. Bow down to nothing but your own higher Self. Until you know that you are that very God of gods, there will never be any freedom for you.

All our past actions are really good, because they lead us to what we ultimately become. Of whom to beg? I am the real existence, and all else is a dream save as it is I. I am the whole ocean; do not call the little wave you have made "I"; know it for nothing but a wave. Satyakâma (lover of truth) heard the inner voice telling him, "You are the infinite, the universal is in you. Control yourself and listen to the voice of your true Self."

The great prophets who do the fighting have to be less perfect than those who live silent lives of holiness, thinking great thoughts and so helping the world. These men, passing out one after another, produce as final outcome the man of power who preaches.

***

Knowledge exists, man only discovers it. The Vedas are the eternal knowledge through which God created the world. They talk high philosophy — the highest — and make this tremendous claim....

Tell the truth boldly, whether it hurts or not. Never pander to weakness. If truth is too much for intelligent people and sweeps them away, let them go; the sooner the better. Childish ideas are for babies and savages; and these are not all in the nursery and the forests, some of them have fallen into the pulpits.

It is bad to stay in the church after you are grown up spiritually. Come out and die in the open air of freedom.

All progression is in the relative world. The human form is the highest and man the greatest being, because here and now we can get rid of the relative world entirely, can actually attain freedom, and this is the goal. Not only we can, but some have reached perfection; so no matter what finer bodies come, they could only be on the relative plane and could do no more than we, for to attain freedom is all that can be done.

The angels never do wicked deeds, so they never get punished and never get saved. Blows are what awaken us and help to break the dream. They show us the insufficiency of this world and make us long to escape, to have freedom....

A thing dimly perceived we call by one name; the same thing when fully perceived we call by another. The higher the moral nature, the higher the perception and the stronger the will.

TUESDAY AFTERNOON

The reason of the harmony between thought and matter is that they are two sides of one thing, call it "x", which divides itself into the internal and the external.

The English word "paradise" comes from the Sanskrit para-desa, which was taken over into the Persian language and means literally "the land beyond", or the other world. The old Aryans always believed in a soul, never that man was the body. Their heavens and hells were all temporary, because no effect can outlast its cause and no cause is eternal; therefore all effects must come to an end.

The whole of the Vedanta Philosophy is in this story: Two birds of golden plumage sat on the same tree. The one above, serene, majestic, immersed in his own glory; the one below restless and eating the fruits of the tree, now sweet, now bitter. Once he ate an exceptionally bitter fruit, then he paused and looked up at the majestic bird above; but he soon forgot about the other bird and went on eating the fruits of the tree as before. Again he ate a bitter fruit, and this time he hopped up a few boughs nearer to the bird at the top. This happened many times until at last the lower bird came to the place of the upper bird and lost himself. He found all at once that there had never been two birds, but that he was all the time that upper bird, serene, majestic, and immersed in his own glory.

XXXVII

RECORDED BY MISS S. E. WALDO, A DISCIPLE

WEDNESDAY, July 31, 1895.

Luther drove a nail into religion when he took away renunciation and gave us morality instead. Atheists and materialists can have ethics, but only believers in the Lord can have religion.

The wicked pay the price of the great soul's holiness. Think of that when you see a wicked man. Just as the poor man's labour pays for the rich man's luxury, so is it in the spiritual world. The terrible degradation of the masses in India is the price nature pays for the production of great souls like Mirâ-bâi, Buddha, etc.

***

"I am the holiness of the holy" (Gita). I am the root, each uses it in his own way, but all is I. "I do everything, you are but the occasion."

Do not talk much, but feel the spirit within you; then you are a Jnani. This is knowledge, all else is ignorance. All that is to be known is Brahman. It is the all. . . .

Sattva binds through the search for happiness and knowledge, Rajas binds through desire, Tamas binds through wrong perception and laziness. Conquer the two lower by Sattva, and then give up all to the Lord and be free.

The Bhakti-Yogi realises Brahman very soon and goes beyond the three qualities. (Gita, Chapter XII.)

The will, the consciousness, the senses, desire, the passions, all these combined make what we call the "soul".

There is first, the apparent self (body); second, the mental self who mistakes the body for himself (the Absolute bound by Maya); third, the Atman, the ever pure, the ever free. Seen partially, It is nature; seen wholly, all nature goes, even the memory of it is lost. There is the changeable (mortal), the eternally changeable (nature), and the Unchangeable (Atman).

Be perfectly hopeless, that is the highest state. What is there to hope for? Burst asunder the bonds of hope, stand on your Self, be at rest, never mind what you do, give up all to God, but have no hypocrisy about it.

Svastha, the Sanskrit word for "standing on your own Self", is used colloquially in India to inquire, "Are you well, are you happy?" And when Hindus would express, "I saw a thing", they say, "I saw a word-meaning (Padârtha)." Even this universe is a "word-meaning".

***

A perfect man's body mechanically does right; it can do only good because it is fully purified. The past momentum that carries on the wheel of body is all good. All evil tendencies are burnt out.

***

"That day is indeed a bad day when we do not speak of the Lord, not a stormy day."

Only love for the Supreme Lord is true Bhakti. Love for any other being, however great, is not

Bhakti. The "Supreme Lord" here means Ishvara, the concept of which transcends what you in the West mean by the personal God. "He from whom this universe proceeds, in whom it rests, and to whom it returns, He is Ishvara, the Eternal, the Pure, the All-Merciful, the Almighty, the Ever-Free, the All-Knowing, the Teacher of all teachers, the Lord who of His own nature is inexpressible Love."

Man does not manufacture God out of his own brain; but he can only see God in the light of his own capacity, and he attributes to Him the best of all he knows. Each attribute is the whole of God, and this signifying the whole by one quality is the metaphysical explanation of the personal God. Ishvara is without form yet has all forms, is without qualities yet has all qualities. As human beings, we have to see the trinity of existence — God, man, nature; and we cannot do otherwise.

But to the Bhakta all these philosophical distinctions are mere idle talk. He cares nothing for argument, he does not reason, he "senses", he perceives. He wants to love himself in pure love of God, and there have been Bhaktas who maintain that this is more to be desired than liberation, who say, "I do not want to be sugar. I want to taste sugar; I want to love and enjoy the Beloved."

In Bhakti-Yoga the first essential is to want God honestly and intensely. We want everything but God, because our ordinary desires are fulfilled by the external world. So long as our needs are confined within the limits of the physical universe, we do not feel any need for God; it is only when we have had hard blows in our lives and are disappointed with everything here that we feel the need for something higher; then we seek God.

Bhakti is not destructive; it teaches that all our faculties may become means to reach salvation. We must turn them all towards God and give to Him that love which is usually wasted on the fleeting objects of sense.

Bhakti differs from your Western idea of religion in that Bhakti admits no elements of fear, no Being to be appeased or propitiated. There are even Bhaktas who worship God as their own child, so that there may remain no feeling even of awe or reverence. There can be no fear in true love, and so long as there is the least fear, Bhakti cannot even begin. In Bhakti there is also no place for begging or bargaining with God. The idea of asking God for anything is sacrilege to a Bhakta. He will not pray for health or wealth or even to go to heaven.

One who wants to love God, to be a Bhakta, must make a bundle of all these desires and leave them outside the door and then enter. He who wants to enter the realms of light must make a bundle of all "shop-keeping" religion and cast it away before he can pass the gates. It is not that you do not get what you pray for; you get everything, but it is low, vulgar, a beggar's religion. "Fool indeed is he, who, living on the banks of the Ganga, digs a little well for water. Fool indeed is the man who, coming to a mine of diamonds, begins to search for glass beads." These prayers for health and wealth and material prosperity are not Bhakti. They are the lowest form of Karma. Bhakti is a higher thing. We are striving to come into the presence of the King of kings. We cannot get there in a beggar's dress. If we wanted to enter the presence of an emperor, would we be admitted in a beggar's rags? Certainly not. The lackey would drive us out of the gates. This is the Emperor of emperors and never can we come before Him in a beggar's garb. Shop-keepers never have admission there, buying and selling will not do there at all. You read in the Bible that Jesus drove the buyers and sellers out of the temple.

So it goes without saying that the first task in becoming a Bhakta is to give up all desires of heaven and so on. Such a heaven would be like this place, this earth, only a little better. The Christian idea of heaven is a place of intensified enjoyment. How can that be God? All this desire to go to heaven is a desire for enjoyment. This has to be given up. The love of the Bhakta must be absolutely pure and unselfish, seeking nothing for itself either here or hereafter.

"Giving up the desire of pleasure and pain, gain or loss, worship God day and night; not a moment is to be lost in vain."

"Giving up all other thoughts, the whole mind day

and night worships God. Thus being worshipped day and night, He reveals Himself and makes His worshippers feel Him."

XXXVIII

RECORDED BY MISS S. E. WALDO, A DISCIPLE

THURSDAY, August 1, 1895.

The real Guru is the one through whom we have our spiritual descent. He is the channel through which the spiritual current flows to us, the link which joins us to the whole spiritual world. Too much faith in personality has a tendency to produce weakness and idolatry, but intense love for the Guru makes rapid growth possible, he connects us with the internal Guru. Adore your Guru if there be real truth in him; that Guru-bhakti (devotion to the teacher) will quickly lead you to the highest.

Sri Ramakrishna's purity was that of a baby. He never touched money in his life, and lust was absolutely annihilated in him. Do not go to great religious teachers to learn physical science, their whole energy has gone to the spiritual. In Sri Ramakrishna Paramahamsa the man was all dead and only God remained; he actually could not see sin, he was literally "of purer eyes than to behold iniquity". The purity of these few Paramahamsa (Monks of the highest order) is all that holds the world together. If they should all die out and leave it, the world would go to pieces. They do good by simply being, and they know it not; they just are....

Books suggest the inner light and the method of bringing that out, but we can only understand them when we have earned the knowledge ourselves. When the inner light has flashed for you, let the books go, and look only within. You have in you all and a thousand times more than is in all the books. Never lose faith in yourself, you can do anything in this universe. Never weaken, all power is yours.

If religion and life depend upon books or upon the existence of any prophet whatsoever, then perish all religion and books! Religion is in us. No books or teachers can do more than help us to find it, and even without them we can get all truth within. You have gratitude for books and teachers without bondage to them; and worship your Guru as God, but do not obey him blindly; love him all you will, but think for yourself. No blind belief can save you, work out your own salvation. Have only one idea of God — that He is an eternal help.

Freedom and highest love must go together, then neither can become a bondage. We can give nothing to God; He gives all to us. He is the Guru of Gurus. Then we find that He is the "Soul of our souls", our very Self. No wonder we love Him, He is the Soul of our souls; whom or what else can we love? We want to be the "steady flame, burning without heat and without smoke". To whom can you do good, when you see only God? You cannot do good to God! All doubt goes, all is, "sameness". If you do good at all, you do it to yourself; feel that the receiver is the higher one. You serve the other because you are lower than he, not because he is low and you are high. Give as the rose gives perfume, because it is its own nature, utterly unconscious of giving.

The great Hindu reformer, Raja Ram Mohan Roy, was a wonderful example of this unselfish work. He devoted his whole life to helping India. It was he who stopped the burning of widows. It is usually believed that this reform was due entirely to the English; but it was Raja Ram Mohan Roy who started the agitation against the custom and succeeded in obtaining the support of the Government in suppressing it. Until he began the movement, the English had done nothing. He also founded the important religious Society called the Brahmo-Samaj, and subscribed a hundred thousand dollars to found a university. He then stepped out and told them to go ahead without him. He cared nothing for fame or for results to himself.

THURSDAY AFTERNOON

There are endless series of manifestations, like "merry-go-round", in which the souls ride, so to speak. The series are eternal; individual souls get out, but the events repeat themselves eternally; and that is how one's past and future can be read, because all is really present. When the soul is in a certain chain, it has to go through the experiences of that chain. From one series souls go to other series; from some series they escape for ever by realising that they are Brahman. By getting hold of one prominent event in a chain and holding on to it, the whole chain can be dragged in and read. This power is easily acquired, but it is of no real value; and to practise it takes just so much from our spiritual forces. Go not after these things, worship God.

XXXIX

RECORDED BY MISS S. E. WALDO, A DISCIPLE

FRIDAY, August 2, 1895.

Nishthâ (devotion to one ideal) is the beginning of realisation. "Take the honey out of all flowers; sit and be friendly with all, pay reverence to all, say to all, 'Yes, brother, yes, brother', but keep firm in your own way." A higher stage is actually to take the position of the other. If I am all, why can I not really and actively sympathise with my brother and see with his eyes? While I am weak, I must stick to one course (Nishthâ), but when I am strong, I can feel with every other and perfectly sympathise with his ideas.

The old idea was: "Develop one idea at the expense of all the rest". The modern way is "harmonious development". A third way is to "develop the mind and control it", then put it where you will; the result will come quickly. This is developing yourself in the truest way. Learn concentration and use it in any direction. Thus you lose nothing. He who gets the whole must have the parts too. Dualism is included in Advaitism (monism).

"I first saw him and he saw me. There was a flash of eye from me to him and from him to me."

This went on until the two souls became so closely united that they actually became one. . . .

There are two kinds of Samadhi — I concentrate on myself, then I concentrate and there is a unity of subject and object.

You must be able to sympathise fully with each particular, then at once to jump back to the highest monism. After having perfected yourself, you limit yourself voluntarily. Take the whole power into each action. Be able to become a dualist for the time being and forget Advaita, yet be able to take it up again at will.

* * *

Cause and effect are all Maya, and we shall grow to understand that all we see is as disconnected as the child's fairy tales now seem to us. There is really no such thing as cause and effect and we shall come to know it. Then if you can, lower your intellect to let any allegory pass through your mind without questioning about connection. Develop love of imagery and beautiful poetry and then enjoy all mythologies as poetry. Come not to mythology with ideas of history and reasoning. Let it flow as a current through your mind, let it be whirled as a candle before your eyes, without asking who holds the candle, and you will get the circle; the residuum of truth will remain in your mind.

The writers of all mythologies wrote in symbols of what they saw and heard, they painted flowing pictures. Do not try to pick out the themes and so destroy the pictures; take them as they are and let them act on you. Judge them only by the effect and get the good out of them.

* * *

Your own will is all that answers prayer, only it appears under the guise of different religious conceptions to each mind. We may call it Buddha, Jesus, Krishna, Jehovah, Allah, Agni, but it is only the Self, the "I". . . .

Concepts grow, but there is no historical value in the allegories which present them. Moses' visions are more likely to be wrong than ours are, because we have more knowledge and are less likely to be deceived by illusions.

Books are useless to us until our own book opens; then all other books are good so far as they confirm our book. It is the strong that understand strength, it is the elephant that understands the lion, not the rat. How can we understand Jesus until we are his equals? It is all in the dream to feed five thousand with two loaves, or to feed two with five loaves; neither is real and neither affects the other. Only grandeur appreciates grandeur, only God realises God. The dream is only the dreamer, it has no other basis. It is not one thing and the dreamer another. The keynote running through the music is — "I am He, I am He", all other notes are but variations and do not affect the real theme. We are the living books and books are but the words we have spoken. Everything is the living God, the living Christ; see it as such. Read man, he is the living poem. We are the light that illumines all the Bibles and Christs and Buddhas that ever were. Without that, these would be dead to us, not living.

Stand on your own Self.

The dead body resents nothing; let us make our bodies dead and cease to identify ourselves with them.

XL

RECORDED BY MISS S. E. WALDO, A DISCIPLE

SATURDAY, August 3, 1895.

Individuals who are to get freedom in this life have to live thousands of years in one lifetime. They have to be ahead of their times, but the masses can only crawl. Thus we have Christs and Buddhas....

There was once a Hindu queen, who so much desired that all her children should attain freedom in this life that she herself took all the care of them; and as she rocked them to sleep, she sang always the one song to them — "Tat tvam asi, Tat tvam asi" ("That thou art, That thou art").

Three of them became Sannyasins, but the fourth was taken away to be brought up elsewhere to become a king. As he was leaving home, the mother gave him a piece of paper which he was to read when he grew to manhood. On that piece of paper was written, "God alone is true. All else is false. The soul never kills or is killed. Live alone or in the company of holy ones." When the young prince read this, he too at once renounced the world and became a Sannyasin.

Give up, renounce the world. Now we are like dogs strayed into a kitchen and eating a piece of meat, looking round in fear lest at any moment some one may come and drive them out. Instead of that, be a king and know you own the world. This never comes until you give it up and it ceases to bind. Give up mentally, if you do not physically. Give up from the heart of your hearts. Have Vairâgya (renunciation). This is the real sacrifice, and without it, it is impossible to attain spirituality. Do not desire, for what you desire you get, and with it comes terrible bondage. It is nothing but bringing "noses on us,"[6]* as in the case of the man who had three boons to ask. We never get freedom until we are self-contained. "Self is the Saviour of self, none else."

Learn to feel yourself in other bodies, to know that we are all one. Throw all other nonsense to the winds. Spit out your actions, good or bad, and never think of them again. What is done is done. Throw off superstition. Have no weakness even in the face of death. Do not repent, do not brood over past deeds, and do not remember your good deeds; be âzâd (free). The weak, the fearful, the ignorant will never reach Atman. You cannot undo, the effect must come, face it, but be careful never to do the same thing again. Give up the burden of all deeds to the Lord; give all, both good and bad. Do not keep the good and give only the bad. God helps those who do not help themselves.

"Drinking the cup of desire, the world becomes mad." Day and night never come together, so desire and the Lord can never come together. Give up desire.

***

There is a vast difference between saying "food, food" and eating it, between saying "water, water" and drinking it. So by merely repeating the words "God, God" we cannot hope to attain realisation. We must strive and practise.

Only by the wave falling back into the sea can it become unlimited, never as a wave can it be so. Then after it has become the sea, it can become the wave again and as big a one as it pleases. Break the identification of yourself with the current and know that you are free.

True philosophy is the systematising of certain perceptions. Intellect ends where religion begins. Inspiration is much higher than reason, but it must not contradict it. Reason is the rough tool to do the hard work; inspiration is the bright light which shows us all truth. The will to do a thing is not necessarily inspiration. . . .

Progression in Maya is a circle that brings you back to the starting point; but you start ignorant and come to the end with all knowledge. Worship of God, worship of the holy ones, concentration and meditation, and unselfish work, these are the ways of breaking away from Maya's net; but we must first have the strong desire to get free. The flash of light that will illuminate the darkness for us is in us; it is the knowledge that is our nature — there is no "birthright", we were never born. All that we have to do is to drive away the clouds that cover it.

Give up all desire for enjoyment in earth or heaven. Control the organs of the senses and control the mind. Bear every misery without even knowing that you are miserable. Think of nothing but liberation. Have faith in Guru, in his teachings, and in the surety that you can get free. Say "Soham, Soham" whatever comes. Tell yourself this even in eating, walking, suffering; tell the mind this incessantly — that what we see never existed, that there is only "I". Flash — the dream will break! Think day and night, this universe is zero, only God is. Have intense desire to get free.

All relatives and friends are but "old dry wells"; we fall into them and get dreams of duty and bondage, and there is no end. Do not create illusion by helping anyone. It is like a banyan tree, that spreads on and on. If you are a dualist, you are a fool to try to help God. If you are a monist, you know that you are God; where find duty? You have no duty to husband, child, friend. Take things as they come, lie still, and when your body floats, go; rise with the rising tide, fall with falling tide. Let the body die; this idea of body is but a worn-out fable. "Be still and know that you are God."

The present only is existent. There is no past or future even in thought, because to think it, you have to make it the present. Give up everything, and let it float where it will. This world is all a delusion, do not let it fool you again. You have known it for what it is not, now know it for what it is. If the body is dragged anywhere, let it go; do not care where the body is. This tyrannical idea of duty is a terrible poison and is destroying the world.

Do not wait to have a harp and rest by degrees; why not take a harp and begin here? Why wait for heaven? Make it here. In heaven there is no marrying or giving in marriage; why not begin at once and have none here? The yellow robe of the Sannyasin is the sign of the free. Give up the beggar's dress of the world; wear the flag of freedom, the ochre robe.

XLI

RECORDED BY MISS S. E. WALDO, A DISCIPLE

SUNDAY, August 4, 1895.

"Whom the ignorant worship, Him I preach unto thee."

This one and only God is the "knownest" of the known. He is the one thing we see everywhere. All know their own Self, all know, "I am", even animals. All we know is the projection of the Self. Teach this to the children, they can grasp it. Every religion has worshipped the Self, even though unconsciously, because there is nothing else.

This indecent clinging to life as we know it here, is the source of all evil. It causes all this cheating and stealing. It makes money a god and all vices and fears ensue. Value nothing material and do not cling to it. If you cling to nothing, not even life, then there is no fear. "He goes from death to death who sees many in this world." There can be no physical death for us and no mental death, when we see that all is one. All bodies are mine; so even body is eternal, because the tree, the animal, the sun, the moon, the universe itself is my body; then how can it die? Every mind, every thought is mine, then how can death come? The Self is never born and never dies. When we realise this, all doubts vanish. "I am, I know, I love" — these can never be doubted. There is no hunger, for all that is eaten is eaten by me. If a hair falls out, we do not think we die; so if one body dies, it is but a hair falling....

The superconscious is God, is beyond speech beyond thought, beyond consciousness.... There are three states, — brutality (Tamas), humanity (Rajas), and divinity (Sattva). Those attaining the highest state simply are. Duty dies there; they only love and as a magnet draw others to them. This is freedom. No more you do moral acts, but whatever you do is moral. The Brahmavit (knower of God) is higher than all gods. The angels came to worship Jesus when he had conquered delusion and had said, "Get thee behind me, Satan." None can help a Brahmavit, the universe itself bows down before him. His every desire is fulfilled, his spirit purifies others; therefore worship the Brahmavit if you wish to attain the highest. When we have the three great "gifts of God" — a human body, intense desire to be free, and the help of a great soul to show us the way — then liberation is certain for us. Mukti is ours.

***

Death of the body for ever is Nirvana. It is the negative side and says, "I am not this, nor this, nor this." Vedanta takes the further step and asserts the positive side — Mukti or freedom. "I am Existence absolute, Knowledge absolute, Bliss absolute, I am He", this is Vedanta, the cap-stone of the perfect arch.

The great majority of the adherents of Northern Buddhism believe in Mukti and are really Vedantists. Only the Ceylonese accept Nirvana as annihilation.

No belief or disbelief can kill the "I". That which comes with belief and goes with disbelief is only delusion. Nothing teaches the Atman. "I salute my own Self." "Self-illuminated, I salute myself, I am Brahman." The body is a dark room; when we enter it, it becomes illuminated, it becomes alive. Nothing can ever affect the illumination; it cannot be destroyed. It may be covered, but never destroyed.

***

At the present time God should be worshipped as "Mother", the Infinite Energy. This will lead to purity, and tremendous energy will come here in America. Here no temples weigh us down, no one suffers as they do in poorer countries. Woman has suffered for aeons, and that has given her infinite patience and infinite perseverance. She holds on to an idea. It is this which makes her the support of even superstitious religions and of the priests in every land, and it is this that will free her. We have to become Vedantists and live this grand thought; the masses must get it, and only in free America can this be done. In India these ideas were brought out by individuals like Buddha, Shankara, and others, but the masses did not retain them. The new cycle must see the masses living Vedanta, and this will have to come through women.

"Keep the beloved beautiful Mother in the heart of your hearts with all care."

"Throw out everything but the tongue, keep that to say, "Mother, Mother!""

"Let no evil counsellors enter; let you and me, my heart, alone see Mother."

"Thou art beyond all that lives!"

"My Moon of life, my Soul of soul!"

SUNDAY AFTERNOON

Mind is an instrument in the hand of Atman, just as body is an instrument in the hand of mind. Matter is motion outside, mind is motion inside. All change begins and ends in time. If the Atman is unchangeable, It must be perfect; if perfect, It must be infinite; and if It be infinite, It must be only One; there cannot be two infinites. So the Atman, the Self, can be only One. Though It seems to be various, It is really only One. If a man were to go toward the sun, at every step he would see a different sun, and yet it would be the same sun after all.

Asti, "isness", is the basis of all unity; and just as soon as the basis is found, perfection ensues. If all colour could be resolved into one colour, painting would cease. The perfect oneness is rest; we refer all manifestations to one Being. Taoists, Confucianists, Buddhists, Hindus, Jews, Mohammedans, Christians, and Zoroastrians, all preached the golden rule and in almost the same words; but only the Hindus have given the rationale, because they saw the reason: Man must love others because those others are himself. There is but One.

Of all the great religious teachers the world has known, only Lao-tze, Buddha, and Jesus transcended the golden rule and said, "Do good to your enemies", "Love them that hate you."

Principles exist; we do not create them, we only discover them. . . . Religion consists solely in realisation. Doctrines are methods, not religion. All the different religions are but applications of the one religion adapted to suit the requirements of different nations. Theories only lead to fighting; thus the name of God that ought to bring peace has been the cause of half the bloodshed of the world. Go to the direct source. Ask God what He is. Unless He answers, He is not; but every religion teaches that He does answer.

Have something to say for yourself, else how can you have any idea of what others have said? Do not cling to old superstitions; be ever ready for new truths. "Fools are they who would drink brackish water from a well that their forefathers have digged and would not drink pure water from a well that others have digged." Until we realise God for ourselves, we can know nothing about Him. Each man is perfect by his nature; prophets have manifested this perfection, but it is potential in us. How can we understand that Moses saw God unless we too see Him? If God ever came to anyone, He will come to me. I will go to God direct; let Him talk to me. I cannot take belief as a basis; that is atheism and blasphemy. If God spake to a man in the deserts of Arabia two thousand years ago, He can also speak to me today, else how can I know that He has not died? Come to God any way you can; only come. But in coming do not push anyone down.

The knowing ones must have pity on the ignorant. One who knows is willing to give up his body even for an ant, because he knows that the body is nothing.

XLII

RECORDED BY MISS S. E. WALDO, A DISCIPLE

MONDAY, August 5, 1895.

The question is: Is it necessary to pass through all the lower stages to reach the highest, or can a plunge be taken at once? The modern American boy takes twenty-five years to attain that which his forefathers took hundreds of years to do. The present-day Hindu gets in twenty years to the height reached in eight thousand years by his ancestors. On the physical side, the embryo goes from the amoeba to man in the womb. These are the teachings of modern science. Vedanta goes further and tells us that we not only have to live the life of all past humanity, but also the future life of all humanity. The man who does the first is the educated man, the second is the Jivanmukta, for ever free (even while living).

Time is merely the measure of our thoughts, and thought being inconceivably swift, there is no limit to the speed with which we can live the life ahead. So it cannot be stated how long it would take to live all future life. It might be in a second, or it might take fifty lifetimes. It depends on the intensity of the desire. The teaching must therefore be modified according to the needs of the taught. The consuming fire is ready for all, even water and chunks of ice quickly consume. Fire a mass of bird-shot, one at least will strike; give a man a whole museum of truths, he will at once take what is suited to him. Past lives have moulded our tendencies; give to the taught in accordance with his tendency. Intellectual, mystical, devotional, practical — make one the basis, but teach the others with it. Intellect must be balanced with love, the mystical nature with reason, while practice must form part of every method. Take every one where he stands and push him forward. Religious teaching must always be constructive, not destructive.

Each tendency shows the life-work of the past, the line or radius along which that man must move. All radii lead to the centre. Never even attempt to disturb anyone's tendencies; to do that puts back both teacher and taught. When you teach Jnana, you must become a Jnani and stand mentally exactly where the taught stands. Similarly in every other Yoga. Develop every faculty as if it were the only one possessed, this is the true secret of so-called harmonious development. That is, get extensity with intensity, but not at its expense. We are infinite. There is no limitation in us, we can be as intense as the most devoted Mohammedan and as broad as the most roaring atheist.

The way to do this is not to put the mind on any one subject, but to develop and control the mind itself; then you can turn it on any side you choose. Thus you keep the intensity and extensity. Feel Jnana as if it were all there was, then do the same with Bhakti, with Raja (-Yoga), with Karma. Give up the waves and go to the ocean, then you can have the waves as you please. Control the "lake" of your own mind, else you cannot understand the lake of another's mind.

The true teacher is one who can throw his whole force into the tendency of the taught. Without real sympathy we can never teach well. Give up the notion that man is a responsible being, only the perfect man is responsible. The ignorant have drunk deep of the cup of delusion and are not sane. You, who know, must have infinite patience with these. Have nothing but love for them and find out the disease that has made them see the world in a wrong light, then help them to cure it and see aright. Remember always that only the free have free will; all the rest are in bondage and are not responsible for what they do. Will as will is bound. The water when melting on the top of the Himalayas is free, but becoming the river, it is bound by the banks; yet the original impetus carries it to the sea, and it regains its freedom. The first is the "fall of man", the second is the "resurrection". Not one atom can rest until it finds its freedom.

Some imaginations help to break the bondage of the rest. The whole universe is imagination, but one set of imaginations will cure another set. Those which tell us that there is sin and sorrow and death in the world are terrible; but the other set which says ever, "I am holy, there is God, there is no pain", these are good and help to break the bondage of the others. The highest imagination that can break all the links of the chain is that of Personal God.

"Om tat sat" is the only thing beyond Maya, but God exists eternally. As long as the Niagara Falls exist, the rainbow will exist; but the water continually flows away. The falls are the universe, and the rainbow is personal God; and both are eternal. While the universe exists, God must exist. God creates the universe, and the universe creates God; and both are eternal. Maya is neither existence nor non-existence. Both the Niagara Falls and the rainbow are eternally changeable. . . . Brahman seen through Maya. Persians and Christians split Maya into two and call the good half "God" and the bad half the "devil". Vedanta takes Maya as a whole and recognises a unity beyond it — Brahman. . . .

Mohammed found that Christianity was straying out from the Semitic fold and his teachings were to show what Christianity ought to be as a Semitic religion, that it should hold to one God. The Aryan idea that "I and my Father are one" disgusted and terrified him. In reality the conception of the Trinity was a great advance over the dualistic idea of Jehovah, who was for ever separate from man. The theory of incarnation is the first link in the chain of ideas leading to the recognition of the oneness of God and man. God appearing first in one human form, then re-appearing at different times in other human forms, is at last recognised as being in every human form, or in all men. Monistic is the highest stage, monotheistic is a lower stage. Imagination will lead you to the highest even more rapidly and easily than reasoning.

Let a few stand out and live for God alone and save religion for the world. Do not pretend to be like Janaka when you are only the "progenitor" of delusions. (The name Janaka means "progenitor" and belonged to a king who, although he still held his kingdom for the sake of his people, had given up everything mentally.) Be honest and say, "I see the ideal but I cannot yet approach it"; but do not pretend to give up when you do not. If you give up, stand fast. If a hundred fall in the fight, seize the flag and carry it on. God is true for all that, no matter who fails. Let him who falls hand on the flag to another to carry on; it can never fall.

When I am washed and clean, why shall impurity be added on to me? Seek first the kingdom of Heaven, and let everything else go. Do not want anything "added into you"; be only glad to get rid of it. Give up and know that success will follow, even if you never see it. Jesus left twelve fishermen, and yet those few blew up the Roman Empire.

Sacrifice on God's altar earth's purest and best. He who struggles is better than he who never attempts. Even to look on one who has given up has a purifying effect. Stand up for God; let the world go. Have no compromise. Give up the world, then alone you are loosened from the body. When it dies, you are âzâd, free. Be free. Death alone can never free us. Freedom must be attained by our own efforts during life; then, when the body falls, there will be no rebirth for the free.

Truth is to be judged by truth and by nothing else. Doing good is not the test of truth; the Sun needs no torch by which to see it. Even if truth destroys the whole universe, still it is truth; stand by it.

Practising the concrete forms of religion is easy and attracts the masses; but really there is nothing in the external.

"As the spider throws her web out of herself and draws it in, even so this universe is thrown out and drawn in by God."

XLIII

RECORDED BY MISS S. E. WALDO, A DISCIPLE

TUESDAY, August 6, 1895.

Without the "I" there can be no "you" outside. From this some philosophers came to the conclusion that the external world did not exist save in the subject; that the "you" existed only in the "I". Others have argued that the "I" can only be known through the "you" and with equal logic. These two views are partial truths, each wrong in part and each right in part. Thought is as much material and as much in nature as body is. Both matter and mind exist in a third, a unity which divides itself into the two. This unity is the Atman, the real Self.

There is being, "x", which is manifesting itself as both mind and matter. Its movements in the seen are along certain fixed lines called law. As a unity, it is free; as many, it is bound by law. Still, with all this bondage, an idea of freedom is ever present, and this is Nivritti, or the "dragging from attachment". The materialising forces which through desire lead us to take an active part in worldly affairs are called Pravritti.

That action is moral which frees us from the bondage of matter and vice versa. This world appears infinite, because everything is in a circle; it returns to whence it came. The circle meets, so there is no rest or peace here in any place. We must get out. Mukti is the one end to be attained....

Evil changes in form but remains the same in quality. In ancient times force ruled, today it is cunning. Misery in India is not so bad as in America, because the poor man here sees the greater contrast to his own bad condition.

Good and evil are inextricably combined, and one cannot be had without the other. The sum total of energy in this universe is like a lake, every wave inevitably leads to a corresponding depression. The sum total is absolutely the same; so to make one man happy is to make another unhappy. External happiness is material and the supply is fixed; so that not one grain can be had by one person without taking from another. Only bliss beyond the material world can be had without loss to any. Material happiness is but a transformation of material sorrow.

Those who are born in the wave and kept in it do not see the depression and what is there. Never think, you can make the world better and happier. The bullock in the oil-mill never reaches the wisp of hay tied in front of him, he only grinds out the oil. So we chase the will-o'-the-wisp of happiness that always eludes us, and we only grind nature's mill, then die, merely to begin again. If we could get rid of evil, we should never catch a glimpse of anything higher; we would be satisfied and never struggle to get free. When man finds that all search for happiness in matter is nonsense, then religion begins. All human knowledge is but a part of religion.

In the human body the balance between good and evil is so even that there is a chance for man to wish to free himself from both.

The free never became bound; to ask how he did, is an illogical question. Where no bondage is, there is no cause and effect. "I became a fox in a dream and a dog chased me." Now how can I ask why the dog chased me? The fox was a part of the dream, and the dog followed as a matter of course; but both belong to the dream and have no existence outside. Science and religion are both attempts to help us out of the bondage; only religion is the more ancient, and we have the superstition that it is the more holy. In a way it is, because it makes morality a vital point, and science does not.

"Blessed are the pure in heart, for they shall see God." This sentence alone would save mankind if all books and prophets were lost. This purity of heart will bring the vision of God. It is the theme of the whole music of this universe. In purity is no bondage. Remove the veils of ignorance by purity, then we manifest ourselves as we really are and know that we were never in bondage. The seeing of many is the great sin of all the world. See all as Self and love all; let all idea of separateness go....

The diabolical man is a part of my body as a wound or a burn is. We have to nurse it and get it better; so continually nurse and help the diabolical man, until he "heals" and is once happy and healthy.

While we think on the relative plane, we have the right to believe that as bodies we can be hurt by relative things and equally that we can be helped by them. This idea of help, abstracted, is what we call God. The sum total of all ideas of help is God.

God is the abstract compound of all that is merciful and good and helpful; that should be the sole idea. As Atman, we have no body; so to say, "I am God, and poison does not hurt me", is an absurdity. While there is a body and we see it, we have not realised God. Can the little whirlpool remain after the river vanishes? Cry for help, and you will get it; and at last you will find that the one crying for help has vanished, and so has the Helper, and the play is over; only the Self remains.

This once done, come back and play as you will. This body can then do no evil, because it is not until the evil forces are all burned out that liberation comes. All dross has been burned out and there remains "flame without heat and without smoke".

The past momentum carries on the body, but it can only do good, because the bad was all gone before freedom came. The dying thief on the cross reaped the effects of his past actions. He had been a Yogi and had slipped; then he had to be born again; again he slipped and became a thief; but the past good he had done bore fruit, and he met Jesus in the moment when liberation could come, and one word made him free.

Buddha set his greatest enemy free, because he, by hating him (Buddha) so much, kept constantly thinking of him; that thought purified his mind, and he became ready for freedom. Therefore think of God all the time, and that will purify you....

(Thus ended the beautiful lessons of our beloved Guru. The following Monday he left Thousand Island Park and returned to New York.)

CONVERSATIONS AND DIALOGUES

FROM THE DIARY OF A DISCIPLE (SHRI SHARAT CHANDRA CHAKRAVARTY, B.A.)

I

Swamiji was staying at the time at the rented garden-house of Nilambar Babu where the Math had been removed from Alambazar. Arrangements had been made for Shri Ramakrishna's Tithipuja (Nativity) on a grand scale. On the morning of the auspicious day, Swamiji personally inspected the preliminaries of the worship. The inspection over, Swamiji asked the disciple, "Well, you have brought the holy threads, I hope?"

Disciple: Yes, sir, I have. Everything is ready, as you desired. But, sir, I can't make out why so many holy threads are in requisition.

Swamiji: Every Dwijati[1] (twice-born) has a right to investiture with the holy thread. The Vedas themselves are authority in this matter. Whoever will come here on this sacred birthday of Shri Ramakrishna, I shall invest him with the holy thread. These people have fallen from their true status, and the scriptures say that after proper expiation, those fallen in the way earn the right to investiture with the holy thread. This is the great day of Shri Ramakrishna's nativity, and men will be purified by taking his name. So the assembled devotees are to be invested with the holy thread today; do you now understand?

Disciple: I have collected, Sir, quite a good number of holy threads according to your instructions, and after the worship I shall with your permission invest the Bhaktas with them.

Swamiji: To the Bhaktas who are not Brahmins, give this Mantra of Gayatri (here Swamiji communicated to the disciple the special Gayatris for them.) By degrees all the people of the land have to be lifted to the position of Brahmins, not to speak of the Bhaktas of Shri Ramakrishna. Each Hindu, I say, is a brother of every other, and it is we who have degraded them by our outcry, "Don't touch, don't touch!" And so the whole country has been plunged to the utmost depths of meanness, cowardice, and ignorance. These men have to be uplifted; words of hope and faith have to be proclaimed to them. We have to tell them, "You are men like us, and you have all the rights that we have." Do you understand?

Disciple: Yes, sir, it should be so.

Swamiji: Now, ask those who will take the holy thread to finish their bath in the Ganga. Than after prostration before Shri Ramakrishna, they will have their investiture.

About forty to fifty Bhaktas then duly received the Gayatri from the disciple and were invested with the holy thread. When receiving them, Swamiji's face beamed with profound delight. A little after this, Shri Girish Chandra Ghosh arrived at the Math from Calcutta.

Now arrangements for music were made at the desire of Swamiji, and Sannyasins of the Math decorated Swamiji as a Yogin.

Swamiji now chanted with the sweetest intonation to the accompaniment of the Tanpura, the Sanskrit hymn beginning with [(Sanskrit)] ("repeating in a low tone the name of Rama" etc.), and when the chanting came to a close, he went on repeating with exquisite charm the holy words "Rama, Rama, Shri Rama, Rama". His eyes were half-closed, and the natural sublimity of his countenance seemed today to have deepened a hundredfold. Everybody remained spelled for over a half an hour.

After the chanting of Shri Rama's name, Swamiji continued to sing a song of Tulsidas on Shri Ramachandra in the same intoxicated strain of mind. Then other music followed.

After this, Swamiji suddenly took to putting off all the decorations he had on his person and began to dress Girish Babu with them. Then he declared, "Paramahamsa-deva used to say our brother is the incarnation of Bhairava[2]. There's no distinction between him and us." Girish Babu sat speechless all

---

1. Brahmins, Kshatriyas, and Vaishyas are the Dwijatis.

2. Divine companion of Shiva.

the time. A piece of gerua cloth was also brought, and he was draped in it and uttered no word of remonstrance. For he had merged his self fully today in the wishes of his brother disciples. Swamiji now said, "Well, G. C., you are to speak to us today about Thakur (Lord). And all of you (turning all round himself) sit quiet and attentive." Even then, Girish Babu sat motionless, voiceless like marble, absolutely lost in joy. And when at last he opened his lips, he did so to say, "Ah, what can this humble self speak of our Lord of unbounded mercy! Verily in this alone I realise his mercy, that to me, this lowly creature, He has extended the privilege of sitting and mixing on the same footing with you Sannyasins, pure from your childhood, who have renounced all lust and lucre." While speaking thus, the words choked in his throat, and he could not speak anything more.

After this, some pieces of Hindu music were rendered by Swamiji. The devotees were now called to partake of refreshments. After refreshments, Swamiji came and took his seat in the parlour on the ground-floor, and all the many visitors sat round him. Accosting a house-holder friend who had his investiture with the holy thread that day, Swamiji said, "Really you all belong to the twice-born castes, only it is long since you lost your status. From this day again you become the twice-born. Repeat the Gayatri at least a hundred times daily, won't you?" The householder expressed his assent.

Meanwhile Srijut Mahendranath Gupta (Master Mahashaya [Venerable], or "M") appeared on the scene. Swamiji cordially received him and made him take his seat. "Master Mahashaya," said Swamiji, "this is the anniversary of Shri Ramakrishna's birthday. So you shall have to relate to us something about him." Master Mahashaya bent his head down smilingly in reply.

Just then it was announced that Swami Akhandananda had come from Murshidabad with two Pantuas[1] which weighed one maund and a half! All of us hurried out to see these prodigious Pantuas. When they were shown to Swamiji, he said, "Take them up to the chapel for offering."

Making Swami Akhandananda the subject of his remarks, Swamiji said to the disciple, "Mark you, what a great hero he is in work! Of fear, death and the like he has no cognisance — doggedly going on doing his own work —'work for the welfare of the many, for the happiness of the many'."

Disciple: Sir, that power must have come to him as the result of a good deal of austerities.

Swamiji: True, power comes of austerities; but again, working for the sake of others itself constitutes Tapasya (practice of austerity). The karma-yogins regard work itself as part of Tapasya. As on the one hand the practice of Tapasya intensifies altruistic feelings in the devotee and actuates him to unselfish work, so also the pursuit of work for the sake of others carries the worker to the last fruition of Tapasya, namely the purification of the heart, and leads him thus to the realisation of the supreme Atman (Self).

Disciple: But, sir, how few of us can work whole-heartedly for the sake of others from the very outset! How difficult it is for such broad-mindedness to come at all as will make men sacrifice the desire for their own happiness and devote their lives for others!

Swamiji: And how many have their minds going after Tapasya? With the attraction for lust and lucre working the other way, how many long for the realisation of God? In fact, disinterested work is quite as difficult as Tapasya. So you have no right to say anything against those who go in for work in the cause of others. If you find Tapasya to be to your liking, well, go on with it. Another may find work as congenial to himself, and you have no right to make a prohibition in his case. You seem to have the settled idea in your mind that work is no Tapasya at all!

Disciple: Yes, sir, before this I used to mean quite a different thing by Tapasya.

Swamiji: As by continuing our religious practices we gradually develop a certain determined tendency for it, so by performing disinterested work over and over again, even unwillingly, we gradually find the will merging itself in it. The inclination to work for others develops in this way, do you see? Just do

---

1. A sweetmeat usually about two inches in length, made mostly of fresh cheese fried in ghee and put in syrup.

some such work even though unwillingly, and then see if the actual fruit of Tapasya is realised within or not. As the outcome of work for the sake of others, the angularities of the mind get smoothed down, and men are gradually prepared for sincere self-sacrifice for the good of others.

Disciple: But, sir, what is the necessity at all for doing good to others?

Swamiji: Well, it is necessary for one's own good. We become forgetful of the ego when we think of the body as dedicated to the service of others — the body with which most complacently we identify the ego. And in the long run comes the consciousness of disembodiness. The more intently you think of the well-being of others, the more oblivious of self you become. In this way, as gradually your heart gets purified by work, you will come to feel the truth that your own Self is pervading all beings and all things. Thus it is that doing good to others constitutes a way, a means of revealing one's own Self or Atman. Know this also to be one of the spiritual practices, a discipline for God-realisation. Its aim also is Self-realisation. Exactly as that aim is attained by Jnana (knowledge), Bhakti (devotion) and so on, also by work for the sake of others.

Disciple: But, sir, if I am to keep thinking of others day and night, when shall I contemplate on the Atman? If I rest wholly occupied with something particular and relative, how can I realise the Atman which is Absolute?

Swamiji: The highest aim of all disciplines, all spiritual paths, is the attainment of the knowledge of Atman. If you, by being devoted to the service of others and by getting your heart purified by such work, attain to the vision of all beings as the Self, what else remains to be attained in the way of Self-realisation? Would you say that Self-realisation is the state of existing as inert matter, as this wall or as this piece of wood, for instance?

Disciple: Though that is not the meaning, yet what the scriptures speak of as the withdrawal of the Self into Its real nature consists in the arresting of all mind-functions and all work.

Swamiji: Yes, this Samadhi of which the scriptures speak is a state not at all easy to attain. When very rarely it appears in somebody, it does not last for long; so what will he keep himself occupied with? Thus it is that after realising that state described in the scriptures, the saint sees the Self in all beings and in that consciousness devotes himself to service, so that any Karma that was yet left to be worked out through the body may exhaust itself. It is this state which has been described by the authors of the Shastras (scriptures) as Jivanmukti, "Freedom while living".

Disciple: So after all it comes about, sir, that unless this state of Jivanmukti is attained, work for the sake of others can never be pursued in the truest sense of the term.

Swamiji: Yes, that is what the Shastras say, but they also say that work or service for the good of others leads to this state of Jivanmukti. Otherwise there would be no need on the part of the Shastras to teach a separate path of religious practice, called the Karma-yoga.

The disciple now understood the point and became silent, and Swamiji giving up the point commenced rendering in a voice of superhuman sweetness the song composed by Babu Girish Chandra Ghosh to commemorate Shri Ramakrishna's Nativity, and beginning:

"Who art Thou lying on the lap of the poor Brahmin matron."

II

Today Swamiji is to perform a sacrifice and install Shri Ramakrishna on the site of the new Math. The disciple has been staying at the Math since the night before, with a view to witnessing the installation ceremony.

In the morning Swamiji had his bath in the Ganga and entered the worship-room. Then he made offerings to the sacred Padukas (slippers) of Shri Ramakrishna and fell to meditation.

Meditation and worship over, preparations were now made for going to the new Math premises. Swamiji himself took on his right shoulder the ashes of Shri Ramakrishna's body preserved in a copper casket, and led the van. The disciple in company with other Sannyasins brought up the rear. There was the music of bells and conchs. On his way Swamiji said to the disciple, "Shri Ramakrishna said to me, 'Wherever you will take me on your shoulders, there I will go and stay, be it under a tree or in a hut.' It is therefore that I am myself carrying him on my shoulders to the new Math grounds. Know it for certain that Shri Ramakrishna will keep his seat fixed there, for the welfare of many, for a long time to come."

Disciple: When was it that he said this to you?

Swamiji: Didn't you hear from them? It was at the Cossipur garden.

Disciple: I see. It was on this occasion, I suppose, that the split took place between Shri Ramakrishna's Sannyasin and householder disciples regarding the privilege of serving him?

Swamiji: Yes, but not exactly a "split"— it was only a misunderstanding, that's all. Rest assured that among those that are Shri Ramakrishna's devotees, and have truly obtained his grace, there is no sect or schism, there cannot be — be they householders or Sannyasins. As to that kind of slight misunderstanding, do you know what it was due to? Well, each devotee colours Shri Ramakrishna in the light of his own understanding and each forms his own idea of him from his peculiar standpoint. He was, as it were, a great Sun and each one of us is eyeing him, as it were, through a different kind of colored glass and coming to look upon that one Sun as particoloured. Of course, it is quite true that this leads to schism in course of time. But then, such schisms rarely occur in the lifetime of those who are fortunate enough to have come in direct contact with an Avatara. The effulgence of that Personality, who takes pleasure only in his Self, dazzles their eyes and sweeps away pride, egotism, and narrow-mindedness from their minds. Consequently they find no opportunity to create sects and party factions. They are content to offer him their heart's worship, each in his own fashion.

Disciple: Sir, do the devotees of the Avatara, then, view him differently notwithstanding their knowing him to be God, and does this lead to the succeeding generations of their followers to limit themselves within narrow bounds and form various little sects?

Swamiji: Quite so. Hence sects are bound to form in course of time. Look, for instance, how the followers of Chaitanya Deva have been divided into two or three hundred sects; and those of Jesus hold thousands of creeds. But all those sects without exception follow Chaitanya Deva or Jesus, and none else.

Disciple: Then, perhaps, Shri Ramakrishna's followers, too, will be divided in course of time into various sects?

Swamiji: Well, of course. But then this Math that we are building will harmonise all creeds, all standpoints. Just as Shri Ramakrishna held highly liberal views, this Math too, will be a center for propagating similar ideas. The blazing light of universal harmony that will emanate from here will flood the whole world.

While all this was going on, the party reached the Math premises. Swamiji took the casket down from his shoulder, placed in on the carpet spread on the ground, and bowed before it touching the ground with his forehead. Others too followed suit.

Then Swamiji again sat for worship. After going through the Puja (worship), he lighted the sacrificial fire, made oblations to it, and himself cooking Payasa (milk-rice with sugar) with the help of his brother-disciples, offered it to Shri Ramakrishna. Probably also he initiated certain householders on the spot that day. All this ceremony being done, Swamiji cordially addressed the assembled gentlemen and said, "Pray today all of you, heart and soul, to the holy feet of Shri Ramakrishna, that the great Avatara of this cycle that he is, he may "For the welfare of the many, and for the happiness of the many — [(Sanskrit)]", reside in this holy spot from this day for a great length of time, and ever continue to make it the unique center of harmony amongst all religions." Everyone prayed like that with folded palms. Swamiji next called the disciple and said, "None of us (Sannyasins) have any longer the right to take back this casket of Shri Ramakrishna, for we have installed him here today. It behoves you, therefore, to take it on your head back (to Nilambar Babu's garden)". Seeing that the disciple hesitated to touch the casket, Swamiji said, "No fear, touch it, you have my order." The disciple gladly obeyed the injunction, lifted the casket on his head, and moved on. He went first, next came Swamiji, and the rest followed. Swamiji said to the disciple on the way, "Shri Ramakrishna has today sat on your head and is blessing you. Take care, never let your mind think of anything transitory, from this day forth." Before crossing a small bridge, Swamiji again said to him, "Beware, now, you must move very cautiously."

Thus all safely reached the Math and rejoiced. Swamiji now entered into a conversation with the disciple, in the course of which he said, "Through the will of Shri Ramakrishna, his Dharmakshetra — sanctified spot — has been established today. A twelve years' anxiety is off my head. Do you know what I am thinking of at this moment?— this Math will be a center of learning and spiritual discipline. Householders of a virtuous turn like yourselves will build houses on the surrounding land and live there, and Sannyasins, men of renunciation, will live in the center, while on that plot of land on the south of the Math, buildings will be erected for English and American disciples to live in. How do you like this idea?

Disciple: Sir, it is indeed a wonderful fancy of yours.

Swamiji: A fancy do you call it? Not at all, everything will come about in time. I am but laying the foundation. There will be lots of further developments in future. Some portion of it I shall live to work out. And I shall infuse into you fellows various ideas, which you will work out in future. It will not do merely to listen to great principles. You must apply them in the practical field, turn them into constant practice. What will be the good of cramming the high-sounding dicta of the scriptures? You have first to grasp the teachings of the Shastras, and then to work them out in practical life. Do you understand? This is called practical religion.

Thus the talk went on, and gradually drifted to the topic of Shankaracharya. The disciple was a great adherent of Shankara, almost to the point of fanaticism. He used to look upon Shankara's Advaita philosophy as the crest of all philosophies and could not bear any criticism of him. Swamiji was aware of this, and, as was his wont, wanted to break this one-sidedness of the disciple.

Swamiji: Shankara's intellect was sharp like the razor. He was a good arguer and a scholar, no doubt of that, but he had no great liberality; his heart too seems to have been like that. Besides, he used to take great pride in his Brahmanism — much like a southern Brahmin of the priest class, you may say. How he has defended in his commentary on the Vedanta-sutras that the non-brahmin castes will not attain to a supreme knowledge of Brahman! And what specious arguments! Referring to Vidura[1] he has said that he became a knower of Brahman by reason of his Brahmin body in the previous incarnation. Well, if nowadays any Shudra attains to a knowledge of Brahman, shall we have to side with your Shankara and maintain that because he had been a Brahmin in his previous birth, therefore he has attained to this knowledge? Goodness! What is the use of dragging in Brahminism with so much ado? The Vedas have entitled any one belonging to the three upper castes to study the Vedas and the realisation of Brahman, haven't they? So Shankara had no need whatsoever of displaying this curious bit of pedantry on this subject, contrary to the Vedas. And such was his heart that he burnt to death lots of Buddhist monks — by defeating them in argument! And the Buddhists, too, were foolish enough to burn themselves to death, simply because they were worsted in argument! What can you call such an action on Shankara's part except fanaticism? But look at Buddha's heart! Ever ready to give his own life to save the life of even a kid — what to speak of "[(Sanskrit)] — for the welfare of the many, for the happiness of the many"! See, what a large heartedness — what a compassion!

Disciple: Can't we call that attitude of the Bud-

---

[1]. Uncle of the Pandava brothers, and a most saintly character, considered to be an incarnation of Dharma.

dha, too, another kind of fanaticism, sir? He went to the length of sacrificing his own body for the sake of a beast!

Swamiji: But consider how much good to the world and its beings came out of that 'fanaticism' of his — how many monasteries and schools and colleges, how many public hospitals and veterinary refuges were established, how developed architecture became — think of that. What was there in this country before Buddha's advent? Only a number of religious principles recorded on bundles of palm leaves — and those too known only to a few. It was Lord Buddha who brought them down to the practical field and showed how to apply them in the everyday life of the people. In a sense, he was the living embodiment of true Vedanta.

Disciple: But, sir, it was he who by breaking down the Varnashrama Dharma (duty according to caste and order of life) brought about a revolution within the fold of Hinduism in India, and there seems to be some truth also in the remark that the religion he preached was for this reason banished in course of time from the soil of India.

Swamiji: It was not through his teachings that Buddhism came to such degradation, it was the fault of his followers. By becoming too philosophic they lost much of their breadth of heart. Then gradually the corruption known as Vamachara (unrestrained mixing with women in the name of religion) crept in and ruined Buddhism. Such diabolical rites are not to be met with in any modern Tantra! One of the principal centres of Buddhism was Jagannatha or Puri, and you have simply to go there and look at the abominable figures carved on the temple walls to be convinced of this. Puri has come under the sway of the Vaishnavas since the time of Ramanuja and Shri Chaitanya. Through the influence of great personages like these the place now wears an altogether different aspect.

Disciple: Sir, the Shastras tell us of various special influences attaching to places of pilgrimage. How far is this claim true?

Swamiji: When the whole world is the Form Universal of the Eternal Atman, the Ishvara (God), what is there to wonder at in special influences attaching to particular places? There are places where He manifests Himself specially, either spontaneously or through the earnest longing of pure souls, and the ordinary man, if he visits those places with eagerness, attains his end quite easily. Therefore it may lead to the development of the Self in time to have recourse to holy places. But know it for certain that there is no greater Tirtha (holy spot) than the body of man. Nowhere else is the Atman so manifest as here. That car of Jagannatha that you see is but a concrete symbol of this corporeal car. You have to behold the Atman in this car of the body. Haven't you read "[(Sanskrit)] — know the Atman to be seated on the chariot" etc., "[(Sanskrit)] — all the gods worship the Vamana (the Supreme Being in a diminutive form) seated in the interior of the body"? The sight of the Atman is the real vision of Jagannatha. And the statement "[(Sanskrit)] — seeing the Vamana on the car, one is no more subject to rebirth", means that if you can visualise the Atman which is within you, and disregarding which you are always identifying yourself with this curious mass of matter, this body of yours — if you can see that, then there is no more rebirth for you. If the sight of the Lord's image on a wooden framework confers liberation on people, then crores of them would be liberated every year — specially with such facility of communication by rail nowadays! But I do not mean to say that the notion which devotees in general entertain towards Shri Jagannatha is either nothing or erroneous. There is a class of people who gradually rise to higher and higher truths with the help of that image. So it is an undoubted fact that in and through that image there is a special manifestation of the Lord.

Disciple: Sir, are there different religions then for the ignorant and the wise?

Swamiji: Quite so. Otherwise why do your scriptures go to such lengths over the specification of the qualifications of an aspirant? All is truth no doubt, but relative truth, different in degrees. Whatever man knows to be truth is of a like nature: some are lesser truths, others, higher ones in comparison with them, while the Absolute Truth is God alone.

This Atman is altogether dormant in matter; in man, designated as a living being, It is partially conscious; while in personages like Shri Krishna, Buddha, and Shankara the same Atman has reached the superconscious stage. There is a state even beyond that, which cannot be expressed in terms of thought or language — [(Sanskrit)].

Disciple: Sir, there are certain Bhakti sects who hold that we must practise devotion by placing ourselves in a particular attitude or relation with God. They do not understand anything about the glory of the Atman and so forth, and exclusively recommend this constant devotional attitude.

Swamiji: What they say is true to their own case. By continued practice along this line, they too shall feel an awakening of Brahman within them. And what we (Sannyasins) are doing is another kind of practice. We have renounced the world. So how will it suit us to practise by putting ourselves in some worldly relation — such as that of mother, or father, or wife or son, and so forth — with God? To us all these ideals appear to be narrow. Of course it is very difficult to qualify for the worship of God in His absolute, unconditioned aspect. But must we go in for poison because we get no nectar? Always talk and hear and reason about this Atman. By continuing to practise in this way, you will find in time that the Lion (Brahman) will wake up in you too. Go beyond all those relative attitudes — mere sports of the mind. Listen to what Yama says in the Katha Upanisad: [(Sanskrit)][1] Arise! Awake! and stop not until the goal is reached!

Here the subject was brought to a close. The bell for taking Prasada (consecrated food) rang, and Swamiji went to partake of it, followed by the disciple.

III

Swamiji has removed the Math from Alambazar to Nilambar Babu's garden at Belur. He is very glad to have come to these new premises. He said to the disciple when the latter came, "See how the Ganga flows by and what a nice building! I like this place. This is the ideal kind of place for a Math." It was then afternoon.

In the evening the disciple found Swamiji alone in the upper storey, and the talk went on, on various topics, in the course of which he wanted to know about Swamiji's boyhood days. Swamiji began to say, "From my very boyhood I was a dare-devil sort of fellow. Otherwise, do you think I could make a tour round the world without a single copper in my pocket?"

In boyhood Swamiji had a great predilection for hearing the chanting of the Ramayana by professional singers. Wherever such chanting would take place in the neighborhood, he would attend it, leaving sport and all. Swamiji related how, while listening to the Ramayana, on some days, he would be so deeply engrossed in it as to forget all about home, and would have no idea that it was late at night, and that he must return home, and so forth. One day during the chant he heard that the monkey-god Hanuman lived in banana orchards. Forthwith he was so much convinced that when the chant was over, he did not go home straight that night, but loitered in a banana orchard close to his house, with the hope of catching sight of Hanuman, till it was very late in the night.

In his student life he used to pass the day-time only in playing and gambolling with his mates, and study at night bolting the doors. And none could know when he prepared his lessons.

The disciple asked, "Did you see any visions, sir, during your school days?"

Swamiji: While at school, one night I was meditating within closed doors and had a fairly deep concentration of mind. How long I meditated in that way, I cannot say. It was over, and I still kept my seat, when from the southern wall of that room a luminous figure stepped out and stood in front of me. There was a wonderful radiance on its visage, yet there seemed to be no play of emotion on it. It was the figure of a Sannyasin absolutely calm, shaven-headed, and staff and Kamandalu (a Sannyasin's wooden water-bowl) in hand. He gazed at me for some time and seemed as if he would address

---

1. Arise, awake, and learn by approaching the elite.

me. I too gazed at him in speechless wonder. Then a kind of fright seized me, I opened the door, and hurried out of the room. Then it struck me that it was foolish of me to run away like that, that perhaps he might say something to me. But I have never met that figure since. Many a time and often I have thought that if again I saw him, I would no more be afraid but would speak to him. But I met him no more.

Disciple: Did you ever think on the matter afterwards?

Swamiji: Yes, but I could find no clue to its solution. I now think it was the Lord Buddha whom I saw.

After a short pause, Swamiji said, "When the mind is purified, when one is free from the attachment for lust and gold, one sees lots of visions, most wonderful ones! But one should not pay heed to them. The aspirant cannot advance further if he sets his mind constantly on them. Haven't you heard that Shri Ramakrishna used to say, 'Countless jewels lie uncared for in the outer courts of my beloved Lord's sanctum'? We must come face to face with the Atman; what is the use of setting one's mind on vagaries like those?"

After saying these words, Swamiji sat silent for a while, lost in thought over something. He then resumed:

"Well, while I was in America I had certain wonderful powers developed in me. By looking into people's eyes I could fathom in a trice the contents of their minds. The workings of everybody's mind would be potent to me, like a fruit on the palm of one's hand. To some I used to give out these things, and of those to whom I communicated these, many would become my disciples; whereas those who came to mix with me with some ulterior motive would not, on coming across this power of mine, even venture into my presence any more. "When I began lecturing in Chicago and other cities, I had to deliver every week some twelve or fifteen or even more lectures at times. This excessive strain on the body and mind would exhaust me to a degree. I seemed to run short of subjects for lectures and was anxious where to find new topics for the morrow's lecture. New thoughts seemed altogether scarce. One day, after the lecture, I lay thinking of what means to adopt next. The thought induced a sort of slumber, and in that state I heard as if somebody standing by me was lecturing — many new ideas and new veins of thought, which I had scarcely heard or thought of in my life. On awaking I remembered them and reproduced them in my lecture. I cannot enumerate how often this phenomenon took place. Many, many days did I hear such lectures while lying in bed. Sometimes the lecture would be delivered in such a loud voice that the inmates of adjacent rooms would hear the sound and ask me the next day, "With whom, Swamiji, were you talking so loudly last night?" I used to avoid the question somehow. Ah, it was a wonderful phenomenon."

The disciple was wonder-struck at Swamiji's words and after thinking deeply on the matter said, "Sir, then you yourself must have lectured like that in your subtle body, and sometimes it would be echoed by the gross body also."

Swamiji listened and replied, "Well, may be."

The topic of his American experiences came up. Swamiji said, "In that country the women are more learned than men. They are all well versed in science and philosophy, and that is why they would appreciate and honour me so much. The men are grinding all day at their work and have very little leisure, whereas the women, by studying and teaching in schools and colleges, have become highly learned. Whichever side you turn your eyes in America, you see the power and influence of women."

Disciple: Well, sir, did not the bigoted Christians oppose you?

Swamiji: Yes, they did. When people began to honour me, then the Padris were after me. They spread many slanders about me by publishing them in the newspapers. Many asked me to contradict these slanders. But I never took the slightest notice of them. It is my firm conviction that no great work is accomplished in this world by low cunning; so without paying any heed to these vile slanders, I used to work steadily at my mission. The upshot I used to find was that often my slanderers, feeling repentant afterwards, would surrender to me and offer apologies, by themselves contradicting the slanders in the papers. Sometimes it so happened that learning that I had been invited to a certain house, somebody would communicate those slanders to my host, who hearing them, would leave home, locking his door. When I went there to attend the invitation, I found it was deserted and nobody was there. Again a few days afterwards, they themselves, learning the truth, would feel sorry for their previous conduct and come to offer themselves as disciples. The fact is, my son, this whole world is full of mean ways of worldliness. But men of real moral courage and discrimination are never deceived by these. Let the world say what it chooses, I shall tread the path of duty — know this to be the line of action for a hero. Otherwise, if one has to attend day and night to what this man says or that man writes, no great work is achieved in this world. Do you know this Sanskrit Shloka: "Let those who are versed in the ethical codes praise or blame, let Lakshmi, the goddess of Fortune, come or go wherever she wisheth, let death overtake him today or after a century, the wise man never swerves from the path of rectitude."[1] Let people praise you or blame you, let fortune smile or frown upon you, let your body fall today or after a Yuga, see that you do not deviate from the path of Truth. How much of tempest and waves one has to weather, before one reaches the haven of Peace! The greater a man has become, the fiercer ordeal he has had to pass through. Their lives have been tested true by the touchstone of practical life, and only then have they been acknowledged great by the world. Those who are faint-hearted and cowardly sink their barks near the shore, frightened by the raging of waves on the sea. He who is a hero never casts a glance at these. Come what may, I must attain my ideal first — this is Purushakara, manly endeavour; without such manly endeavor no amount of Divine help will be of any avail to banish your inertia.

Disciple: Is, then, reliance on Divine help a sign of weakness?

Swamiji: In the Shastras real self-surrender and reliance on God has been indicated as the culmination of human achievement. But in your country nowadays the way people speak of Daiva or reliance on Divine dispensation is a sign of death, the outcome of great cowardliness; conjuring up some monstrous idea of God-head and trying to saddle that with all your faults and shortcomings. Haven't you heard Shri Ramakrishna's story about "the sin of killing a cow"?[2] In the end the owner of the garden had to suffer for the sin of killing the cow. Nowadays everybody says: "I am acting as I am being directed by the Lord", and thus throws the burden of both his sins and virtues on the Lord. As if he is himself the lotus-leaf in the water (untouched by it)! If everybody can truly live always in this mood, then he is a Free Soul. But what really happens is that for the "good" I have the credit, but the "bad" Thou, God, art responsible! Praise be to such reliance on God! Without the attainment of the fullness of Knowledge or Divine Love, such a state of absolute reliance on the Lord does not come. He who is truly and sincerely reliant on the Lord goes beyond all idea of the duality of good and bad. The brightest example of the attainment of this state among us at the present time is Nag Mahashaya.[3]

Then the conversation drifted to the subject of Nag Mahashaya. Swamiji said, "One does not find a second devoted Bhakta like him — oh, when shall I see him again!"

Disciple: He will soon come to Calcutta to meet you, so mother (Nag Mahashaya's wife) has written to me.

Swamiji: Shri Ramakrishna used to compare him to King Janaka. A man with such control over all

---

1. Bhartrihari's Nitishataka.

2. A man had laid out a beautiful garden into which a cow strayed one day and did much injury. The man in rage gave some blows to the cow which killed her. Then to avoid the terrible sin he bethought himself of a trick; knowing that Indra was the presiding deity of the hand, he tried to lay the blame on him. Indra perceiving his sophistry appeared on the scene in the guise of a Brahmin and by a number of questions drew from him the answer that each and every item in connection with that garden was the man's own handiwork; whereupon Indra exposed his cunning with the cutting remark, "Well, everything here has been done by you, and Indra alone is responsible for the killing of the cow, eh!"

3. Durga Charan Nag, a disciple of Shri Ramakrishna.

the senses one does not hear of even, much less come across. You must associate with him as much as you can. He is one of Shri Ramakrishna's nearest disciples.

Disciple: Many in our part of the country call him a madcap. But I have known him to be a great soul since the very first day of my meeting him. He loves me much, and I have his fervent blessings.

Swamiji: Since you have attained the company of such a Mahapurusha (holy soul), what more have you to fear about? As an effect of many lives of Tapasya one is blessed with the company of such a great soul. How does he live at home?

Disciple: Sir, he has got no business or anything of the kind. He is always busy in serving the guests who come to his house. Beyond the small sum the Pal Babus give him, he has no other means of subsistence; his expenses, however, are like those in a rich family. But he does not spend a pice for his own enjoyment, all that expense is for the service of others. Service — service of others — this seems to be the great mission of his life. It sometimes strikes me that realising the Atman in all creatures, he is engrossed in serving the whole world as a part and parcel of himself. In the service of others he works incessantly and is not conscious even of his body. I suppose, he always lives on the plane which you, sir, call the superconscious state of the mind.

Swamiji: Why should not that be? How greatly was he beloved of Shri Ramakrishna! In your East Bengal, one of Shri Ramakrishna's divine companions has been born in the person of Nag Mahashaya. By his radiance Eastern Bengal has become effulgent.

IV

It is two or three days since Swamiji has returned from Kashmir. His health is indifferent. When the disciple came to the Math, Swami Brahmananda said, "Since returning from Kashmir, Swamiji does not speak to anybody, he sits in one place rapt in thought; you go to him and by conversation try to draw his mind a little towards worldly objects."

The disciple coming to Swamiji's room in the upper storey found him sitting as if immersed in deep mediation. There was no smile on his face, his brilliant eyes had no outward look, as if intent on seeing something within. Seeing the disciple, he only said, "You have come, my son? Please take your seat", and lapsed into silence. The disciple seeing the inside of his left eye reddened asked, "How is it that your eye is red?" "That is nothing", said Swamiji and was again silent. When even after along time Swamiji did not speak, the disciple was a little troubled at heart and touching his feet said, "Won't you relate to me what things you have seen at Amarnath?" By the disciple's touching his feet, the tensity of his mood was broken a little, as if his attention was diverted a little outwards. He said, "Since visiting Amarnath, I feel as if Shiva is sitting on my head for twenty-four hours and would not come down." The disciple heard it with speechless wonder.

Swamiji: I underwent great religious austerities at Amarnath and then in the temple of Kshir Bhavani. Go and prepare me some tobacco, I will relate everything to you.

The disciple joyfully obeyed the order. Swamiji slowly smoking began to say, "On the way to Amarnath, I made a very steep ascent on the mountain. Pilgrims do not generally travel by that path. But the determination came upon me that I must go by that path, and so I did. The labour of the strenuous ascent has told on my body. The cold there is so biting that you feel it like pin-pricks."

Disciple: I have heard that it is the custom to visit the image of Amarnath naked; is it so?

Swamiji: Yes, I entered the cave with only my Kaupina on and my body smeared with holy ash; I did not then feel any cold or heat. But when I came out of the temple, I was benumbed by the cold.

Disciple: Did you see the holy pigeons? I have heard, in that cold no living creatures are found to live, but a flight of pigeons from some unknown place frequents the place occasionally.

Swamiji: Yes, I saw three or four white pigeons; whether they live in the cave or the neighboring hills, I could not ascertain.

Disciple: Sir, I have heard people say that the

sight of pigeons on coming out of the temple indicates that one has really been blessed with the vision of Shiva.

Swamiji: I have heard that the sight of the pigeons brings to fruition whatever desires one may have.

Then Swamiji said that on the way back he returned to Srinagar by the common route by which the pilgrims return. A few days after returning to Srinagar, he went to visit Kshir Bhavani Devi and staying there for seven days worshipped the Devi and made Homa to her with offerings of Kshira (condensed milk). Every day he used to worship the Devi with a maund of Kshira as offering. One day, while worshipping, the thought arose in Swamiji's mind: "Mother Bhavani has been manifesting Her Presence here for untold years. The Mohammedans came and destroyed her temple, yet the people of the place did nothing to protect Her. Alas, if I were then living I could never have borne it silently." When, thinking in this strain, his mind was much oppressed with sorrow and anguish, he distinctly heard the voice of the Mother saying, "It was according to My desire that the Mohammedans destroyed this temple. It is My desire that I should live in a dilapidated temple, otherwise, can I not immediately erect a seven-storeyed temple of gold here if I like? What can you do? Shall I protect you or shall you protect me!" Swamiji said, "Since hearing that divine voice, I cherish no more plans. The idea of building Maths etc. I have given up; as Mother wills, so it will be." The disciple, speechless with wonder, began to think, "Did he not one day tell me that whatever I saw and heard was but the echo of the Atman within me, that there was nothing outside?"— and fearlessly spoke it out also —"Sir, you used to say that Divine Voices are the echo of our inward thoughts and feelings." Swamiji gravely said, "Whether it be internal or external, if you actually hear with your ears such a disembodied voice, as I have done, can you deny it and call it false? Divine Voices are actually heard, just as you and I are talking."

The disciple, without controverting accepted Swamiji's words, for his words always carried conviction.

He then brought up the subject of departed spirits, and said, "Sir, these ghosts and departed spirits we hear about — which the Shastras also amply corroborate — are all these true or not?

Swamiji: Certainly they are true. Whatever you don't see, are they all false for that? Beyond your sight, millions of universes are revolving at great distances. Because you do not see them, are they non-existent for that? But then, do not put your mind on these subjects of ghosts and spirits. Your mental attitude towards them should be one of indifference. You duty is to realise the Atman within this body. When you realise the Atman, ghosts and spirits will be your slaves.

Disciple: But sir, I think that, if one sees them, it strengthens one's belief in the hereafter, and dispels all doubts about it.

Swamiji: You are heroes; do you mean to say that even you shall have to strengthen your belief in the hereafter by seeing ghosts and spirits! You have read so many sciences and scriptures — have mastered so many secrets of this infinite universe — even with such knowledge, you have to acquire the knowledge of the Atman by seeing ghosts and spirits! What a shame!

Disciple: Well, sir, have you ever seen ghosts and spirits?

Swamiji narrated that a certain deceased relative of his used to come to him as a disembodied spirit. Sometimes it used to bring him information about distant events. But on verification, some of its information was not found to be correct. Afterwards at a certain place of pilgrimage Swamiji prayed for it mentally, wishing it might be released — since then he did not see it again. The disciple then questioned Swamiji if Shraddha or other obsequial ceremonies appeased the departed spirits in any way. Swamiji replied, "That is not impossible." On the disciple's asking for the grounds of that belief Swamiji said, "I will explain the subject to you at length some day. There are irrefutable arguments to prove that the Shraddha ceremony appeases the departed beings. Today I don't feel well. I shall explain it to you another day." But the disciple did not get another opportunity to ask that question to Swamiji.

V

The Math is still situated in Nilambar Babu's garden house at Belur. It is the month of November. Swamiji is now much engaged in the study and discussion of Sanskrit scriptures. The couplet beginning with "Achandala-pratihatarayah", he composed about this time. Today Swamiji composed the hymn, "Om Hring Ritam "etc., and handing it over to the disciple said, "See if there is any metrical defect in these stanzas." The disciple made a copy of the poem for this purpose.

On this day it seemed as if the goddess of learning had manifested herself on his tongue. With the disciple he fluently talked about two hours at a stretch in exceedingly melodious Sanskrit. After the disciple had copied the hymn, Swamiji said, "You see, as I write immersed in thought, grammatical slips sometimes occur; therefore I ask you all to look over them."

Disciple: Sir, these are not slips, but the licence of genius.

Swamiji: You may say so; but why will other people assent to that? The other day I wrote an essay on "What is Hinduism", and some amongst you even are complaining that it was written in a very stiff Bengali. I think, language and thought also, like all other things, become lifeless and monotonous in course of time. Such a state seems to have happened now in this country. On the advent of Shri Ramakrishna, however, a new current has set in, in thought and language. Everything has now to be recast in new moulds. Everything has to be propagated with the stamp of new genius. Look, for example, how the old modes of Sannyasins are breaking, yielding place to a new mould by degrees. The Sannyasins of the present day have to go to distant countries for preaching, and if they go in an ash-besmeared, half-nude body like the Sadhus (holy men) of old, in the first place they won't be taken on board the ships, and even if they anyhow reach foreign countries in that dress, they will have to stay in jail. Everything requires to be changed a little according to place, time, and civilisation. Henceforth I am thinking of writing essays in Bengali. Litterateurs will perhaps rail at them. Never mind — I shall try to cast the Bengali language in a new mould. Nowadays, Bengali writers use too many verbs in their writings; this takes away the force of the language. If one can express the ideas of verbs with adjectives, it adds to the force of the language; henceforth try to write in that style. Try to write articles in that style in the Udbodhan. Do you know the meaning of the use of verbs in language? It gives a pause to the thought; hence the use of too many verbs in language is the sign of weakness, like quick breathing, and indicates that there is not much vitality in the language; that is why one cannot lecture well in the Bengali language. He who has control over his language, does not make frequent breaks in his thoughts. As your physique has been rendered languid by living on a dietary of boiled rice and dal, similar is the case with your language. In food, in modes of life, in thought, and in language, energy has to be infused. With the infusion of vitality all round and the circulation of blood in all arteries and veins, one should feel the throbbing of new life in everything — then only will the people of this land be able to survive the present terrible struggle for existence; otherwise the country and the race will vanish in the enveloping shadows of death at no distant date.

Disciple: Sir, the constitution of the people of this country has been moulded in a peculiar way through long ages. Is it possible to change that within a short time?

Swamiji: If you have known the old ways to be wrong, then why don't you, as I say, learn to live in a better way? By your example ten other people will follow suit, and by theirs another fifty people will learn. By this process in course of time the new idea will awaken in the hearts of the whole race. But even if after understanding, you do not act accordingly, I shall know that you are wise in words only — but practically you are fools.

Disciple: Your words, sir, infuse great courage, enthusiasm, energy and strength into the heart.

Swamiji: By degrees the heart has to be strengthened. If one man is made, it equals the result of a hundred thousand lectures. Making the mind and lips at one, the ideas have to be practised in life. This is what Shri Ramakrishna meant by "allowing no theft in the chamber of thought". You have to be practical in all spheres of work. The whole country has been ruined by masses of theories. He who is the true son of Shri Ramakrishna will manifest the practical side of religious ideas and will set to work with one-pointed devotion without paying heed to the prattling of men or of society. Haven't you heard of the couplet of Tulsidas: "The elephant walks the market-place and a thousand curs bark at him; so the Sadhus have no ill-feeling if worldly people slander them." You have to walk in this way. No count should be taken of the words of people. If one has to pay heed to their praise or blame, no great work can be accomplished in this life. "नायमात्मा बलहीनेन लभ्य:— the Atman is not to be gained by the weak." If there is no strength in the body and mind, the Atman cannot be realised. First you have to build the body by good nutritious food — then only will the mind be strong. The mind is but the subtle part of the body. You must retain great strength in your mind and words. "I am low, I am low"— repeating these ideas in the mind, man belittles and degrades himself. Therefore, the Shastra (Ashtavakra Samhita, I.11) says:

मुक्ताभिमानी मुक्तो हि बद्धो बद्धाभिमान्यपि।
किम्वदन्तीह सत्येयं या मतिः सा गतिर्भवेत्॥

— He who thinks himself free, free he becomes; he who thinks himself bound, bound he remains — this popular saying is true: 'As one thinks, so one becomes'." He alone who is always awake to the idea of freedom, becomes free; he who thinks he is bound, endures life after life in the state of bondage. It is a fact. This truth holds good both in spiritual and temporal matters. Those who are always down-hearted and dispirited in this life can do no work; from life to life they come and go wailing and moaning. "The earth is enjoyed by heroes"— this is the unfailing truth. Be a hero. Always say, "I have no fear." Tell this to everybody —"Have no fear". Fear is death, fear is sin, fear is hell, fear is unrighteousness, fear is wrong life. All the negative thoughts and ideas that are in this world have proceeded from this evil spirit of fear. This fear alone has kept the sun, air and death in their respective places and functions, allowing none to escape from their bounds. Therefore the Shruti says (Katha Upanishad, II.iii,3) says:

"भयादस्याग्निपिति भयात्तपति सूर्य:।
भयादिन्द्रश्च वायुश्च मृत्युर्धावति पञ्चम:॥

— Through fear of this, fire burns, the sun heats; through fear Indra and Vayu are carrying on their functions, and Death stalks upon this earth." When the gods Indra, Chandra, Vayu, Varuna will attain to fearlessness, then will they be one with Brahman, and all this phantasm of the world will vanish. Therefore I say, "Be fearless, be fearless."

Swamiji, in saying these words, appeared in the eyes of the disciple like the very embodiment of "fearlessness", and he thought, "How in his presence even the fear of death leaves one and vanishes into nothingness!"

Swamiji continued: In this embodied existence, you will be tossed again and again on the waves of happiness and misery, prosperity and adversity — but know them all to be of momentary duration. Never care for them. "I am birthless, the deathless Atman, whose nature is Intelligence"— implanting this idea firmly in your heart, you should pass the days of your life. "I have no birth, no death, I am the Atman untouched by anything"— lose yourself completely in this idea. If you can once become one with this idea, then in the hour of sorrow and tribulation, it will rise of itself in your mind, and you will not have to strive with difficulty to bring it up. The other day, I was a guest of Babu Priyanath Mukherjee at Baidyanath. There I had such a spell of asthma that I felt like dying. But from within, with every breath arose the deep-toned sound, "I am He, I am He". Resting on the pillow, I was waiting for the vital breath to depart, and observing all the time that from within was being heard the sound of "I am He, I am He!" I could hear all along "एकमेवाद्वयं ब्रह्म नेह नानास्ति किञ्चन — the Brahman, the One without a second, alone exists, nothing manifold exists in the world."

The disciple, struck with amazement said, "Sir, talking with you and listening to your realisations, I feel no necessity for the study of scriptures."

Swamiji: No! Scriptures have to be studied also. For the attainment of Jnana, study of scriptures is essential. I shall soon open classes in the Math for them. The Vedas, Upanishads, the Gita, and Bhagavata should be studied in the classes, and I shall teach the Panini's Ashtadhyayai.

Disciple: Have you studied the Ashtadhayayi of Panini?

Swamiji: When I was in Jaipur, I met a great grammarian and felt a desire to study Sanskrit grammar with him. Although he was a great scholar in that branch, he had not much aptitude for teaching. He explained to me the commentary on the first aphorism for three days continuously, still I could not grasp a bit of it. On the fourth day the teacher got annoyed and said, "Swamiji, I could not make you understand the meaning of the first aphorism even in three days; I fear, you will not be much benefited by my teaching." Hearing these words, a great self-reproach came over me. Putting food and sleep aside, I set myself to study the commentary on the first aphorism independently. Within three hours the sense of the commentary stood explained before me as clearly as anything; then going to my teacher I gave him the sense of the whole commentary. My teacher, hearing me, said, "How could you gather the sense so excellently within three hours, which I failed to explain to you in three days?" After that, every day I began to read chapter after chapter, with the greatest ease. Through concentration of mind everything can be accomplished — even mountains can be crushed to atoms.

Disciple: Sir, everything is wonderful about you.

Swamiji: There is nothing wonderful in this universe. Ignorance constitutes the only darkness, which confers all things and makes them look mysterious. When everything is lighted by Knowledge, the sense of mystery vanishes from the face of things. Even such an inscrutable thing as Maya, which brings the most impossible things to pass, disappears. Know Him, think of Him, by knowing whom everything else is known. And when that Atman is realised, the purport of all scriptures will be perceived as clearly as a fruit on the palm of one's hand. The Rishis of old attained realisation, and must we fail? We are also men. What has happened once in the life of one individual must, through proper endeavour, be realised in the life of others. History repeats itself. This Atman is the same in all, there is only a difference of manifestation in different individuals. Try to manifest this Atman, and you will see your intellect penetrating into all subjects. The intellect of one who has not realised the Atman is one-sided, whereas the genius of the knower of Atman is all-embracing. With the manifestation of the Atman you will find that science, philosophy, and everything will be easily mastered. Proclaim the glory of the Atman with the roar of a lion, and impart fearlessness unto all beings by saying, "Arise, awake, and stop not till the goal is reached."

VI

The disciple is staying with Swamiji at the garden-house of Nilambar Babu at Belur for the last two days.

Today, Swamiji has given permission to the disciple to stay in his room at night. When the disciple was serving Swamiji and massaging his feet, he spoke to him: "What folly! Leaving such a place as this, you want to go back to Calcutta! See what an atmosphere of holiness is here — the pure air of the Ganga — what an assemblage of Sadhus — will you find anywhere a place like this!"

Disciple: Sir, as the fruition of great austerities in past lives, I have been blessed with your company. Now bless me that I may not be overcome by ignorance and delusion any more. Now my mind sometimes is seized with a great longing for some direct spiritual realisation.

Swamiji: I also felt like that many times. One day in the Cossipore garden, I had expressed my prayer to Shri Ramakrishna with great earnestness. Then in the evening, at the hour of meditation, I lost the consciousness of the body, and felt that it was absolutely non-existent. I felt that the sun, moon, space, time, ether, and all had been reduced to a homogeneous mass and then melted far away into the unknown; the body-consciousness had almost vanished, and I had nearly merged in the Supreme. But I had just a trace of the feeling of Ego, so I could again return to the world of relativity from the Samadhi. In this state of Samadhi all the difference between "I" and the "Brahman" goes away, everything is reduced into unity, like the waters of the Infinite Ocean — water everywhere, nothing else exists — language and thought, all fail there. Then only is the state "beyond mind and speech" realised in its actuality. Otherwise, so long as the religious aspirant thinks or says, "I am the Brahman" — "I" and "the Brahman", these two entities persist — there is the involved semblance of duality. After that experience, even after trying repeatedly, I failed to bring back the state of Samadhi. On informing Shri Ramakrishna about it, he said, "If you remain day and night in that state, the work of the Divine Mother will not be accomplished; therefore you won't be able to induce that state again; when your work is finished, it will come again."

Disciple: On the attainment of the absolute and transcendent Nirvikalpa Samadhi can none return to the world of duality through the consciousness of Egoism?

Swamiji: Shri Ramakrishna used to say that the Avataras alone can descend to the ordinary plane from that state of Samadhi, for the good of the world. Ordinary Jivas do not; immersed in that state, they remain alive for a period of twenty-one days; after that, their body drops like a sere leaf from the tree of Samsara (world).

Disciple: When in Samadhi the mind is merged, and there remain no waves on the surface of consciousness, where then is the possibility of mental activity and returning to the world through the consciousness of Ego? When there is no mind, then who will descend from Samadhi to the relative plane, and by what means?

Swamiji: The conclusion of the Vedanta is that when there is absolute samadhi and cessation of all modifications, there is no return from that state; as the Vedanta Aphorism says: "अनावृत्तिः शब्दात्— there is non-return, from scriptural texts." But the Avataras cherish a few desires for the good of the world. By taking hold of that thread, they come down from the superconscious to the conscious state.

Disciple: But, sir, if one or two desires remain, how can that state be called the absolute, transcendent Samadhi? For the scriptures say that in that state all the modifications of the mind and all desires are stamped out.

Swamiji: How then can there be projection of the universe after Mahapralaya (final dissolution)? At Maha-pralaya everything is merged in the Brahman. But even after that, one hears and reads of creation in the scriptures, that projection and contraction (of the universe) go on in wave forms. Like the fresh creation and dissolution of the universe after Mahapralaya, the superconscious and conscious states of Avataras also stand to reason.

Disciple: If I argue that at the time of dissolution the seeds of further creation remain almost merged in Brahman, and that it is not absolute dissolution or Nirvikalpa Samadhi?

Swamiji: Then I shall ask you to answer how the projection of the universe is possible from Brahman in which there is no shadow of any qualification — which is unaffected and unqualified.

Disciple: Why, this is but a seeming projection. The reply to the question is given in the scriptures in this way, that the manifestation of creation from Brahman is only an appearance like the mirage in the desert, but really there has been no creation or anything of the kind. This illusion is produced by Maya, which is the negation of the eternally existing Brahman, and hence unreal.

Swamiji: If the creation is false, then you can also regard the Nirvikalpa Samadhi of Jiva and his return therefrom as seeming appearances. Jiva is Brahman by his nature. How can he have any experience of bondage? Your desire to realise the truth that you are Brahman is also a hallucination in that case — for the scripture says, "You are already that."

Therefore, "अयमेव हि ते बन्ध समाधिमनुतिष्ठसि — this is verily your bondage that you are practising the attainment of Samadhi."

Disciple: This is a great dilemma. If I am Brahman, why don't I always realise it?

Swamiji: In order to attain to that realisation in the conscious plane, some instrumentality is required. The mind is that instrument in us. But it is a non-intelligent substance. It only appears to be intelligent through the light of the Atman behind. Therefore the author of the Panchadashi (III.40) says: "चिच्छायावेशत: शक्तिश्चेतनेव विभाति सा — the Shakti appears to be intelligent by the reflection of the intelligence of the Atman." Hence the mind also appears to us like an intelligent substance. Therefore it is certain that you won't be able to know the Atman, the Essence of Intelligence, through the mind. You have to go beyond the mind — for only the Atman exists there — there the object of knowledge becomes the same as the instrument of knowledge. The knower, knowledge, and the instrument of knowledge become one and the same. It is therefore that the Shruti says, "विज्ञातारमरे केन विजानीयात् — through what are you to know the Eternal Subject?" The real fact is that there is a state beyond the conscious plane, where there is no duality of the knower, knowledge, and the instrument of knowledge etc. When the mind is merged, that state is perceived. I say it is "perceived," because there is no other word to express that state. Language cannot express that state. Shankaracharya has styled it "Transcendent Perception" (Aparokshanubhuti). Even after that transcendent perception Avataras descend to the relative plane and give glimpses of that — therefore it is said that the Vedas and other scriptures have originated from the perception of Seers. The case of ordinary Jivas is like that of the salt-doll which attempting to sound the depths of the ocean melted into it. Do you see? The sum and substance of it is — you have only got to know that you are Eternal Brahman.

You are already that, only the intervention of a non-intelligent mind (which is called Maya in the scriptures) is hiding that knowledge. When the mind composed of subtle matter is quelled, the Atman is effulgent by Its own radiance. One proof of the fact that Maya or mind is an illusion is that the mind by itself is non-intelligent and of the nature of darkness; and it is the light of the Atman behind, that makes it appear as intelligent. When you will understand this, the mind will merge in the unbroken Ocean of Intelligence; then you will realise: "[(Sanskrit)] — this Atman is Brahman."

Then Swamiji, addressing the disciple, said, "You feel sleepy, then go to sleep."

In the night the disciple had a wonderful dream, as a result of which he earnestly begged Swamiji's permission to worship him. Swamiji had to acquiesce, and after the ceremony was over he said to the disciple, "Well, your worship is finished, but Premananda will be in a rage at your sacrilegious act of worshipping my feet in the flower-tray meant for Shri Ramakrishna's worship." Before his words were finished, Swami Premananda came there, and Swamiji said to him, "See what a sacrilege he has committed! With the requisites of Shri Ramakrishna's worship, he has worshipped me!" Swami Premananda, smiling, said, "Well done! Are you and Shri Ramakrishna different?" — hearing which the disciple felt at ease.

The disciple is an orthodox Hindu. Not to speak of prohibited food, he does not even take food touched by another. Therefore Swamiji sometimes used to refer to him as "priest". Swamiji, while he was eating biscuits with his breakfast, said to Swami Sadananda, "Bring the priest in here." When the disciple came to Swamiji, he gave some portion of his food to him to eat. Finding the disciple accepting it without any demur, Swamiji said, "Do you know what you have eaten now? These are made from eggs." In reply, the disciple said, "Whatever may be in it, I have no need to know; taking this sacramental food from you, I have become immortal."

Thereupon Swamiji said, "I bless you that from this day all your egoism of caste, colour, high birth, religious merit and demerit, and all, may vanish for ever!"...

VII

The disciple has come to the Math this morning. As soon as he stood after touching the feet of Swamiji, Swamiji said, "What's the use of your continuing in service any more? Why not go in for some business?" The disciple was then employed as a private tutor in some family. Asked about the profession of teaching, Swamiji said, "If one does the work of teaching boys for a long time, one gets blunt in intellect; one's intelligence is not manifested. If one stays among a crowd of boys day and night, gradually one gets obtuse. So give up the working of teaching boys."

Disciple: What shall I do, then?

Swamiji; Why, if you want to live the life of a worldly man and have a desire for earning money, then go over to America. I shall give you directions for business. You will find that in five years you will get together a lot of money.

Disciple: What business shall I go in for? And where am I to get the money from?

Swamiji: What nonsense are you talking? Within you lies indomitable power. Only thinking, "I am nothing, I am nothing", you have become powerless. Why, you alone! The whole race has become so. Go round the world once, and you will find how vigorously the life-current of other nations is flowing. And what are you doing? Even after learning so much, you go about the doors of others, crying, "Give me employment". Trampled under others' feet doing slavery for others, are you men any more? You are not worth a pin's head! In this fertile country with abundant water-supply, where nature produces wealth and harvest a thousand times more than in others, you have no food for your stomach, no clothes to cover your body! In this country of abundance, the produce of which has been the cause of the spread of civilisation in other countries, you are reduced to such straits! Your condition is even worse than that of a dog. And you glory in your Vedas and Vedanta! A nation that cannot provide for its simple food and clothing, which always depends on others for its subsistence — what is there for it to vaunt about? Throw your religious observances overboard for the present and be first prepared for the struggle for existence. People of foreign countries are turning out such golden results from the raw materials produced in your country, and you, like asses of burden, are only carrying their load. The people of foreign countries import Indian raw goods, manufacture various commodities by bringing their intelligence to bear upon them, and become great; whereas you have locked up your intelligence, thrown away your inherited wealth to others, and roam about crying piteously for food.

Disciple: In what way, sir, can the means of subsistence be procured?

Swamiji: Why, the means are in your hands. You blindfold your eyes, and said, "I am blind and can see nothing." Tear off the folds from your eyes and you will see the whole world lighted by the rays of the midday sun. If you cannot procure money, go to foreign countries, working your passage as a Lascar. Take Indian cloth, towels, bamboo-work, and other indigenous products, and peddle in the streets of Europe and America; you will find how greatly Indian products are appreciated in foreign markets even now. In America I found, some Mohammedans of the Hooghly district had grown rich by peddling Indian commodities in this way. Have you even less intelligence than they? Take, for example, such excellent fabric as the Varanasi-made Saris of India, the like of which are not produced anywhere else in the world. Go to America with this cloth. Have gowns made out of this fabric and sell them, and you will see how much you earn.

Disciple: Sir, why will they wear gowns made of the Saris of Varanasi? I have heard that clothes designed diversely are not to the taste of the ladies in those countries.

Swamiji: Whether they will receive or not, I shall look to that. It is for you to exert yourself and go over there. I have many friends in that country, to whom I shall introduce you. At first I shall request them to take this cloth up among themselves. Then you will find many will follow suit, and at last you won't be able to keep the supply up to the enormous demand.

Disciple: Where shall I get the capital for the business?

Swamiji: I shall somehow give you a start; for the rest you must depend on your own exertions. "If you die, you get to heaven; and if you win, you enjoy the earth" (Gita). Even if you die in this attempt, well and good, many will take up the work, following your example. And if you succeed, you will live a life of great opulence.

Disciple: Yes, sir, so it is. But I cannot muster sufficient courage.

Swamiji: That is what I say, my son, you have no Shraddha — no faith in yourselves. What will you achieve? You will have neither material nor spiritual advancement. Either put forth your energy in the way I have suggested and be successful in life, or give up all and take to the path we have chosen. Serve the people of all countries through spiritual instruction — then only will you get your dole of food like us. If there is no mutual exchange, do you think anybody cares for anybody else? You observe in our case, that because we give the householders some spiritual instructions, they in return give us some morsels of food. If you do nothing, why will they give you food? You observe so much misery in mere service and slavery of others, still you are not waking up; and so your misery also is never at an end. This is certainly the delusive power of Maya! In the West I have found that those who are in the employment of others have their seats fixed in the back rows in the Parliament, while the front seats are reserved for those who have made themselves famous by self-exertion, or education, or intelligence. In Western countries there is no botheration of caste. Those on whom Fortune smiles for their industry and exertion are alone regarded as leaders of the country and the controllers of its destiny. Whereas in your country, you are simply vaunting your superiority in caste, till at last you cannot even get a morsel of food! You have not the capacity to manufacture a needle, and you dare to criticise the English! Fools! Sit at their feet and learn from them the arts, industries, and the practicality necessary for the struggle for existence. You will be esteemed once more when you will become fit. Then they too will pay heed to your words. Without the necessary preparation, what will mere shouting in the Congress avail?

Disciple: But, sir, all the educated men of the country have joined it.

Swamiji: Well, you consider a man as educated if only he can pass some examinations and deliver good lectures. The education which does not help the common mass of people to equip themselves for the struggle for life, which does not bring out strength of character, a spirit of philanthropy, and the courage of a lion — is it worth the name? Real education is that which enables one to stand on one's own legs. The education that you are receiving now in schools and colleges is only making you a race of dyspeptics. You are working like machines merely, and living a jelly-fish existence.

The peasant, the shoemaker, the sweeper, and such other lower classes of India have much greater capacity for work and self-reliance than you. They have been silently working through long ages and producing the entire wealth of the land, without a word of complaint. Very soon they will get above you in position. Gradually capital is drifting into their hands, and they are not so much troubled with wants as you are. Modern education has changed your fashion, but new avenues of wealth lie yet undiscovered for want of the inventive genius. You have so long oppressed these forbearing masses; now is the time for their retribution. And you will become extinct in your vain search for employment, making it the be — all and end — all of your life.

Disciple: Sir, although our power of originality is less than that of other countries, still the lower classes of India are being guided by our intelligence. So where will they get the power and culture to overcome the higher classes in the struggle for existence?

Swamiji: Never mind if they have not read a few books like you — if they have not acquired your tailor-made civilisation. What do these matter? But they are the backbone of the nation in all countries. If these lower classes stop work, from where will you get your food and clothing? If the sweepers of

Calcutta stop work for a day, it creates a panic; and if they strike for three days, the whole town will be depopulated by the outbreak of epidemics. If the labourers stop work, your supply of food and clothes also stops. And you regard them as low-class people and vaunt your own culture!

Engrossed in the struggle for existence, they had not the opportunity for the awakening of knowledge. They have worked so long uniformly like machines guided by human intelligence, and the clever educated section have taken the substantial part of the fruits of their labour. In every country this has been the case. But times have changed. The lower classes are gradually awakening to this fact and making a united front against this, determined to exact their legitimate dues. The masses of Europe and America have been the first to awaken and have already begun the fight. Signs of this awakening have shown themselves in India, too, as is evident from the number of strikes among the lower classes nowadays. The upper classes will no longer be able to repress the lower, try they ever so much. The well-being of the higher classes now lies in helping the lower to get their legitimate rights.

Therefore I say, set yourselves to the task of spreading education among the masses. Tell them and make them understand, "You are our brothers — a part and parcel of our bodies, and we love you and never hate you." If they receive this sympathy from you, their enthusiasm for work will be increased a hundredfold. Kindle their knowledge with the help of modern science. Teach them history, geography, science, literature, and along with these the profound truths of religion. In exchange for that teaching, the poverty of the teachers will also disappear. By mutual exchange both parties will become friendly to each other.

Disciple: But, sir, with the spread of learning among them, they too will in course of time have fertile brains but become idle and inactive like us and live on the fruits of the labour of the next lower classes.

Swamiji: Why shall it be so? Even with the awakening of knowledge, the potter will remain a potter, the fisherman a fisherman, the peasant a peasant. Why should they leave their hereditary calling? "(Sanskrit) — don't give up the work to which you were born, even if it be attended with defects." If they are taught in this way, why should they give up their respective callings? Rather they will apply their knowledge to the better performance of the work to which they have been born. A number of geniuses are sure to arise from among them in the course of time. You (the higher classes) will take these into your own fold. The Brahmins acknowledged the valiant king Vishvamitra as a Brahmin, and think how grateful the whole Kshatriya race became to the Brahmins for this act! By such sympathy and co-operation even birds and beasts become one's own — not to speak of men!

Disciple: Sir, what you say is true, but there yet seems to be a wide gulf between the higher and lower classes. To bring the higher classes to sympathise with the lower seems to be a difficult affair in India.

Swamiji: But without that there is no well-being for your upper classes. You will be destroyed by internecine quarrels and fights — which you have been having so long. When the masses will wake up, they will come to understand your oppression of them, and by a puff of their mouth you will be entirely blown away! It is they who have introduced civilisation amongst you; and it is they who will then pull it down. Think how at the hands of the Gauls the mighty ancient Roman civilisation crumbled into dust! Therefore I say, try to rouse these lower classes from slumber by imparting learning and culture to them. When they will awaken — and awaken one day they must — they also will not forget your good services to them and will remain grateful to you.

After such conversation Swamiji, addressing the disciple, said: Let these subjects drop now — come, tell me what you have decided. Do something, whatever it be. Either go in for some business, or like us come to the path of real Sannyasa, "[(Sanskrit)] — for one's own liberation and for the good of the world." The latter path is of course the best way there is. What good will it do to be a worthless householder? You have understood that everything in life is transitory: "[(Sanskrit)] — life is as unstable as the water on the lotus leaf." Therefore if you have the enthusiasm for acquiring this knowledge of the Atman, do not wait any more but come forward immediately. "[(Sanskrit)] — the very day that you feel dispassion for the world, that very day renounce and take to Sannyasa" (Jabalopanishad, 4). Sacrifice your life for the good of others and go round to the doors of people carrying this message of fearlessness "[(Sanskrit)] — arise, awake, and stop not till the goal is reached."

VIII

Swamiji accompanied by Sister Nivedita, Swami Yogananda, and others has come to visit the Zoological Gardens at Alipur in the afternoon. Rai Rambrahma Sanyal Bahadur, Superintendent of the Gardens, cordially received them and took them round the Gardens. Swamiji, as he went on seeing the various species of animals, casually referred to the Darwinian theory of the gradual evolution of animals. The disciple remembers how, entering the room for snakes, he pointed to a huge python with circular rings on its body, with the remark: "From this the tortoise has evolved in course of time. That very snake, by remaining stationary at one spot for a long time, has gradually turned hard-backed." He further said in fun to the disciple, "You eat tortoises, don't you? Darwin holds that it is this snake that has evolved into the tortoise in the process of time — then you eat snakes too!" The disciple protested, "Sir, when a thing is metamorphosed into another thing through evolution, it has no more its former shape and habits; then how can you say that eating tortoise means eating snakes also?"

This answer created laughter among the party. After seeing some other things, Swamiji went to Rambrahma Babu's quarters in the Gardens, where he took tea, and others also did the same. Finding that the disciples hesitated to sit at the same table and partake of the sweets and tea which Sister Nivedita had touched, Swamiji repeatedly urged him to take them, which he was induced to do, and drinking water himself, he gave the rest of it to the disciple to drink. After this there was a short conversation on Darwin's evolution theory.

Rambrahma Babu: What is your opinion of the evolution theory of Darwin and the causes he has put forward for it?

Swamiji: Taking for granted that Darwin is right, I cannot yet admit that it is the final conclusion about the causes of evolution.

Rambrahma Babu: Did the ancient scholars of our country discuss this subject?

Swamiji: The subject has been nicely discussed in the Samkhya Philosophy. I am of opinion that the conclusion of the ancient Indian philosophers is the last word on the causes of evolution. Rambrahma Babu: I shall be glad to hear of it, if it can be explained in a few words.

Swamiji: You are certainly aware of the laws of struggle for existence, survival of the fittest, natural selection, and so forth, which have been held by the Western scholars to be the causes of elevating a lower species to a higher. But none of these has been advocated as the cause of that in the system of Patanjali. Patanjali holds that the transformation of one species into another is effected by the "in-filling of nature" [(Sanskrit)]. It is not that this is done by the constant struggle against obstacles. In my opinion, struggle and competition sometimes stand in the way of a being's attaining its perfection. If the evolution of an animal is effected by the destruction of a thousand others, then one must confess that this evolution is doing very little good to the world. Taking it for granted that it conduces to physical well-being, we cannot help admitting that it is a serious obstacle to spiritual development. According to the philosophers of our country, every being is a perfect Soul, and the diversity of evolution and manifestation of nature is simply due to the difference in the degree of manifestation of this Soul. The moment the obstacles to the evolution and manifestation of nature are completely removed, the Soul manifests Itself perfectly. Whatever may happen in the lower strata of nature's evolutions, in the higher strata at any rate, it is not true that it is only by constantly struggling against obstacles that one has to go beyond them. Rather it is observed that there the obstacles give way and a greater manifestation of the Soul takes place through education and culture, through concentration and meditation, and above all through sacrifice. Therefore, to designate the obstacles not as the effects but as the causes of the Soul-manifestation, and describe them as aiding this wonderful diversity of nature, is not consonant with reason. The attempt to remove evil from the world by killing a thousand evil-doers, only adds to the evil in the world. But if the people can be made to desist from evil-doing by means of spiritual instruction, there is no more evil in the world. Now, see how horrible the Western struggle theory becomes!

Rambrahma Babu was astonished to hear Swamiji's words and said at length, "India badly needs at the present moment men well versed in the Eastern and Western philosophies like you. Such men alone are able to point out the mistakes of the educated people who see only one side of the shield. I am extremely delighted to hear your original explanation of the evolution theory."

Shortly after, Swamiji with the party left for Baghbazar and reached Balaram Bose's house at about 8 p.m. After a short rest, he came to the drawing-room, where there was a small gathering, all eager to hear of the conversation at the Zoological Gardens in detail. When Swamiji came to the room, the disciple, as the spokesman of the meeting, raised that very topic.

Disciple: Sir, I have not been able to follow all your remarks about the evolution theory at the Zoo. Will you kindly recapitulate them in simple words?

Swamiji: Why, which points did you fail to grasp?

Disciple: You have often told us that it is the power to struggle with the external forces which constitutes the sign of life and the first step towards improvement. Today you seem to have spoken just the opposite thing.

Swamiji: Why should I speak differently? It was you who could not follow me. In the animal kingdom we really see such laws as struggle for existence, survival of the fittest, etc., evidently at work. Therefore Darwin's theory seems true to a certain extent. But in the human kingdom, where there is the manifestation of rationality, we find just the reverse of those laws. For instance, in those whom we consider really great men or ideal characters, we scarcely observe any external struggle. In the animal kingdom instinct prevails; but the more a man advances, the more he manifests rationality. For this reason, progress in the rational human kingdom cannot be achieved, like that in the animal kingdom, by the destruction of others! The highest evolution of man is effected through sacrifice alone. A man is great among his fellows in proportion as he can sacrifice for the sake of others, while in the lower strata of the animal kingdom, that animal is the strongest which can kill the greatest number of animals. Hence the struggle theory is not equally applicable to both kingdoms. Man's struggle is in the mental sphere. A man is greater in proportion as he can control his mind. When the mind's activities are perfectly at rest, the Atman manifests Itself. The struggle which we observe in the animal kingdom for the preservation of the gross body obtains in the human plane of existence for gaining mastery over the mind or for attaining the state of balance. Like a living tree and its reflection in the water of a tank, we find opposite kinds of struggle in the animal and human kingdoms.

Disciple: Why then do you advocate so much the improvement of our physique?

Swamiji: Well, do you consider yourselves as men? You have got only a bit of rationality — that's all. How will you struggle with the mind unless the physique be strong? Do you deserve to be called men any longer — the highest evolution in the world? What have you got besides eating, sleeping, and satisfying the creature-comforts? Thank your stars that you have not developed into quadrupeds yet! Shri Ramakrishna used to say, "He is the man who is conscious of his dignity". You are but standing witnesses to the lowest class of insect-like existence of which the scripture speaks, that they simply undergo the round of births and deaths without being allowed to go to any of the higher spheres! You are simply living a life of jealousy among yourselves and are objects of hatred in the eyes of the foreigner. You are animals, therefore I recommend you to struggle. Leave aside theories and all that. Just reflect calmly on your own everyday acts and dealings with others and find out whether you are not a species of beings intermediate between the animal and human planes of existence! First build up your own physique. Then only you can get control over the mind. "नायमात्मा बलहीनेन लभ्य: — this Self is not to be attained by the weak" (Katha Upanishad, I.ii.23).

Disciple: But, sir, the commentator (Shankara) has interpreted the word "weak" to mean "devoid of Brahmacharya or continence".

Swamiji: Let him. I say, "The physically weak are unfit for the realisation of the Self."

Disciple: But many dull-headed persons also have strong bodies.

Swamiji: If you can take the pains to give them good ideas once, they will be able to work them out sooner than physically unfit people. Don't you find that in a weak physique it is difficult to control the sex-appetite or anger? Lean people are quickly incensed and are quickly overcome by the sex instinct.

Disciple: But we find exceptions to the rule also.

Swamiji: Who denies it? Once a person gets control over the mind, it matters little whether the body remains strong or becomes emaciated. The gist of the thing is that unless one has a good physique one can never aspire to Self-realisation. Shri Ramakrishna used to say, "One fails to attain realisation if there be but a slight defect in the body".

Finding that Swamiji had grown excited, the disciple did not dare to push the topic further, but remained quiet accepting Swamiji's view. Shortly after, Swamiji, addressing those present, said, "By the bye, have you heard that this `priest' has today taken food which was touched by Nivedita? That he took the sweets touched by her did not matter so much, but — here he addressed the disciple — "how did you drink the water she had touched?"

Disciple: But it was you, sir, who ordered me to do so. Under the Guru's orders I can do anything. I was unwilling to drink the water though. But you drank it and I had to take it as Prasada.

Swamiji: Well, your caste is gone for ever. Now nobody will respect you as a Brahmin of the priest class.

Disciple: I don't care if they do not. I can take the rice from the house of a Pariah if you order me to.

These words set Swamiji and all those present in a roar of laughter.

The conversation lasted till it was past midnight, when the disciple came back to his lodging, only to find it bolted. So he had to pass the night out of doors.

The wheel of Time has rolled on in its unrelenting course, and Swamiji, Swami Yogananda, and Sister Nivedita are now no more on earth. Only the sacred memory of their lives remains — and the disciple considers himself blessed to be able to record, in ever so meagre a way, these reminiscences.

IX

The disciple has come to the Math (monastery) today. It has now been removed to Nilambar Babu's garden-house, and the site of the present Math has recently been purchased. Swamiji is out visiting the new Math-grounds at about four o'clock, taking the disciple with him. The site was then mostly jungle, but on the north side of it there was a one-storeyed brick-built house. Swamiji began to walk over the site and to discuss in the course of conversation the plan of work of the future Math and its rules and regulations.

Reaching by degrees the veranda on the east side of the one-storeyed house, Swamiji said, "Here would be the place for the Sadhus to live. It is my wish to convert this Math into a chief centre of spiritual practices and the culture of knowledge. The power that will have its rise from here will flood the whole world and turn the course of men's lives into different channels; from this place will spring forth ideals which will be the harmony of Knowledge, Devotion, Yoga, and Work; at a nod from the men of this Math a life-giving impetus will in time be given to the remotest corners of the globe;

while all true seekers after spirituality will in course of time assemble here. A thousand thoughts like these are arising in my mind. "Yonder plot of land on the south side of the Math will be the centre of learning, where grammar, philosophy, science, literature, rhetoric, the Shrutis, Bhakti scriptures, and English will be taught. This Temple of Learning will be fashioned after the Tols of old days. Boys who are Brahmacharins from their childhood will live there and study the scriptures. Their food and clothing and all will be supplied from the Math. After a course of five years' training these Brahmacharins may, if they like, go back to their homes and lead householders' lives; or they may embrace the monastic life with the sanction of the venerable Superiors of the Math. The authorities of the Math will have the power to turn out at once any of these Brahmacharins who will be found refractory or of a bad character. Teaching will be imparted here irrespective of caste or creed, and those who will have objection to this will not be admitted. But those who would like to observe their particular caste-rites, should make separate arrangements for their food, etc. They will only attend the classes along with the rest. The Math authorities shall keep a vigilant watch over the character of these also. None but those that are trained here shall be eligible for Sannyasa. Won't it be nice when by degrees this Math will begin to work like this?"

Disciple: Then you want to reintroduce into the country the ancient institution of living a Brahmacharin's life in the house of the Guru?

Swamiji: Exactly. The modern system of education gives no facility for the development of the knowledge of Brahman. We must found Brahmacharya Homes as in times of old. But now we must lay their foundations on a broad basis, that is to say, we must introduce a good deal of change into it to suit the requirements of the times. Of this I shall speak to you later on. "That piece of land to the south of the Math," Swamiji resumed, "we must also purchase in time. There we shall start an Annasatra — a Feeding Home. There arrangements will be made for serving really indigent people in the spirit of God. The Feeding Home will be named after Shri Ramakrishna. Its scope will at first be determined by the amount of funds. For the matter of that, we may start it with two or three inmates. We must train energetic Brahmacharins to conduct this Home. They will have to collect the funds for its maintenance — ay, even by begging. The Math will not be allowed to give any pecuniary help in this matter. The Brahmacharins themselves shall have to raise funds for it. Only after completing their five years' training in this Home of Service, will they be allowed to join the Temple of Learning branch. After a training of ten years — five in the Feeding Home and five in the Temple of Learning — they will be allowed to enter the life of Sannyasa, having initiation from the Math authorities — provided of course they have a mind to become Sannyasins and the Math authorities consider them fit for Sannyasa and are willing to admit them into it. But the Head of the Math will be free to confer Sannyasa on any exceptionally meritorious Brahmacharin, at any time, in defiance of this rule. The ordinary Brahmacharins, however, will have to qualify themselves for Sannyasa by degrees, as I have just said. I have all these ideas in my brain."

Disciple: Sir, what will be the object of starting three such sections in the Math?

Swamiji: Didn't you understand me? First of all, comes the gift of food; next is the gift of learning, and the highest of all is the gift of knowledge. We must harmonise these three ideals in the Math. By continuously practising the gift of food, the Brahmacharins will have the idea of practical work for the sake of others and that of serving all beings in the spirit of the Lord firmly impressed on their minds. This will gradually purify their minds and lead to the manifestation of Sattvika (pure and unselfish) ideas. And having this the Brahmacharins will in time acquire the fitness for attaining the knowledge of Brahman and become eligible for Sannyasa.

Disciple: Sir, if, as you say, the gift of (spiritual) knowledge is the highest, why then start sections for the gift of food and the gift of learning?

Swamiji: Can't you understand this point even now? Listen. If in these days of food scarcity you can, for the disinterested service of others, get together a few morsels of food by begging or any other means, and give them to the poor and suffering, that will not only be doing good to yourself and the world, but you will at the same time get everybody's sympathy for this noble work. The worldly-minded people, tied down to lust and wealth, will have faith in you for this labour of love and come forward to help you. You will attract a thousand times as many men by this unasked-for gift of food, as you will by the gift of learning or of (spiritual) knowledge. In no other work will you get so much public sympathy as you will in this. In a truly noble work, not to speak of men, even God Himself befriends the doer. When people have thus been attracted, you will be able to stimulate the desire for learning and spirituality in them. Therefore the gift of food comes first.

Disciple; Sir, to start Feeding Homes we want a site first, then buildings, and then the funds to work them. Where will so much money come from?

Swamiji: The southern portion of the Math premises I am leaving at your disposal immediately, and I am getting a thatched house erected under that Bael tree. You just find out one or two blind or infirm people and apply yourself to their service. Go and beg food for them yourself; cook with your own hands and feed them. If you continue this for some days, you will find that lots of people will be coming forward to assist you with plenty of money. "[(Sanskrit)] — never, my son, does a doer of good come to grief." (Gita, VI.40)

Disciple: Yes, it is true. But may not that kind of continuous work become a source of bondage in the long run?

Swamiji: If you have no eye to the fruits of work, and if you have a passionate longing to go beyond all selfish desires, then these good works will help to break your bonds, I tell you. How thoughtless of you to say that such work will lead to bondage! Such disinterested work is the only means of rooting out the bondage due to selfish work. "[(Sanskrit)] There is no other way out" (Shvetasvatara Upanishad, III.8).

Disciple: Your words encourage me to hear in detail about your ideas of the Feeding Home and Home of Service.

Swamiji: We must build small well-ventilated rooms for the poor. Only two or three of them will live in each room. They must be given good bedding, clean clothes, and so on. There will be a doctor for them, who will inspect them once or twice a week according to his convenience. The Sevashrama (Home of Service) will be as a ward attached to the Annasatra, where the sick will be nursed. Then, gradually, as funds will accumulate, we shall build a big kitchen. The Annasatra must be astir with constant shouts of food demanded and supplied. The rice-gruel must run into the Ganga and whiten its water! When I see such a Feeding Home started, it will bring solace to my heart.

Disciple: When you have this kind of desire, most likely it will materialise into action in course of time.

Hearing the disciple's words, Swamiji remained motionless for a while, gazing on the Ganga. Then with a beaming countenance he addressed the disciple, saying: "Who knows which of you will have the lion roused up in him, and when? If in a single one amongst you Mother rouses the fire, there will be hundreds of Feeding Homes like that. Knowledge and Power and Devotion — everything exists in the fullest measure in all beings. We only notice the varying degrees of their manifestation and call one great and another little. In the minds of all creatures a screen intervenes as it were and hides the perfect manifestation from view. The moment that is removed, everything is settled; whatever you want, whatever you will desire, will come to pass."

Swamiji continued: "If the Lord wills, we shall make this Math a great centre of harmony. Our Lord is the visible embodiment of the harmony of all ideals. He will be established on earth if we keep alive that spirit of harmony here. We must see to it that people of all creeds and sects, from the Brahmana down to the Chandala, may come here and find their respective ideals manifested. The other day when I installed Shri Ramakrishna on the Math grounds, I felt as if his ideas shot forth from this place and flooded the whole universe, sentient and insentient. I, for one, am doing my best, and shall continue to do so — all of you too explain to people the liberal ideas of Shri Ramakrishna; what is the use of merely reading the Vedanta? We must prove the truth of pure Advaitism in practical life. Shankara left this Advaita philosophy in the hills and forests, while I have come to bring it out of those places and scatter it broadcast before the workaday world and society. The lion-roar of Advaita must resound in every hearth and home, in meadows and groves, over hills and plains. Come all of you to my assistance and set yourselves to work."

Disciple: Sir, it appeals to me rather to realise that state through meditation than to manifest it in action.

Swamiji: That is but a state of stupefaction, as under liquor. What will be the use of merely remaining like that? Through the urge of Advaitic realisation, you should sometimes dance wildly and sometimes remain lost to outward sense. Does one feel happy to taste of a good thing by oneself? One should share it with others. Granted that you attain personal liberation by means of the realisation of the Advaita, but what matters it to the world? You must liberate the whole universe before you leave this body. Then only you will be established in the eternal Truth. Has that bliss any match, my boy? You will be established in that bliss of the Infinite which is limitless like the skies. You will be struck dumb to find your presence everywhere in the world of soul and matter. You will feel the whole sentient and insentient world as your own self. Then you can't help treating all with the same kindness as you show towards yourself. This is indeed practical Vedanta. Do you understand me? Brahman is one, but is at the same time appearing to us as many, on the relative plane. Name and form are at the root of this relativity. For instance, what do you find when you abstract name and form from a jar? Only earth, which is its essence. Similarly, through delusion you are thinking of and seeing a jar, a cloth, a monastery, and so on. The phenomenal world depends on this nescience which obstructs knowledge and which has no real existence. One sees variety such as wife, children, body, mind — only in the world created by nescience by means of name and form. As soon as this nescience is removed, the realisation of Brahman which eternally exists is the result.

Disciple: Where has the nescience come from?

Swamiji: Where it has come from I shall tell you later on. When you began to run, mistaking the rope for the snake, did the rope actually turn into a snake? Or was it not your ignorance which put you to flight in that way?

Disciple: I did it from sheer ignorance.

Swamiji: Well, then, consider whether, when you will again come to know the rope as rope, you will not laugh at your previous ignorance. Will not name and form appear to be a delusion then?

Disciple: They will.

Swamiji: If that be so, the name and form turn out to be unreal. Thus Brahman, the Eternal Existence, proves to be the only reality. Only through this twilight of nescience you think this is your wife, that is your child, this is your own, that is not your own, and so on, and fail to realise the existence of the Atman, the illuminator of everything. When through the Guru's instructions and your own conviction you will see, not this world of name and form, but the essence which lies as its substratum then only you will realise your identity with the whole universe from the Creator down to a clump of grass, then only you will get the state in which "[(Sanskrit)] — the knots of the heart are cut asunder and all doubts are dispelled".

Disciple: Sir, one wishes to know of the origin and cessation of this nescience.

Swamiji: You have understood, I presume, that a thing that ceases to exist afterwards is a phenomenon merely? He who has truly realised Brahman will say — where is nescience, in faith? He sees the rope as rope only, and never as the snake. And he laughs at the alarm of those who see it as the snake. For this reason, nescience has no absolute reality. You can call nescience neither real nor unreal; "[(Sanskrit)] — neither real, nor unreal, nor a mixture of both". About a thing that is thus proved to be false, neither question nor answer is of any significance. Moreover, any question on such a thing is unreasonable. I shall explain how. Are not this question and answer made from the standpoint of name and form, of time and space? And can you explain Brahman which transcends time and space, by means of questions and answers? Hence the Shastras and Mantras and such other things are only relatively, and not absolutely, true. Nescience has verily no essence to call its own; how then can you understand it? When Brahman will manifest Itself, there will be no more room for such questions. Have you not heard that story of Shri Ramakrishna about the shoemaker coolie?[1] The moment one recognises nescience, it vanishes.

Disciple: But, sir, whence has this nescience come?

Swamiji: How can that come which has no existence at all? It must exist first, to admit the possibility of coming.

Disciple: How then did this world of souls and matter originate?

Swamiji: There is only one Existence — brahman. You are but seeing That under different forms and names, through the veil of name and form which are unreal.

Disciple: But why this unreal name and form? Whence have they come?

Swamiji: The Shastras have described this ingrained notion or ignorance as almost endless in a series. But it has a termination, while Brahman ever remains as It is, without suffering the least change, like the rope which causes the delusion of the snake. Therefore the conclusion of the Vedanta is that the whole universe has been superimposed on Brahman — appearing like a juggler's trick. It has not caused the least aberration of Brahman from Its real nature. Do you understand me?

Disciple: One thing I cannot yet understand.

Swamiji: What is that?

Disciple: You have just said that creation, maintenance, and dissolution, etc. are superimposed on Brahman, and have no absolute existence. But how can that be? One can never have the delusion of something that one has not already experienced. Just as one who has never seen a snake cannot mistake a rope for a snake, so how can one who has not experienced this creation, come to mistake Brahman for the creation? Therefore creation must have been, or is, to have given rise to the delusion of creation. But this brings in a dualistic position.

Swamiji: The man of realisation will in the first place refute your objection by stating that to his vision creation and things of that sort do not at all appear. He sees Brahman and Brahman alone. He sees the rope and not the snake. If you argue that you, at any rate, are seeing this creation, or snake — then he will try to bring home to you the real nature of the rope, with a view to curing your defective vision. When through his instructions and your reasoning you will be able to realise the truth of the rope, or Brahman, then this delusive idea of the snake, or creation, will vanish. At that time, what else can you call this delusive idea of creation, maintenance, and dissolution, but a superimposition on the Brahman? If this appearance of creation etc. has continued as a beginningless series, let it do so; no advantage will be gained by settling this question. Until Brahman is realised as vividly as a fruit on the palm of one's hand this question cannot be adequately settled, and then neither such a question crops up, nor is there need for a solution. The tasting of the reality of Brahman is then like a dumb man tasting something nice, but without the power to express his feelings.

Disciple: What then will be the use of reasoning about it so much?

Swamiji: Reasoning is necessary to understand the point intellectually. But the Reality transcends

---

1. Once a Brahmin, desirous of going to a disciple's house, was in need of a coolie to carry his load. Not finding anyone belonging to a good caste, he at last asked a shoemaker to perform the function. The man at first refused on the ground that he was a man belonging to an untouchable caste. But the Brahmin insisted on engaging him, telling him that he would escape detection by keeping perfectly silent. The man was at last persuaded to go, and when the party reached their destination, someone asked the shoemaker-servant to remove a pair of shoes. The servant who thought it best to keep silent, as instructed, paid no attention to the order, which was repeated, whereupon the man getting annoyed shouted out, "Why dost thou not hear me, sirrah? Art thou a shoemaker?" "O Master," cried the bewildered shoemaker, "I am discovered. I cannot stay any longer." Saying this he immediately took to his heels.

reasoning: "[(Sanskrit)] — this conviction cannot be reached through reasoning."

In the course of such conversation Swamiji reached the Math, accompanied by the disciple. Swamiji then explained to the Sannyasins and Brahmacharins of the Math the gist of the above discussion on Brahman. While going upstairs, he remarked to the disciple, "[(Sanskrit)] — this Atman cannot be attained by the weak."

X

The Bengali fortnightly magazine, Udbodhan, was just started by Swami Trigunatita under the direction of Swamiji for spreading the religious views of Shri Ramakrishna among the general public. After the first number came out the disciple came to the Math at Nilambar Babu's garden one day. Swamiji started the following conversation with him about the Udbodhan.

Swamiji: (Humorously caricaturing the name of the magazine) Have you seen the Udbandhana[2]?

Disciple: Yes, sir; it is a good number.

Swamiji: We must mould the ideas, language, and everything of this magazine in a new fashion.

Disciple: How?

Swamiji: Not only must we give out Shri Ramakrishna's ideas to all, but we must also introduce a new vigour into the Bengali language. For instance, the frequent use of verbs diminishes the force of a language. We must restrict the use of verbs by the use of adjectives. Begin to write articles in that way, and show them to me before you give them to print in the Udbodhan.

Disciple: Sir, it is impossible for any other man to labour for this magazine in the way Swami Trigunatita does.

Swamiji: Do you think these Sannyasin children of Shri Ramakrishna are born simply to sit under trees lighting Dhuni-fires? Whenever any of them will take up some work, people will be astonished to see their energy. Learn from them how to work. Here, for instance, Trigunatita has given up his spiritual practices, his meditation and everything, to carry out my orders, and has set himself to work. Is this a matter of small sacrifice? What an amount of love for me is at the back of this spirit of work, do you see? He will not stop short of success! Have you householders such determination?

Disciple: But, sir, it looks rather odd in our eyes that Sannyasins in ochre robe should go about from door to door as the Swami is doing.

Swamiji: Why? The circulation of the magazine is only for the good of the householders. By the spread of new ideas within the country the public at large will be benefited. Do you think this unselfish work is any way inferior to devotional practices? Our object is to do good to humanity. We have no idea of making money from the income of this paper. We have renounced everything and have no wives or children to provide for after our death. If the paper be a success, the whole of its income will be spent in the service of humanity. Its surplus money will be profitably spent in the opening of monasteries and homes of service in different places and all sorts of work of public utility. We are not certainly working like householders with the plan of filling our own pockets. Know for certain that all our movements are for the good of others.

Disciple: Even then, all will not be able to appreciate this spirit.

Swamiji: What if they cannot? It neither adds nor takes away anything from us. We do not take up any work with an eye to criticism.

Disciple: So this magazine will be a fortnightly. We should like it to be a weekly.

Swamiji: Yes, but where are the funds? If through the grace of Shri Ramakrishna funds are raised, it can be made into a daily even, in future. A hundred thousand copies may be struck off daily and distributed free in every street and lane of Calcutta.

Disciple: This idea of yours is a capital one.

Swamiji: I have a mind to make the paper self-supporting first, and then set you up as its editor. You have not yet got the capacity to make any enterprise stand on its legs. That is reserved only for these all-renouncing Sannyasins to do. They will

---
2. The word means "suicide by hanging".

work themselves to death, but never yield. Whereas a little resistance or just a trifle of criticism is bewildering to you.

Disciple: Sir, the other day I saw that Swami Trigunatita worshipped the photograph of Sri Ramakrishna in the Press before opening the work and asked for your blessings for the success of the work.

Swamiji: Well, Shri Ramakrishna is our centre. Each one of us is a ray of that light-centre. So Trigunatita worshipped Shri Ramakrishna before beginning the work, did he? It was excellently done. But he told me nothing of it.

Disciple: Sir, he fears you and yesterday he told me to come to you and ask your opinion of the first issue of the magazine, after which, he said, he would see you.

Swamiji: Tell him when you go that I am exceedingly delighted with his work. Give him my loving blessings. And all of you help him as far as you can. You will be doing Shri Ramakrishna's work by that.

Immediately after saying these words Swamiji called Swami Brahmananda to him and directed him to give Swami Trigunatita more money for the Udbodhan if it was needed.

The same evening, after supper, Swamiji again referred to the topic of Udbodhan in the following words: "In the Udbodhan we must give the public only positive ideas. Negative thoughts weaken men. Do you not find that where parents are constantly taxing their sons to read and write, telling them they will never learn anything, and calling them fools and so forth, the latter do actually turn out to be so in many cases? If you speak kind words to boys and encourage them, they are bound to improve in time. What holds good of children, also holds good of children in the region of higher thoughts. If you can give them positive ideas, people will grow up to be men and learn to stand on their own legs. In language and literature, in poetry and the arts, in everything we must point out not the mistakes that people are making in their thoughts and actions, but the way in which they will gradually be able to do these things better. Pointing out mistakes wounds a man's feelings. We have seen how Shri Ramakrishna would encourage even those whom we considered as worthless and change the very course of their lives thereby! His very method of teaching was a unique phenomenon."

After a short pause, Swamiji continued, "Never take the preaching of religion to mean the turning up of one's nose at everything and at everybody. In matters physical, mental, and spiritual — in everything we must give men positive ideas and never hate anybody. It is your hatred of one another that has brought about your degradation. Now we shall have to raise men by scattering broadcast only positive thoughts. First we must raise the whole Hindu race in this way and then the whole world. That is why Shri Ramakrishna incarnated. He never destroyed a single man's special inclinations. He gave words of hope and encouragement even to the most degraded of persons and lifted them up. We too must follow in his footsteps and lift all up, and rouse them. Do you understand? "Your history, literature, mythology, and all other Shastras are simply frightening people. They are only telling them, 'You will go to hell, you are doomed!' Therefore has this lethargy crept into the very vitals of India. Hence we must explain to men in simple words the highest ideas of the Vedas and the Vedanta. Through the imparting of moral principles, good behaviour, and education we must make the Chandala come up to the level of the Brahmana. Come, write out all these things in the Udbodhan and awaken everyone, young and old, man and woman. Then only shall I know that your study of the Vedas and Vedanta has been a success. What do you say? Will you be able to do this?"

Disciple: Through your blessings and command I think I shall succeed in everything.

Swamiji: Another thing. You must learn to make the physique very strong and teach the same to others. Don't you find me exercising every day with dumb-bells even now? Walk in the morning and evenings and do physical labour. Body and mind must run parallel. It won't do to depend on others in everything. When the necessity of strengthening the physique is brought home to people, they will exert themselves of their own accord. It is to make them feel this need that education is necessary at the present moment.

XI

Disciple: Why is it, Swamiji, that our society and country have come to such degradation?

Swamiji: It is you who are responsible for it.

Disciple: How, sir? You surprise me.

Swamiji: You have been despising the lower classes of the country for a very long time and, as a result, you have now become the objects of contempt in the eyes of the world.

Disciple: When did you find us despising them?

Swamiji: Why, you priest-class never let the non-brahmin class read the Vedas and Vedanta and all such weighty Shastras — never touch them even. You have only kept them down. It is you who have always done like that through selfishness. It was the Brahmins who made a monopoly of the religious books and kept the question of sanction and prohibition in their own hands. And repeatedly calling the other races of India low and vile, they put this belief into their heads that they were really such. If you tell a man, "You are low, you are vile", in season and out of season, then he is bound to believe in course of time that he is really such. This is called hypnotism. The non-brahmin classes are now slowly rousing themselves. Their faith in Brahminical scriptures and Mantras is getting shaken. Through the spread of Western education all the tricks of the Brahmins are giving way, like the banks of the Padma in the rainy season. Do you not see that?

Disciple: Yes, sir, the stricture of orthodoxy is gradually lessening nowadays.

Swamiji: It is as it should be. The Brahmins, in fact, gradually took a course of gross immorality and oppression. Through selfishness they introduced a large number of strange, non-vedic, immoral, and unreasonable doctrines — simply to keep intact their own prestige. And the fruits of that they are reaping forthwith.

Disciple: What may these fruits be, sir?

Swamiji: Don't you perceive them? It is simply due to your having despised the masses of India that you have now been living a life of slavery for the last thousand years; it is therefore that you are the objects of hatred in the eyes of foreigners and are looked upon with indifference by your countrymen.

Disciple: But, sir, even now it is the Brahmins who direct all ceremonials, and people are observing them according to the opinions of the Brahmins. Why then do you speak like that?

Swamiji: I don't find it. Where do the tenfold Samskaras or purifying ceremonies enjoined by the Shastras obtain still? Well, I have travelled the whole of India, and everywhere I have found society to be guided by local usages which are condemned by the Shrutis and Smritis. Popular customs, local usages, and observances prevalent among women only — have not these taken the place of the Smritis everywhere? Who obeys, and whom? If you can but spend enough money, the priest-class is ready to write out whatever sanctions or prohibitions you want! How many of them read the Vedic Kalpa (Ritual), Grihya and Shrauta Sutras? Then, look, here in Bengal the code of Raghunandana is obeyed; a little farther on you will find the code of Mitakshara in vogue; while in another part the code of Manu holds sway! You seem to think that the same laws hold good everywhere! What I want therefore is to introduce the study of the Vedas by stimulating a greater regard for them in the minds of the people, and to pass everywhere the injunctions of the Vedas.

Disciple: Sir, is it possible nowadays to set them going?

Swamiji: It is true that all the ancient Vedic laws will not have a go, but if we introduce additions and alterations in them to suit the needs of the times, codify them, and hold them up as a new model to society, why will they not pass current?

Disciple: Sir, I was under the impression that at least the injunctions of Manu were being obeyed all over India even now.

Swamiji: Nothing of the kind. Just look to your own province and see how the Vamachara (immoral practices) of the Tantras has entered into your very marrow. Even modern Vaishnavism, which is the skeleton of the defunct Buddhism, is saturated with Vamachara! We must stem the tide of this Vamachara, which is contrary to the spirit of the Vedas.

Disciple: Sir, is it possible now to cleanse this Aegean stable?

Swamiji: What nonsense do you say, you coward! You have well-nigh thrown the country into ruin by crying, 'It is impossible, it is impossible!' What cannot human effort achieve?

Disciple: But, sir, such a state of things seems impossible unless sages like Manu and Yajnavalkya are again born in the country.

Swamiji: Goodness gracious! Was it not purity and unselfish labour that made them Manu and Yajnavalkya, or was it something else? Well, we ourselves can be far greater than even Manu and Yajnavalkya if we try to; why will not our views prevail then?

Disciple: Sir, it is you who said just now that we must revive the ancient usages and observances within the country. How then can we think lightly of sages like Manu and the rest?

Swamiji: What an absurd deduction! You altogether miss my point. I have only said that the ancient Vedic customs must be remodelled according to the need of the society and the times, and passed under a new form in the land. Have I not?

Disciple: Yes, sir.

Swamiji: What, then, were you talking? You have read the Shastras, and my hope and faith rest in men like you. Understand my words in their true spirit, and apply yourselves to work in their light.

Disciple: But, sir, who will listen to us? Why should our countrymen accept them?

Swamiji: If you can truly convince them and practise what you preach, they must. If, on the contrary, like a coward you simply utter Shlokas as a parrot, be a mere talker and quote authority only, without showing them in action — then who will care to listen to you?

Disciple: Please give me some advice in brief about social reform.

Swamiji: Why, I have given you advice enough; now put at least something in practice. Let the world see that your reading of the scriptures and listening to me has been a success. The codes of Manu and lots of other books that you have read — what is their basis and underlying purpose? Keeping that basis intact, compile in the manner of the ancient Rishis the essential truths of them and supplement them with thoughts that are suited to the times; only take care that all races and all sects throughout India be really benefited by following these rules. Just write out a Smriti like that; I shall revise it.

Disciple: Sir, it is not an easy task; and even if such a Smriti be written, will it be accepted?

Swamiji: Why not? Just write it out. "[(Sanskrit)] — time is infinite, and the world is vast." If you write it in the proper way, there must come a day when it will be accepted. Have faith in yourself. You people were once the Vedic Rishis. Only, you have come in different forms, that's all. I see it clear as daylight that you all have infinite power in you. Rouse that up; arise, arise — apply yourselves heart and soul, gird up your loins. What will you do with wealth and fame that are so transitory? Do you know what I think? I don't care for Mukti and all that. My mission is to arouse within you all such ideas; I am ready to undergo a hundred thousand rebirths to train up a single man.

Disciple: But, sir, what will be the use of undertaking such works? Is not death stalking behind?

Swamiji: Fie upon you! If you die, you will die but once. Why will you die every minute of your life by constantly harping on death like a coward?

Disciple: All right, sir, I may not think of death, but what good will come of any kind of work in this evanescent world?

Swamiji: My boy, when death is inevitable, is it not better to die like heroes than as stocks and stones? And what is the use of living a day or two more in this transitory world? It is better to wear out than to rust out — specially for the sake of doing the least good to others.

Disciple: It is true, sir. I beg pardon for troubling

you so much.

Swamiji: I don't feel tired even if I talk for two whole nights to an earnest inquirer; I can give up food and sleep and talk and talk. Well, if I have a mind, I can sit up in Samadhi in a Himalayan cave. And you see that nowadays through the Mother's grace I have not to think about food, it comes anyhow. Why then don't I do so? And why am I here? Only the sight of the country's misery and the thought of its future do not let me remain quiet any more!— even Samadhi and all that appear as futile — even the sphere of Brahma with its enjoyments becomes insipid! My vow of life is to think of your welfare. The day that vow will be fulfilled, I shall leave this body and make a straight run up!

Hearing Swamiji's words the disciple sat speechless for a while, gazing at him, wondering in his heart. Then, with a view to taking his leave, he saluted Swamiji reverently and asked his permission to go.

Swamiji: Why do you want to go? Why not live in the Math? Your mind will again be polluted if you go back to the worldly-minded. See here, how fresh is the air, there is the Ganga, and the Sadhus (holy men) are practising meditation, and holding lofty talks! While the moment you will go to Calcutta, you will be thinking of nasty stuff.

The disciple joyfully replied, "All right, sir, I shall stay today at the Math."

Swamiji: Why "today"? Can't you live here for good? What is the use of going back to the world?

The disciple bent down his head, hearing Swamiji's words. Various thoughts crowded into his brain and kept him speechless.

XII

Today Swamiji is walking round the new Math grounds in the afternoon in company with the disciple. Standing at a little distance off the Bael tree Swamiji took to singing slowly a Bengali song[1]: "O Himalaya,

---
1. This is one of the songs sung in the homes of Bengal on the eve of Durga Puja.

Ganesh is auspicious to me" etc., ending with the line —"And many Dandis (Sannyasins) and Yogis with matted hair will also come." While singing the song Swamiji repeated this line to the disciple and said, "Do you understand? In course of time many Sadhus and Sannyasins will come here." Saying this he sat under the tree and remarked, "The ground under the Bilva tree is very holy. Meditating here quickly brings about an awakening of the religious instinct. Shri Ramakrishna used to say so."

Disciple: Sir, those who are devoted to the discrimination between the Self and not-self — have they any need to consider the auspiciousness of place, time, and so forth?

Swamiji: Those who are established in the knowledge of the Atman have no need for such discrimination, but that state is not attained off-hand. It comes as the result of long practice. Therefore in the beginning one has to take the help of external aids and learn to stand on one's own legs. Later on, when one is established in the knowledge of the Atman, there is no more need for any external aid.

The various methods of spiritual practice that have been laid down in the scriptures are all for the attainment of the knowledge of the Atman. Of course these practices vary according to the qualifications of different aspirants. But they also are a kind of work, and so long as there is work, the Atman is not discovered. The obstacles to the manifestation of the Atman are overcome by practices as laid down in the scriptures; but work has no power of directly manifesting the Atman, it is only effective in removing some veils that cover knowledge. Then the Atman manifests by Its own effulgence. Do you see? Therefore does your commentator (Shankara) say, "In our knowledge of Brahman, there cannot be the least touch of work."

Disciple: But, sir, since the obstacles to Self-manifestation are not overcome without the performance of work in some form or other, therefore indirectly work stands as a means to knowledge.

Swamiji: From the standpoint of the causal chain, it so appears prima facie . Taking up this view it is stated in the Purva-mimamsa that work for a definite end infallibly produces a definite result. But the vision of the Atman which is Absolute is not to be compassed by means of work. For the rule with regard to a seeker of the Atman is that he should undergo spiritual practice, but have no eye to its results. It follows thence that these practices are simply the cause of the purification of the aspirant's mind. For if the Atman could be directly realised as a result of these practices, then scriptures would not have enjoined on the aspirant to give up the results of work. So it is with a view to combating the Purva-mimamsa doctrine of work with motive producing results, that the philosophy of work without motive has been set forth in the Gita. Do you see?

Disciple: But, sir, if one has to renounce the fruits of work, why should one be induced to undertake work which is always troublesome?

Swamiji: In this human life, one cannot help doing some kind of work always. When man has perforce to do some work, Karma-yoga enjoins on him to do it in such a way as will bring freedom through the realisation of the Atman. As to your objection that none will be induced to work — the answer is, that whatever work you do has some motive behind it; but when by the long performance of work, one notices that one work merely leads to another, through a round of births and rebirths, then the awakened discrimination of man naturally begins to question itself, "Where is the end to this interminable chain of work?" It is then that he appreciates the full import of the words of the Lord in the Gita: "Inscrutable is the course of work." Therefore when the aspirant finds that work with motive brings no happiness, then he renounces action. But man is so constituted that to him the performance of work is a necessity, so what work should he take up? He takes up some unselfish work, but gives up all desire for its fruits. For he has known then that in those fruits of work lie countless seeds of future births and deaths. Therefore the knower of Brahman renounces all actions. Although to outward appearances he engages himself in some work, he has no attachment to it. Such men have been described in the scriptures as Karma-yogins.

Disciple: Is then the work without motive of the unselfish knower of Brahman like the activities of a lunatic?

Swamiji: Why so? Giving up the fruits of work means not to perform work for the good of one's own body or mind. The knower of Brahman never seeks his own happiness. But what is there to prevent him from doing work for the welfare of others? Whatever work he does without attachment for its fruits brings only good to the world — it is all "for the good of the many, for the happiness of the many". Shri Ramakrishna used to say, "They never take a false step". Haven't you read in the Uttara-rama-charita "[(Sanskrit)]" — the words of the ancient Rishis have always some meaning, they are never false?" When the mind is merged in the Atman by the suppression of all modifications, it produces "a dispassion for the enjoyment of fruits of work here or hereafter"; there remains no desire in the mind for any enjoyment here, or, after death, in any heavenly sphere. There is no action and interaction of desires in the mind. But when the mind descends from the superconscious state into the world of "I and mine", then by the momentum of previous work or habit, or Samskaras (impressions), the functions of the body go on as before. The mind then is generally in the superconscious state; eating and other functions of the body are done from mere necessity, and the body-consciousness is very much attenuated. Whatever work is done after reaching this transcendental state is done rightly; it conduces to the real well-being of men and the world; for then the mind of the doer is not contaminated by selfishness or calculation of personal gain or loss. The Lord has created this wonderful universe, remaining always in the realm of superconsciousness; therefore there is nothing imperfect in this world. So I was saying that the actions which the knower of the Atman does without attachment for fruits are never imperfect, but they conduce to the real well-being of men and the world.

Disciple: Sir, you said just now that knowledge and work are contradictory, that in the supreme knowledge there is no room at all for work, or in other words, that by means of work the realisation of Brahman cannot be attained. Why then do you now and then speak words calculated to awaken great Rajas (activity)? You were telling me the other day, "Work, work, work — there is no other way."

Swamiji: Going round the whole world, I find that people of this country are immersed in great Tamas (inactivity), compared with people of other countries. On the outside, there is a simulation of the Sattvika (calm and balanced) state, but inside, downright inertness like that of stocks and stones — what work will be done in the world by such people? How long can such an inactive, lazy, and sensual people live in the world? First travel in Western countries, then contradict my words. How much of enterprise and devotion to work, how much enthusiasm and manifestation of Rajas are there in the lives of the Western people! While, in your own country, it is as if the blood has become congealed in the heart, so that it cannot circulate in the veins — as if paralysis has overtaken the body and it has become languid. So my idea is first to make the people active by developing their Rajas, and thus make them fit for the struggle for existence. With no strength in the body, no enthusiasm at heart, and no originality in the brain, what will they do — these lumps of dead matter! By stimulating them I want to bring life into them — to this I have dedicated my life. I will rouse them through the infallible power of Vedic Mantras. I am born to proclaim to them that fearless message —"Arise! Awake!" Be you my helpers in this work! Go from village to village, from one portion of the country to another, and preach this message of fearlessness to all, from the Brahmin to the Chandala. Tell each and all that infinite power resides within them, that they are sharers of immortal Bliss. Thus rouse up the Rajas within them — make them fit for the struggle for existence, and then speak to them about salvation. First make the people of the country stand on their legs by rousing their inner power, first let them learn to have good food and clothes and plenty of enjoyment — then tell them how to be free from this bondage of enjoyment.

Laziness, meanness, and hypocrisy have covered the whole length and breadth of the country. Can an intelligent man look on all this and remain quiet? Does it not bring tears to the eyes? Madras, Bombay, Punjab, Bengal — whichever way I look, I see no signs of life. You are thinking yourselves highly educated. What nonsense have you learnt? Getting by heart the thoughts of others in a foreign language, and stuffing your brain with them and taking some university degrees, you consider yourselves educated! Fie upon you! Is this education? What is the goal of your education? Either a clerkship, or being a roguish lawyer, or at the most a Deputy Magistracy, which is another form of clerkship — isn't that all? Open your eyes and see what a piteous cry for food is rising in the land of Bharata, proverbial for its wealth! Will your education fulfil this want? Never.

With the help of Western science set yourselves to dig the earth and produce food-stuffs — not by means of mean servitude of others — but by discovering new avenues to production, by your own exertions aided by Western science. Therefore I teach the people of this country to be full of activities, so as to be able to produce food and clothing for themselves. For want of food and clothing and plunged in anxiety for it, the country has come to ruin — what are you doing to remedy this? Throw aside your scriptures in the Ganga and teach the people first the means of procuring their food and clothing, and then you will find time to read to them the scriptures. If their material wants are not removed by the rousing of intense activity, none will listen to words of spirituality. Therefore I say, first rouse the inherent power of the Atman within you, then, rousing the faith of the general people in that power as much as you can, teach them first of all to make provision for food, and then teach them religion. There is no time to sit idle — who knows when death will overtake one?

While saying these words, a mingled expression of remorse, sorrow, compassion, and power shone on his face. Looking at his majestic appearance, the disciple was awed into silence. A little while afterwards Swamiji said again, "That activity and self-reliance must come in the people of the country in time — I see it clearly. There is no escape. The intelligent man can distinctly see the vision of the next three Yugas (ages) ahead. Ever since the advent of Shri Ramakrishna the eastern horizon has been aglow with the dawning rays of the sun which in course of time will illumine the country with the splendour of the midday sun."

XIII

The present Math buildings are almost complete now.

Swamiji is not in good health; therefore doctors have advised him to go out on a boat in the mornings and evenings on the Ganga.

Today is Sunday. The disciple is sitting in Swamiji's room and conversing with him. About this time Swamiji framed certain rules for the guidance of the Sannyasins and Brahmacharins of the Math, the object of which was to keep them from indiscriminate mixing with worldly people. The conversation turned on this topic.

Swamiji: Nowadays I feel a peculiar smell of lax self-control in the dress and clothes of worldly people; therefore I have made it a rule in the Math that householders should not sit or lie on the beds of Sadhus. Formerly I used to read in the Shastras that such a smell is felt, and therefore Sannyasins cannot bear the smell of householders. Now I see it is true. By strictly observing the rules that have been framed, the Brahmacharins will in time grow into genuine Sannyasins. When they are established in the ideal of Sannyasa, they will be able to mix on an equal footing with worldly men without any harm. But now if they are not kept within the barriers of strict rules, they will all go wrong. In order to attain to ideal Brahmacharya one has in the beginning to observe strict rules regarding chastity. Not only should one keep oneself strictly aloof from the least association with the opposite sex, but also give up the company of married people even.

The disciple who was a householder was awed at these words of Swamiji, felt dejected that he would not be able to associate freely as before with the Sadhus of the Math and said, "Sir, I feel more intimacy with the Math and its inmates than with my own family. As if they are known to me from a long time. The unbounded freedom that I enjoy in the Math, I feel nowhere else in the world."

Swamiji: All those who are pure in spirit will feel like that here. Those who do not feel so must be taken as not belonging to this Math and its ideals. That is the reason why many people come here out of mere sensation-mongering and then run away. Those who are devoid of continence and are running after money day and night will never be able to appreciate the ideals of the Math, nor regard the Math people as their own. The Sannyasins of this Math are not like those of old, ash-besmeared, with matted hair and iron tongs in their hands, and curing disease by medicinal titbits; therefore seeing the contrast, people cannot appreciate them. The ways, movements and ideas of our Master were all cast in a new mould, so we are also of a new type. Sometimes dressed like gentlemen, we are engaged in lecturing; at other times, throwing all aside, with "Hara, Hara, Vyom Vyom" on the lips, ash-clad, we are immersed in meditation and austerities in mountains and forests.

Now it won't do to merely quote the authority of our ancient books. The tidal wave of Western civilisation is now rushing over the length and breadth of the country. It won't do now simply to sit in meditation on mountain tops without realising in the least its usefulness. Now is wanted — as said in the Gita by the Lord — intense Karma-yoga, with unbounded courage and indomitable strength in the heart. Then only will the people of the country be roused, otherwise they will continue to be as much in the dark as you are.

The day is nearly ended. Swamiji came downstairs, dressed for the boating excursion on the Ganga. Swamiji, accompanied by the disciple and two others, boarded the boat, which passed the Dakshineswar temple and reached Panihati where it was anchored below the garden-house of Babu Govinda Kumar Chaudhury. It has once been proposed to rent this house for the use of the Math. Swamiji descended from the boat, went round the house and the garden and looking over the place minutely said, "The garden is nice but is at a great distance from Calcutta. The devotees of Shri Ramakrishna would have been put to trouble to walk such a long distance from Calcutta. It is fortunate that the Math has not been established here." The boat then returned to the Math amid the enveloping darkness.

XIV

The disciple has today come to the Math with Nag Mahashaya in company.

Swamiji to Nag Mahashaya (saluting him): You are all right, I hope?

Nag Mahashaya: I have come today to visit you. Glory to Shankara! Glory to Shankara! I am blessed today verily with the sight of Shiva!

Saying these words, Nag Mahashaya out of reverence stood with joined hands before him.

Swamiji: How is your health?

Nag Mahashaya: Why are you asking about this trifling body — this cage of flesh and bones? Verily I am blessed today to see you.

Saying these words, Nag Mahashaya prostrated before Swamiji.

Swamiji (lifting him up): Why are you doing that to me?

Nag Mahashaya: I see with my inner eye that today I am blessed with the vision of Shiva Himself. Glory to Ramakrishna!

Swamiji (addressing the disciple): Do you see? How real Bhakti transforms human nature! Nag Mahashaya has lost himself in the Divine, his body-consciousness has vanished altogether. (To Swami Premananda) Get some Prasada for Nag Mahashaya.

Nag Mahashaya: Prasada! (To Swamiji with folded hands) Seeing you, all my earthly hunger has vanished today.

The Brahmacharins and Sannyasins of the Math were studying the Upanishads. Swamiji said to them, "Today a great devotee of Shri Ramakrishna has come amongst us. Let it be a holiday in honour of Nag Mahashaya's visit to the Math." So all closed their books and sat in a circle round Nag Mahashaya; Swamiji also sat in front of him.

Swamiji (addressing all): Do you see? Look at Nag Mahashaya; he is a householder, yet he has no knowledge of the mundane existence; he always lives lost in Divine consciousness. (To Nag Mahashaya) Please tell us and these Brahmacharins something about Shri Ramakrishna.

Nag Mahashaya (in reverence): What do you say, sir? What shall I say? I have come to see you — the hero, the helper in the divine play of Shri Ramakrishna. Now will people appreciate his message and teachings. Glory to Ramakrishna!

Swamiji: It is you who have really appreciated and understood Shri Ramakrishna. We are only spent in useless wanderings.

Nag Mahashaya: What do you say, sir? You are the image of Shri Ramakrishna — the obverse and reverse of the same coin. Those who have eyes, let them see.

Swamiji: Is the starting of these Maths and Ashramas etc. a step in the right direction?

Nag Mahashaya: I am an insignificant being, what do I understand? Whatever you do, I know for a certainty, will conduce to the well-being of the world — ay, of the world.

Many out of reverence proceeded to take the dust of Nag Mahashaya's feet, which made him much agitated. Swamiji, addressing all, said, "Don't act so as to cause pain to Nag Mahashaya; he feels uncomfortable." Hearing this everybody desisted.

Swamiji: Do please come and stay at the Math. You will be an object-lesson to the boys here.

Nag Mahashaya: I once asked Shri Ramakrishna about that, to which he replied, "Stay as a householder as you are doing." Therefore I am continuing in that life. I see you all occasionally and feel myself blessed.

Swamiji: I will go to your place once.

Nag Mahashaya, mad with joy, said, "Shall such a day dawn? My place will be made holy by your visit, like Varanasi. Shall I be so fortunate as that!"

Swamiji: Well, I have the desire. Now it depends

on "Mother" to take me there.

Nag Mahashaya: Who will understand you? Unless the inner vision opens, nobody can understand you. Only Shri Ramakrishna understood you; all else have simply put faith in his words, but none has understood you really.

Swamiji: Now my one desire is to rouse the country — the sleeping leviathan that has lost all faith in his power and makes no response. If I can wake it up to a sense of the Eternal Religion then I shall know that Shri Ramakrishna's advent and our birth are fruitful. That is the one desire in my heart: Mukti and all else appear of no consequence to me. Please give me your blessings that I may succeed.

Nag Mahashaya: Your will and his have become one. Whatever is your will is his. Glory to Shri Ramakrishna!

Swamiji: To work one requires a strong body; since coming to this country, I am not doing well; in the West I was in very good health.

Nag Mahashaya: "Whenever one is born in a body," Shri Ramakrishna used to say, "one has to pay the house tax." Disease and sorrow are the tax. But your body is a box of gold mohurs, and very great care should be taken of it. But who will do it? Who will understand? Only Shri Ramakrishna understood. Glory to Ramakrishna!

Swamiji: All at the Math take great care of me.

Nag Mahashaya: It will be to their good if they do it, whether they know it or not. If proper attention is not paid to your body, then the chances are that it will fall off.

Swamiji: Nag Mahashaya, I do not fully understand whether what I am doing is right or not. At particular times I feel a great inclination to work in a certain direction, and I work according to that. Whether it is for good or evil, I cannot understand.

Nag Mahashaya: Well, Shri Ramakrishna said, "The treasure is now locked."— therefore he does not let you know fully. The moment you know it, your play of human life will be at an end.

Swamiji was pondering something with steadfast gaze. Then Swami Premananda brought some Prasada for Nag Mahashaya who was ecstatic with joy. Shortly after Nag Mahashaya found Swamiji slowly digging the ground with a spade near the pond, and held him by the hand saying, "When we are present, why should you do that?" Swamiji leaving the spade walked about the garden talking the while, and began to narrate to a disciple, "After Shri Ramakrishna's passing away we heard one day that Nag Mahashaya lay fasting in his humbled tiled lodgings in Calcutta. Myself, Swami Turiyananda, and another went together and appeared at Nag Mahashaya's cottage. Seeing us he rose from his bed. We said, `We shall have our Bhiksha (food) here today.' At once Nag Mahashaya brought rice, cooking pot, fuel, etc. from the bazaar and began to cook. We thought that we would eat and make Nag Mahashaya also eat. Cooking over, he gave the food to us; we set apart something for him and then sat down to eat. After this, we requested him to take food; he at once broke the pot of rice and striking his forehead began to say: `Shall I give food to the body in which God has not been realised?' Seeing this we were struck with amazement. Later on after much persuasion we induced him to take some food and then returned."

Swamiji: Will Nag Mahashaya stay in the Math tonight?

Disciple: No, he has some work; he must return today.

Swamiji: Then look for a boat. It is getting dark. When the boat came, the disciple and Nag Mahashaya saluted

XV

Swamiji is now in very good health. The disciple has come to the Math on a Sunday morning. After visiting Swamiji he has come downstairs and is discussing the Vedantic scriptures with Swami Nirmalananda. At this moment Swamiji himself came downstairs and addressing the disciple, said, "What were you discussing with Nirmalananda?"

Disciple: Sir, he was saying, "The Brahman of the Vedanta is only known to you and your Swamiji. We on the contrary know that "(Sanskrit)— shri

Krishna is the Lord Himself."

Swamiji: What did you say?

Disciple: I said that the Atman is the one Truth, and that Krishna was merely a person who had realised this Atman. Swami Nirmalananda is at heart a believer in the Advaita Vedanta, but outwardly he takes up the dualistic side. His first idea seems to be to moot the personal aspect of the Ishvara and then by a gradual process of reasoning to strengthen the foundations of Vedanta.

But as soon as he calls me a "Vaishnava" I forget his real intention and begin a heated discussion with him.

Swamiji: He loves you and so enjoys the fun of teasing you. But why should you be upset by his words? You will also answer, "You, sir, are an atheist, a believer in Nihility."

Disciple: Sir, is there any such statement in the Upanishads that Ishvara is an all-powerful Person? But people generally believe in such an Ishvara.

Swamiji: The highest principle, the Lord of all, cannot be a Person. The Jiva is an individual and the sum total of all Jivas is the Ishvara. In the Jiva, Avidya, or nescience, is predominant, but Ishvara controls Maya composed of Avidya and Vidya and independently projects this world of moving and immovable things out of Himself. But Brahman transcends both the individual and collective aspects, the Jiva and Ishvara. In Brahman there is no part. It is for the sake of easy comprehension that parts have been imagined in It. That part of Brahman in which there is the superimposition of creation, maintenance and dissolution of the universe has been spoken of as Ishvara in the scriptures, while the other unchangeable portion, with reference to which there is no thought of duality, is indicated as Brahman. But do not on that account think that Brahman is a distinct and separate substance from the Jivas and the universe. The Qualified Monists hold that it is Brahman that has transformed Itself into Jivas and the universe. The Advaitins on the contrary maintain that Jivas and the universe have been merely superimposed on Brahman. But in reality there has been no modification in Brahman. The Advaitin says that the universe consists only of name and form. It endures only so long as there are name and form. When through meditation and other practices name and form are dissolved, then only the transcendent Brahman remains. Then the separate reality of Jivas and the universe is felt no longer. Then it is realised that one is the Eternal Pure Essence of Intelligence, or Brahman. The real nature of the Jiva is Brahman. When the veil of name and form vanishes through meditation etc., then that idea is simply realised. This is the substance of pure Advaita. The Vedas, the Vedanta and all other scriptures only explain this idea in different ways.

Disciple: How then is it true that Ishvara is an almighty Person?

Swamiji: Man is man in so far as he is qualified by the limiting adjunct of mind. Through the mind he has to understand and grasp everything, and therefore whatever he thinks must be limited by the mind. Hence it is the natural tendency of man to argue, from the analogy of his own personality, the personality of Ishvara (God). Man can only think of his ideal as a human being. When buffeted by sorrow in this world of disease and death he is driven to desperation and helplessness, then he seeks refuge with someone, relying on whom he may feel safe. But where is that refuge to be found? The omnipresent Atman which depends on nothing else to support It is the only Refuge. At first man does not find that. When discrimination and dispassion arise in the course of meditation and spiritual practices, he comes to know it. But in whatever way he may progress on the path of spirituality, everyone is unconsciously awakening Brahman within him. But the means may be different in different cases. Those who have faith in the Personal God have to undergo spiritual practices holding on to that idea. If there is sincerity, through that will come the awakening of the lion of Brahman within. The knowledge of Brahman is the one goal of all beings but the various ideas are the various paths to it. Although the real nature of the Jiva is Brahman, still as he has identification with the qualifying adjunct of the mind, he suffers from all sorts of doubts and difficulties, pleasure and pain. But everyone from Brahma down to a blade of grass is advancing towards the realisation of his real nature. And none can escape the round of births and deaths until he realises his identity with Brahman. Getting the human birth, when the desire for freedom becomes very strong, and along with it comes the grace of a person of realisation, then man's desire for Self-knowledge becomes intensified. Otherwise the mind of men given to lust and greed never inclines that way. How should the desire to know Brahman arise in one who has the hankering in his mind for the pleasures of family life, for wealth and for fame? He who is prepared to renounce all, who amid the strong current of the duality of good and evil, happiness and misery, is calm, steady, balanced, and awake to his Ideal, alone endeavours to attain to Self-knowledge. He alone by the might of his own power tears asunder the net of the world. "[(Sanskrit)] — breaking the barriers of Maya, he emerges like a mighty lion."

Disciple: Well then, is it true that without Sannyasa, there can be no knowledge of Brahman?

Swamiji: That is true, a thousand times. One must have both internal and external Sannyasa — renunciation in spirit as also formal renunciation. Shankaracharya, in commenting on the Upanishadic text, "Neither by Tapas (spiritual practice) devoid of the necessary insignia",[1] has said that by practising Sadhana without the external badge of Sannyasa (the Gerua-robe, the staff, Kamandalu, etc.), Brahman, which is difficult to attain, is not realised. Without dispassion for the world, without renunciation, without giving up the desire for enjoyment, absolutely nothing can be accomplished in the spiritual life. "It is not like a sweetmeat in the hands of a child which you can snatch by a trick."[2]

Disciple: But, sir, in the course of spiritual practices, that renunciation may come.

Swamiji: Let those to whom it will come gradually have it that way. But why should you sit and wait for that? At once begin to dig the channel which will bring the waters of spirituality to your life. Shri Ramakrishna used to deprecate lukewarmness in spiritual attainments as, for instance, saying that religion would come gradually, and that there was no hurry for it. When one is thirsty, can one sit idle? Does he not run about for water? Because your thirst for spirituality has not come, therefore you are sitting idly. The desire for knowledge has not grown strong, therefore you are satisfied with the little pleasures of family life.

Disciple: Really I do not understand why I don't get that idea of renouncing everything. Do make some way for that, please.

Swamiji: The end and the means are all in your hands. I can only stimulate them. You have read so many scriptures and are serving and associating with such Sadhus who have known Brahman; if even this does not bring the idea of renunciation, then your life is in vain. But it will not be altogether vain; the effects of this will manifest in some way or other in time.

The disciple was much dejected and again said to Swamiji: "Sir, I have come under your refuge, do open the path of Mukti for me — that I may realise the Truth in this body."

Swamiji: What fear is there? Always discriminate — your body, your house, these Jivas and the world are all absolutely unreal like a dream. Always think that this body is only an inert instrument. And the self-contained Purusha within is your real nature. The adjunct of mind is His first and subtle covering, then, there is this body which is His gross, outer covering. The indivisible changeless, self-effulgent Purusha is lying hidden under these delusive veils, therefore your real nature is unknown to you. The direction of the mind which always runs after the senses has to be turned within. The mind has to be killed. The body is but gross — it dies and dissolves into the five elements. But the bundle of mental impressions, which is the mind, does not die soon. It remains for some time in seed-form and then sprouts and grows in the form of a tree — it takes on another physical body and goes the round of birth and death, until Self-knowledge arises. Therefore

---

1. Mundaka Upanishad, III. ii. 4.

2. Song of Ramprasad.

I say, by meditation and concentration and by the power of philosophical discrimination plunge this mind in the Ocean of Existence-knowledge-bliss Absolute. When the mind dies, all limiting adjuncts vanish and you are established in Brahman.

Disciple: Sir, it is so difficult to direct this uncontrolled mind towards Brahman.

Swamiji: Is there anything difficult for the hero? Only men of faint hearts speak so. "[(Sanskrit)] — mukti is easy of attainment only to the hero — but not to cowards." Says the Gita (VI. 35), "[(Sanskrit)] — by renunciation and by practice is the mind brought under control, O Arjuna." The Chitta or mind-stuff is like a transparent lake, and the waves which rise in it by the impact of sense-impressions constitute Manas or the mind. Therefore the mind consists of a succession of thought-waves. From these mental waves arises desire. Then that desire transforms itself into will and works through its gross instrument, the body. Again, as work is endless, so its fruits also are endless. Hence the mind is always being tossed by countless myriads of waves — the fruits of work. This mind has to be divested of all modifications (Vrittis) and reconverted into the transparent lake, so that there remains not a single wave of modification in it. Then will Brahman manifest Itself. The scriptures give a glimpse of this state in such passages as: "Then all the knots of the heart are cut asunder", etc. Do you understand?

Disciple: Yes, sir, but meditation must base itself on some object?

Swamiji: You yourself will be the object of your meditation. Think and meditate that you are the omnipresent Atman. "I am neither the body, nor the mind, nor the Buddhi (determinative faculty), neither the gross nor the subtle body"— by this process of elimination, immerse your mind in the transcendent knowledge which is your real nature. Kill the mind by thus plunging it repeatedly in this. Then only you will realise the Essence of Intelligence, or be established in your real nature. Knower and known, meditator and the object meditated upon will then become one, and the cessation of all phenomenal superimpositions will follow.

This is styled in the Shastras as the transcendence of the triad or relative knowledge (Triputibheda). There is no relative or conditioned knowledge in this state. When the Atman is the only knower, by what means can you possibly know It? The Atman is Knowledge, the Atman is Intelligence, the Atman is Sachchidananda. It is through the inscrutable power of Maya, which cannot be indicated as either existent or non-existent, that the relative consciousness has come upon the Jiva who is none other than Brahman. This is generally known as the conscious state. And the state in which this duality of relative existence becomes one in the pure Brahman is called in the scriptures the superconscious state and described in such words as, "[(Sanskrit)] — it is like an ocean perfectly at rest and without a name" (Vivekachudamani, 410).

Swamiji spoke these words as if from the profound depths of his realisation of Brahman.

Swamiji: All philosophy and scriptures have come from the plane of relative knowledge of subject and object. But no thought or language of the human mind can fully express the Reality which lies beyond the plane of relative Knowledge! Science, philosophy, etc. are only partial truths. So they can never be the adequate channels of expression for the transcendent Reality. Hence viewed from the transcendent standpoint, everything appears to be unreal — religious creeds, and works, I and thou, and the universe — everything is unreal! Then only it is perceived: "I am the only reality; I am the all-pervading Atman, and I am the proof of my own existence." Where is the room for a separate proof to establish the reality of my existence? I am, as the scriptures say, "[(Sanskrit)] — always known to myself as the eternal subject" (Vivekachudamani, 409). I have seen that state, realised it. You also see and realise it and preach this truth of Brahman to all. Then only will you attain to peace.

While speaking these words, Swamiji's face wore a serious expression and he was lost in thought. After some time he continued: "Realise in your own life this knowledge of Brahman which comprehends all theories and is the rationale of all truths, and preach it to the world. This will conduce to your own good and the good of others as well. I have told you today the essence of all truths; there is nothing higher than this."

Disciple: Sir, now you are speaking of Jnana; but sometimes you proclaim the superiority of Bhakti, sometimes of Karma, and sometimes of Yoga. This confuses our understanding.

Swamiji: Well, the truth is this. The knowledge of Brahman is the ultimate goal — the highest destiny of man. But man cannot remain absorbed in Brahman all the time. When he comes out of it, he must have something to engage himself. At that time he should do such work as will contribute to the real well-being of people. Therefore do I urge you in the service of Jivas in a spirit of oneness. But, my son, such are the intricacies of work, that even great saints are caught in them and become attached.

Therefore work has to be done without any desire for results. This is the teaching of the Gita. But know that in the knowledge of Brahman there is no touch of any relation to work. Good works, at the most, purify the mind. Therefore has the commentator Shankara so sharply criticised the doctrine of the combination of Jnana and Karma. Some attain to the knowledge of Brahman by the means of unselfish work. This is also a means, but the end is the realisation of Brahman. Know this thoroughly that the goal of the path of discrimination and of all other modes of practice is the realisation of Brahman.

Disciple: Now, sir, please tell me about the utility of Raja-yoga and Bhakti-yoga.

Swamiji: Striving in these paths also some attain to the realisation of Brahman. The path of Bhakti or devotion of God is a slow process, but is easy of practice. In the path of Yoga there are many obstacles; perhaps the mind runs after psychic powers and thus draws you away from attaining your real nature. Only the path of Jnana is of quick fruition and the rationale of all other creeds; hence it is equally esteemed in all countries and all ages. But even in the path of discrimination there is the chance of the mind getting stuck in the interminable net of vain argumentation. Therefore along with it, meditation should be practised. By means of discrimination and meditation, the goal or Brahman has to be reached. One is sure to reach the goal by practising in this way. This, in my opinion, is the easy path ensuring quick success.

Disciple: Now please tell me something about the doctrine of Incarnation of God.

Swamiji: You want to master everything in a day, it seems!

Disciple: Sir, if the doubts and difficulties of the mind be solved in one day, then I shall not have to trouble you time and again.

Swamiji: Those by whose grace the knowledge of Atman, which is extolled so much in the scriptures, is attained in a minute are the moving Tirthas (seats of holiness)— the Incarnations. From their very birth they are knowers of Brahman, and between Brahman and the knower of Brahman there is not the least difference. "[(Sanskrit)] — he who knows the Brahman becomes the Brahman" (Mundaka, III.ii.9). The Atman cannot be known by the mind for It is Itself the Knower — this I have already said. Therefore man's relative knowledge reached up to the Avataras — those who are always established in the Atman. The highest ideal of Ishvara which the human mind can grasp is the Avatara. Beyond this there is no relative knowledge. Such knowers of Brahman are rarely born in the world. And very few people can understand them. They alone are the proof of the truths of the scriptures — the towers of light in the ocean of the world. By the company of such Avataras and by their grace, the darkness of the mind disappears in a trice and realisation flashes immediately in the heart. Why or by what process it comes cannot be ascertained. But it does come. I have seen it happen like that. Shri Krishna spoke the Gita, establishing Himself in the Atman. Those passages of the Gita where He speaks with the word "I", invariably indicate the Atman: "Take refuge in Me alone" means, "Be established in the Atman". This knowledge of the Atman is the highest aim of the Gita. The references to Yoga etc. are but incidental to this realisation of the Atman. Those who have not this knowledge of the Atman are "suicides". "They kill themselves by the clinging to the unreal"; they lose their life in the noose of sense-pleasures. You are also men, and can't you ignore this trash of sensual enjoyment that won't last for two days? Should you also swell the ranks of those who are born and die in utter ignorance? Accept the "beneficial" and discard the "pleasant". Speak of this Atman to all, even to the lowest. By continued speaking your own intelligence also will clear up. And always repeat the great Mantras —"[(Sanskrit)] — thou art That", "[(Sanskrit)] — I am That", "[(Sanskrit)] — all this is verily Brahman"— and have the courage of a lion in the heart. What is there to fear? Fear is death — fear is the greatest sin. The human soul, represented by Arjuna, was touched with fear. Therefore Bhagavan Shri Krishna, established in the Atman, spoke to him the teachings of the Gita. Still his fear would not leave him. Later, when Arjuna saw the Universal Form of the Lord, and became established in the Atman, then with all bondages of Karma burnt by the fire of knowledge, he fought the battle.

Disciple: Sir, can a man do work even after realisation?

Swamiji: After realisation, what is ordinarily called work does not persist. It changes its character. The work which the Jnani does only conduces to the well-being of the world. Whatever a man of realisation says or does contributes to the welfare of all. We have observed Shri Ramakrishna; he was, as it were "[(Sanskrit)] — in the body, but not of it!" About the motive of the actions of such personages only this can be said: "[(Sanskrit)] — everything they do like men, simply by way of sport" (Brahma-Sutras, II.i.33).

XVI

The disciple has come to the Math today accompanied by Shri Ranadaprasad Das Gupta, the founder and professor of the Jubilee Art Academy, Calcutta. Ranada Babu is an expert artist, a learned man and an admirer of Swamiji. After the exchange of courtesies Swamiji began to talk with Ranada Babu on various topics relating to art.

Swamiji: I had the opportunity of seeing the beauties of art of nearly every civilised country in the world, but I saw nothing like the development of art which took place in our country during the Buddhistic period. During the regime of the Mogul Emperors also, there was a marked development of art — and the Taj and the Jumma Masjid etc. are standing monuments of that culture.

Art has its origin in the expression of some idea in whatever man produces. Where there is no expression of idea, however much there may be a display of colours and so on, it cannot be styled as true art. Even the articles of everyday use, such as water vessels, or cups and saucers, should be used to express an idea. In the Paris Exhibition I saw a wonderful figure carved in marble. In explanation of the figure, the following words were inscribed underneath: Art unveiling Nature. That is how art sees the inner beauty of nature by drawing away with its own hands the covering veils. The work has been so designed as to indicate that the beauty of nature has not yet become fully unveiled; but the artist is fascinated, as it were, with the beauty of the little that has become manifest. One cannot refrain from praising the sculptor who has tried to express this exquisite idea. You should also try to produce something original like this.

Ranada Babu: Yes, I also have the desire to do some original modelling at leisure. But I meet with no encouragement in this country; it is a poor country and there is want of appreciation. Swamiji: If you can with your whole heart produce one real thing, if you can rightly express a single idea in art, it must win appreciation in course of time. A real thing never suffers from want of appreciation in this world. It is also heard that some artists have gained appreciation for their works a thousand years after their death!

Ranada Babu: That is true. But we have become so worthless that we haven't got the courage to spend a lot of energy to no purpose. Through these five years' struggle I have succeeded to some extent. Bless me that my efforts be not in vain.

Swamiji: If you set to work in right earnest, then

you are sure to be successful. Whoever works at a thing heart and soul not only achieves success in it, but through his absorption in that he also realises the supreme Truth — brahman. Whoever works at a thing with his whole heart receives help from God.

Ranada Babu: What difference did you find between the art of the West and that of India?

Swamiji: It is nearly the same everywhere. Originality is rarely found. In those countries pictures are painted with the help of models obtained by photographing various objects. But no sooner does one take the help of machinery than all originality vanishes — one cannot give expression to one's ideas. The ancient artists used to evolve original ideas from their brains and try to express them in their paintings. Now the picture being a likeness of photographs, the power of originality and the attempt to develop are getting scarce. But each nation has a characteristic of its own. In its manners and customs, in its mode of living, in painting and sculpture is found the expression of that characteristic idea. For instance, music and dancing in the West are all pointed in their expression. In dance, they look as if jerking the limbs; in instrumental music, the sounds prick the ear like a sword thrust, as it were; so also in vocal music. In this country, on the other hand, the dance has a rolling wave-like movement, and there is the same rounded movement in the varieties of pitch in vocal song. So also in instrumental music. Hence with regard to art also, a different expression is found among different people. People who are very materialistic take nature as their ideal, and try to express in art ideas allied thereto, while the people whose ideal is the transcendent Reality beyond nature try to express that in art through the powers of nature. With regard to the former class of people, nature is the primary basis of art, while with the second class, ideality is the principal motive of artistic development. Thus, though starting with two different ideals in art, they have advanced in it each in its own way. Seeing some paintings in the West you will mistake them for real natural objects. With respect to this country also, when in ancient times sculpture attained a high degree of perfection, if you look at a statue of the period it will make you forget the material world and transport you to a new ideal world. As in Western countries paintings like those of former times are not produced now, so in our country also, attempts to give expression to original ideas in art are no longer seen. For example, the paintings from your art school have got no expression, as it were. It would be well if you try to paint the objects of everyday meditation of the Hindus by giving in them the expression of ancient ideals.

Ranada Babu: I feel much encouraged by your words. I shall try to act up to your suggestions.

Swamiji: Take, for instance, the figure of Mother Kali. In it there is the union of the blissful and the terrible aspects. But in none of the pictures can be seen the true expression of these two aspects. Far from this, there is no attempt to express adequately even one of these two aspects! I have tried to put down some ideas of the terrible aspects of Mother Kali in my English poem, Kali the Mother. Can you express those ideas in a picture?

Ranada Babu: Please let me know them.

Swamiji had the poem brought from the library, and began to read it out most impressively to Ranada Babu. Ranada Babu silently listened to the poem, and after a while, as if visualising the figure with his mind's eye, he turned to Swamiji with a frightened look.

Swamiji: Well, will you be able to express this idea in the picture?

Ranada Babu: Yes, I shall try[1]; but it turns one's head even to imagine the idea.

Swamiji: After drawing the picture, please show it to me. Then I will tell you about the points necessary to perfect it.

Then Swamiji had the design which he had sketched for the seal[2] of the Ramakrishna Mission brought, showed it to Ranada Babu and asked his opinion on it. It depicted a lake in which a lotus blossomed, and there was a swan, and the whole was encircled by a serpent. Ranada Babu at first could

---

1. Ranada Babu began to paint this picture the very next day, but it was never finished, nor shown to Swamiji.

2. Printed on the title-page of this volume.

not catch the significance of it and asked Swamiji to explain. Swamiji said, "The wavy waters in the picture are symbolic of Karma; the lotus, of Bhakti; and the rising-sun, of Jnana. The encircling serpent is indicative of Yoga and the awakened Kundalini Shakti, while the swan in the picture stands for the Paramatman (Supreme Self). Therefore the idea of the picture is that by the union of Karma, Jnana, Bhakti, and Yoga, the vision of the Paramatman is obtained."

Ranada Babu kept silent, gratified to hear the motif of the picture. After a while he said, "I wish I could learn about art from you!"

Then Swamiji showed to Ranada Babu a drawing, depicting his plan of the future Ramakrishna Temple and Math. Then he began to say, "In the building of this prospective Temple and Math I have the desire to bring together all that is best in Eastern and Western art. I shall try to apply in its construction all the ideas about architecture which I have gathered in my travels all over the world. A big prayer-hall will be built with roof supported on numerous clustered pillars. In its walls, hundreds of lotuses will be in full bloom. It must be big enough to accommodate a thousand persons sitting in meditation. The Ramakrishna temple and prayer-hall should be built together in such a way that from a distance it would taken for a representation of the symbol, "Om". Within the temple there would be a figure of Shri Ramakrishna seated on a swan. On the two sides of the door will be represented the figure of a lion and a lamb licking each other's body in love-expressing the idea that great power and gentleness have become united in love. I have these ideas in my mind; and if I live long enough I shall carry them out. Otherwise future generations will try if they can do it by degrees. It is my opinion that Shri Ramakrishna was born to vivify all branches of art and culture in this country. Therefore this Math has to be built up in such a way that religion, work, learning, Jnana, and Bhakti may spread over the world from this centre. Be you my helpers in this work."

Ranada Babu and the assembled Sannyasins and Brahmacharins listened to Swamiji in mute wonder.

After a while Swamiji resumed, "I am discussing the subject at length with you as you are yourself an adept in the line. Now please tell me what you have learnt about the highest ideals of art as the result of your long study of it."

Ranada Babu: What new thing can I tell you? On the contrary, it is you who have opened my eyes on this subject. I have never heard such instructive words on the subject of art in my life. Bless me, sir, that I can work out the ideas that I have got from you.

Then Swamiji got up from his seat and paced the lawn, remarking to the disciple, "He is a very spirited young man."

Disciple: Sir, he is astonished to hear your words.

Swamiji, without answering the disciple, began to hum the lines of a song which Shri Ramakrishna used to sing, "The controlled mind is a great treasure, the philosopher's stone, which yields whatever you want."

After walking a while, Swamiji, washing his face, entered his room with the disciple in company and read the article on Art in the Enclyclopaedia Britannica for some time. After finishing it, he began to make fun with the disciple, caricaturing the words and accents of East Bengal.

XVII

Swamiji has just returned from East Bengal and Assam a few days back. He is ill, and his feet have swollen. Coming to the Math, the disciple went upstairs and prostrated himself at Swamiji's feet. In spite of his ill health, Swamiji wore his usual smiling face and affectionate look.

Disciple: How are you, Swamiji?

Swamiji: What shall I speak of my health, my son? The body is getting unfit for work day by day. It has been born on the soil of Bengal, and some disease or other is always overtaking it. The physique of this country is not at all good. If you want to do some strenuous work, it cannot bear the strain. But the few days that the body lasts, I will work for you. I shall die in harness. Disciple: If you give up work for some time and take rest, then you will be all right. Your life means good to the world.

Swamiji: Am I able to sit quiet, my son! Two or three days before Shri Ramakrishna's passing away, She whom he used to call "Kali" entered this body. It is She who takes me here and there and makes me work, without letting me remain quiet or allowing me to look to my personal comforts.

Disciple: Are you speaking metaphorically?

Swamiji: Oh, no; two or three days before his leaving the body, he called me to his side one day, and asking me to sit before him, looked steadfastly at me and fell into Samadhi. Then I really felt that a subtle force like an electric shock was entering my body! In a little while, I also lost outward consciousness and sat motionless. How long I stayed in that condition I do not remember; when consciousness returned I found Shri Ramakrishna shedding tears. On questioning him, he answered me affectionately, "Today, giving you my all, I have become a beggar. With this power you are to do many works for the world's good before you will return." I feel that power is constantly directing me to this or that work. This body has not been made for remaining idle.

Hearing these words with speechless wonder the disciple thought — who knows how common people will take these words? Thereupon he changed the topic and said, "Sir, how did you like our East Bengal?"

Swamiji: I liked it on the whole. The fields, I saw, were rich in crops, the climate also is good, and the scenery on the hill-side is charming. The Brahmaputra Valley is incomparable in its beauty. The people of East Bengal are a little stronger and more active than those of this part. It may be due to their taking plenty of fish and meat. Whatever they do, they do with great persistence. They use a great deal of oil and fat in their food, which is not good, because taking too much of oily and fatty food produces fat in the body.

Disciple: How did you find their religious consciousness?

Swamiji: About religious ideas, I noticed the people are very conservative, and many have turned into fanatics in trying to be liberal in religion. One day a young man brought to me, in the house of Mohini Babu at Dacca, a photograph and said, "Sir, please tell me who he is. Is he an Avatara?" I told him gently many times that I know nothing of it. When even on my telling him three or four times the boy did not cease from his persistent questioning, I was constrained to say at last, "My boy, henceforth take a little nutritious food and then your brain will develop. Without nourishing food, I see your brain has become dried up." At these words the young man may have been much displeased. But what could I do? Unless I spoke like this to the boys, they would turn into madcaps by degrees.

Disciple: In our East Bengal a great many Avataras have cropped up recently.

Swamiji: People may call their Guru an Avatara; they may have any idea of him they like. But Incarnations of God are not born anywhere and everywhere and at all seasons. At Dacca itself I heard there were three or four Avataras!

Disciple: How did you find the women of that side?

Swamiji: The women are very nearly the same everywhere. I found Vaishnavism strong at Dacca. The wife of H__ seemed to be very intelligent. With great care she used to prepare food and send it to me.

Disciple: I heard you have been to Nag Mahashaya's place.

Swamiji: Yes, going so far, should I not visit the birthplace of such a great soul? His wife fed me with many delicacies prepared by her own hand. The house is charming, like a peace retreat. There I took a swimming bath in a village pond. After that I had such a sound sleep that I woke at half past two in the afternoon. Of the few days I had sound sleep in my life, that in Nag Mahashaya's house was one. Rising from sleep I had a plentiful repast. Nag Mahashaya's wife presented me a cloth which I tied round my head as a turban and started for Dacca. I found that the photograph of Nag Mahashaya was being worshipped there. The place where his remains lie interred ought to be well kept. Even now it is not as it should be.

Disciple: The people of that part have not been able to appreciate Nag Mahashaya.

Swamiji: How can ordinary people appreciate a great man like him? Those who had his company are blessed indeed.

Disciple: What did you see at Kamakhya?

Swamiji: The Shillong hills are very beautiful. There I met Sir Henry Cotton, the Chief Commissioner of Assam. He asked me, "Swamiji, after travelling through Europe and America, what have you come to see here in these distant hills?" Such a good and kind-hearted man as Sir Henry Cotton is rarely found. Hearing of my illness, he sent the Civil Surgeon and inquired after my health mornings and evenings. I could not do much lecturing there, because my health was very bad. On the way Nitai served and looked after me nicely.

Disciple: What did you find the religious ideas of that part to be?

Swamiji: It is the land of the Tantras. I heard of one "Hankar Deva" who is worshipped there as an Avatara. I heard his sect is very wide-spread. I could not ascertain if "Hankar Deva" was but another form of the name Shankaracharya. They are monks — perhaps Tantrika Sannyasins, or perhaps one of the Shankara sects.

Disciple: The people of East Bengal have not been able to appreciate you as is the case with Nag Mahashaya.

Swamiji: Whether they appreciate me or not, the people there are more active and energetic than those of these parts. In time it will develop more. What are nowadays known as refined or civilised ways have not yet thoroughly entered those parts. Gradually they will. In all times, etiquette and fashion spread to the countryside from the capital. And this is happening in East Bengal also. The land that has produced a great soul like Nag Mahashaya is blessed and has a hopeful future. By the light of his personality Eastern Bengal is radiant.

Disciple: But, sir, ordinary people did not know him as a great soul. He hid himself in great obscurity.

Swamiji: There they used to make much fuss about my food and say, "Why should you eat that food or eat from the hands of such and such?" — and so on. To which I had to reply, "I am a Sannyasin and a mendicant friar and what need have I to observe so much outward formality with regard to food etc.? Do not your scriptures say, "[(Sanskrit)] — one should beg one's food from door to door, ay even from the house of an outcast"? But of course external forms are necessary in the beginning, for the inner realisation of religion, in order to make the truth of the scriptures practical in one's life. Haven't you heard of Shri Ramakrishna's story of "wringing out the almanac for water"?[1] Outward forms and observances are only for the manifestation of the great inner powers of man. The object of all scriptures is to awaken those inner powers and make him understand and realise his real nature. The means are of the nature of ordinances and prohibitions. If you lose sight of the ideal fight over the means only, what will it avail? In every country I have visited, I find this fighting over the means going on, and people have no eye on the ideal. Shri Ramakrishna came to show the truth of this.

Realisation of the truth is the essential thing. Whether you bathe in the Ganga for a thousand years or live on vegetable food for a like period, unless it helps towards the manifestation of the Self, know that it is all of no use. If on the other hand, any one can realise the Atman, without the observance of outward forms, then that very non-observance of forms is the best means. But even after the realisation of Atman, one should observe outward forms to a certain extent for setting an example to the people. The thing is you must make the mind steadfast on something. If it is steadfast on one object, it attains to concentration, that is, its other modifications die out and there is a uniform flow in one direction. Many become wholly preoccupied with the outward forms and observances merely and fail to direct their mind to thoughts of the Atman! If

---

1. The Bengali almanac makes a forecast of the annual rainfall but not a drop comes out of squeezing its pages! Similarly scriptures are useless unless their truths are realised in life.

you remain day and night within the narrow groove of ordinances and prohibitions, how will there be any expression of the soul? The more one has advanced in the realisation of the Atman, the less is he dependent on the observances of forms. Shankaracharya also has said, "[(Sanskrit)] — where is there any ordinance or prohibition for him whose mind is always above the play of the Gunas?" Therefore the essential truth is realisation. Know that to be the goal. Each distinct creed is but a way to the Truth. The test of progress is the amount of renunciation that one has attained. Where you find the attraction for lust and wealth considerably diminished, to whatever creed he may belong, know that his inner spirit is awakening. The door of Self-realisation has surely opened for him. On the contrary if you observe a thousand outward rules and quote a thousand scriptural texts, still, if it has not brought the spirit of renunciation in you, know that your life is in vain. Be earnest over this realisation and set your heart on it. Well, you have read enough of scriptures. But tell me, of what avail has it been? Some perhaps thinking of money have become millionaires, whereas you have become a Pundit by thinking of scriptures. But both are bondages. Attain the supreme knowledge and go beyond Vidya and Avidya, relative knowledge and ignorance.

Disciple: Sir, through your grace I understand it all, but my past Karma does not allow me to assimilate these teachings.

Swamiji: Throw aside your Karma and all such stuff. If it is a truth that by your own past action you have got this body; then, nullifying the effects of evil works by good works, why should you not be a Jivanmukta in this very body? Know that freedom or Self-knowledge is in your own hands. In real knowledge there is no touch of work. But those who work after being Jivanmuktas do so for the good of others. They do not look to the results of works. No seed of desire finds any room in their mind. And strictly speaking it is almost impossible to work like that for the good of the world from the householder's position. In the whole of Hindu scriptures there is the single instance of King Janaka in this respect. But you nowadays want to pose as Janakas (lit. fathers) in every home by begetting children year after year, while he was without the body-consciousness!

Disciple: Please bless me that I may attain Self-realisation in this very life.

Swamiji: What fear? If there is sincerity of spirit, I tell you, for a certainty, you will attain it in this very life. But manly endeavour is wanted. Do you know what it is? "I shall certainly attain Self-knowledge. Whatever obstacles may come, I shall certainly overcome them"— a firm determination like this is Purushakara. "Whether my mother, father, friends, brothers, wife, and children live or die, whether this body remains or goes, I shall never turn back till I attain to the vision of the Atman"— this resolute endeavour to advance towards one's goal, setting at naught all other considerations, is termed manly endeavour. Otherwise, endeavour for creature comforts even beasts and birds show. Man has got this body simply to realise Self-knowledge. If you follow the common run of people in the world and float with the general current, where then is your manliness? Well, the common people are going to the jaws of death! But you have come to conquer it! Advance like a hero. Don't be thwarted by anything. How many days will this body last, with its happiness and misery? When you have got the human body, then rouse the Atman within and say — I have reached the state of fearlessness! Say — I am the Atman in which my lower ego has become merged for ever. Be perfect in this idea; and then as long as the body endures, speak unto others this message of fearlessness: "Thou art That", "Arise, awake, and stop not till the goal is reached!" If you can achieve this, then shall I know that you are really a tenacious East Bengal man.

XVIII

Swamiji is in indifferent health since his return to the Math from the Shillong Hills. His feet have swollen. All this has made his brother-disciples very anxious. At the request of Swami Niranjanananda, Swamiji has agreed to take Ayurvedic medicine. He is to begin this treatment from next Tuesday and entirely give up taking water and salt. Today is Sunday. The disciple asked him, "Sir, it is terribly hot now and you drink water very frequently; it will be unbearable for you now to stop taking water altogether for this treatment."

Swamiji: What do you say? I shall make a firm resolve, on the morning of the day I shall begin this treatment, not to take any water. After that no water shall pass down the throat any more. For three weeks not a drop of water shall be able to go down the throat. The body is but an outer covering of the mind and whatever the mind will dictate to it, it will have to carry out. So there is nothing to be afraid of. At the request of Niranjan I have to undergo this treatment. Well, I cannot be indifferent to the request of my brother-disciples.

It is now about ten o'clock. Swamiji cheerfully raised the topic of his future Math for women, saying, "With the Holy Mother as the centre of inspiration, a Math is to be established on the eastern bank of the Ganga. As Brahmacharins and Sadhus will be trained in this Math here, so in the other Math also, Brahmacharinis and Sadhvis will be trained."

Disciple: Sir, history does not tell us of any Maths for women in India in ancient times. Only during the Buddhistic period one hears of Maths for women; but from it in course of time many corruptions arose. The whole country was overrun by great evil practices.

Swamiji: It is very difficult to understand why in this country so much difference is made between men and women, whereas the Vedanta declares that one and the same conscious Self is present in all beings. You always criticise the women, but say what have you done for their uplift? Writing down Smritis etc., and binding them by hard rules, the men have turned the women into mere manufacturing machines! If you do not raise the women, who are the living embodiment of the Divine Mother, don't think that you have any other way to rise.

Disciple: Women are a bondage and a snare to men. By their Maya they cover the knowledge and dispassion of men. It is for this, I suppose, that scriptural writers hint that knowledge and devotion are difficult of attainment to them.

Swamiji: In what scriptures do you find statements that women are not competent for knowledge and devotion? In the period of degradation, when the priests made other castes incompetent for the study of the Vedas, they deprived the women also of all their rights. Otherwise you will find that in the Vedic or Upanishad age Maitreyi, Gargi, and other ladies of revered memory have taken the places of Rishis through their skill in discussing about Brahman. In an assembly of a thousand Brahmanas who were all erudite in the Vedas, Gargi boldly challenged Yajnavalkya in a discussion about Brahman. Since such ideal women were entitled to spiritual knowledge, why shall not the women have the same privilege now? What has happened once can certainly happen again. History repeats itself. All nations have attained greatness by paying proper respect to women. That country and that nation which do not respect women have never become great, nor will ever be in future. The principal reason why your race has so much degenerated is that you have no respect for these living images of Shakti. Manu says, "Where women are respected, there the gods delight; and where they are not, there all works and efforts come to naught."[1] There is no hope of rise for that family or country where there is no estimation of women, where they live in sadness. For this reason, they have to be raised first; and an ideal Math has to be started for them.

Disciple: Sir, when you first returned from the West, in your lecture at the Star Theatre you sharply criticised the Tantras. Now by your supporting the worship of women, as taught in the Tantras, you are contradicting yourself.

Swamiji: I denounced only the present corrupted form of Vamachara of the Tantras. I did not denounce the Mother-worship of the Tantras, or even the real Vamachara. The purport of the Tantras is to worship women in a spirit of Divinity. During the downfall of Buddhism, the Vamachara became very much corrupted, and that corrupted form obtains to the present day. Even now the Tantra literature

1. Manu, III. 56.

of India is influenced by those ideas. I denounced only these corrupt and horrible practices — which I do even now. I never objected to the worship of women who are the living embodiment of Divine Mother, whose external manifestations, appealing to the senses have maddened men, but whose internal manifestations, such as knowledge, devotion, discrimination and dispassion make man omniscient, of unfailing purpose, and a knower of Brahman. "सैषा प्रसन्ना वरदा नृणां भवति मुक्तये — she, when pleased, becomes propitious and the cause of the freedom of man" (Chandi, I. 57). Without propitiating the Mother by worship and obeisance, not even Brahma and Vishnu have the power to elude Her grasp and attain to freedom. Therefore for the worship of these family goddesses, in order to manifest the Brahman within them, I shall establish the women's Math.

Disciple: It may be a good idea but where will you get the women inmates? With the present hard restrictions of society, who will permit the ladies of their household to join your Math?

Swamiji: Why so? Even now there are women disciples of Shri Ramakrishna. With their help I shall start this Math. The Holy Mother will be their central figure and the wives and daughters of the devotees of Shri Ramakrishna will be its first inmates. For they will easily appreciate the usefulness of such a Math. After that, following their example, many householders will help in their noble work.

Disciple: The devotees of Shri Ramakrishna will certainly join this work. But I don't think the general public will help in this work.

Swamiji: No great work has been done in the world without sacrifice. Who on seeing the tiny sprout of the banyan can imagine that in course of time it will develop into a gigantic banyan tree? At present I shall start the Math in this way. Later on you will see that after a generation or two people of this country will appreciate the worth of this Math. My women disciples will lay down their lives for it. Casting off fear and cowardice, you also be helpers in this noble mission and hold this high ideal before all. You will see, it will shed its lustre over the whole country in time.

Disciple: Sir, please tell me all about your plan of this Math for women.

Swamiji: On the other side of the Ganga a big plot of land will be acquired, where unmarried girls or Brahmacharini widows will live; devout married women will also be allowed to stay now and then. Men will have no concern with this Math. The elderly Sadhus of the Math will manage the affairs of this Math from a distance. There shall be a girls' school attached to this women's Math, in which religious scriptures, literature, Sanskrit, grammar, and even some amount of English should be taught. Other matters such as sewing, culinary art, rules of domestic work, and upbringing of children, will also be taught while Japa, worship, meditation, etc. shall form an indispensable part of the teaching. Those who will be able to live here permanently, renouncing home and family ties, will be provided with food and clothing from the Math. Those who will not be able to do that will be allowed to study in this Math as day-scholars. With the permission of the head of the Math, the latter will be allowed even to stay in the Math occasionally, and during such stay will be maintained by the Math. The elder Brahmacharinis will take charge of the training of the girl students in Brahmacharya. After five or six years' training in this Math, the guardians of the girls may marry them. If deemed fit for Yoga and religious life, with the permission of the guardians they will be allowed to stay in this Math, taking the vow of celibacy. These celibate nuns will in time be the teachers and preachers of the Math. In villages and towns they will open centres and strive for the spread of female education. Through such devout preachers of character there will be the real spread of female education in the country. So long as the students will remain in association with this Math, they must observe Brahmacharya as the basic ideal of this Math.

Spirituality, sacrifice, and self-control will be the motto of the pupils of this Math, and service or Seva-dharma the vow of their life. In view of such ideal lives, who will not respect and have faith in them? If the life of the women of this country be moulded in such fashion, then only will there be the reappearance of such ideal characters as Sita, Savitri and Gargi. To what straits the strictures of local usages have reduced the women of this country, rendering them lifeless and inert, you could understand if only you visited the Western countries. You alone are responsible for this miserable condition of the women, and it rests with you also to raise them again. Therefore I say, set to work. What will it do to memorise a few religious books like the Vedas and so on?

Disciple: Sir, if the girl students after being trained in this Math marry, how will one find ideal characters in them? Will it not be better if the rule is made that those who will be educated in this Math shall not marry?

Swamiji: Can that be brought about all at once? They must be given education and left to themselves. After that they will act as they think best. Even after marriage and entering the world, the girls educated as above will inspire their husbands with noble ideals and be the mothers of heroic sons. But there must be this rule that the guardians of the students in the women's Math must not even think of marrying them before they attain the age of fifteen.

Disciple: Sir, then those girls will not command reputation in society. Nobody would like to marry them.

Swamiji: Why will not they be wanted in marriage? You have not yet understood the trend of society. These learned and accomplished girls will never be in want of bridegrooms. Society nowadays does not follow the texts recommending child-marriage nor will do so in future. Even now don't you see?

Disciple: But there is sure to be a violent opposition against this in the beginning.

Swamiji: Let it be. What is there to be afraid of in that? Opposition to a righteous work initiated with moral courage will only awaken the moral power of the initiators the more. That which meets with no obstruction, no opposition, only takes men to the path of moral death. Struggle is the sign of life.

Disciple: Yes, sir.

Swamiji: In the highest reality of the Parabrahman, there is no distinction of sex. We notice this only in the relative plane. And the more the mind becomes introspective, the more that idea of difference vanishes. Ultimately, when the mind is wholly merged in the homogeneous and undifferentiated Brahman, such ideas as this is a man or that a woman do not remain at all. We have actually seen this in the life of Shri Ramakrishna. Therefore do I say that though outwardly there may be difference between men and women, in their real nature there is none. Hence, if a man can be a knower of Brahman, why cannot a woman attain to the same knowledge? Therefore I was saying that if even one amongst the women became a knower of Brahman, then by the radiance of her personality thousands of women would be inspired and awakened to truth, and great well-being of the country and society would ensue. Do you understand?

Disciple: Sir, your teachings have opened my eyes today.

Swamiji: Not fully yet. When you realise that all-illumining reality of the Atman, then you will see that this idea of sex-distinction has vanished altogether, then only will you look upon women as the veritable manifestation of Brahman. We have seen in Shri Ramakrishna how he had this idea of divine motherhood in every woman, of whatever caste she might be, or whatever might be her worth. It is because I have seen this that I ask you all so earnestly to do likewise and open girls' schools in every village and try to uplift them. If the women are raised, then their children will by their noble actions glorify the name of the country — then will culture, knowledge, power, and devotion awaken in the land.

Disciple: But, sir, contrary results appear to have come out of the present female education. With just a smattering of education, they take merely to the Western modes of living, but it is not clear how far they are advancing in the spirit of renunciation, self-control, austerity, Brahmacharya and other qualities conducive to Brahmajnana.

Swamiji: In the beginning a few mistakes like that are unavoidable. When a new idea is preached in the country, some, failing to grasp it properly, go wrong in that way. But what matters it to the well-being of society at large? Well, those who are pioneers of the little bit of female education that now obtains in the country were undoubtedly very great-hearted. But the truth is that some defect or other must creep into that learning or culture which is not founded on a religious basis. But now female education is to be spread with religion as its centre. All other training should be secondary to religion. Religious training, the formation of character and observance of the vow of celibacy — these should be attended to. In the female education which has obtained up till now in India, it is religion that has been made a secondary concern, hence those defects you were speaking of have crept in. But no blame attaches therefore to the women. Reformers having proceeded to start female education without being Brahmacharins themselves have stumbled like that. Founders of all good undertakings, before they launch on their desired work, must attain to the knowledge of the Atman through rigorous self-discipline. Otherwise defects are bound to occur in their work.

Disciple: Yes, sir, it is observed that many educated women spend their time in reading novels and so on; but in East Bengal even with education women have not given up their religious observances. Is it so here in this part?

Swamiji: In every country, nations have their good and bad sides. Ours is to do good works in our lives and hold an example before others. No work succeeds by condemnation. It only repels people. Let anybody say what he likes, don't contradict him. In this world of Maya, whatever work you will take up will be attended with some defect. "[(Sanskrit)] — all works are covered with defects as fire is with smoke" (Gita, XVIII.48). Every fire has a chance of being attended with smoke. But will you, on that account, sit inactive? As far as you can, you must go on doing good work.

Disciple: What is this good work?

Swamiji: Whatever helps in the manifestation of Brahman is good work. Any work can be done so as to help, if not directly, at least indirectly, the manifestation of the Atman. But following the path laid down by the Rishis, that knowledge of the Atman manifests quickly; on the contrary, the doing of works which have been indicated by the scriptural writers as wrong, brings only bondage of the soul and sometimes this bondage of delusion does not vanish even in many lives. But in all ages and climes, freedom is sure to be attained by Jivas ultimately. For the Atman is the real nature of the Jiva. Can anybody give up his own nature? If you fight with your shadow for a thousand years, can you drive it away from you? — it will always remain with you.

Disciple: But, sir, according to Shankara, Karma is antagonistic to Jnana. He has variously refuted the intermingling of Jnana and Karma. So how can Karma be helpful to the manifestation of Jnana?

Swamiji: Shankara after saying so has again described Karma as indirect help to the manifestation of Jnana and the means for the purification of the mind. But I do not contradict his conclusion that in transcendent knowledge there is no touch of any work whatsoever. So long as man is within the realm of the consciousness of action, agent, and the result of action, he is powerless to sit idle without doing some work. So, as work is thus ingrained in the very nature of man, why don't you go on doing such works as are helpful to the manifestation of the knowledge of the Atman? That all work is the effect of ignorance may be true from the absolute standpoint, but within the sphere of relative consciousness it has a great utility. When you will realise the Atman, the doing or non-doing of work will be within your control, and whatever you will do in that state will be good work, conducive to the well-being of Jivas and the world. With the manifestation of Brahman, even the breath you draw will be to the good of Jiva. Then you will no longer have to work by means of conscious planning. Do you understand?

Disciple: Yes, it is a beautiful conclusion reconciling Karma and Jnana from the Vedantic standpoint.

At this time, the bell for supper rang, and the disciple, before going to partake of it, prayed with folded hands, "Bless me, sir, that I may attain to the knowledge of Brahman in this very life." Swamiji placing his hand on the disciple's head said, "Have no fear, my son. You are not like ordinary worldly men — neither householders, nor exactly Sannyasins — but quite a new type."

XIX

Swamiji is in indifferent health. At the earnest request of Swami Niranjanananda he has been taking Ayurvedic medicines for six or seven days. According to this treatment, the drinking of water is strictly forbidden. He has to appease his thirst with milk.

The disciple has come to the Math early in the day. Swamiji on seeing him spoke with affection, "Oh, you have come? Well done, I was thinking of you."

Disciple: I hear that you are living on milk for the last six or seven days.

Swamiji: Yes, at the earnest entreaty of Niranjan, I had to take to this medicine! I cannot disregard their request.

Disciple: You were in the habit of taking water very frequently. How could you give it up altogether?

Swamiji: When I heard that according to this treatment water had to be given up, I made a firm resolve immediately not to take water. Now the idea of drinking water does not even occur to the mind.

Disciple: The treatment is doing you good I hope?

Swamiji: That I don't know. I am simply obeying the orders of my brother-disciples.

Disciple: I think that indigenous drugs such as the Vaidyas use, are very well-suited to our constitution.

Swamiji: My idea is that it is better even to die under the treatment of a scientific doctor than expect recovery from the treatment of laymen who know nothing of modern science, but blindly go by the ancient books, without gaining a mastery of the subject — even though they may have cured a few cases.

Swamiji cooked certain dishes, one of which was prepared with vermicelli. When the disciple, who partook of it, asked Swamiji what it was, he replied, "It is a few English earthworms which I have brought dried from London." This created laughter among those present at the expense of the disciple. Despite his spare food and scanty sleep, Swamiji is very active. A few days ago, a new set of the Encyclopaedia Brittanica had been bought for the Math. Seeing the new shining volumes, the disciple said to Swamiji, "It is almost impossible to read all these books in a single lifetime." He was unaware that Swamiji had already finished ten volumes and had begun the eleventh.

Swamiji: What do you say? Ask me anything you like from these ten volumes, and I will answer you all.

The disciple asked in wonder, "Have you read all these books?" Swamiji: Why should I ask you to question me otherwise?

Being examined, Swamiji not only reproduced the sense, but at places the very language of the difficult topics selected from each volume. The disciple, astonished, put aside the books, saying, "This is not within human power!"

Swamiji: Do you see, simply by the observance of strict Brahmacharya (continence) all learning can be mastered in a very short time — one has an unfailing memory of what one hears or knows but once. It is owing to this want of continence that everything is on the brink of ruin in our country.

Disciple: Whatever you may say, sir, the manifestation of such superhuman power cannot be the result of mere Brahmacharya, something else there must be.

Swamiji did not say anything in reply.

Then Swamiji began to explain lucidly to the disciple the arguments and conclusions about the difficult points in all philosophies. In course of the conversation Swami Brahmananda entered the room and said to the disciple, "You are a nice man! Swamiji is unwell, and instead of trying to keep his mind cheerful by light talk, you are making him talk incessantly, raising the most abstruse subjects!" The disciple was abashed. But Swamiji said to Swami Brahmananda, "Keep your regulation of Ayurvedic treatment aside. These are my children; and if my body goes in teaching them, I don't care." After this, some light talk followed. Then arose the topic of the place of Bharatchandra in Bengali literature. From the beginning Swamiji began to ridicule Bharatchandra in various ways and satirised the life, manners, marriage-customs, and other usages of society at the time of Bharatchandra, who was an advocate of child-marriage. He expressed the opinion that the poems of Bharatchandra, being full of bad taste and obscenities, had not found acceptance in any cultured society except in Bengal, and he said, "Care should be taken that such books do not come into the hands of boys." Then raising the topic of Michael Madhusudan Dutt, he added, "That was a wonderful genius born in your province. There is not another epic in Bengali literature like the Meghnabadh, no mistake in that; and it is difficult to come across a poem like that in the whole of modern European literature."

Disciple: But, sir, I think Michael was very fond of a bombastic style.

Swamiji: Well, if anybody in your country does anything new, you at once hoot him. First examine well what he is saying, but instead of that, the people of the country will chase after anything which is not quite after the old modes. For example, in order to bring to ridicule this Meghnabadh Kavya, which is the gem of Bengali literature, the parody of Chhuchhundaribadh Kavya (The Death of a Mole) was written. They may caricature as much as they like, it does not matter. But the Meghnabadh Kavya still stands unshaken in its reputation like the Himalayas while the opinions and writings of carping critics who are busy picking holes in it have been washed away into oblivion. What will the vulgar public understand of this epic Michael has written in such a vigorous diction and an original metre? And at the present time

Girish Babu is writing wonderful books in a new metre which your overwise Pundits are criticising and finding fault with. But does G.C. care for that? People will appreciate the book afterwards.

Thus speaking on the subject of Michael he said, "Go and get the Meghnadbadh Kavya from the library downstairs." On the disciple's bringing it he said, "Now read, let me see how you can read it."

The disciple read a portion, but the reading not being to the liking of Swamiji, he took the book and showed him how to read and asked him to read again. Then he asked him, "Now, can you say which portion of the Kavya is best?" The disciple failing to answer, Swamiji said, "That portion of the book which describes how Indrajit has been killed in battle and Mandodari, beside herself with grief, is dissuading Ravana from the battle — but Ravana casting off forcibly from his mind the grief for his son is firmly resolved on battle like a great hero, and forgetting in a fury of rage and vengeance all about his wife and children, is ready to rush out for battle — that is the most finely conceived portion of the book. Come what may, I shall not forget my duty, whether the world remains or dissolves — these are the words of a great hero. Inspired by such feelings, Michael has written that portion."

Saying this, Swamiji opened the particular passage and began to read it in the most impressive manner.

XX

Swamiji is much better under the Ayurvedic treatment. The disciple is at the Math. While attending on Swamiji, he asked, "The Atman is all-pervading, the very life of the life of all beings, and so very near. Still why is It not perceived?"

Swamiji: Do you see yourself that you have eyes?

When others speak of the eyes, then you are reminded that you have got eyes. Again when dust or sand enters into them and sets up an irritation, then you feel quite well that you have got eyes. Similarly the realisation of this universal Atman which is inner than the innermost is not easily attained. Reading from scriptures or hearing from the lips of the preceptor, one has some idea of It, but when the hard lashes of the bitter sorrow and pain of the world make the heart sore, when on the death of one's near and dear relatives, man thinks himself helpless, when the impenetrable and insurmountable darkness about the future life agitates his mind, then does the Jiva pant for a realisation of the Atman. Therefore is sorrow helpful to the knowledge of the Atman. But one should remember the bitter lesson of experience. Those who die, merely suffering the woes of life like cats and dogs, are they men? He is a man who even when agitated by the sharp interaction of pleasure and pain is discriminating, and knowing them to be of an evanescent nature, becomes passionately devoted to the Atman. This is all the difference between men and animals. That which is nearest is least observed. The Atman is the nearest of the near, therefore the careless and unsteady mind of man gets no clue to It. But the man who is alert, calm, self-restrained, and discriminating, ignores the external world and diving more and more into the inner world, realises the glory of the Atman and becomes great. Then only he attains to the knowledge of the Atman and realises the truth of such scriptural texts as, "I am the Atman", "Thou art That, O Shvetaketu," and so on. Do you understand?

Disciple: Yes, sir. But why this method of attaining Self-knowledge through the path of pain and suffering? Instead of all this, it would have been well if there had been no creation at all. We were all at one time identified with Brahman. Why then this desire for creation on the path of Brahman? Why again this going forth of the Jiva (who is no other than Brahman) along the path of birth and death, amidst the interaction of the dualities of life?

Swamiji: When a man is intoxicated, he sees many hallucinations; but when the intoxication goes off, he understands them as the imaginations of a heated brain. Whatever you see of this creation which is without a beginning, but has an end, is only an effect of your state of intoxication; when that passes off, such questions will not arise at all.

Disciple: Then is there no reality in the creation, and preservation, etc. of the Universe?

Swamiji: Why should not there be? So long as you identify yourself with the body and have the ego-consciousness, all these will remain. But when you are bereft of the body-consciousness and devoted to the Atman and live in the Atman, then with respect to you none of these will remain, and such questions as whether there is any creation or birth or death will have no room. Then you will have to say — [Sanskrit] — "Where is it gone, by whom is it taken, wherein is the world merged? It was just observed by me and is it non-existent now? What a wonder!" (Vivekachudamani 483).

Disciple: If there is no knowledge of the existence of the universe, how can it be said, "Wherein is the world merged?"

Swamiji: Because one has to express the idea in language, therefore that mode of expression has been used. The author has tried to express in thought and language about the state where thought or language cannot reach, and therefore he has stated the fact that the world is wholly unreal, in a relative mode like the above. The world has no absolute reality which only belongs to Brahman, which is beyond the reach of mind and speech. Say what more you have to ask. Today I will put an end to all your arguments.

The bell of the evening service in the worship-room rang at the time, and everybody made for it. But the disciple stayed in Swamiji's room, noticing which Swamiji said, "Won't you go to the worship-room?"

Disciple: I should like to stay here.

Swamiji: All right.

After some time the disciple looking outside of the room said, "It is the new-moon night and all the quarters are overspread with darkness. It is the night for the worship of Mother Kali."

Swamiji without saying anything gazed at the eastern sky for some time and said, "Do you see what a mysterious and solemn beauty there is in this darkness!" Saying this and continuing to look at the dense mass of darkness, he stood enwrapt. After some minutes had passed, Swamiji slowly began to sing a Bengali song, "O Mother, in deep darkness flashes Thy formless beauty", etc. After the song Swamiji entered his room and sat down with an occasional word like "Mother, Mother", or "Kali, Kali", on his lips.

Uneasy at Swamiji's profoundly abstracted mood, the disciple said, "Now, sir, please speak with me."

Swamiji smilingly said, "Can you fathom the beauty and profundity of the Atman whose external manifestation is so sweet and beautiful?" The disciple wished for a change of topic, noticing which, Swamiji began another song of Kali: "O Mother, Thou flowing stream of nectar, in how many forms and aspects dost Thou play in manifestation!" After the song he said, "This Kali is Brahman in manifestation. Haven't you heard Shri Ramakrishna's illustration of the `snake moving and the snake at rest' (representing the dynamic and static aspects of the same thing)?"

Disciple: Yes, sir.

Swamiji: This time, when I get well, I shall worship the Mother with my heart's blood, then only will She be pleased. Your Raghunandan also says like that. The Mother's child shall be a hero, a Mahavira. In unhappiness, sorrow, death, and desolation, the Mother's child shall always remain fearless.

XXI

Swamiji is staying at the Math nowadays. His health is not very good, but he goes out for a walk in the mornings and evenings. The disciple, after bowing at the feet of Swamiji, inquired about his health.

Swamiji: Well, this body is in such a pitiable condition, but none of you are stepping forward to help in my work! What shall I do single-handed? This time the body has come out of the soil of Bengal, so can it bear the strain of much work? You who come here are pure souls; and if you do not become my helpers in this work, what shall I do alone?

Disciple: Sir, these self-sacrificing Brahmacharins and Sannyasins are standing behind you, and I think that each one of them can devote his life to your work — still why do you speak in this way?

Swamiji: Well, I want a band of young Bengal — who alone are the hope of this country. My hope of the future lies in the youths of character — intelligent, renouncing all for the service of others, and obedient — who can sacrifice their lives in working out my ideas and thereby do good to themselves and the country at large. Otherwise, boys of the common run are coming in groups and will come. Dullness is written on their faces — their hearts are devoid of energy, their bodies feeble and unfit for work, and minds devoid of courage. What work will be done by these? If I get ten or twelve boys with the faith of Nachiketa, I can turn the thoughts and pursuits of this country in a new channel.

Disciple: Sir, so many young men are coming to you, and do you find none among them of such a nature?

Swamiji: Among those who appear to me to be of good calibre, some have bound themselves by matrimony; some have sold themselves for the acquisition of worldly name, fame, or wealth; while some are of feeble bodies. The rest, who form the majority, are unable to receive any high idea. You are no doubt fit to receive my high ideas, but you are not able to work them out in the practical field. For these reasons sometimes an anguish comes into the mind, and I think that taking this human body, I could not do much work through untowardness of fortune. Of course, I have not yet wholly given up hope, for, by the will of God, from among these very boys may arise in time great heroes of action and spirituality who will in future work out my ideas.

Disciple: It is my firm belief that your broad and liberal ideas must find universal acceptance some day or other. For I see they are all-sided and infusing vigour into every department of thought and activity. And the people of the country are accepting, either overtly or covertly, your ideas, and teaching them to the people.

Swamiji: What matters it if they acknowledge my name or not? It is enough if they accept my ideas. Ninety-nine per cent of the Sadhus, even after renouncing lust and wealth, get bound at the last by the desire of name and fame. "Fame . . . that last infirmity of noble mind"— haven't you read? We shall have to work, giving up altogether all desire for results. People will call us both good and bad. But we shall have to work like lions, keeping the ideal before us, without caring whether "the wise ones praise or blame us".

Disciple: What ideal should we follow now?

Swamiji: You have now to make the character of Mahavira your ideal. See how at the command of Ramachandra he crossed the ocean. He had no care for life or death! He was a perfect master of his senses and wonderfully sagacious. You have now to build your life on this great ideal of personal service. Through that, all other ideals will gradually manifest in life. Obedience to the Guru without questioning, and strict observance of Brahmacharya — this is the secret of success. As on the one hand Hanuman represent the ideal of service, so on the other hand he represents leonine courage, striking the whole world with awe. He has not the least hesitation in sacrificing his life for the good of Rama. A supreme indifference to everything except the service of Rama, even to the attainment of the status of Brahma and Shiva, the great World-gods! Only the carrying out of Shri Rama's best is the one vow of this life! Such whole-hearted devotion is wanted. Playing on the Khol and Kartal and dancing in the frenzy of Kirtana has degenerated the whole people. They are, in the first place, a race of dyspeptics — and if in addition to this they dance and jump in that way, how can they bear the strain? In trying to imitate the highest Sadhana, the preliminary qualification for which is absolute purity, they have been swallowed in dire Tamas. In every district and village you may visit, you will find only the sound of the Khol and Kartal! Are not drums made in the country? Are not trumpets and kettle-drums available in India? Make the boys hear the deep-toned sound of these instruments. Hearing from boyhood the sound of these effeminate forms of music and listening to the kirtana, the country is well-nigh converted into a country of women. What more degradation can you expect? Even the poet's imagination fails to draw this picture! The Damaru[1] and horn have to be sounded, drums are to be beaten so as to raise the deep and martial notes, and with "Mahavira, Mahavira" on your lips and shouting "Hara, Hara, Vyom, Vyom", the quarters are to be reverberated. The music which awakens only the softer feelings of man is to be stopped now for some time. Stopping the light tunes such as Kheal and Tappa for some time, the people are to be accustomed to hear the Dhrupad music. Through the thunder-roll of the dignified Vedic hymns, life is to be brought back into the country. In everything the austere spirit of heroic manhood is to be revived. In following such an ideal lies the good of the people and the country. If you can build your character after such an ideal, then a thousand others will follow. But take care that you do not swerve an inch from the ideal. Never lose heart. In eating, dressing, or lying, in singing or playing, in enjoyment or disease, always manifest the highest moral courage. Then only will you attain the grace of Mahashakti, the Divine Mother.

Disciple: Sir, at times I am overcome by low spirits, I don't know how.

Swamiji: Then think like this: "Whose child am I? I associate with him and shall I have such weak-mindedness and lowness of spirits?" Stamping down such weakness of mind and heart, stand up, saying, "I am possessed of heroism — I am possessed of a steady intellect — I am a knower of Brahman, a man of illumination." Be fully conscious of your dignity by remembering, "I am the disciple of such and such who is the companion-in-life of Shri Ramakrishna, the conqueror of lust and wealth." This will produce a good effect. He who has not this pride has no awakening of Brahman within him. Haven't you heard Ramprasad's song? He used to say, "Whom do I fear in the world, whose sovereign is the Divine Mother!" Keep such a pride always awake in the mind. Then weakness of mind and heart will no longer be able to approach you. Never allow weakness to overtake your mind. Remember Mahavira, remember the Divine Mother! And you will see that all weakness, all cowardice will vanish at once.

Saying these words, Swamiji came downstairs and took his accustomed seat on a cot in the courtyard. Then, addressing the assembled Sannyasins and

---

1. An hour-glass-shaped drum, held in Shiva's hand.

Brahmacharins, he said, "Here is the unveiled presence of Brahman. Fie upon those who disregarding It set their mind on other things! Ah! here is Brahman as palpable as a fruit in one's palm. Don't you see? Here!"

These words were spoken in such an appealing way, that every one stood motionless like a figure painted on canvas and felt as if he were suddenly drawn into the depth of meditation. . . . After some time that tension of feeling passed and they regained their normal consciousness.

Next, in the course of a walk, Swamiji spoke to the disciple. "Did you see how everybody had become concentrated today? These are all children of Shri Ramakrishna, and on the very uttering of the words, they felt the truth."

Disciple: Sir, not to speak of them, even my heart was overflowing with an unearthly bliss! But now it appears like a vanished dream.

Swamiji: Everything will come in time. Now, go on working. Set yourself to some work for the good of men sunk in ignorance and delusion. You will see that such experiences will come of themselves.

Disciple: I feel nervous to enter into its labyrinths — neither have I the strength. The scriptures also say, "Impenetrable is the path of Karma".

Swamiji: What do you wish to do then?

Disciple: To live and hold discussion with one like you, who has realised the truth of all scriptures and through hearing, thinking, and meditating on the Truth to realise Brahman in this very life. I have no enthusiasm, nor perhaps the strength, for anything else.

Swamiji: If you love that, well, you can go on doing it. And speak about your thoughts and conclusions about the Shastras to others, it will benefit them. So long as there is the body, one cannot live without doing some work or other; therefore one should do such work as is conducive to the good of others. Your own realisations and conclusions about scriptural truths may benefit many a seeker after Truth. Put them into writing which may help many others.

Disciple: First let me realise the Truth, then I shall write. Shri Ramakrishna used to say; "Without the badge of authority, none will listen to you."

Swamiji: There may be many in the world who have got stuck in that stage of spiritual discipline and reasoning through which you are passing, without being able to pass beyond that stage. Your experience and way of thinking, if recorded, may be of benefit to them at least. If you put down in easy language the substance of the discussions which you hold with the Sadhus of this Math, it may help many.

Disciple: Since you wish it, I shall try to do it.

Swamiji: What is the good of that spiritual practice or realisation which does not benefit others, does not conduce to the well-being of people sunk in ignorance and delusion, does not help in rescuing them from the clutches of lust and wealth? Do you think, so long as one Jiva endures in bondage, you will have any liberation? So long as he is not liberated — it may take several lifetimes — you will have to be born to help him, to make him realise Brahman. Every Jiva is part of yourself — which is the rationale of all work for others. As you desire the whole-hearted good of your wife and children, knowing them to be your own, so when a like amount of love and attraction for every Jiva will awaken in you, then I shall know that Brahman is awakening in you, not a moment before. When this feeling of the all-round good of all without respect for caste or colour will awaken in your heart, then I shall know you are advancing towards the ideal.

Disciple: Sir, it is a most tremendous statement that without the salvation of all, there shall be no salvation for an individual! I have never heard of such a wonderful proposition.

Swamiji: There is a class of Vedantists who hold such a view. They say that individual liberation is not the real and perfect form of liberation, but universal and collective liberation is true Mukti. Of course, both merits and defects can be pointed out in that view.

Disciple: According to Vedanta, the state of individualised existence is the root of bondage, and the Infinite Intelligence, through desires and effects of works, appears bound in that limiting condition. When by means of discrimination that limiting condition vanishes and the Jiva is bereft of all adjuncts, then how can there be bondage for the Atman which is of the essence of transcendent Intelligence? He for whom the idea of the Jiva and the world is a persisting reality may think that without the liberation of all he has no liberation. But when the mind becomes bereft of all limiting adjuncts and is merged in Brahman, where is there any differentiation for him? So nothing can operate as a bar to his Mukti.

Swamiji: Yes, what you say is right, and most Vedantins hold that view, which is also flawless. In that view, individual liberation is not barred. But just consider the greatness of his heart who thinks that he will take the whole universe with him to liberation!

Disciple: Sir, it may indicate boldness of heart, but it is not supported by the scriptures.

Swamiji was in an abstracted mood and did not listen to the words. After some time he said: "Day and night think and meditate on Brahman, meditate with great one-pointedness of mind. And during the time of awakeness to outward life, either do some work for the sake of others or repeat in your mind, 'Let good happen to Jivas and the world!' 'Let the mind of all flow in the direction of Brahman!' Even by such continuous current of thought the world will be benefited. Nothing good in the world becomes fruitless, be it work or thought. Your thought-currents will perhaps rouse the religious feeling of someone in America."

Disciple: Sir, please bless me that my mind may be concentrated on the Truth.

Swamiji: So it will be. If you have earnestness of desire, it will certainly be.

XXII

At the time Belur Math was established, many among the orthodox Hindus were wont to make sharp criticism of the ways of life in the Math. Hearing the report of such criticism from the disciple, Swamiji would say (in the words of the couplet of Tulasidas), "The elephant passes in the market-place, and a thousand curs begin barking after him; so the Sadhus have no ill-feeling when worldly people slander then." Or again he would say, "Without persecution no beneficent idea can enter into the heart of a society." He would exhort everybody, "Go on working without an eye to results. One day you are sure to reap the fruits of it." Again, on the lips of Swamiji were very often heard the words of the Gita, "A doer of good never comes to grief, my son."

In May or June, 1901, seeing the disciple at the Math Swamiji said, "Bring me a copy of Ashtavimshati-tattva (Twenty-eight Categories) of Raghunandan at an early date."

Disciple: Yes, sir, but what will you do with the Raghunandan Smriti, which the present educated India calls a heap of superstition?

Swamiji: Why? Raghunandan was a wonderful scholar of his time. Collecting the ancient Smritis, he codified the customs and observances of the Hindus, adapting them to the needs of the changed times and circumstances. All Bengal is following the rules laid down by him. But in the iron grip of his rules regulating the life of a Hindu from conception to death, the Hindu society was much oppressed. In matters of eating and sleeping, in even the ordinary functions of life, not to speak of the important ones, he tried to regulate every one by rules. In the altered circumstances of the times, that did not last long. At all times in all countries the Karma-kanda, comprising the social customs and observances, changes form. Only the Jnana-kanda endures. Even in the Vedic age you find that the rituals gradually changed in form. But the philosophic portion of the Upanishads has remained unchanged up till now — only there have been many interpreters, that is all.

Disciple: What will do you with the Smriti of Raghunandan?

Swamiji: This time I have a desire to celebrate the Durga Puja (worship of goddess Durga). If the expenses are forthcoming, I shall worship the Mahamaya. Therefore I have a mind to read the ceremonial forms of that worship. When you come to the Math next Sunday, you must bring a copy of the book with you.

Disciple: All right, sir.

Next Saturday the disciple brought a copy of the book, and Swamiji was much pleased to get it. Meeting the disciple a week after this he said, "I have finished the Raghunandan Smriti presented by you. If possible, I shall celebrate the Puja of the Divine Mother."

The Durga Puja took place with great eclat at the proper time.

Shortly after this Swamiji performed a Homa before the Mother Kali at Kalighat. Referring this incident he spoke to the disciple, "Well, I was glad to see that there was yet a liberality of view at Kalighat. The temple authorities did not object in the least to my entering the temple, though they knew that I was a man who had returned from the West. On the contrary, they very cordially took me into the holy precincts and helped me to worship the Mother to my heart's content."

XXIII

Today is the anniversary celebration of Shri Ramakrishna — the last that Swamiji ever saw. The disciple presented an invocatory hymn on Shri Ramakrishna to Swamiji. He then proceeded to rub Swamiji's feet gently. Before starting to read the poem, Swamiji spoke to him: "Do it very gently as the feet have become very tender."

After reading the poem Swamiji said, "It is well done."

Swamiji's illness had increased so much that the disciple, observing it, felt sore at heart. Understanding his inner feeling, Swamiji said, "What are you thinking? This body is born and it will die. If I have been able to instil a few of my ideas into you all, then I shall know that my birth has not been in vain."

Disciple: Are we fit objects of your mercy? If you bless me, without taking my fitness into consideration, then I will consider myself fortunate.

Swamiji: Always remember that renunciation is the root idea. Unless one is initiated into this idea, not even Brahma and the World-gods have the power to attain Mukti.

Disciple: It is a matter of deep regret that even hearing this from you almost every day, I have not been able to realise it.

Swamiji: Renunciation must come, but in the fulness of time. "[(Sanskrit)] — in the fulness of time one attains to knowledge within himself." When the few Samskaras (tendencies) of the previous life are spent, then renunciation sprouts up in the heart.

After some time he said, "Why should you go outside and see the big concourse of people? Stay with me now. And ask Niranjan to sit at the door, so that nobody may disturb me today."

Then the following conversation took place between Swamiji and the disciple:

Swamiji: I think that it will be better if from now the anniversary is celebrated in a different way. The celebration should extend to four or five days instead of one. On the first day, there may be study and interpretation of scriptures; on the second, discussion on the Vedas and the Vedanta and the solution of the problems in connection with them; on the third day, there may be a question class. The fourth day may be fixed for lectures. On the last day, there will be a festival on the present lines. This will be like the Durga Puja extending over four or five days. Of course, if the celebration is on the above lines, none but the devotees of Shri Ramakrishna will be able to attend on the other days except the last. But that does not matter. A large promiscuous crowd of people does not mean a great propagation of the message of Shri Ramakrishna.

Disciple: Sir, it is a beautiful idea. Next time it will be done according to your wishes.

Swamiji: Now, my son, you all will carry them out. I have no more inclination for these things.

Disciple: Sir, this year many Kirtana parties have come.

Hearing these words Swamiji stood up holding the iron bars of the window and looked at the assembled crowd of devotees. After some time he sat down.

Swamiji: You are the actors in the Divine Lila (play) of Shri Ramakrishna. After this, not to speak of ours, people will take your names also. These hymns which you are writing will afterwards be read by people for the acquirement of love and knowledge. Know that the attainment of the knowledge of the Atman is the highest object of life. If you have devotion for the Avataras who are the world-teachers, that knowledge will manifest of itself in time.

Disciple: Sir, shall I attain to such knowledge?

Swamiji: By the blessings of Shri Ramakrishna you shall attain to divine love and knowledge. You will not find much happiness in the worldly life.

Disciple: Sir, if you condescend to destroy the weakness of my mind, then only there is hope for me.

Swamiji: What fear! When you have chanced to come here, you shall be free.

Disciple (with great entreaty): You must save me and lift me from ignorance in this very life.

Swamiji: Say, who can save anybody? The Guru can only take away some covering veils. When these veils are removed, the Atman shines in Its own glory and manifests like the sun.

Disciple: Then why do we find mention of grace in the scriptures?

Swamiji: Grace means this. He who has realised the Atman becomes a storehouse of great power. Making him the centre and with a certain radius a circle is formed, and whoever comes within the circle becomes animated with the ideas of that saint, i.e. they are overwhelmed by his ideas. Thus without much religious striving, they inherit the results of his wonderful spirituality. If you call this grace, you may do so.

Disciple: Is there no other grace than this?

Swamiji: Yes, there is. When the Avatara comes, then with him are born liberated persons as helpers in his world-play. Only Avataras have the power to dispel the darkness of a million souls and give them salvation in one life. This is known as grace. Do you understand?

Disciple: Yes, sir. But what is the way for those who have not been blessed with the sight of him?

Swamiji: The way for them is to call on him. Calling on him, many are blessed with his vision — can see him in human form just like ours and obtain his grace.

Disciple: Have you ever had a vision of Shri Ramakrishna after his passing away?

Swamiji: After leaving the body, I associated for some time with Pavhari Baba of Ghazipur. There was a garden not far distant from his Ashrama where I lived. People used to say it was a haunted garden, but as you know, I am a sort of demon myself and have not much fear of ghosts. In the garden there were many lemon trees which bore numerous fruits. At that time I was suffering from diarrhoea, and there no food could be had except bread. So, to increase the digestive powers, I used to take plenty of lemons. Mixing with Pavhari Baba, I liked him very much, and he also came to love me deeply. One day I thought that I did not learn any art for making this weak body strong, even though I lived with Shri Ramakrishna for so many years. I had heard that Pavhari Baba knew the science of Hatha-yoga. So I thought I would learn the practices of Hatha-yoga from him, and through them strengthen the body. You know, I have a dogged resolution, and whatever I set my heart on, I always carry out. On the eve of the day on which I was to take initiation, I was lying on a cot thinking; and just then I saw the form of Sri Ramakrishna standing on my right side, looking steadfastly at me, as if very much grieved. I had dedicated myself to him, and at the thought that I was taking another Guru I was much ashamed and kept looking at him. Thus perhaps two or three hours passed, but no words escaped from my mouth. Then he disappeared all on a sudden. My mind became upset seeing Shri Ramakrishna that night, so I postponed the idea of initiation from Pavhari Baba for the day. After a day or two again the idea of initiation from Pavhari Baba arose in the mind — and again in the night there was the appearance of Shri Ramakrishna as on the previous occasion. Thus when for several nights in succession I had the vision of Shri Ramakrishna, I gave up the idea of initiation altogether, thinking that as every time I resolved on it, I was getting such a vision, then no good but harm would come from it.

After some time he addressed the disciple, saying, "Those who have seen Shri Ramakrishna are really blessed. Their family and birth have become purified by it. All of you will also get his vision. The very fact that you have come here, shows that you are very near to him. Nobody has been able to understand who came on earth as Sri Ramakrishna. Even his own nearest devotees have got no real clue to it. Only some have got a little inkling of it. All will understand it afterwards."

The conversation was thus going on when Swami Niranjanananda knocked at the door. The disciple rose and inquired, "Who has come?" Swami Niranjanananda replied, "Sister Nivedita and some other English ladies." They were admitted into the room, sat on the floor and inquired about the health of Swamiji. After a few more words they went away. Then Swamiji said to the disciple, "See how cultured they are! If they were Bengalis, they would have made me talk at least for half an hour, even though they found me unwell."

It is about half past two now, and there is a great gathering of people outside. Understanding the disciple's mind, Swamiji said, "Just go and have a look round — but come back soon."

XXIV

After returning from Eastern Bengal Swamiji stayed in the Math and lived a simple childlike life. Every year some Santal labourers used to work in the Math. Swamiji would joke and make fun with them and loved to hear their tales of weal and woe. One day several noted gentlemen of Calcutta came to visit Swamiji in the Math. That day Swamiji had started such a warm talk with the Santals that, when he was informed of the arrival of those gentlemen, he said, "I shan't be able to go now. I am happy with these men." Really that day Swamiji did not leave the poor Santals to see those visitors.

One among the Santals was named Keshta. Swamiji loved Keshta very much. Whenever Swamiji came to talk with them, Keshta used to say to Swamiji, "O my Swamiji, do not come to us when we are working, for while talking with you our work stops and the supervising Swami rebukes us afterwards." Swamiji would be touched by these words and say, "No, no, he will not say anything; tell me a little about your part of the country"— saying which he used to introduce the topic of their worldly affairs.

One day Swamiji said to Keshta, "Well, will you take food here one day?" Keshta said, "We do not take food touched by you; if you put salt in our food and we eat it, we shall lose our caste." Swamiji said, "Why should you take salt? We will prepare curry for you without salt, will you then take it?" Keshta agreed to it. Then at orders of Swamiji, bread, curry, sweets, curd, etc. were arranged for the Santals, and he made them sit before him to eat. While eating, Keshta said, "Whence have you got such a thing? We never tasted anything like this." Feeding them sumptuously, Swamiji said, "You are Narayanas, God manifest; today I have offered food to Narayana." The service of "Daridra Narayana"— god in the poor — about which Swamiji spoke, he himself performed one day like this.

After their meal, the Santals went for rest, and Swamiji, addressing the disciple, said, "I found them the veritable embodiment of God — such simplicity, such sincere guileless love I have seen nowhere else." Then, addressing the Sannyasins of the Math, he said, "See how simple they are. Can you mitigate their misery a little? Otherwise, of what good is the wearing of the Gerua robe? Sacrifice of everything for the good of others is real Sannyasa. They have never enjoyed any good thing in life. Sometimes I feel a desire to sell the Math and everything, and distribute the money to the poor and destitute. We have made the tree our shelter. Alas! the people of the country cannot get anything to eat, and how can we have the heart to raise food to our mouths? When I was in the Western countries, I prayed to the Divine Mother, "People here are sleeping on a bed of flowers, they eat all kinds of delicacies, and what do they not enjoy, while people in our country are dying of starvation. Mother, will there be no way for them! One of the objects of my going to the West to preach religion was to see if I could find any means for feeding the people of this country. "Seeing the poor people of our country starving for food, a desire comes to me to overthrow all ceremonial worship and learning, and go round from village to village collecting money from the rich by convincing them through force of character and Sadhana, and to spend the whole life in serving the poor. "Alas! nobody thinks of the poor of this land. They are the backbone of the country, who by their labour are producing food — these poor people, the sweepers and labourers, who if they stop work for one day will create a panic in the town. But there is none to sympathise with them, none to console them in their misery. Just see, for want of sympathy from the Hindus, thousands of Pariahs in Madras are turning Christians. Don't think this is simply due to the pinch of hunger; it is because they do not get any sympathy from us. We are day and night calling out to them, 'Don't touch us! Don't touch us!' Is there any compassion or kindliness of heart in the country? Only a class of 'Don't-touchists'; kick such customs out! I sometimes feel the urge to break the barriers of 'Don't-touchism', to go at once and call out, 'Come, all who are poor, miserable, wretched, and down-trodden', and to bring them all together in the name of Shri Ramakrishna. Unless they rise, the Mother won't awaken. We could not make any provision for food and clothes for these — what have we done then? Alas! they know nothing of worldliness, and therefore even after working day and night cannot provide themselves with food and clothes. Let us open their eyes. I see clear as daylight that there is the one Brahman in all, in them and in me — one Shakti dwells in all. The only difference is of manifestation. Unless the blood circulates over the whole body, has any country risen at any time? If one limb is paralysed, then even with the other limbs whole, not much can be done with that body — know this for certain."

Disciple: Sir, there is such a diversity of religions and ideas among the people of this country that it is a difficult affair to bring harmony among them.

Swamiji (in anger): If you think any work difficult, then do not come here. Through the grace of God all paths become easy. Your work is to serve the poor and miserable, without any distinction of caste or colour, and you have no need to think about the results. Your duty is to go on working, and then everything will follow of itself. My method of work is to construct and not to pull down. Read the history of the world, and you will find that a great soul stood as the central figure in a certain period of a country. Animated by his ideas, hundreds of people did good to the world. You are all intelligent boys, and have been coming here for a long time. Say, what have you done? Couldn't you give one life for the service of others? In the next life you may read Vedanta and other philosophies. Give this life for the service of others, then I shall know that your coming here has not been in vain.

Saying these words, Swamiji sat silent, wrapt in deep thought. After some time, he added, "After so much austerity, I have understood this as the real truth — god is present in every Jiva; there is no other God besides that. 'Who serves Jiva, serves God indeed'." After some pause Swamiji, addressing the disciple, said, "What I have told you today, inscribe in your heart. See that you do not forget it."

XXV

It was Saturday, and the disciple came to the Math just before evening. An austere routine was being followed now at the Math regarding spiritual practices. Swamiji had issued an order that all Brahmacharins and Sannyasins should get up very early in the morning and practise Japa and meditation in the worship-room. Swamiji was having little sleep during these days, and would rise from bed at three in the morning.

On the disciple saluting Swamiji just after his appearance at the Math, he said, "Well, see how they are practising religious exercises here nowadays. Everyone passes a considerable time in Japa and meditation on mornings and evenings. Look there — a bell has been procured, which is used for rousing all from sleep. Everyone has to get up before dawn. Shri Ramakrishna used to say, 'In the morning and evening the mind remains highly imbued with Sattva ideas; those are the times when one should meditate with earnestness.' "After the passing away of Shri Ramakrishna we underwent a lot of religious practice at the Baranagore Math. We used to get up at 3 a.m. and after washing our face etc.— some after bath, and others without it — we would sit in the worship-room and become absorbed in Japa and meditation. What a strong spirit of dispassion we had in those days! We had no thought even as to whether the world existed or not. Ramakrishnananda busied himself day and night with the duties pertaining to Shri Ramakrishna's worship and service, and occupied the same position in the Math as the mistress of the house does in a family. It was he who would procure, mostly by begging, the requisite articles for Shri Ramakrishna's worship and our subsistence. There have been days when the Japa and meditation continued from morning till four or five in the afternoon. Ramakrishnananda waited and waited with our meals ready, till at last he would come and snatch us from our meditation by sheer force. Oh, what a wonderful constancy of devotion we have noticed in him!"

Disciple: Sir, how did you use to meet the Math expenses then?

Swamiji: What a question! Well, we were Sadhus, and what would come by begging and other means, would be utilised for defraying the Math expenses. Today both Suresh Babu (Surendra Nath Mitra) and Balaram Babu are no more; had they been alive they would have been exceedingly glad to see this Math. You have doubtless heard Suresh Babu's name. It was he who used to bear all the expenses of the Baranagore Math. It was this Suresh Mitra who used to think most for us in those days. His devotion and faith have no parallel!

Disciple; Sir, I have heard that you did not see him very often while he was dying.

Swamiji: We could only do so if we were allowed (by his relatives). Well, it is a long tale. But know this for certain that among worldly people it is of little count to your relatives and kinsmen whether you live or die. If you succeed in leaving some property, you will find even in your lifetime that there has been set up a brawl over it in your household. You will have no one to console you in your deathbed — not even your wife and sons! Such is the way of the world!

Referring to the past condition of the Math, Swamiji went on, "Owing to want of funds I would sometimes fight for abolishing the Math altogether. But I could never induce Ramakrishnananda to accede to the proposal. Know Ramakrishnananda to be the central figure of the Math. There have been days when the Math was without a grain of food. If some rice was collected by begging, there was no salt to take it with! On some days there would be only rice and salt, but nobody cared for it in the least. We were then being carried away by a tidal wave of spiritual practice. Boiled Bimba leaves, rice, and salt — this was the menu for a month at a stretch. Oh, those wonderful days! The austerities of that period were enough to dismay supernatural beings, not to speak of men. But it is a tremendous truth that if there be real worth in you, the more are circumstances against you, the more will that inner power manifest itself. But the reason why I have provided for beds and a tolerable living in this Math is that the Sannyasins that are enrolling themselves nowadays will not be able to bear so much strain as we did. There was the life of Shri Ramakrishna before us, and that was why we did not care much for privations and hardships. Boys of this generation will not be able to undergo so much hardship. Hence it is that I have provided for some sort of habitation and a bare subsistence for them. If they get just enough food and clothing, the boys will devote themselves to religious practice and will learn to sacrifice their lives for the good of humanity."

Disciple: Sir, outside people say a good deal against this sort of bedding and furniture.

Swamiji: Let them say. Even in jest they will at least once think of this Math. And they say, it is easier to attain liberation through cherishing a hostile spirit. Shri Ramakrishna used to say, "Men should be ignored like worms." Do you mean we have to conduct ourselves according to the chance opinion of others? Pshaw!

Disciple: Sir, you sometimes say, "All are Narayanas, the poor and the needy are my Narayanas", and again you say, "Men should be ignored like worms." What do you really mean?

Swamiji: Well, there is not the least doubt that all are Narayanas. But all Narayanas do not criticise the furniture of the Math. I shall go on working for the good of men, without caring in the least for the criticisms of others — it is in this sense that the expression, "Men are to be ignored like worms", has been used. He who has a dogged determination like that shall have everything. Only some may have it sooner, and others a little later, that is all. But one is bound to reach the goal. It is because we had such a determination that we have attained the little that we have. Otherwise, what dire days of privation we have had to pass through! One day, for want of food I fainted in the outer platform of a house on the roadside and quite a shower of rain had passed over my head before I recovered my senses! Another day, I had to do odd jobs in Calcutta for the whole day without food, and had my meal on my return to the Math at ten or eleven in the night. And these were not solitary instances.

Saying these words, Swamiji sat for a while pursuing some trend of thought. Then he resumed:

Real monasticism is not easy to attain. There is no order of life so rigorous as this. If you stumble ever so little, you are hurled down a precipice — and are smashed to pieces. One day I was travelling on foot from Agra to Vrindaban. There was not a farthing with me. I was about a couple of miles from Vrindaban when I found a man smoking on the roadside, and I was seized with a desire to smoke. I said to the man, "Hallo, will you let me have a puff at your Chillum?" He seemed to be hesitating greatly and said, "Sire, I am a sweeper." Well, there was the influence of old Samskaras, and I immediately stepped back and resumed my journey without smoking. I had gone a short distance when the thought occurred to me that I was a Sannyasin, who had renounced caste, family, prestige, and everything — and still I drew back as soon as the man gave himself out as a sweeper, and could not smoke at the Chillum touched by him! The thought made me restless at heart; then I had walked on half a mile. Again I retraced my steps and came to the sweeper whom I found still sitting there. I hastened to tell him, "Do prepare a Chillum of tobacco for me, my dear friend." I paid no heed to his objections and insisted on having it. So the man was compelled to prepare a Chillum for me. Then I gladly had a puff at it and proceeded to Vrindaban. When one has embraced the monastic life, one has to test whether one has gone beyond the prestige of caste and birth, etc. It is so difficult to observe the monastic vow in right earnest! There must not be the slightest divergence between one's words and actions.

Disciple: Sir, you sometimes hold before us the

householder's ideal and sometimes the ideal of the Sannyasin. Which one are we to adopt?

Swamiji: Well, go on listening to all. Then stick to that one which appeals to you — grip it hard like a bulldog.

Swamiji came downstairs accompanied by the disciple, while speaking these words, and began to pace to and fro, uttering now and then the name of Shiva or humming a song on the Divine Mother, such as, "Who knows how diversely Thou playest, O Mother, Thou flowing stream of nectar", and so on.

XXVI

The disciple passed the preceding night in Swamiji's room. At 4 a.m. Swamiji roused him and said "Go and knock up the Sadhus and Brahmacharins from sleep with the bell." In pursuance of the order, the disciple rang the bell near the Sadhus who slept. The monastic inmates hastened to go to the worship-room for meditation.

According to Swamiji's instructions, the disciple rang the bell lustily near Swami Brahmananda's bed, which made the latter exclaim, "Good heavens! The Bangal[1] has made it too hot for us to stay in the Math!" On the disciple's communicating this to

---

1. Meaning an East Bengal man, used as a term of endearing reproach for the disciple.

Swamiji, he burst out into a hearty laugh, saying, "Well done!"

Then Swamiji, too, washed his face and entered the chapel accompanied by the disciple.

The Sannyasins — swami Brahmananda and others — were already seated for meditation. A separate seat was kept for Swamiji, on which he sat facing the east, and pointing to a seat in front to the disciple, said, "Go and meditate, sitting there."

Shortly after taking his seat, Swamiji became perfectly calm and motionless, like a statue, and his breathing became very slow. Everyone else kept his seat.

After about an hour and a half, Swamiji rose from meditation with the words "Shiva, Shiva". His eyes were flushed, the expression placid, calm, and grave. Bowing before Shri Ramakrishna he came downstairs and paced the courtyard of the Math. After a while he said to the disciple. "Do you see how the Sadhus are practising meditation etc. nowadays? When the meditation is deep, one sees many wonderful things. While meditating at the Baranagore Math, one day I saw the nerves Ida and Pingala. One can see them with a little effort. Then, when one has a vision of the Shushumna, one can see anything one likes. If a man has unflinching devotion to the Guru, spiritual practices — meditation, Japa, and so forth — come quite naturally; one need not struggle for them. 'The Guru is Brahma, the Guru is Vishnu, and the Guru is Shiva Himself.'"

Then the disciple prepared tobacco for Swamiji and when he returned with it, Swamiji spoke as he puffed at it, "Within there is the lion — the eternally pure, illumined, and ever free Atman; and directly one realises Him through meditation and concentration, this world of Maya vanishes. He is equally present in all; and the more one practises, the quicker does the Kundalini (the 'coiled-up' power) awaken in him. When this power reaches the head, one's vision is unobstructed — one realises the Atman."

Disciple: Sir, I have only read of these things in the scriptures, but nothing has been realised as yet.

Swamiji: कालेत्मनि वनिदति — it is bound to come in time. But some attain this early, and others are a little late. One must stick to it — determined never to let it go. This is true manliness. You must keep the mind fixed on one object, like an unbroken stream of oil. The ordinary man's mind is scattered on different objects, and at the time of meditation, too, the mind is at first apt to wander. But let any desire whatever arise in the mind, you must sit calmly and watch what sort of ideas are coming. By continuing to watch in that way, the mind becomes calm, and there are no more thought-waves in it. These waves represent the thought-activity of the mind. Those things that you have previously thought deeply, have transformed themselves into a subconscious current, and therefore these come up in the mind in meditation. The rise of these waves, or thoughts, during meditation is an evidence that your mind is tending towards concentration. Sometimes the mind is concentrated on a set of ideas — this is called meditation with Vikalpa or oscillation. But when the mind becomes almost free from all activities, it melts in the inner Self, which is the essence of infinite Knowledge, One, and Itself Its own support. This is what is called Nirvikalpa Samadhi, free from all activities. In Shri Ramakrishna we have again and again noticed both these forms of Samadhi. He had not to struggle to get these states. They came to him spontaneously, then and there. It was a wonderful phenomenon. It was by seeing him that we could rightly understand these things. Meditate every day alone. Everything will open up of itself. Now the Divine Mother — the embodiment of illumination — is sleeping within, hence you do not understand this. She is the Kundalini. When, before meditating, you proceed to "purify the nerves", you must mentally strike hard on the Kundalini in the Muladhara (sacral plexus), and repeat, "Arise, Mother, arise!" One must practise these slowly. During meditation, suppress the emotional side altogether. This is a great source of danger. Those that are very emotional no doubt have their Kundalini rushing quickly upwards, but it is as quick to come down as to go up. And when it does come down, it leaves the devotee in a state of utter ruin. It is for this reason that Kirtanas and other auxiliaries to emotional development have a great drawback. It is true that by dancing and jumping, etc. through a momentary impulse, that power is made to course upwards, but it is never enduring. On the contrary when it traces back its course, it rouses violent lust in the individual. Listening to my lectures in America, through temporary excitement many among the audience used to get into an ecstatic state, and some would even become motionless like statues. But on inquiry I afterwards found that many of them had an excess of the carnal instinct immediately after that state. But this happens simply owing to a lack of steady practice in meditation and concentration.

Disciple: Sir, in no scriptures have I ever read these secrets of spiritual practice. Today I have heard quite new things.

Swamiji: Do you think the scriptures contain all the secrets of spiritual practice? These are being handed down secretly through a succession of Gurus and disciples. Practise meditation and concentration with the utmost care. Place fragrant flowers in front and burn incense. At the outset take such external help as will make the mind pure. As you repeat the name of your Guru and Ishta, say, "Peace be to all creatures and the universe!" First send impulses of these good wishes to the north, south, east, west, above, below — in all directions, and then sit down to meditate. One has to do this during the early stages. Then sitting still (you may face in any direction), meditate in the way I have taught you while initiating. Don't leave out a single day. If you have too much pressing work, go through the spiritual exercises for at least a quarter of an hour. Can you reach the goal without steadfast devotion, my son?

Now Swamiji went upstairs, and as he did so, he said, "You people will have your spiritual insight opened without much trouble. Now that you have chanced to come here, you have liberation and all under your thumb. Besides practising meditation, etc., set yourselves heart and soul to remove to a certain extent the miseries of the world, so full of wails. Through hard austerities I have almost ruined this body. There is hardly any energy left in this pack of bones and flesh. You set yourselves to work now, and let me rest a while. If you fail to do anything else, well, you can tell the world at large about the scriptural truths you have studied so long. There is no higher gift than this, for the gift of knowledge is the highest gift in the world."

XXVII

Swamiji was now staying at the Math. The disciple came to the Math and towards the evening accompanied Swamiji and Swami Premananda for a walk. Finding Swamiji absorbed in thought, the disciple entered into a conversation with Swami Premananda on what Shri Ramakrishna used to say of Swamiji's greatness. After walking some distance Swamiji turned to go back to the Math. Seeing Swami Premananda and the disciple near by, he said, "Well, what were you talking?" The disciple said, "We were talking about Shri Ramakrishna and his words." Swamiji only heard the reply, but again lapsed into thought and walking along the road returned to the Math. He sat on the camp-cot placed under the mango-tree and, resting there some time, washed his face and then, pacing the upper verandah, spoke to the disciple thus: "Why do you not set about propagating Vedanta in your part of the country? There Tantrikism prevails to a fearful extent. Rouse and agitate the country with the lion-roar of Advaitavada (monism). Then I shall know you to be a Vedantist. First open a Sanskrit school there and teach the Upanishads and the Brahma-sutras. Teach the boys the system of Brahmacharya. I have heard that in your country there is much logic-chopping of the Nyaya school. What is there in it? Only Vyapti (pervasiveness) and Anumana (inference)— on these subjects the Pandits of the Nyaya school discuss for months! What does it help towards the Knowledge of the Atman? Either in your village or Nag Mahashaya's, open a Chatushpathi (indigenous school) in which the scriptures will be studied and also the life and teachings of Shri Ramakrishna. In this way you will advance your own good as well as the good of the people, and your fame will endure.

Disciple: Sir, I cherish no desire for name or fame.

Only, sometimes I feel to do as you are saying. But by marriage I have got so entangled in the world that I fear my desire will always remain in the mind only.

Swamiji: What if you have married? As you are maintaining your parents and brothers with food and clothing, so do for your wife likewise; and by giving her religious instruction draw her to your path. Think her to be a partner and helper in the living of your religious life. At other times look upon her with an even eye with others. Thinking thus all the unsteadiness of the mind will die out. What fear?

The disciple felt assured by these words. After his meal, Swamiji sat on his own bed, and the disciple had an opportunity of doing some personal service for him.

Swamiji began to speak to the disciple, enjoining him to be reverential to the Math members: "These children of Shri Ramakrishna whom you see, are wonderful Tyagis (selfless souls), and by service to them you will attain to the purification of mind and be blessed with the vision of the Atman. You remember the words of the Gita: `By interrogation and service to the great soul'. Therefore you must serve them, by which you will attain your goal; and you know how much they love you."

Disciple: But I find it very difficult to understand them. Each one seems to be of a different type.

Swamiji: Shri Ramakrishna was a wonderful gardener. Therefore he has made a bouquet of different flowers and formed his Order. All different types and ideas have come into it, and many more will come. Shri Ramakrishna used to say, "Whoever has prayed to God sincerely for one day, must come here." Know each of those who are here to be of great spiritual power. Because they remain shrivelled before me, do not think them to be ordinary souls. When they will go out, they will be the cause of the awakening of spirituality in people. Know them to be part of the spiritual body of Shri Ramakrishna, who was the embodiment of infinite religious ideas. I look upon them with that eye. See, for instance, Brahmananda, who is here — even I have not the spirituality which he has. Shri Ramakrishna looked upon him as his mind-born son; and he lived and walked, ate and slept with him. He is the ornament of our Math — our king. Similarly Premananda, Turiyananda, Trigunatitananda, Akhandananda, Saradananda, Ramakrishnananda, Subodhananda, and others; you may go round the world, but it is doubtful if you will find men of such spirituality and faith in God like them. They are each a centre of religious power, and in time that power will manifest.

The disciple listened in wonder, and Swamiji said again: "But from your part of the country, except Nag Mahashaya none came to Shri Ramakrishna. A few others who saw Shri Ramakrishna could not appreciate him." At the thought of Nag Mahashaya, Swamiji kept silent for some time. It was only four or five months since he had passed away. Swamiji had heard that on one occasion a spring of Ganga water rose in the house of Nag Mahashaya, and recollecting this he asked the disciple, "Well, how did that event take place? Tell me about it."

Disciple: I only heard about it, but did not see it with my own eyes. I heard that in a Mahavaruni Yoga Nag Mahashaya started with his father for Calcutta.

But not getting any accommodation in the railway train he stayed for three or four days in Narayangunge in vain and returned home. Then Nag Mahashaya said to his father, "If the mind is pure, then the Mother Ganga will appear here." Then at the auspicious hour of the holy bath, a jet of water rose, piercing the ground of his courtyard. Many of those who saw it are living today. But that was many years before I met him.

Swamiji: There was nothing strange in it. He was a saint of unfalsified determination. I do not consider such a phenomenon at all strange in his case.

Saying this, Swamiji, feeling sleepy, lay on his side. At this the disciple came down to take his supper.

XXVIII

While walking on the banks of the Ganga at Calcutta one afternoon, the disciple saw a Sannyasin in the distance approaching towards Ahiritola Ghat. While he came near, the disciple found the Sannyasin to be no other than his Guru, Swami Vivekananda. In his left hand he had a leaf receptacle containing fried gram, which he was eating like a boy, and was walking in great joy. When he stood before him, the disciple fell at his feet and asked the reason for his coming to Calcutta unexpectedly.

Swamiji: I came on business. Come, will you go to the Math? Eat a little of the fried gram. It has a nice saline and pungent taste. The disciple took the food with gladness and agreed to go to the Math with him.

Swamiji: Then look for a boat.

The disciple hurried to hire a boat. He was settling the amount of the boat-hire with the boatman, who demanded eight annas, when Swamiji also appeared on the scene and stopped the disciple saying, "Why are you higgling with them?" and said to the boatman, "Very well, I will give you eight annas", and got into the boat. That boat proceeded slowly against the current and took nearly an hour and half to reach the Math. Being alone with Swamiji in the boat, the disciple had an opportunity of asking him freely about all subjects. Raising the topic of the glorificatory poem which the disciple had recently composed singing the greatness of the devotees of Shri Ramakrishna, Swamiji asked him, "How do you know that those whom you have named in your hymn are the near and intimate disciples of Shri Ramakrishna?"

Disciple: Sir, I have associated with the Sannyasin and householder disciples of Shri Ramakrishna for so many years; I have heard from them that they are all devotees of Shri Ramakrishna.

Swamiji: Yes, they are devotees of Shri Ramakrishna. But all devotees do not belong to the group of his most intimate and nearest disciples. Staying in the Cossipore Garden, Shri Ramakrishna said to us, "The Divine Mother showed me that all of these are not my inner devotees." Shri Ramakrishna said so that day with respect to both his men and women devotees.

Then speaking of the way Shri Ramakrishna would indicate different grades among devotees, high and low, Swamiji began to explain to the disciple at length the great difference there is between the householder's and the Sannyasin's life.

Swamiji: Is it possible that one would serve the path of lust and wealth and understand Shri Ramakrishna aright at the same time? Or will it ever be possible? Never put your faith in such words. Many among the devotees of Shri Ramakrishna are now proclaiming themselves as Ishvara-koti (of Divine class), Antaranga (of inner circle), etc. They could not imbibe his great renunciation or dispassion, yet they say they are his intimate devotees! Sweep away all such words. He was a prince of Tyagis (self-renouncers), and obtaining his grace can anybody spend his life in the enjoyment of lust and wealth?

Disciple: Is it then, sir, that those who came to him at Dakshineswar were not his devotees?

Swamiji: Who says that? Everybody who has gone to Shri Ramakrishna has advanced in spirituality, is advancing, and will advance. Shri Ramakrishna used to say that the perfected Rishis of a previous Kalpa (cycle) take human bodies and come on earth with the Avataras. They are the associates of the Lord. God works through them and propagates His religion. Know this for a truth that they alone are the associates of the Avatara who have renounced all self for the sake of others, who, giving up all sense-enjoyments with repugnance, spend their lives for the good of the world, for the welfare of the Jivas. The disciples of Jesus were all Sannyasins. The direct recipients of the grace of Shankara, Ramanuja, Shri Chaitanya and Buddha were the all-renouncing Sannyasins. It is men of this stamp who have been through succession of disciples spreading the Brahma-vidya (knowledge of Brahman) in the world. Where and when have you heard that a man being the slave of lust and wealth has been able to liberate another or to show the path of God to him? Without himself free, how can he make others free? In Veda, Vedanta, Itihasa (history), Purana (ancient tradition), you will find everywhere that the Sannyasins have been the teachers of religion in all ages and climes. History repeats itself. It will also be likewise now. The capable Sannyasin children of Shri Ramakrishna, the teacher of the great synthesis of religions, will be honoured everywhere as the teachers of men. The words of others will dissipate in the air like an empty sound. The real self-sacrificing Sannyasins of the Math will be the centre of the preservation and spread of religious ideas. Do you understand?

Disciple: Then is it not true — what the householder devotees of Shri Ramakrishna are preaching about him in diverse ways?

Swamiji: It can't be said that they are altogether false; but what they are saying about Shri Ramakrishna is only partial truth. According to one's own capacity, one has understood Shri Ramakrishna and so is discussing about him. It is not bad either to do so. But if any of his devotees has concluded that what he has understood of him is the only truth, then he is an object of pity. Some are saying that Shri Ramakrishna was a Tantrika and Kaula, some that he was Shri Chaitanya born on earth to preach "Naradiya Bhakti" (Bhakti as taught by Narada); some again that to undertake spiritual practices is opposed to faith in him as an Avatara while some are opining that it is not agreeable to his teachings to take to Sannyasa. You will hear such words from the householder devotees, but do not listen to such one-sided estimates. He was the concentrated embodiment of how many previous Avataras! Even spending the whole life in religious austerity, we could not understand it. Therefore one has to speak about him with caution and restraint. As are one's capacities, so he fills one with spiritual ideas. One spray from the full ocean of his spirituality, if realised, will make gods of men. Such a synthesis of universal ideas you will not find in the history of the world again. Understand from this who was born in the person of Shri Ramakrishna. When he used to instruct his Sannyasin disciples, he would rise from his seat and look about to see if any householder was coming that way or not. If he found none, then in glowing words he would depict the glory of renunciation and austerity. As a result of the rousing power of that fiery dispassion, we have renounced the world and become averse to worldliness.

Disciple: He used to make such distinctions between householders and Sannyasins!

Swamiji: Ask and learn from the householder devotees themselves about it. And you yourself can think and know which are greater — those of his children who for the realisation of God have renounced all enjoyments of the worldly life and are spending themselves in the practice of austerities on hills and forests, Tirthas and Ashramas (holy places and hermitages), or those who are praising and glorifying his name and practising his remembrance, but are not able to rise above the delusion and bondage of the world? Which are greater — those who are coming forward in the service of humanity, regarding them as the Atman, those who are continent since early age, who are the moving embodiments of renunciation and dispassion, or those who like flies are at one time sitting on a flower, and at the next moment on a dung heap? You can yourself think and come to a conclusion.

Disciple: But, sir, what does the world really mean to those who have obtained his grace? Whether they remain in the householder's life or take to Sannyasa, it is immaterial — so it appears to me.
Swamiji: The mind of those who have truly received his grace cannot be attached to worldliness. The test of his grace is — unattachment to lust or wealth. If that has not come in anyone's life, then he has not truly received his grace.

When the above discussion ended thus, the disciple raising another topic, asked Swamiji, "Sir, what is the outcome of all your labours here and in foreign countries?"

Swamiji: You will see only a little manifestation of what has been done. In time the whole world must accept the universal and catholic ideas of Shri Ramakrishna and of this, only the beginning has been made. Before this flood everybody will be swept off.

Disciple: Please tell me more about Shri Ramakrishna. I like very much to hear of him from your lips.

Swamiji: You are hearing so much about him all the time, what more? He himself is his own parallel. Has he any exemplar?

Disciple: What is the way for us who have not seen him?

Swamiji: You have been blessed with the company of these Sadhus who are the direct recipients of his grace. How then can you say you have not seen him? He is present among his Sannyasin disciples. By service to them, he will in time be revealed in your heart. In time you will realise everything.

Disciple: But, sir, you speak about others who have received his grace, but never about what he used to say about yourself.

Swamiji: What shall I say about myself? You see, I must be one of his demons. In his presence even, I would sometimes speak ill of him, hearing which he would laugh.

Saying thus Swamiji's face assumed a grave aspect, and he looked towards the river with an absent mind and sat still for some time. Within a short time the evening fell and the boat also reached the Math. Swamiji was then humming a tune to himself, "Now in the evening of life, take the child back to his home."

When the song was finished, Swamiji said, "In your part of the country (East Bengal) sweet-voiced singers are not born. Without drinking the water of mother Ganga, a sweet, musical voice is not acquired."

After paying the hire, Swamiji descended from the boat and taking off his coat sat in the western verandah of the Math. His fair complexion and ochre robe presented a beautiful sight.

XXIX

Today is the first of Asharh (June-july). The disciple has come to the Math before dusk from Bally, with his office-dress on, as he has not found time to change it. Coming to the Math, he prostrated himself at the feet of Swamiji and inquired about his health. Swamiji replied that he was well, but looking at his dress, he said, "You put on coat and trousers, why don't you put on collars?" Saying this, he called Swami Saradananda who was near and said, "Give him tomorrow two collars from my stock."

Swami Saradananda bowed assent to his order.

The disciple then changed his office-dress and came to Swamiji, who, addressing him, said, "By giving up one's national costume and ways of eating and living, one gets denationalised. One can learn from all, but that learning which leads to denationalisation does not help one's uplift but becomes the cause of degradation."

Disciple: Sir, one cannot do without putting on dress approved by superior European officers in official quarters.

Swamiji: No one prevents that. In the interests of your service, you put on official dress in official quarters. But on returning home you should be a regular Bengali Babu — with flowing cloth, a native shirt, and with the Chudder on the shoulder. Do you understand?

Disciple: Yes, sir.

Swamiji: You go about from house to house only with the European shirt on. In the West, to go about visiting people with simply the shirt on is ungentlemanly — one is considered naked. Without putting on a coat over the shirt, you will not be welcomed in a gentleman's house. What nonsense have you learnt to imitate in the matter of dress! Boys and young men nowadays adopt a peculiar manner of dress which is neither Indian nor Western, but a queer combination.

After such talk Swamiji began to pace the bank of the river, and the disciple was alone with him. He was hesitating to ask Swamiji a question about religious practices.

Swamiji: What are you thinking? Out with it.

The disciple with great delicacy said, "Sir, I have been thinking that if you can teach me some method by which the mind becomes calm within a short time, by which I may be immersed in meditation quickly, I shall feel much benefited. In the round of worldly duties, I feel it difficult to make the mind steady in meditation at the time of spiritual practice."

Swamiji seemed delighted at this humility and earnestness of the disciple. In reply he affectionately said, "After some time come to me when I am alone upstairs, I will talk to you about it."

Coming up shortly after, the disciple found that Swamiji was sitting in meditation, facing the west. His face wore a wonderful expression, and his whole body was completely motionless. The disciple stood by, looking with speechless wonder on the figure of Swamiji in meditation, and when even after standing long he found no sign of external consciousness in Swamiji, he sat noiselessly by. After half an hour, Swamiji seemed to show signs of a return to external consciousness. The disciple found that his folded hands began to quiver, and a few minutes later Swamiji opened his eyes and looking at the disciple said, "When did you come?"

Disciple: A short while ago.

Swamiji: Very well, get me a glass of water.

The disciple hurriedly brought a glass of water and Swamiji drinking a little, asked the disciple to put the glass back in its proper place. The disciple did so and again sat by Swamiji.

Swamiji: Today I had a very deep meditation.

Disciple: Sir, please teach me so that my mind also may get absorbed in meditation.

Swamiji: I have already told you all the methods. Meditate every day accordingly, and in the fulness of time you will feel like that. Now tell me what form of Sadhana appeals to you most.

Disciple: Sir, I practise every day as you have told me, still I don't get a deep meditation. Sometimes I think it is useless for me to practise meditation. So I feel that I shall not fare well in it, and therefore now desire only eternal companionship with you.

Swamiji: Those are weaknesses of the mind. Always try to get absorbed in the eternally present Atman. If you once get the vision of the Atman, you will get everything — the bonds of birth and death will be broken.

Disciple: You bless me to attain to it. You asked me, still I don't get a deep meditation. By some means, do please make my mind steady.

Swamiji: Meditate whenever you get time. If the mind once enters the path of Sushumna, everything will get right. You will not have to do much after that.

Disciple: You encourage me in many ways. But shall I be blessed with a vision of the Truth? Shall I get freedom by attaining true knowledge?

Swamiji: Yes, of course. Everybody will attain Mukti, from a worm up to Brahma, and shall you alone fail? These are weaknesses of the mind; never think of such things.

After this, he said again: "Be possessed of Shraddha (faith), of Virya (courage), attain to the knowledge of the Atman, and sacrifice your life for the good of others — this is my wish and blessing."

The bell for the meal ringing at this moment, Swamiji asked the disciple to go and partake of it. The disciple, prostrating himself at the feet of Swamiji, prayed for his blessings. Swamiji putting his hand on his head blessed him and said, "If my blessings be of any good to you, I say — may Bhagavan Shri Ramakrishna give you his grace! I know of no blessing higher than this." After meals, the disciple did not go upstairs to Swamiji, who had retired early that night. Next morning the disciple, having to return to Calcutta in the interests of his business appeared before Swamiji upstairs.

Swamiji: Will you go immediately?

Disciple: Yes, sir.

Swamiji: Come again next Sunday, won't you?

Disciple: Yes, certainly.

Swamiji: All right, there is a boat coming.

The disciple took leave of Swamiji. He did not know that this was to be his last meeting with his Ishtadeva (chosen Ideal) in the physical body. Swamiji with a glad heart bade him farewell and said, "Come on Sunday." The disciple replied, "Yes, I will," and got downstairs.

The boatmen were calling for him, so he ran for the boat. Boarding it, he saw Swamiji pacing the upper verandah, and saluting him he entered the boat.

Seven days after this, Swamiji passed away from mortal life. The disciple had no knowledge of the impending catastrophe. Getting the news on the second day of Swamiji's passing away, he came to the Math, and therefore he had not the good fortune to see his physical form again!

SHRI PRIYA NATH SINHA

XXX

of Swamiji had a talk with him one day at the Math on this subject. Swamiji remarked, "You see, we have an old adage: 'If your son is not inclined to study, put him in the Durbars (Sabha).' The word Sabha here does not mean social meetings, such as take place occasionally at people's houses — it means royal Durbars. In the days of the independent kings of Bengal, they used to hold their courts mornings and evenings. There all the affairs of the State were discussed in the morning — and as there were no newspapers at that time, the king used to converse with the leading gentry of the capital and gather from them all information regarding the people and the State. These gentlemen had to attend these meetings, for if they did not do so, the king would inquire into the reason of their non-attendance. Such Durbars were the centres of culture in every country and not merely in ours. In the present day, the western parts of India, especially Rajputana, are much better off in this respect than Bengal, as something similar to these old Durbars still obtains there."

Q.— then, Maharaj, have our people lost their own good manners because we have no kings of our own?

Swamiji: It is all a degeneration which has its root in selfishness. That in boarding a steamer one follows the vulgar maxim, "Uncle, save thy own precious skin", and in music and moments of recreation everyone tries to make a display of himself, is a typical picture of our mental state. Only a little training in self-sacrifice would take it away. It is the fault of the parents who do not teach their children good manners. Self-sacrifice, indeed, is the basis of all civilisation.

On the other hand, owing to the undue domination exercised by the parents, our boys do not get free scope for growth. The parents consider singing as improper. But the son, when he hears a fine piece of music, at once sets his whole mind on how to learn it, and naturally he must look out for an Adda.[1] Then again, "It is a sin to smoke!" So what else can the young man do than mix with the servants of the house, to indulge in this habit in secret? In everyone there are infinite tendencies, which require proper scope for satisfaction. But in our country that is not allowed; and to bring about a different order of things would require a fresh training of the parents. Such is the condition! What a pity! We have not yet developed a high grade of civilisation; and in spite of this, our educated Babus want the British to hand over the government to them to manage! It makes me laugh and cry as well. Well, where is that martial spirit which, at the very outset, requires one to know how to serve and obey and to practise self-restraint! The martial spirit is not self-assertion but self-sacrifice. One must be ready to advance and lay down one's life at the word of command, before he can command the hearts and lives of others. One must sacrifice himself first.

A devotee of Shri Ramakrishna once passed some severe remarks, in a book written by him, against those who did not believe in Shri Ramakrishna as an Incarnation of God. Swamiji summoned the writer to his presence and addressed him thus in a spirited manner:

What right had you to write like that, abusing others? What matters it if they do not believe in your Lord? Have we created a sect? Are we Ramakrishnites, that we should look upon anyone who will not worship him, as our enemy? By your bigotry you have only lowered him, and made him small. If your Lord is God Himself, then you ought to know that in whatsoever name one is calling upon him, it is his worship only — and who are you to abuse others? Do you think they will hear you if you inveigh against them? How foolish! You can only win others' hearts when you have sacrificed yourself to them, otherwise why should they hear you?

Regaining his natural composure after a short

while, Swamiji spoke in a sorrowful tone:

Can anyone, my dear friend, have faith or resignation in the Lord, unless he himself is a hero? Never can hatred and malice vanish from one's heart unless one becomes a hero, and unless one is free from these, how can one become truly civilised? Where in this country is that sturdy manliness, that spirit of heroism? Alas, nowhere. Often have I looked for that, and I found only one instance of it, and only one.

Q.— in whom have you found it, Swamiji?

Swamiji: In G. C. alone I have seen that true resignation — that true spirit of a servant of the Lord. And was it not because he was ever ready to sacrifice himself that Shri Ramakrishna took upon himself all his responsibility? What a unique spirit of resignation to the Lord! I have not met his parallel. From him have I learnt the lesson of self-surrender.

So saying, Swamiji raised his folded hands to his head out of respect to him.

XXXI

Swamiji: A very funny thing happened today. I went to a friend's house. He has had a picture painted, the subject of which is "Shri Krishna addressing Arjuna on the battlefield of Kurukshetra". Shri Krishna stands on the chariot, holding the reins in His hand and preaching the Gita to Arjuna. He showed me the picture and asked me how I liked it. "Fairly well", I said. But as he insisted on having my criticism on it, I had to give my honest opinion by saying, "There is nothing in it to commend itself to me; first, because the chariot of the time of Shri Krishna was not like the modern pagoda-shaped car, and also, there is no expression in the figure of Shri Krishna."

Q.— Was not the pagoda-chariot in use then?

Swamiji: Don't you know that since the Buddhistic era, there has been a great confusion in everything in our country? The kings never used to fight in pagoda-chariots. There are chariots even today in Rajputana that greatly resemble the chariots of old. Have you seen the chariots in the pictures of Grecian mythology? They have two wheels, and one mounts them from behind; we had that sort of chariot. What good is it to paint a picture if the details are wrong? An historical picture comes up to a standard of excellence when after making proper study and research, things are portrayed exactly as they were at that period. The truth must be represented, otherwise the picture is nothing. In these days, our young men who go in for painting are generally those who were unsuccessful at school, and who have been given up at home as good-for-nothing; what work of art can you expect from them? To paint a really good picture requires as much talent as to produce a perfect drama.

Q.— how then should Shri Krishna be represented in the picture in question?

Swamiji: Shri Krishna ought to be painted as He really was, the Gita personified; and the central idea of the Gita should radiate from His whole form as He was teaching the path of Dharma to Arjuna, who had been overcome by infatuation and cowardice.

So saying Swamiji posed himself in the way in which Shri Krishna should be portrayed, and continued: "Look here, thus does he hold the bridle of the horses — so tight that they are brought to their haunches, with their forelegs fighting the air, and their mouths gaping. This will show a tremendous play of action in the figure of Shri Krishna. His friend, the world-renowned hero, casting aside his bow and arrows, has sunk down like a coward on the chariot, in the midst of the two armies. And Shri Krishna, whip in one hand and tightening the reins with the other, has turned Himself towards Arjuna, with his childlike face beaming with unworldly love and sympathy, and a calm and serene look — and is delivering the message of the Gita to his beloved comrade. Now, tell me what idea this picture of the Preacher of the Gita conveys to you."

The friend: Activity combined with firmness and serenity.

Swamiji: Ay, that's it! Intense action in the whole body, and withal a face expressing the profound calmness and serenity of the blue sky. This is the central idea of the Gita — to be calm and steadfast in all circumstances, with one's body, mind, and soul centred at His hallowed Feet! [(Sanskrit)] (Gita IV.18)

He who even while doing action can keep his mind calm, and in whom, even when not doing any outward action, flows the current of activity in the form of the contemplation of Brahman, is the intelligent one among men, he indeed is the Yogi, he indeed is the perfect worker.

At this moment, the man who had been sent to arrange a boat returned and said that it was ready; so Swamiji told his friend, "Now let us go to the Math.

You must have left word at home that you were going there with me?"

They continued their talk as they walked to the boat.

Swamiji: This idea must be preached to everyone — work, work, endless work — without looking at results, and always keeping the whole mind and soul steadfast at the lotus feet of the Lord!

Q.— but is this not Karma-yoga?

Swamiji: Yes, this is Karma-yoga; but without spiritual practices you will never be able to do this Karma-yoga. You must harmonise the four different Yogas; otherwise how can you always keep your mind and heart wholly on the Lord?

Q.— it is generally said that work according to the Gita means the performance of Vedic sacrifices and religious exercises; any other kind of work is futile.

Swamiji: All right; but you must make it more comprehensive. Who is responsible for every action you do, every breath you take, and every thought you think? Isn't it you yourself?

The friend: Yes and no. I cannot solve this clearly. The truth about it is that man is the instrument and the Lord is the agent. So when I am directed by His will, I am not at all responsible for my actions.

Swamiji: Well, that can be said only in the highest state of realisation. When the mind will be purified by work and you will see that it is He who is causing all to work, then only you will have a right to speak like that. Otherwise it is all bosh, a mere cant.

Q.— why so, if one is truly convinced by reasoning that the Lord alone is causing all actions to be done?

Swamiji: It may hold good when one has been so convinced. But it only lasts for that moment, and not a whit afterwards. Well, consider this thoroughly, whether all that you do in your everyday life, you are not doing with an egoistic idea that you yourself are the agent.

How long do you remember that it is the Lord who is making you work? But then, by repeatedly analysing like that, you will come to a state when the ego will vanish and in its place the Lord will come in. Then you will be able to say with justice "Thou, Lord, art guarding all my actions from within." But, my friend, if the ego occupies all the space within your heart, where forsooth will there be room enough for the Lord to come in? The Lord is verily absent!

Q.— But it is He who is giving me the wicked impulse?

Swamiji: No, by no means. It would be blaspheming the Lord to think in that way. He is not inciting you to evil action, it is all the creation of your desire for self-gratification. If one says the Lord is causing everything to be done, and wilfully persists in wrong-doing, it only brings ruin on him. That is the origin of self-deception. Don't you feel an elation after you have done a good deed? You then give yourself the credit of doing something good — you can't help it, it is very human. But how absurd to take the credit of doing the good act on oneself and lay the blame for the evil act on the Lord! It is a most dangerous idea — the effect of ill-digested Gita and Vedanta. Never hold that view. Rather say that He is causing the good work to be done while you are responsible for the evil action. That will bring on devotion and faith, and you will see His grace manifested at every step. The truth about it is that no one has created you — you have created yourself. This is discrimination, this is Vedanta.

But one does not understand it before realisation. Therefore the aspirant should begin with the dualistic standpoint, that the Lord is causing the good actions, while he is doing the evil. This is the easiest way to the purification of the mind. Hence you find dualism so strong among the Vaishnavas. It is very difficult to entertain Advaitic (non-dualistic) ideas at the outset. But the dualistic standpoint gradually leads to the realisation of the Advaita.

Hypocrisy is always a dangerous thing. If there is no wilful self-deception, that is to say, if one sincerely believes that the most wicked impulse is also prompted by the Lord, rest assured that one will not have to do those mean acts for long. All the impurities of the mind are quickly destroyed. Our ancient scriptural writers understood this well. And I think that the Tantrika form of worship originated from the time that Buddhism began to decline and, through the oppression of the Buddhists, people began to perform their Vedic sacrifices in secret. They had no more opportunity to conduct them for two months at a stretch, so they made clay images, worshipped them, and consigned them to the water — finishing everything in one night, without leaving the least trace! Man longs for a concrete symbol, otherwise his heart is not satisfied. So in every home that one-night sacrifice began to take place. As Shri Ramakrishna used to say, "Some enter the house by the scavenger's entrance", so the spiritual teachers of that time saw that those who could not perform any religious rite owing to their evil propensities, also needed some way of coming round by degrees to the path of virtue. For them those queer Tantrika rites came to be invented.

Q.— They went on doing evil actions thinking them to be good. So how could this remove their evil tendencies?

Swamiji: Why, they gave a different direction to their propensities; they did them, but with the object of realising the Lord.

Q.— Can this really be done?

Swamiji: It comes to the same thing. The motive must be right. And what should prevent them from succeeding?

Q.— But many are caught in the temptation for wine, meat, etc. in trying to get along with such means.

Swamiji: It was therefore that Shri Ramakrishna came. The days of practising the Tantra in that fashion are gone. He, too, practised the Tantra, but not in that way. Where there is the injunction of drinking wine, he would simply touch his forehead with a drop of it. The Tantrika form of worship is a very slippery ground. Hence I say that this province has had enough of the Tantra. Now it must go beyond. The Vedas should be studied. A harmony of the four kinds of Yogas must be practised and absolute chastity must be preserved.

Q.— What do you mean by the harmony of the four Yogas?

Swamiji: Discrimination between the real and the unreal, dispassion and devotion, work and practices in concentration, and along with these there must be a reverential attitude towards women.

Q.— How can one look with reverence on women?

Swamiji: Well, they are the representatives of the Divine Mother. And real well-being of India will commence from the day that the worship of the Divine Mother will truly begin, and every man will sacrifice himself at the altar of the Mother. . . .

Q.— Swamiji, in your boyhood, when we asked you to marry, you would reply, "I won't, but you will see what I shall become." You have actually verified your words.

Swamiji: Yes, dear brother, you saw how I was in want of food, and had to work hard besides. Oh, the tremendous labour! Today the Americans out of love have given me this nice bed, and I have something to eat also. But, also, I have not been destined to enjoy physically — and lying on the mattress only aggravates my illness. I feel suffocated, as it were. I have to come down and lie on the floor for relief!

MISCELLANEOUS

Vengeance Of History (Mrs. Wright)
XXXII

"It was the other day," he said, in his musical voice, "only just the other day — not more than four hundred years ago." And then followed tales of cruelty and oppression, of a patient race and a suffering people, and of a judgment to come! "Ah, the English!" he said. "Only just a little while ago they were savages, the vermin crawled on the ladies' bodies, . . . and they scented themselves to disguise the abominable odour of their persons. . . . Most hor-r-ible! Even now they are barely emerging from barbarism." "Nonsense," said one of his scandalised hearers, "that was at least five hundred years ago." "And did I not say `a little while ago'? What are a few hundred years when you look at the antiquity of the human soul?" Then with a turn of tone, quite reasonable and gentle, "They are quite savage", he said. "The frightful cold, the want and privation of their northern climate", going on more quickly and warmly, "has made themwild . They only think to kill. . . . Where is their religion? They take the name of that Holy One, they claim to love their fellowmen, they civilise — by Christianity!— no! It is their hunger that has civilised them, not their God. The love of man is on their lips, in their hearts there is nothing but evil and every violence. `I love you my brother, I love you!' . . . and all the while they cut his throat! Their hands are red with blood." . . . Then, going on more slowly, his beautiful voice deepening till it sounded like a bell, "But the judgment of God will fall upon them. `Vengeance is mine; I will repay, saith the Lord', and destruction is coming. What are your Christians? Not one third of the world. Look at those Chinese, millions of them. They are the vengeance of God that will light upon you. There will be another invasion of the Huns", adding, with a little chuckle, "they will sweep over Europe, they will not leave one stone standing upon another. Men, women, children, all will go and the dark ages will come again." His voice was indescribably sad and pitiful; then suddenly and flippantly, dropping the seer, "Me — i don't care! The world will rise up better from it, but it is coming. The vengeance of God, it is coming soon." "Soon?" they all asked.

"It will not be a thousand years before it is done."

They drew a breath of relief. It did not seem imminent.

"And God will have vengeance", he went on. "You may not see it in religion, you may not see it in politics, but you must see it in history, and as it has been; it will come to pass. If you grind down the people, you will suffer. We in India are suffering the vengeance of God. Look upon these things. They ground down those poor people for their own wealth, they heard not the voice of distress, they ate from gold and silver when the people cried for bread, and the Mohammedans came upon them slaughtering and killing: slaughtering and killing they overran them. India has been conquered again and again for years, and last and worst of all came the Englishman. You look about India, what has the Hindu left? Won-derful temples, everywhere. What has the Mohammedan left? Beautiful palaces. What has the Englishman left? Nothing but mounds of broken brandy bottles! And God has had no mercy upon my people because they had no mercy. By their cruelty they degraded the populace; and when they needed them, the common people had no strength to give for their aid. If man cannot believe in the Vengeance of God, he certainly cannot deny the Vengeance of History. And it will come upon the English; they have their heels on our necks, they have sucked the last drop of our blood for their own pleasures, they have carried away with them millions of our money, while our people have starved by villages and provinces. And now the Chinaman is the vengeance that will fall upon them; if the Chinese rose today and swept the English into the sea, as they well deserve, it would be no more than justice."

And then, having said his say, the Swami was silent. A babble of thin-voiced chatter rose about him, to which he listened, apparently unheeding. Occasionally he cast his eye up to the roof and repeated softly, "Shiva! Shiva!" and the little company, shaken and disturbed by the current of powerful feelings and vindictive passion which seemed to be flowing like molten lava beneath the silent surface of this strange being, broke up, perturbed.

He stayed days [actually it was only a long weekend].... All through, his discourses abounded in picturesque illustrations and beautiful legends....

One beautiful story he told was of a man whose wife reproached him with his troubles, reviled him because of the success of others, and recounted to him all his failures. "Is this what your God has done for you", she said to him, "after you have served Him so many years?" Then the man answered, "Am I a trader in religion? Look at the mountain. What does it do for me, or what have I done for it? And yet I love it be-cause I am so made that I love the beautiful. Thus I love God."... There was another story he told of a king who offered a gift to a Rishi. The Rishi refused, but the king insisted and begged that he would come with him. When they came to the palace, he heard the king praying, and the king begged for wealth, for power, for length of days from God. The Rishi listened, wondering, until at last he picked up his mat and started away. Then the king opened his eyes from his prayers and saw him. "Why are you going?" he said. "You have not asked for your gift." "I", said the Rishi, "ask from a beggar?"

When someone suggested to him that Christianity was a saving power, he opened his great dark eyes upon him and said, "If Christianity is a saving power in itself, why has it not saved the Ethiopians, the Abyssinians?"

Often on Swamiji's lips was the phrase, "They would not dare to do this to a monk."... At times he even expressed a great longing that the English government would take him and shoot him. "It would be the first nail in their coffin", he would say, with a little gleam of his white teeth. "and my death would run through the land like wild fire."

His great heroine was the dreadful [?] Ranee of the Indian mutiny, who led her troops in person. Most of the old mutineers, he said, had become monks in order to hide themselves, and this accounted very well for the dangerous quality of the monks' opinions. There was one man of them who had lost four sons and could speak of them with composure, but whenever he mentioned the Ranee, he would weep, with tears streaming down his face. "That woman was a goddess", he said, "a devi. When overcome, she fell on her sword and died like a man." It was strange to hear the other side of the Indian mutiny, when you would never believe that there was another side to it, and to be assured that a Hindu could not possibly kill a woman....

Religion, Civilisation, And Miracles (The Appeal-Avalanche) XXXIII

"I am a monk," he said, as he sat in the parlors of La Salette Academy, (On January 21, 1894.) which is his home while in Memphis, "and not a priest. When at home I travel from place to place, teaching the people of the villages and towns through which I pass. I am dependent upon them for my sustenance, as I am not allowed to touch money."

"I was born," he continued, in answer to a question, "in Bengal and become a monk and a celibate from choice. At my birth my father had a horoscope taken of my life, but would never tell me what it was. Some years ago when I visited my home, my father having died, I came across the chart among some papers in my mother's possession and saw from it that I was destined to become a wanderer on the face of the earth."

There was a touch of pathos in the speaker's voice and a murmur of sympathy ran around the group of listeners. Kananda (American reporters generally spelt his name as Vivekananda in those days.) knocked the ashes from his cigar and was silent for a space.

Presently some one asked:

"If your religion is all that you claim it is, if it is the only true faith, how is it that your people are not more advanced in civilisation than we are? Why has it not elevated them among the nations of the world?"

"Because that is not the sphere of any religion,"

replied the Hindu gravely. "My people are the most moral in the world, or quite as much as any other race. They are more considerate of their fellow man's rights, and even those of dumb animals, but they are not materialists. No religion has ever advanced the thought or inspiration of a nation or people. In fact, no great achievement has ever been attained in the history of the world that religion has not retarded. Your boasted Christianity has not proven an exception in this respect. Your Darwins, your Mills, your Humes, have never received the endorsement of your prelates. Why, then, criticise my religion on this account?"

"I would not give a fig for a faith that does not tend to elevate mankind's lot on earth as well as his spiritual condition," said one of the group, 'and therein I am not prepared to admit the correctness of your statements. Christianity has founded colleges, hospitals and raised the degenerate. It has elevated the downcast and helped its followers to live."

"You are right there to a certain extent," replied the monk calmly, "and yet it is not shown that these things are directly the result of your Christianity. There are many causes operating in the West to produce these results.

"Religious thought should be directed to developing man's spiritual side. Science, art, learning and metaphysical research all have their proper functions in life, but if you seek to blend them, you destroy their individual characteristics until, in time, you eliminate the spiritual, for instance, from the religious altogether. You Americans worship what? The dollar. In the mad rush for gold, you forget the spiritual until you have become a nation of materialists. Even your preachers and churches are tainted with the all-pervading desire. Show me one in the history of your people, who has led the spiritual lives that those whom I can name at home have done. Where are those who, when death comes, could say, 'O Brother Death, I welcome thee.' Your religion helps you to build Ferris wheels and Eiffel towers, but does it aid you in the development of your inner lives?"

The monk spoke earnestly, and his voice, rich and well modulated, came through the dusk that pervaded the apartment, half-sadly, half-accusingly. There was something of the weird in the comments of this stranger from a land whose history dates back 6,000 years upon the civilisation of the Nineteenth Century America.

"But, in pursuing the spiritual, you lost sight of the demands of the present," said some one. "Your doctrine does not help men to live."

"It helps them to die," was the answer.

"We are sure of the present."

"You are sure of nothing."

"The aim of the ideal religion should be to help one to live and to prepare one to die at the same time."

"Exactly," said the Hindu, quickly, "and it is that which we are seeking to attain. I believe that the Hindu faith has developed the spiritual in its devotees at the expense of the material, and I think that in the Western world the contrary is true. By uniting the materialism of the West with the spiritualism of the East I believe much can be accomplished. It may be that in the attempt the Hindu faith will lose much of its individuality."

"Would not the entire social system of India have to be revolutionised to do what you hope to do?"

"Yet, probably, still the religion would remain unimpaired."

The conversation here turned upon the form of worship of the Hindus, and Kananda gave some interesting information on this subject. There are agnostics and atheists in India as well as elsewhere. "Realisation" is the one thing essential in the lives of the followers of Brahma. Faith is not necessary. Theosophy is a subject with which Kananda is not versed, nor is it a part of his creed unless he chooses to make it so. It is more of a separate study. Kananda never met Mme. Blavatsky, but has met Col. Olcott of the American Theosophical Society. He is also acquainted with Annie Besant. Speaking of the "fakirs" of India, the famous jugglers or musicians [magicians?], whose feats have made for them a world-wide reputation, Kananda told of a few episodes that had come within his observation and which almost surpass belief.

"Five months ago," he said, when questioned on this subject, "or just one month before I left India to come to this country, I happened in company in a caravan or party of 25 to sojourn for a space in a city in the interior. While there we learned of the marvellous work of one of these itinerant magicians and had him brought before us. He told us he would produce for us any article we desired. We stripped him, at his request, until he was quite naked and placed him in the corner of the room. I threw my travelling blanket about him and then we called upon him to do as he had promised. He asked what we should like, and I asked for a bunch of California [?] grapes, and straightway the fellow brought them forth from under his blanket. Oranges and other fruits were produced, and finally great dishes of steaming rice."

Continuing, the monk said he believed in the existence of a "sixth sense" and in telepathy. He offered no explanation of the feats of the fakirs, merely saying that they were very wonderful. The subject of idols came up and the monk said that idols formed a part of his religion insomuch as the symbol is concerned.

"What do you worship?" said the monk, "What is your idea of God?"

"The spirit," said a lady quietly.

"What is the spirit? Do you Protestants worship the words of the Bible or something beyond? We worship the God through the idol."

"That is, you attain the subjective through the objective," said a gentleman who had listened attentively to the words of the stranger.

"Yes, that is it," said the monk, gratefully.

Vivekananda discussed further in the same strain until the call terminated as the hour for the Hindu's lecture approached.

"I was born," he continued, in answer to a question, "in Bengal and become a monk and a celibate from choice. At my birth my father had a horoscope taken of my life, but would never tell me what it was. Some years ago when I visited my home, my father having died, I came across the chart among some papers in my mother's possession and saw from it that I was destined to become a wanderer on the face of the earth."

There was a touch of pathos in the speaker's voice and a murmur of sympathy ran around the group of listeners. Kananda[1] knocked the ashes from his cigar and was silent for a space.

Presently some one asked:

"If your religion is all that you claim it is, if it is the only true faith, how is it that your people are not more advanced in civilisation than we are? Why has it not elevated them among the nations of the world?" "Because that is not the sphere of any religion," replied the Hindu gravely. "My people are the most moral in the world, or quite as much as any other race. They are more considerate of their fellow man's rights, and even those of dumb animals, but they are not materialists. No religion has ever advanced the thought or inspiration of a nation or people. In fact, no great achievement has ever been attained in the history of the world that religion has not retarded. Your boasted Christianity has not proven an exception in this respect. Your Darwins, your Mills, your Humes, have never received the endorsement of your prelates. Why, then, criticise my religion on this account?" "I would not give a fig for a faith that does not tend to elevate mankind's lot on earth as well as his spiritual condition," said one of the group, 'and therein I am not prepared to admit the correctness of your statements. Christianity has founded colleges, hospitals and raised the degenerate. It has elevated the downcast and helped its followers to live." "You are right there to a certain extent," replied the monk calmly, "and yet it is not shown that these things are directly the result of your Christianity. There are many causes operating in the West to produce these results. "Religious thought should be directed to developing man's spiritual side. Science, art, learning and metaphysical research all have their proper functions in life, but if you seek to blend them, you destroy their in-

---

1. American reporters generally spelt his name as Vive Kananda in those days.

dividual characteristics until, in time, you eliminate the spiritual, for instance, from the religious altogether. You Americans worship what? The dollar. In the mad rush for gold, you forget the spiritual until you have become a nation of materialists. Even your preachers and churches are tainted with the all-pervading desire. Show me one in the history of your people, who has led the spiritual lives that those whom I can name at home have done. Where are those who, when death comes, could say, 'O Brother Death, I welcome thee.' Your religion helps you to build Ferris wheels and Eiffel towers, but does it aid you in the development of your inner lives?"

The monk spoke earnestly, and his voice, rich and well modulated, came through the dusk that pervaded the apartment, half-sadly, half-accusingly. There was something of the weird in the comments of this stranger from a land whose history dates back 6,000 years upon the civilisation of the Nineteenth Century America. "But, in pursuing the spiritual, you lost sight of the demands of the present," said some one. "Your doctrine does not help men to live." "It helps them to die," was the answer.

"We are sure of the present."

"You are sure of nothing."

"The aim of the ideal religion should be to help one to live and to prepare one to die at the same time." "Exactly," said the Hindu, quickly, "and it is that which we are seeking to attain. I believe that the Hindu faith has developed the spiritual in its devotees at the expense of the material, and I think that in the Western world the contrary is true. By uniting the materialism of the West with the spiritualism of the East I believe much can be accomplished. It may be that in the attempt the Hindu faith will lose much of its individuality." "Would not the entire social system of India have to be revolutionised to do what you hope to do?" "Yet, probably, still the religion would remain unimpaired."

The conversation here turned upon the form of worship of the Hindus, and Kananda gave some interesting information on this subject. There are agnostics and atheists in India as well as elsewhere. "Realisation" is the one thing essential in the lives of the followers of Brahma. Faith is not necessary. Theosophy is a subject with which Kananda is not versed, nor is it a part of his creed unless he chooses to make it so. It is more of a separate study. Kananda never met Mme. Blavatsky, but has met Col. Olcott of the American Theosophical Society. He is also acquainted with Annie Besant. Speaking of the "fakirs" of India, the famous jugglers or musicians [magicians?], whose feats have made for them a world-wide reputation, Kananda told of a few episodes that had come within his observation and which almost surpass belief. "Five months ago," he said, when questioned on this subject, "or just one month before I left India to come to this country, I happened in company in a caravan or party of 25 to sojourn for a space in a city in the interior. While there we learned of the marvellous work of one of these itinerant magicians and had him brought before us. He told us he would produce for us any article we desired. We stripped him, at his request, until he was quite naked and placed him in the corner of the room. I threw my travelling blanket about him and then we called upon him to do as he had promised. He asked what we should like, and I asked for a bunch of California [?] grapes, and straightway the fellow brought them forth from under his blanket. Oranges and other fruits were produced, and finally great dishes of steaming rice." Continuing, the monk said he believed in the existence of a "sixth sense" and in telepathy. He offered no explanation of the feats of the fakirs, merely saying that they were very wonderful. The subject of idols came up and the monk said that idols formed a part of his religion insomuch as the symbol is concerned.

"What do you worship?" said the monk, "What is your idea of God?" "The spirit," said a lady quietly.

"What is the spirit? Do you Protestants worship the words of the Bible or something beyond? We worship the God through the idol." "That is, you attain the subjective through the objective," said a gentleman who had listened attentively to the words of the stranger. "Yes, that is it," said the monk, gratefully.

Vivekananda discussed further in the same strain until the call terminated as the hour for the Hindu's lecture approached.

Religious Harmony (The Detroit Free Press, February 14, 1894)
XXXIV

"I make the distinction between religion and creed. Religion is the acceptance of all existing creeds, seeing in them the same striving towards the same destination. Creed is something antagonistic and combative. There are different creeds, because there are different people, and the creed is adapted to the commonwealth where it furnishes what people want. As the world is made up of infinite variety of persons of different natures, intellectually, spiritually, and materially, so these people take to themselves that form of belief in the existence of a great and good moral law, which is best fitted for them. Religion recognizes and is glad of the existence of all these forms because of the beautiful underlying principle.

The same goal is reached by different routes and my way would not be suited perhaps to the temperament of my Western neighbour, the same that his route would not commend itself to my disposition and philosophical way of thinking. I belong to the Hindu religion. That is not the Buddhists' creed, one of the sects of the Hindu religion. We never indulge in missionary work. We do not seek to thrust the principles of our religion upon anyone. The fundamental principles of our religion forbid that. Nor do we say anything against any missionaries whom you send from this country anywhere. For all of us they are entirely welcome to penetrate the innermost recesses of the earth. Many come to us, but we do not struggle for them; we have no missionaries striving to bring anyone to our way of thinking. With no effort from us many forms of the Hindu religion are spreading far and wide, and these manifestations have taken the form of Christian science, theosophy, and Edwin Arnold's Light of Asia. Our religion is older than most religions and the Christian creed — i do not call it religion, because of its antagonistic features — came directly from the Hindu religion. It is one of the great offshoots. The Catholic religion also takes all its forms from us — the confessional, the belief in saints and so on — and a Catholic priest who saw this absolute similarity and recognised the truth of the origin of the Catholic religion was dethroned from his position because he dared to publish a volume explaining all that he observed and was convinced of." "You recognise agnostics in your religion?" was asked.

"Oh, yes; philosophical agnostics and what you call infidels. When Buddha, who is with us a saint, was asked by one of his followers: 'Does God exist?' He replied: 'God. When have I spoken to you about God? This I tell you, be good and do good.' The philosophical agnostics — there are many of us — believe in the great moral law underlying everything in nature and in the ultimate perfection. All the creeds which are accepted by all people are but the endeavours of humanity to realise that infinity of Self which lies in the great future." "Is it beneath the dignity of your religion to resort to missionary effort?"

For reply the visitor from the Orient turned to a little volume and referred to an edict among other remarkable edicts. "This," he said, "was written 200 B.C., and will be the best answer I can give you on that question."

In delightfully clear, well modulated tones, he read:

"The King Piyadasi, beloved of the gods, honours all sects, both ascetics and householders; he propitiates them by alms and other gifts, but he attaches less importance to gifts and honours than to endeavour to promote the essential moral virtues. It is true the prevalence of essential virtues differs in different sects, but there is a common basis. That is, gentleness, moderation in language and morality. Thus one should not exalt one's own sect and decry others, but tender them on every occasion the honour they deserve. Striving thus, one promotes the welfare of his own sect, while serving the others. Striving otherwise, one does not serve his own sect, while disserving others; and whosoever, from attachment to his own sect and with a view to promoting it, decries others, only deals rude blows to his own sect. Hence concord alone is meritorious, so that all bear and love to bear the beliefs of each other. It is with this purpose that this edict has been inscribed; that all people, whatever their fate may be, should be encouraged to promote the essential moral doctrines in each and mutual respects for all other sects. It is with this object that the ministers of religion, the inspectors and other bodies of officers should all work."

After reading this impressive passage Swami Vive Kananda remarked that the same wise king who had caused this edict to be inscribed had forbidden the indulgence of war, as its horrors were antagonistic to all the principles of the great and universal moral doctrine. "For this reason," remarked the visitor, "India has suffered in its material aspect. Where brute strength and bloodshed has advanced other nations, India has deprecated such brutal manifestations; and by the law of the survival of the fittest, which applies to nations as well as to individuals, it has fallen behind as a power on the earth in the material sense." "But will it not be an impossibility to find in the great combative Western countries, where such tremendous energy is needed to develop the pressing practical necessities of the nineteenth century, this spirit which prevails in placid India?"

The brilliant eyes flashed, and a smile crossed the features of the Eastern brother. "May not one combine the energy of the lion with the gentleness of the lamb?" he asked.

Continuing, he intimated that perhaps the future holds the conjunction of the East and the West, a combination which would be productive of marvellous results. A condition which speaks well for the natures of the Western nation is the reverence in which women are held and the gentle consideration with which they are treated.

He says with the dying Buddha, "Work out your own salvation. I cannot help you. No man can help you. Help yourself." Harmony and peace, and not dissension, is his watchword.

The following story is one which he related recently regarding the practice of fault-finding among creeds: "A frog lived in a well. It had lived there for a long time. It was born there and brought up there, and yet was a little, small frog. Of course the evolutionists were not there to tell us whether the frog lost its eyes or not, but, for our story's sake, we must take it for granted that it had eyes, and that it every day cleansed the waters of all the worms and bacilli that lived in it, with an energy that would give credit to our modern bacteriologists. In this way it went on and became a little sleek and fat — perhaps as much so as myself. Well, one day another frog that lived in the sea, came and fell into the well. "'Whence are you from?'

"'I am from the sea.'

"'The sea? How big is that? Is it as big as my well?' and he took a leap from one side of the well to the other. "'My friend,' says the frog of the sea, `how do you compare the sea with your little well?' "Then the frog took another leap and asked; `Is your sea so big?' "'What nonsense you speak to compare the sea with your well.' "'Well, then,' said the frog of the well, `nothing can be bigger than my well; there can be nothing bigger than this; this fellow is a liar, so turn him out.' "That has been the difficulty all the while.

"I am a Hindu. I am sitting in my own little well, and thinking that the world is my well. The Christian sits in his little well and the whole world is his well. The Mohammedan sits in his well and thinks the whole world that. I have to thank you of America for the great attempt you are making to break down the barriers of this little world of ours, and hope that, in the future, the Lord will help you to accomplish that purpose."

Fallen Women (The Detroit Tribune, March 17, 1894) XXXV

The story of which the sentences that precede this one are a paragraph, was written in India. They were written by Rudyard Kipling, from whom most of us have learned all that we definitely know about India, with the exception of the fact that India raises wheat enough to be a great competitor of our own farmers, that men work there for two cents a day and that women throw their babies into the Ganga, which is the sacred river of the country.

But Vive Kananda, since he came to this country, has exploded the story about the women of India feeding their babies to the alligators, and now he says that he never heard of Rudyard Kipling until he came to America, and that it is not proper in India to talk of such a profession as that of Lalun, out of which Mr. Kipling has made one of his most delightful and instructive tales. "In India," said Kananda yesterday, "we do not discuss such things. No one ever speaks of those unfortunate women. When a woman is discovered to be unchaste in India, she is hurled out from her caste. No one thereafter can touch or speak to her. If she went into the house, they would take up and clean the carpets and wash the walls she breathed against. No one can have anything to do with such a person. There are no women who are not virtuous in Indian society. It is not at all as it is in this country. Here there are bad women living side by side with virtuous women in your society. One cannot know who is bad and who is good in America. But in India once a woman slips, she is an outcast for ever — she and her children, sons and daughters. It is terrible, I admit, but it keeps society pure." "How about the men?" was asked. "Does the same rule hold in regard to them? Are they outcast when they are proven to be unchaste?" "Oh, no. It is quite different with them. It would be so, perhaps, if they could be found out. But the men move about. They can go from place to place. It is not possible to discover them. The women are shut up in the house. They are certainly discovered if they do anything wrong. And when they are discovered, they are thrown out. Nothing can save them. Sometimes it is very hard when a father has to give up his daughter or a husband his wife. But if they do not give them up, they will be banished with them too. It is very different in this country. Women cannot go about there and make associations as they do here. It is very terrible, but it makes society pure. "I think that unchastity is the one great sin of your country. It must be so, there is so much luxury here. A poor girl would sell herself for a new bonnet. It must be so where there is so much luxury."

Mr. Kipling says this about Lalun and her profession:

"Lalun's real husband, for even ladies of Lalun's profession have husbands in the East, was a great, big jujube tree. Her mama, who had married a fig, spent ten thousand rupees on Lalun's wedding, which was blessed by forty-seven clergymen of mama's church, and distributed 5,000 rupees in charity to the poor. And that was a custom of the land."

In India when a woman is unfaithful to her husband she loses her caste, but none of her civil or religious rights. She can still own property and the temples are still open to her. 'Yes," said Kananda, "a bad woman is not allowed to marry. She cannot marry any one without their being an outcast like herself, so she marries a tree, or sometimes a sword. It is the custom. Sometimes these women grow very rich and become very charitable, but they can never regain their caste. In the interior towns, where they still adhere to the old customs, she cannot ride in a carriage, no matter how wealthy she may be; the best that she is allowed is a pair of bullocks. And then in India she has to wear a dress of her own, so that she can be distinguished. You can see these people going by, but no one ever speaks to them. The greatest number of these women is in the cities. A good many of them are Jews too, but they all have different quarters of the cities, you know. They all live apart. It is a singular thing that, bad as they are, wretched as some of these women are, they will not admit a Christian lover. They will not eat with them or touch them — the `omnivorous barbarians', as they call them. They call them that because they eat everything. Do you know what that disease, the unspeakable disease, is called in India? It is called `Bad Faringan', which means `the Christian disease'. It was the Christian that brought it into India. "Has there been any attempt in India to solve this question? Is it a public question the way it is in America?" "No, there has been very little done in India. There is a great field for women missionaries if they would convert prostitutes in India. They do nothing in India — very little. There is one sect, the Veshnava [Vaishnava][1], who try to reclaim these women. This is a religious sect. I think about 90 per cent [?] of all prostitutes belong to this sect. This sect does not believe in caste and they go everywhere without reference to caste. There are certain temples, as the temple of Jagatnot [Jagannath], where there is no caste. Everybody who goes into that town takes off his caste while he is there, because that is holy ground and everything is supposed to be pure there. When he goes outside, he resumes it again, for caste is a mere worldly thing. You know some of the castes are so particular that they will not eat any food unless it is prepared by themselves. They will not touch any one outside their caste. But in the city they all live together. This is the only sect in India that makes proselytes. It makes everybody a member of its church. It goes into the Himalayas and converts the wild men. You perhaps did not know that there were wild men in India. Yes, there are. They dwell at the foot of the Himalayas." "Is there any ceremony by which a woman is declared unchaste, a civil process?" Kananda was asked. "No, it is not a civil process. It is just custom. Sometimes there is a formal ceremony and sometimes there is not. They simply make pariahs out of them. When any woman is suspected sometimes they get together and give her a sort of trial, and if it is decided that she is guilty, then a note is sent around to all the other members of the caste, and she is banished. "Mind you," he exclaimed, "I do not mean to say that this is a solution of the question. The custom is terribly rigid. But you have no solution of the question, either. It is a terrible thing. It is a great wrong of the Western world."

---

1. Words in square brackets are ours.- ed.

TRANSLATION OF WRITINGS

Swami Vivekananda left Calcutta for the West, for the second time, on the 20th June, 1899, by the BISN steamship Golconda. In reading these pages the reader should remember that Swamiji wrote them in alight, humorous tone in Bengali, which it is impossible to render in English.

The second section of these memoirs, relates to his return journey from the West at the end of 1900.

These were originally published in the Udbodhan.

-EDITOR.

MEMOIRS OF EUROPEAN TRAVEL

I

Om Namo Nârâyanâya, ("Salutations to the Lord"; the usual form of addressing a Sannyasin. These memoirs of his second journey to the West were addressed to Swami Trigunatitananda, Editor, Udbodhan and hence this form of address.) Swâmi. — Pronounce the last syllable of the second word in a high pitch, brother, in the Hrishikesh fashion. For seven days we have been on board the ship and every day I think of writing to you something about our mode of life, and of writing materials also you have given me enough, but the characteristic lethargy of a Bengali stands in the way and foils everything. In the first place, there is idleness; every day I think of writing — what do you call it — a diary, but then, on account of various preoccupations, it is postponed to the endless "tomorrow", and does not progress an inch. In the second place, I do not remember the dates etc., at all; you must do me the favour to fill these up yourselves. And, besides, if you be very generous, you may think that like the great devotee, Hanuman, it is impossible for me to remember dates and such other trivialities — owing to the presence of the Lord in the heart. But the real truth is that it is due to my foolishness and idleness.

What nonsense! What comparison can there be between "the Solar Dynasty" (Swamiji here refers to Kâlidâsa's famous line of the Raghuvamsham: "O the difference between the majestic Solar Dynasty and my poor intellect!") — I beg your pardon — between Hanuman with his whole heart given to Shri Râma, the crown of the Solar Dynasty, and me, the lowest of the low! But then he crossed at one bound the ocean extending a hundred Yojanas, while we are crossing it confined within a wooden house, so to say, being pitched this side and that and somehow keeping ourselves on our feet with the help of posts and pillars. But there is one point of superiority on our side in that he had the blessed sight of Râkshasas and Râkshasis after reaching Lankâ, whereas we are going in company with them. At dinner time that glittering of a hundred knives and the clattering of a hundred forks frightened brother T __ (Turiyananda) out of his wits. He now and then started lest his neighbour with auburn hair and grey, cat-like eyes, through inadvertence might plunge her knife into his flesh, and the more so, as he is rather sleek and fat. I say, did Hanuman have sea-sickness while crossing the sea? Do the ancient books say anything on that? You are all well-read men, proficient in the Ramayana and other scriptures, so you may settle that question. But our modern authorities are silent on that point. Perhaps he had not; but then the fact of his having entered into the jaws of somebody raises a doubt. Brother T__ is also of opinion that when the prow of the ship suddenly heaves up towards heaven as if to consult with the king of gods, and immediately after plunges to the bottom of the ocean as if to pierce king Vali, residing in the nether worlds — he at that time feels that he is being swallowed by the terrible and wide-gaping jaws of somebody.

I beg your pardon, you have entrusted your work to a nice man! I owe you a description of the sea-voyage for seven days which will be full of poetry and interest, and be written in a polished, rhetorical style, but instead of that I am talking at random. But the fact is, having striven all my life to eat the kernel of Brahman, after throwing away the shell of Maya, how shall I now get the power of appreciating nature's beauties all of a sudden? All my life I have been on the move all over India, "from Varanasi to Kashmir, and thence to Khorasan, and Gujarat (Tulsidâs.)". How many hills and rivers, mountains and springs, and valleys and dales, how many cloud-belted peaks covered in perpetual snow, and oceans tempestuous, roaring and foamy, have I not seen, and heard of, and crossed! But sitting on a shabby wooden bedstead in a dark room of the ground floor, requiring a lamp to be lighted in the day-time, with the walls variegated by the stain of chewed betel leaves and made noisy by the squeaking and tickling of rats and moles and lizards, by the side of the main street resounding with the rattle of hackneys and tram-cars and darkened by clouds of dust — in such poetic environment, the pictures of the Himalayas, oceans, meadows, deserts, etc., that poet Shyamacharan, puffing at the all too familiar hookah, has drawn with such life-like precision, to the glory of the Bengalis — it is vain for us to try to imitate them! Shyamacharan in his boyhood went for a change to the up-country, where the water is so stimulating to the digestive functions that if you drink a tumblerful of it even after a very heavy meal, every bit of it will be digested and you will feel hungry again. Here it was that Shyamacharan's intuitive genius caught a glimpse of the sublime and beautiful aspects of nature. But there is one fly in the pot — they say that Shyamacharan's peregrinations extended as far as Burdwan (in Bengal) and no further!

But at your earnest request and also to prove that I am not wholly devoid of the poetic instinct either, I set myself to the task with God's name, and you, too, be all attention.

No ship generally leaves the port in the night — specially from a commercial port like Calcutta and in a river like the Hooghly or Ganga. Until the ship reaches the sea, it is in the charge of the pilot, who acts as the Captain, and he gives the command. His duty ends in either piloting the ship down to the sea or, if it be an incoming ship, from the mouth of the sea to the port. We have got two great dangers towards the mouth of the Hooghly — first, the James and Mary Banks near Budge-Budge, and second, the sandbank near the entrance to Diamond Harbour. Only in the high tide and during the day, the pilot can very carefully steer his ship, and in no other condition; consequently it took us two days to get out of the Hooghly.

Do you remember the Ganga at Hrishikesh? That clear bluish water — in which one can count the fins of fishes five yards below the surface — that wonderfully sweet, ice-cold "charming water of the Ganga (From Valmiki's hymn.)", and that wonderful sound of "Hara, Hara" of the running water, and the echo of "Hara, Hara" from the neighbouring mountain-falls? Do you remember that life in the forest, the begging of Mâdhukari (Meaning, collected from door to door, in small bits.) alms, eating on small islands of rock in the bed of the Ganga, hearty drinking of that water with the palms, and the fearless wandering of fishes all round for crumbs of bread? You remember that love for Ganga water, that glory of the Ganga, the touch of its water that makes the mind dispassionate, that Ganga flowing over the Himalayas, through Srinagar, Tehri, Uttarkasi, and Gangotri — some of you have seen even the source of the Ganga! But there is a certain unforgettable fascination in our Ganga of Calcutta, muddy, and whitish — as if from contact with Shiva's body — and bearing a large number of ships on her bosom. Is it merely patriotism or the impressions of childhood? — Who knows? What wonderful relation is this between mother Ganga and the Hindus? Is it merely superstition? May be. They spend their lives with the name of Ganga on their lips, they die immersed in the waters of the Ganga, men from far off places take away Ganga water with them, keep it carefully in copper vessels, and sip drops of it on holy festive occasions. Kings and princes keep it in jars, and at considerable expense take the water from Gangotri to pour it on the head of Shiva at Rameshwaram! The Hindus visit foreign countries — Rangoon, Java, Hongkong, Madagascar, Suez, Aden, Malta — and they take with them Ganga water and the Gitâ.

The Gita and the sacred waters of the Ganga constitute the Hinduism of the Hindus. Last time I went to the West, I also took a little of it with me, fearing it might be needed, and whenever opportunities occurred I used to drink a few drops of it. And every time I drank, in the midst of the stream of humanity, amid that bustle of civilisation, that hurry of frenzied footsteps of millions of men and women in the West, the mind at once became calm and still, as it were. That stream of men, that intense activity of the West, that clash and competition at every step, those seats of luxury and celestial opulence — Paris, London, New York, Berlin, Rome — all would disappear and I used to hear that wonderful sound of "Hara, Hara", to see that lonely forest on the sides of the Himalayas, and feel the murmuring heavenly river coursing through the heart and brain and every artery of the body and thundering forth, "Hara, Hara, Hara!"

This time you, too, I see, have sent Mother Ganga, for Madras. But, dear brother, what a strange vessel have you put Mother in! Brother T__ is a Brahmachârin from his boyhood, and looks "like burning fire through the force of his spirituality (Kâlidâsa's Kumârasambhavam.)". Formerly as a Brâhmana he used to be saluted as "Namo Brahmané", and now it is — oh, the sublimity of it! — "Namo Nârâyanâya", as he is a Sannyâsin. And it is perhaps due to that, that Mother, in his custody, has left her seat in the Kamandalu of Brahmâ, and been forced to enter a jar! Anyhow, getting up from bed late at night I found that Mother evidently could not bear staying in that awkward vessel and was trying to force her passage out of it. I thought it most dangerous, for if Mother chose to re-enact here those previous scenes of her life, such as piercing the Himalayas, washing away the great elephant Airâvata, and pulling down the hut of the sage Jahnu, then it would be a terrible affair. I offered many prayers to Mother and said to her in various supplicatory phrases, "Mother, do wait a little, let us reach Madras tomorrow, and there you can do whatever you like. There are many there more thick-skulled than elephants — most of them with huts like that of Jahnu — while those half-shaven, shining heads with ample hair-tufts are almost made of stone, compared to which even the Himalayas would be soft as butter! You may break them as much as you like; now pray wait a little." But all my supplications were in vain. Mother would not listen to them. Then I hit upon a plan, and said to her, "Mother, look at those turbaned servants with jackets on, moving to and fro on the ship, they are Mohammedans, real, beef-eating Mohammedans, and those whom you find moving about sweeping and cleaning the rooms etc., are real scavengers, disciples of Lâl Beg; and if you do not hear me, I will call them and ask them to touch you! Even if that is not sufficient to quiet you, I will just send you to your father's home; you see that room there, if you are shut in there, you will get back to your primitive condition in the Himalayas, when all your restlessness will be silenced, and you shall remain frozen into a block of ice." That silenced her. So it is everywhere, not only in the case of gods, but among men also — whenever they get a devotee, they take an undue advantage over him.

See, how I have again strayed from my subject and am talking at random. I have already told you at the outset that those things are not in my line, but if you bear with me, I shall try again.

There is a certain beauty in one's own people which is not to be found anywhere else. Even the denizens of Paradise cannot compare in point of beauty with our brothers and sisters, or sons and daughters, however uncouth they may be. But, if, even roaming over Paradise and seeing the people there, you find your own people coming out really beautiful, then there is no bound to your delight. There is also a special beauty in our Bengal, covered with endless verdant stretches of grass, and bearing as garlands a thousand rivers and streams. A little of this beauty one finds in Malabar, and also in Kashmir. Is there not beauty in water? When there is water everywhere, and heavy showers of rain are running down arum leaves, while clumps of cocoanut and date palms slightly bend their heads under that downpour, and there is the continuous croaking of frogs all round — is there no beauty in such a scene as this? And one cannot appreciate the beauty of the banks of our Ganga, unless one is returning from foreign countries and entering the river by its mouth at Diamond Harbour. That blue, blue sky, containing in its bosom black clouds, with golden-fringed whitish clouds below them, underneath which clumps of cocoanut and date palms toss their tufted heads like a thousand chowries, and below them again is an assemblage of light, deep, yellowish, slightly dark, and other varieties of green massed together — these being the mango, lichi, blackberry, and jack-fruit trees, with an exuberance of leaves and foliage that entirely hide the trunk, branches, and twigs — while, close by, clusters of bamboos toss in the wind, and at the foot of all lies that grass, before whose soft and glossy surface the carpets of Yarkand, Persia, and Turkistan are almost as nothing — as far as the eye can reach that green, green grass looking as even as if some one had trimmed and pruned it, and stretching right down to the edge of the river — as far down the banks as where the gentle waves of the Ganga have submerged and are pushing playfully against, the land is framed with green grass, and just below this is the sacred water of the Ganga. And if you sweep your eye from the horizon right up to the zenith, you will notice within a single line such a play of diverse colours, such manifold shades of the same colour, as you have witnessed nowhere else. I say, have you ever come under the fascination of colours — the sort of fascination which impels the moths to die in the flame, and the bees to starve themselves to death in the prison of flowers? I tell you one thing — if you want to enjoy the beauty of Gangetic scenery, enjoy it to your heart's content now, for very soon the whole aspect will be altered. In the hands of money-grabbing merchants, everything will disappear. In place of that green grass, brick kilns will be reared and burrow-pits for the brickfields will be sunk. Where, now, the tiny wavelets of the Ganga are playing with the grass, there will be moored the jute-laden flats and those cargo-boats; and those variegated colours of cocoa-nuts and palms, of mangoes and lichis, that blue sky, the beauty of the clouds — these you will altogether miss hereafter; and you will find instead the enveloping smoke of coal, and standing ghostlike in the midst of that smoke, the half-distinct chimneys of the factories!

Now our ship has reached the sea. The description, which you read in Kalidasa's Raghuvamsham of the shores "of the sea appearing blue with forests of palm and other trees" and "looking like a slender rim of rust on the tyre of an iron wheel" etc. — is not at all accurate and faithful. With all my respects for the great poet, it is my belief that he never in his life saw either the ocean or the Himalayas. (Swamiji afterwards changed his opinion with regard to the last part, i.e. Kalidasa's acquaintance with the Himalayas.)

Here there is a blending of white and black waters, somewhat resembling the confluence of the Ganga and Jamuna at Allahabad. Though Mukti (liberation) may be rare in most places, it is sure at "Hardwar, Allahabad, and the mouth of the Ganga". But they say that this is not the real mouth of the river. However, let me salute the Lord here, for "He has His eyes, and head and face everywhere (Gita, XIII, 13.)".

How beautiful! As far as the eye reaches, the deep blue waters of the sea are rising into foamy waves and dancing rhythmically to the winds. Behind us lie the sacred waters of the Ganga, whitened with the ashes of Shiva's body, as we read in the description, "Shiva's matted locks whitened by the foam of the Ganga (Shankaracharya's hymn.)". The water of the Ganga is comparatively still. In front of us lies the parting line between the waters. There ends the white water. Now begin the blue waters of the ocean — before, behind and all round there is only blue, blue water everywhere, breaking incessantly into waves. The sea has blue hair, his body is of a blue complexion, and his garment is also blue. We read in the Puranas that millions of Asuras hid themselves under the ocean through fear of the gods. Today their opportunity has come, today Neptune is their ally, and Aeolus is at their back. With hideous roars and thundering shouts they are today dancing a terrible war-dance on the surface of the ocean, and the foamy waves are their grim laughter! In the midst of this tumult is our ship, and on board the ship, pacing the deck with lordly steps, are men and women of that nation which rules the sea-girt world, dressed in charming attire, with a complexion like the moonbeams — looking like self-reliance and self-confidence personified, and appearing to the black races as pictures of pride and haughtiness. Overhead, the thunder of the cloudy monsoon sky, on all sides the dance and roar of foam-crested waves, and the din of the powerful engines of our ship setting at naught the might of the sea — it was a grand conglomeration of sounds, to which I was listening, lost in wonder, as if in a half-waking state, when, all of a sudden, drowning all these sounds, there fell upon my ears the deep and sonorous music of commingled male and female voices singing in chorus the national anthem, "Rule Britannia, Britannia rules the waves!" Startled, I looked around and found that the ship was rolling heavily, and brother T__, holding his head with his hands was struggling against an attack of sea-sickness.

In the second class are two Bengali youths going to the West for study, whose condition is worse. One of them looks so frightened that he would be only too glad to scuttle straight home if he were allowed to land. These two lads and we two are the only Indians on the ship — the representatives of modern India. During the two days the ship was in the Ganga, brother T__, under the secret instructions of the Editor, Udbodhan, used to urge me very much to finish my article on "Modern India" quickly. I too found an opportunity today and asked him, "Brother, what do you think is the condition of modern India?" And he, casting a look towards the second class and another at himself, said, with a sigh, "Very sad, getting very much muddled up!"

The reason why so much importance is attached to the Hooghly branch of the Ganga, instead of the bigger one, Padmâ, is, according to many, that the Hooghly was the primary and principal course of the river, and latterly the river shifted its course, and created an outlet by the Padma. Similarly the present "Tolley's Nullah" represents the ancient course of the Ganga, and is known as the Âdi-Gangâ. The sailing merchant, the hero of Kavikankan's work, makes his voyage to Ceylon along that channel. Formerly the Ganga was navigable for big ships up to Triveni. The ancient port of Saptagrâm was situated a little distance off Triveni ghat, on the river Saraswati. From very ancient times Saptagram was the principal port for Bengal's foreign trade. Gradually the mouth of the Saraswati got silted up. In the year 1539 it silted up so much that the Portuguese settlers had to take up a site further down the Ganga, for their ships to come up. The site afterwards developed into the famous town of Hooghly. From the commencement of the sixteenth century both Indian and foreign merchants were feeling much anxiety about the silting up of the Ganga. But what of that? Human engineering skill has hitherto proved ineffectual against the gradual silting up of the river-bed which continues to the present day. In 1666 a French Missionary writes that the Ganga near Suti got completely silted up at the time. Holwell, of Black-Hole fame, on his way to Murshidabad was compelled to resort to small country-boats on account of the shallowness of the river at Santipur. In 1797 Captain Colebrook writes that country-boats could not ply in the Hooghly and the Jalangi during summer. During the years 1822-1884, the Hooghly was closed to all boat-traffic. For twenty-four years within this period the water was only two or three feet deep. In the seventeenth century, the Dutch planted a trade settlement at Chinsura, one mile below Hooghly. The French, who came still later, established their settlement at Chandernagore, still further down the river. In 1723 the German Ostend Company opened a factory at Bankipore, five miles below Chandernagore on the other side of the river. In 1616 the Danes had started a factory at Serampore, eight miles below Chandernagore, and then the English established the city of Calcutta still further down the river. None of the above places are now accessible to ships, only Calcutta being open now. But everybody is afraid of its future.

There is one curious reason why there remains so much water in the Ganga up to about Santipur even during summer. When the flow of the surface water has ceased, large quantities of water percolating through the subsoil find their way into the river. The bed of the Ganga is even now considerably below the level of the land on either side. If the level of the river-bed should gradually rise owing to the subsidence of fresh soil, then the trouble will begin. And there is talk about another danger. Even near Calcutta, through earthquakes or other causes, the river at times dried up so much that one could wade across. It is said that in 1770 such a state of things happened. There is another report that on Thursday, the 9th October, 1734, during ebb-tide in the noon, the river dried up completely. Had it happened a little later, during the inauspicious last portion of the day, I leave it to you to infer the result. Perhaps then the river would not have returned to its bed again.

So far, then, as regards the upper portion of the Hooghly; now as regards the portion below Calcutta. The great dangers to be faced in this portion are the James and Mary Banks. Formerly the river Damodar had its confluence with the Ganga thirty miles above Calcutta, but now, through the curious transformations of time, the confluence is over thirty-one miles to the south of it. Some six miles below this point the Rupnarayan pours its waters into the Ganga. The fact is there, that these two feeders rush themselves into the Ganga in happy combination — but how shall this huge quantity of mud be disposed of? Consequently big sandbanks are formed in the bed of the river, which constantly shift their position and are sometimes rather loose and sometimes a compact mass, causing no end of fear. Day and night soundings of the river's depth are being taken, the omission of which for a few days, through carelessness, would mean the destruction of ships. No sooner will a ship strike against them than it will either capsize or be straightway swallowed up in them! Cases are even recorded that within half an hour of a big three-masted ship striking one of these sandbanks, the whole of it disappeared in the sand, leaving only the top of the masts visible. These sandbanks may rightly be considered as the mouth of the Damodar-Rupnarayan. (There is a pun on the words Damodar-Rupnarayan which not only imply the two rivers, but also mean "Narayana as Damodara, or swallowing everything (Damodara-rupa-Narayana).") The Damodar is not now satisfied with Santhal villages, and is swallowing ships and steamers etc. as a sauce by way of variety. In 1877 a ship named "County of Sterling", with a cargo of 1,444 tons of wheat from Calcutta, had no sooner struck one of these terrible sandbanks than within eight minutes there was no trace left of it. In 1874 a steamer carrying a load of 2,400 tons suffered the same fate in two minutes. Blessed be thy mouth, O Mother Ganga! I salute thee for allowing us to get off scot-free. Brother T__ says, "Sir, a goat ought to be offered to the Mother for her benignity." I replied, "Exactly so, brother, but why offer only one day, instead of everyday!" Next day brother T__ readverted to the topic, but I kept silent. The next day after that I pointed out to him at dinner-time to what an extent the offering of goats was progressing. Brother seemed rather puzzled and said, "What do you mean? It is only you who are eating." Then at considerable pains I had to explain to him how it was said that a youth of Calcutta once visited his father-in-law's place in a remote village far from the Ganga. There at dinner-time he found people waiting about with drums etc., and his mother-in-law insisted on his taking a little milk before sitting to dinner. The son-in-law considered it might perhaps be a local custom which he had better obey; but no sooner had he taken a sip of the milk than the drums began to play all around and his mother-in-law, with tears of joy, placed her hand on his head and blessed him, saying, "My son, you have really discharged the duties of a son today; look here, you have in your stomach the water of the Ganga, as you live on its banks, and in the milk there was the powdered bone of your deceased father-in-law; so by this act of yours his bones have reached the Ganga and his spirit has obtained all the merits thereof." So here was a man from Calcutta, and on board the ship there was plenty of meat preparations and every time one ate them, meat was being offered to mother Ganga. So he need not be at all anxious on the subject. Brother T__ is of such a grave disposition that it was difficult to discover what impression the lecture made on him.

What a wonderful thing a ship is! The sea, which from the shore looks so fearful, in the heart of which the sky seems to bend down and meet, from whose bosom the sun slowly rises and in which it sinks again, and the least frown of which makes the heart quail — that sea has been turned into a highway, the cheapest of all routes, by ships. Who invented the ship? No one in particular. That is to say, like all machinery indispensable to men — without which they cannot do for a single moment, and by the combination and adjustment of which all kinds of factory plants have been constructed — the ship also is the outcome of joint labour. Take for instance the wheels; how absolutely indispensable they are! From the creaking bullock-cart to the car of Jagannath, from the spinning wheel to the stupendous machinery of factories, everywhere there is use for the wheel. Who invented the wheel? No one in particular, that is to say, all jointly. The primitive man used to fell trees with axes, roll big trunks along inclined planes; by degrees they were cut into the shape of solid wheels, and gradually the naves and spokes of the modern wheel came into vogue. Who knows how many millions of years it took to do this? But in India all the successive stages of improvement are preserved. However much they may be improved or transformed, there are always found men to occupy the lower stages of evolution, and consequently the whole series is preserved. First of all a musical instrument was formed with a string fixed to a piece of bamboo. Gradually it came to be played by a horsehair bow, and the first violin was made; then it passed through various transformations, with different sorts of strings and guts, and the bow also assumed different forms and names, till at last the highly finished guitar and sarang etc., came into existence. But in spite of this, do not the Mohammedan cabmen even now with a shabby horsehair bow play on the crude instrument made of a bamboo pipe fixed to an earthen pot, and sing the story of Majwar Kahar weaving his fishing net? Go to the Central Provinces, and you will find even now solid wheels rolling on the roads — though it bespeaks a dense intellect on the part of the people, specially in these days of rubber tyres.

In very ancient times, that is, in the golden age, when the common run of people were so sincere and truthful that they would not even cover their bodies for fear of hypocrisy — making the exterior look different from the interior — would not marry lest they might contract selfishness, and banishing all ideas of distinction between meum and tuum always used to look upon the property of others "as mere clods of earth", on the strength of bludgeons, stones, etc. (Swamiji is ironically describing the naked primitive man, to whom marriage was unknown, and who had no respect for person or property.); — in those blessed times, for voyaging over water, they constructed canoes and rafts and so forth, burning out the interior of a tree, or by fastening together a few logs of trees. Haven't you seen catamarans along the sea-coast from Orissa to Colombo? And you must have observed how far into the sea the rafts can go. There you have rudiments of ship-building.

And that boat of the East Bengal boatmen boarding which you have to call on the five patron-saints of the river for your safety; your house-boat manned by Chittagong boatmen, which even in a light storm makes its helmsmen declare his inability to control the helm, and all the passengers are asked to take the names of their respective gods as a last resort; that big up-country boat with a pair of fantastic brass eyes at the prow, rowed by the oarsmen in a standing posture; that boat of merchant Shrimanta's voyage (according to Kavikankan, Shrimanta crossed the Bay of Bengal simply by rowing, and was about to be drowned owing to his boat getting caught in the antennae of a shoal of lobsters, and almost capsizing! Also he mistook a shell for a tiny fish, and so on), in other words the Gangasagar boat — nicely roofed above and having a floor of split bamboos, and containing in its hold rows of jars filled with Ganga water (which is deliciously cool, I beg your pardon, you visit Gangasagar during hard winter, and the chill north wind drives away all your relish for cooling drinks); and that small-sized boat which daily takes the Bengali Babus to their office and brings them back home, and is superintended over by the boatman of Bally, very expert and very clever — no sooner does he sight a cloud so far away as Konnagar than he puts the boat in safety! — they are now passing into the hands of the strong-bodied men from Jaunpur who speak a peculiar dialect, and whom your Mahant Maharaj, out of fun ordered to catch a heron — which he facetiously styled as "Bakâsur (A demon of the shape of a big heron, mentioned in the Bhagavâta.)", and this puzzled them hopelessly and they stammered out, "Please, sire, where are we to get this demon? It is an enigma to us"; then that bulky, slow-moving (cargo) boat nicknamed "Gâdhâ (donkey)" in Bengali, which never goes straight, but always goes sideways; and that big species of boats, like the schooner, having from one to three masts, which imports cargoes of cocoanuts, dates and dried fish from Ceylon, the Maldives, or Arabia; — these and many others too numerous to mention, represent the subsequent development in naval construction.

To steer a ship by means of sails is a wonderful discovery. To whichever direction the wind may be blowing, by a clever manipulation of the sails, the ship is sure to reach her destination. But she takes more time when the wind is contrary. A sailing ship is a most beautiful sight, and from a distance looks like a many-winged great bird descending from the skies. Sails, however, do not allow a ship to steer straight ahead, and if the wind is a little contrary, she has to take a zigzag course. But when there is a perfect lull, the ship is helpless and has to lower her sails and stand still. In the equatorial regions it frequently happens even now. Nowadays sailing ships also have very little of wood in them and are mostly made of iron. It is much more difficult to be the captain or sailor of a sailing ship than in a steamer, and no one can be a good captain in sailing ship without experience. To know the direction of the wind at every step and to be on one's guard against danger-spots long ahead — these two qualifications are indispensably necessary in a sailing ship, more than in a steamer. A steamer is to a great extent under human control — the engines can be stopped in a moment. It can be steered ahead, or astern, sideways or in any desired direction, within a very short time, but the sailing ship is at the mercy of the wind. By the time the sails can be lowered or the helm turned, the ship may strike a bank or run up on a submarine rock or collide with another ship. Nowadays sailing ships very seldom carry passengers, except coolies. They generally carry cargo, and that also inferior stuff, such as salt etc. Small sailing ships such as the schooner, do coasting trade. Sailing ships cannot afford to hire steamers to tow them along the Suez Canal and spend thousands of rupees as toll, so they can go to England in six months by rounding Africa.

Due to all these disadvantages of sailing ships, naval warfare in the past was a risky affair. A slight change in the course of the wind or in the ocean-current would decide the fate of a battle. Again, those ships, being made of wood, would frequently catch fire, which had to be put out. Their construction also was of a different type; one end was flat and very high, with five or six decks. On the uppermost deck at this end there used to be a wooden verandah, in front of which were the commander's room and office and on either side were the officers' cabins. Then there was a large open space, at the other end of which were a few cabins. The lower decks also had similar roofed halls, one underneath the other. In the lowermost deck or hold were the sailor's sleeping and dining rooms, etc. On either side of each deck were ranged cannon, their muzzles projecting through the rows of apertures in the ships' walls; and on both sides were heaps of cannon balls (and powder bags in times of war). All the decks of these ancient men-of-war had very low roofs and one had to carry his head down when moving about. Then it was a troublesome business to secure marines for naval warfare. There was a standing order of the Government to enlist men by force or guile wherever they could be found. Sons were violently snatched away from their mothers, and husbands from their wives. Once they were made to board the ship, (which perhaps the poor fellows had never done in their lives), they were ordered straightway to climb the masts! And if through fear they failed to carry out the order, they were flogged. Some would also die under the ordeal. It was the rich and influential men of the country who made these laws, it was they who would appropriate the benefits of commerce, or ravage, or conquest of different countries, and the poor people were simply to shed their blood and sacrifice their lives — as has been the rule throughout the world's history!

Now those laws exist no longer, and the name of the Pressgang does not now send a shiver through the hearts of the peasantry and poor folk. Now it is voluntary service, but many juvenile criminals are trained as sailors in men-of-war, instead of being thrown into prison.

Steam-power has revolutionised all this, and sails are almost superfluous ornaments in ships nowadays. They depend very little on winds now, and there is much less danger from gales and the like. Ships have now only to take care that they do not strike against submarine rocks. And men-of-war of the present day are totally different from those of the past. In the first place, they do not at all look like ships, but rather like floating iron fortresses of varying dimensions. The number of cannon also has been much reduced, but compared with the modern turret-guns, those of the past were mere child's play. And how fast these men-of-war are! The smallest of these are the torpedo-boats; those that are a little bigger are for capturing hostile merchant-ships, and the big ones are the ponderous instruments for the actual naval fight.

During the Civil War of the United States of America, the Unionist party fixed rows of iron rails against the outer walls of a wooden ship so as to cover them. The enemy's cannon-balls striking against them were repulsed without doing any harm to the ship. After this, as a rule, the ship's sides began to be clad in iron, so that hostile balls might not penetrate the wood. The ship's cannon also began to improve — bigger and bigger cannon were constructed and the work of moving, loading, and firing them came to be executed by machinery, instead of with the hand. A cannon which even five hundred men cannot move an inch, can now be turned vertically or horizontally, loaded and fired by a little boy pressing a button, and all this in a second! As the iron wall of ships began to increase in thickness, so cannon with the power of thunder also began to be manufactured. At the present day, a battle-ship is a fortress with walls of steel, and the guns are almost as Death itself. A single shot is enough to smash the biggest ship into fragments. But this "iron bridal-chamber" — which Nakindar's father (in the popular Bengali tale) never even dreamt of, and which, instead of standing on the top of "Sâtâli Hill" moves dancing on seventy thousand mountain-like billows, even this is mortally afraid of torpedoes! The torpedo is a tube somewhat shaped like a cigar, and if fired at an object travels under water like a fish. Then, the moment it hits its object, the highly explosive materials it contains explode with a terrific noise, and the ship under which this takes place is reduced to its original condition, that is, partly into iron and wooden fragments, and partly into smoke and fire! And no trace is found of the men who are caught in this explosion of the torpedo — the little that is found, is almost in a state of mince-meat! Since the invention of these torpedoes, naval wars cannot last long. One or two fights, and a big victory is scored or a total defeat. But the wholesale loss of men of both parties in naval fight which men apprehended before the introduction of these men-of-war has been greatly falsified by facts.

If a fraction of the volley of balls discharged during a field-fight from the guns and rifles of each hostile army on the opponents hit their aim, then both rival armies would be killed to a man in two minutes. Similarly if only one of five hundred shots fired from a battle-ship in action hit its mark, then no trace would be left of the ships on both sides. But the wonder is that, as guns and rifles are improving in quality, as the latter are being made lighter, and the rifling in their barrels finer, as the range is increasing, as machinery for loading is being multiplied, and rate of firing quickened — the more they seem to miss their aim! Armed with the old fashioned unusually long-barrelled musket — which has to be supported on a two-legged wooden stand while firing, and ignited by actually setting fire and blowing into it — the Barakhjais and the Afridis can fire with unerring precision, while the modern trained soldier with the highly complex machine-guns of the present day fires 150 rounds in a minute and serves merely to heat the atmosphere! Machinery in a small proportion is good, but too much of it kills man's initiative and makes a lifeless machine of him. The men in factories are doing the same monotonous work, day after day, night after night, year after year, each batch of men doing one special bit of work — such as fashioning the heads of pins, or uniting the ends of threads, or moving backwards or forwards with the loom — for a whole life. And the result is that the loss of that special job means death to them — they find no other means of living and starve. Doing routine work like a machine, one becomes a lifeless machine. For that reason, one serving as a schoolmaster or a clerk for a whole lifetime ends by turning a stupendous fool.

The form of merchantmen and passenger-ships is of a different type. Although some merchant-ships are so constructed that in times of war they can easily be equipped with a few guns and give chase to unarmed hostile merchant-ships, for which they get remuneration from their respective Governments, still they generally differ widely from warships. These are now mostly steamships and generally so big and expensive that they are seldom owned by individuals, but by companies. Among the carrying companies for Indian and European trade, the P. & O. Company is the oldest and richest, then comes the B. I. S. N. Company, and there are many others. Among those of foreign nationalities, the Messageries Maritimes (French) the Austrian Lloyd, the German Lloyd, and the Rubattino Company (Italian), are the most famous. Of these the passenger-ships of the P. & O. Company are generally believed to be the safest and fastest. And the arrangements of food in the Messageries Maritimes are excellent.

When we left for Europe this time, the last two companies had stopped booking "native" passengers for fear of the plague-infection. And there is a law of the Indian Government that no "native" of India can go abroad without a certificate from the Emigration Office, in order to make sure that nobody is enticing him away to foreign countries to sell him as a slave or to impress him as a coolie, but that he is going of his own free will. This written document must be produced before they will take him into the ship. This law was so long silent against the Indian gentry going to foreign countries. Now on account of the plague epidemic it has been revived, so that the Government may be informed about every "native" going out. Well, in our country we hear much about some people belonging to the gentry and some to the lower classes. But in the eyes of the Government all are "natives" without exception. Maharajas, Rajas, Brahmins, Kshatriyas, Vaishyas, Shudras — all belong to one and the same class — that of "natives". The law, and the test which applies to coolies, is applicable to all "natives" without distinction. Thanks to you, O English Government, through your grace, for a moment at least I feel myself one with the whole body of "natives". It is all the more welcome, because this body of mine having come of a Kâyastha family, I have become the target of attack of many sections. Nowadays we hear it from the lips of people of all castes in India that they are all full-blooded Aryans — only there is some difference of opinion amongst them about the exact percentage of Aryan blood in their veins, some claiming to have the full measure of it, while others may have one ounce more or less than another — that is all. But in this they are all unanimous that their castes are all superior to the Kayastha! And it is also reported that they and the English race belong to the same stock — that they are cousins-german to each other, and that they are not "natives". And they have come to this country out of humanitarian principles, like the English. And such evil customs as child-marriage, polygamy, image-worship, the sutti, the zenana-system, and so forth have no place in their religion — but these have been introduced by the ancestors of the Kayasthas, and people of that ilk. Their religion also is of the same pattern as that of the English! And their forefathers looked just like the English, only living under the tropical sun of India has turned them black! Now come forward with your pretensions, if you dare! "You are all natives", the Government says. Amongst that mass of black, a shade deeper or lighter cannot be distinguished. The Government says, "They are all natives". Now it is useless for you to dress yourselves after the English fashion. Your European hats etc., will avail you little henceforth. If you throw all the blame on the Hindus, and try to fraternise with the English, you would thereby come in for a greater share of cuffs and blows and not less. Blessings to you, O English Government! You have already become the favoured child of Fortune; may your prosperity increase ever more! We shall be happy once more to wear our loin-cloth and Dhoti — the native dress. Through your grace we shall continue to travel from one end of the country to the other, bare-headed, and barefooted, and heartily eat our habitual food of rice and Dâl with our fingers, right in the Indian fashion. Bless the Lord! We had well-nigh been tempted by Anglo-Indian fashions and been duped by its glamour. We heard it said that no sooner did we give up our native dress, native religion, and native manners and customs, than the English people would take us on their shoulders and lionise us. And we were about to do so, when smack came the whip of the Englishman and the thud of British boots — and immediately men were seized by a panic and turned away, bidding good-bye to English ways, eager to confess their "native" birth.

"The English ways we'd copy with such pains, The British boots did stamp out from our brains!"

Blessed be the English Government! May their throne be firm and their rule permanent. And the little tendency that remained in me for taking to European ways vanished, thanks to the Americans. I was sorely troubled by an overgrown beard, but no sooner did I peep into a hair-cutting saloon than somebody called out, "This is no place for such shabby-looking people as you." I thought that perhaps seeing me so quaintly dressed in turban and Gerua cloak, the man was prejudiced against me. So I should go and buy an English coat and hat. I was about to do this when fortunately I met an American gentleman who explained to me that it was much better that I was dressed in my Gerua cloak, for now the gentlemen would not take me amiss, but if I dressed in European fashion, everybody would chase me away. I met the same kind of treatment in one or two other saloons. After which I began the practice of shaving with my own hands. Once I was burning with hunger, and went into a restaurant, and asked for a particular thing, whereupon the man said, "We do not stock it." "Why, it is there." "Well, my good man, in plain language it means there is no place here for you to sit and take your meal." "And why?" "Because nobody will eat at the same table with you, for he will be outcasted." Then America began to look agreeable to me, somewhat like my own caste-ridden country. Out with these differences of white and black, and this nicety about the proportion of Aryan blood among the "natives"! How awkward it looks for slaves to be over-fastidious about pedigree! There was a Dom (a man of the sweeper-caste) who used to say, "You won't find anywhere on earth a caste superior to ours. You must know we are Dom-m-m-s!" But do you see the fun of it? The excesses about caste distinctions obtain most among peoples who are least honoured among mankind.

Steamships are generally much bigger than sailing ships. The steamships that ply across the Atlantic are just half as much bigger than the "Golconda". (The B. I. S. N. steamer in which Swami Vivekananda went to the West for the second time.) The ship on which I crossed the Pacific from Japan was also very big. In the centre of the biggest ships are the first class compartments with some open space on either side; then comes the second class, flanked by the "steerage" on either side. At one end are the sailors' and servants' quarters. The steerage corresponds to the third class, in which very poor people go as passengers, as, for instance, those who are emigrating to America, Australia, etc. The accommodation for them is very small and the food is served not on tables but from hand to hand. There is no steerage in ships which ply between England and India, but they take deck-passengers. The open space between the first and second classes is used by them for sitting or sleeping purposes. But I did not notice a single deck-passenger bound for a long journey. Only in 1893, on my way to China, I found a number of Chinamen going as deck-passengers from Bombay to Hongkong.

During stormy weather, the deck-passengers suffer great inconvenience, and also to a certain extent at ports when the cargo is unloaded. Excepting in the hurricane-deck which is on top of all, there is a square opening in all other decks, through which cargo is loaded and unloaded, at which times the deck-passengers are put to some trouble. Otherwise, it is very pleasant on the deck at night from Calcutta to Suez, and in summer, through Europe also. When the first and second class passengers are about to melt in their furnished compartments on account of the excessive heat, then the deck is almost a heaven in comparison. The second class in ships of this type is very uncomfortable. Only, in the ships of the newly started German Lloyd Company plying between Bergen, in Germany and Australia, the second class arrangements are excellent; there are cabins even in the hurricane-deck, and food arrangements are almost on a par with those of the first class in the "Golconda". That line touches Colombo on the way.

In the "Golconda" there are only two cabins on the hurricane-deck, one on each side; one is for the doctor, and the other was allotted to us. But owing to the excessive heat, we had to take shelter in the lower deck, for our cabin was just above the engine-room of the ship. Although the ship is made of iron, yet the passengers' cabins are made of wood. And there are many holes along the top and bottom of the wooden walls of these, for the free passage of air. The walls are painted over with ivory-paint which has cost nearly £25 per room. There is a small carpet spread on the floor and against one of the walls are fixed two frameworks somewhat resembling iron bedsteads without legs, one on top of the other. Similarly on the opposite wall. Just opposite the entrance there is a wash-basin, over which there is a looking-glass, two bottles, and two tumblers for drinking water. Against the sides of each bed is attached a netting in brass frames which can be fixed up to the wall and again lowered down. In it the passengers put their watch and other important personal necessaries before retiring. Below the lower bedstead, there is room for storing the trunks and bags. The second class arrangements are on a similar plan, only the space is narrower and the furniture of an inferior quality. The shipping business is almost a monopoly of the English. Therefore in the ships constructed by other nations also, the food arrangements, as well as the regulation of the time, have to be made in the English fashion, to suit the large number of English passengers in them. There are great differences between England, France, Germany, and Russia, as regards food and time. Just as in our country, there are great differences between Bengal, Northern India, the Mahratta country, and Gujarat. But these differences are very little observed in the ships, because there, owing to a majority of English-speaking passengers, everything is being moulded after the English fashion.

The Captain is the highest authority in a ship. Formerly the Captain used to rule in the ship in the high seas, punishing offenders, hanging pirates, and so forth. Now he does not go so far, but his word is law on board a ship. Under him are four officers (or malims, in Indian vernacular). Then come four or five engineers, the chief engineer ranking equally with an officer and getting first class food. And there are four or five steersmen (sukanis, in Indian vernacular) who hold the helm by turns — they are also Europeans. The rest, comprising the servants, the sailors, and the coalmen are all Indian, and all of them Mohammedans; Hindu sailors I saw only on the Bombay side, in P. & O. ships. The servants and the sailors are from Calcutta, while the coalmen belong to East Bengal; the cooks also are Catholic Christians of East Bengal. There are four sweepers besides, whose duty it is to clear out dirty water from the compartments, make arrangements for bath and keep the latrines etc. clean and tidy. The Mohammedan servants and lascars do not take food cooked by Christians; besides, every day there are preparations of ham or bacon on board the ship. But they manage to set up some sort of privacy for themselves. They have no objection to taking bread prepared in the ship's kitchen, and those servants from Calcutta who have received the "new light" of civilisation, do not observe any restrictions in matters of food. There are three messes for the men, one for the servants, one for the sailors, and one for the coalmen. The company provides each mess with a cook and a servant; every mess has got a separate place for cooking. A few Hindu passengers, were going from Calcutta to Colombo, and they used to do their cooking in one of these kitchens after the servants had finished theirs. The servants draw their own drinking water. On every deck two pumps are fixed against the wall, one on each side; the one is for sweet and the other for salt water, and the Mohammedans draw sweet water from this for their own use. Those Hindus who have no objection to taking pipe-water can very easily go on these ships to England and elsewhere, observing all their orthodoxy in matters of food and drink. They can get a kitchen, and drinking water free from the touch of any, and even the bathing water need not be touched by anybody else; all kinds of food such as rice, pulse, vegetables, fish, meat, milk, and ghee are available on the ship, especially on these ships where mostly Indians are employed, to whom rice, pulse, radish, cabbage, and potato, etc. have to be supplied every day. The one thing necessary is money. With money you can proceed anywhere alone, observing full orthodoxy.

These Bengali servants are employed nowadays in almost all ships that ply between Calcutta and Europe. They are gradually forming into a class by themselves. Several nautical terms also are being coined by them; for instance, the captain is termed bariwallah (landlord); the officer malim; the mast 'dôl'; a sail sarh; bring down aria; raise habish (heave), etc.

The body of lascars and coalmen have each a head who is called serang, under whom are two or three tindals, and under these come the lascars and coalmen.

The head of the khansamas, or "boys", is the butler, over whom there is a European steward. The lascars wash and cleanse the ship, throw or wind up the cables, set down or lift the boats and hoist or strike sail (though this last is a rare occurrence in steamships) and do similar kind of work. The Serang and the Tindal are always moving about watching them and assisting in their work. The coalmen keep the fire steady in the engine-room; their duty is to fight day and night with fire and to keep the engines neat and clean. And it is no easy task to keep that stupendous engine and all its parts neat and tidy. The Serang and his assistant (or "Brother", in the lascar's parlance) are from Calcutta and speak Bengali; they look gentlemanly and can read and write, having studied in school; they speak tolerable English also. The Serang has a son, thirteen years of age, who is a servant of the Captain and waits at his door as an orderly. Seeing these Bengali lascars, coalmen, servants, and boys at work, the feeling of despair with regard to my countrymen which I had, was much abated. How they are slowly developing their manhood, with a strong physique — how fearless, yet docile! That cringing, sycophant attitude common to "natives" even the sweepers do not possess — what a transformation!

The Indian lascars do excellent work without murmur, and go on a quarter of a European sailor's pay. This has dissatisfied many in England, especially as many Europeans are losing their living thereby. They sometimes set up an agitation. Having nothing else to say against them — for the lascars are smarter in work than Europeans — they only complain that in rough weather, when the ship is in danger, they lose all courage. Good God! In actual circumstances, that infamy is found to be baseless. In times of danger, the European sailors freely drink through fear and make themselves stupid and out of use. Indian sailors never take a drop of liquor in their life, and up to now, not one of them has ever shown cowardice in times of great danger. Does the Indian soldier display any cowardice on the field of battle? No, but they must have leaders. An English friend of mine, named General Strong, was in India during the Sepoy Mutiny. He used to tell many stories about it. One day, in the course of conversation, I asked him how it was that the sepoys who had enough of guns, ammunition, and provisions at their disposal, and were also trained veterans, came to suffer such a defeat. He replied that the leaders among them, instead of advancing forward, only kept shouting from a safe position in the rear, "Fight on, brave lads", and so forth; but unless the commanding officer goes ahead and faces death, the rank and file will never fight with heart. It is the same in every branch. "A captain must sacrifice his head," they say. If you can lay down your life for a cause, then only you can be a leader. But we all want to be leaders without making the necessary sacrifice. And the result is zero — nobody listens to us!

However much you may parade your descent from Aryan ancestors and sing the glories of ancient India day and night, and however much you may be strutting in the pride of your birth, you, the upper classes of India, do you think you are alive? You are but mummies ten thousand years old! It is among those whom your ancestors despised as "walking carrion" that the little of vitality there is still in India is to be found; and it is you who are the real "walking corpses". Your houses, your furniture, look like museum specimens, so lifeless and antiquated they are; and even an eye-witness of your manners and customs, your movements and modes of life, is inclined to think that he is listening to a grandmother's tale! When, even after making a personal acquaintance with you, one returns home, one seems to think one had been to visit the paintings in an art gallery! In this world of Maya, you are the real illusions, the mystery, the real mirage in the desert, you, the upper classes of India! You represent the past tense, with all its varieties of form jumbled into one. That one still seems to see you at the present time, is nothing but a nightmare brought on by indigestion. You are the void, the unsubstantial nonentities of the future. Denizens of the dreamland, why are you loitering any longer? Fleshless and bloodless skeletons of the dead body of Past India you are, why do you not quickly reduce yourselves into dust and disappear in the air? Ay, on your bony fingers are some priceless rings of jewel, treasured up by your ancestors, and within the embrace of your stinking corpses are preserved a good many ancient treasure-chests. Up to now you have not had the opportunity to hand them over. Now under the British rule, in these days of free education and enlightenment, pass them on to your heirs, ay, do it as quickly as you can. You merge yourselves in the void and disappear, and let New India arise in your place. Let her arise — out of the peasants' cottage, grasping the plough; out of the huts of the fisherman, the cobbler, and the sweeper. Let her spring from the grocer's shop, from beside the oven of the fritter-seller. Let her emanate from the factory, from marts, and from markets. Let her emerge from groves and forests, from hills and mountains.

These common people have suffered oppression for thousands of years — suffered it without murmur, and as a result have got wonderful fortitude. They have suffered eternal misery, which has given them unflinching vitality. Living on a handful of grain, they can convulse the world; give them only half a piece of bread, and the whole world will not be big enough to contain their energy; they are endowed with the inexhaustible vitality of a Raktabija. (A demon, in the Durgâ-Saptashati, every drop of whose blood falling on the ground produced another demon like him.) And, besides, they have got the wonderful strength that comes of a pure and moral life, which is not to be found anywhere else in the world. Such peacefulness, such contentment, such love, such power of silent and incessant work, and such manifestation of lion's strength in times of action — where else will you find these! Skeletons of the Past, there, before you, are your successors, the India that is to be. Throw those treasure-chests of yours and those jewelled rings among them, as soon as you can; and you vanish into the air, and be seen no more — only keep your ears open. No sooner will you disappear than you will hear the inaugural shout of Renaissant India, ringing with the voice of a million thunders and reverberating throughout the universe, "Wah Guru Ki Fateh" — victory to the Guru!

Our ship is now in the Bay of Bengal, which is reported to be very deep. The little of it that was shallow has been silted up by the Ganga crumbling the Himalayas and washing down the North-Western Provinces (U.P.). That alluvial region is our Bengal. There is no indication of Bengal extending further beyond the Sunderbans. Some say that the Sunderbans were formerly the site of many villages and towns and were an elevated region. But many do not admit this now. However, the Sunderbans and the northern part of the Bay of Bengal have been the scene of many historic events. These were the rendezvous of the Portuguese pirates; the king of Arakan made repeated attempts to occupy this region, and here also the representative of the Mogul Emperor tried his best to punish the Portuguese pirates headed by Gonzalez; and this has frequently been the scene of many fights between the Christians, Moguls, Mugs, and Bengalis.

The Bay of Bengal is naturally rough, and to add to this, it is the monsoon season, so our ship is rolling heavily. But then, this is only the beginning and there is no knowing what is to follow, as we are going to Madras. The greater part of Southern India belongs now to the Madras Presidency. What is there in mere extent of land? Even a desert turns into heaven when it falls to the care of a fortunate owner. The unknown petty village of Madras, formerly called Chinnapattanam or Madraspattanam, was sold by the Raja of Chandragiri to a company of merchants. Then the English had their principal trade in Java, and Bantam was the centre of England's Asiatic trade. Madras and other English trade settlements in India were under the control of Bantam. Where is that Bantam now? And what development that Madras has made! It is not whole truth to say that fortune favours the enterprising man; behind there must be the strength that comes of the Divine Mother. But I also admit that it is the enterprising men unto whom Mother gives strength.

Madras reminds one of a typical South Indian province; though even at the Jagannath Ghat of Calcutta, one can get a glimpse of the South by seeing the Orissa Brahmin with his border-shaven head and tufted hair, his variously painted forehead, the involuted slippers, in which only the toes may enter; that nose irritated with snuff and with that habit of covering the bodies of their children with sandalpaste prints. The Gujarati Brahmin, the jet-black Maharashtra Brahmin, and the exceptionally fair, cat-eyed square-headed Brahmin of Konkan — though all of them dress in the same way, and are all known as Deccanis, yet the typical southern Brahmin is to be found in Madras. That forehead covered over with the ample caste-mark of the Ramanuja sect — which to the uninitiated looks anything but sublime, (and whose imitation — the caste-mark of the Ramananda sect of Northern India — is hailed with many a facetious rhyme — and which completely throws into the shade the custom prevailing in Bengal among leaders of the Vaishnavite sect, of frightfully imprinting their whole body); that Telugu, Tamil, and Malayalam speech of which you won't understand a single syllable even if you hear it spoken for six years and in which there is a play of all possible varieties of 'l' and 'd' sounds; that eating of rice with 'black-peppered dal soup' — each morsel of which sends a shiver through the heart (so pungent and so acid!); that addition of margosa leaves, oats, etc., by way of flavour, that taking of "rice-and-curd" etc., that bath with gingili oil rubbed over the body, and the frying of fish in the same oil — without these how can one conceive the southern country?

Again, the South has Hinduism alive during the Mohammedan rule and even for some time previous to it. It was in the South that Shankaracharya was born, among that caste who wear a tuft on the front of the head and eat food prepared with cocoanut oil: this was the country that produced Ramanuja: it was also the birthplace of Madhva Muni. Modern Hinduism owes its allegiance to these alone. The Vaishnavas of the Chaitanya sect form merely a recension of the Madhva sect; the religious reformers of the North such as Kabir, Dadu, Nanak, and Ramsanehi are all an echo of Shankaracharya; there you find the disciples of Ramanuja occupying Ayodhya and other places. These Brahmins of the South do not recognise those of the North as true Brahmins, nor accept them as disciples, and even to the other day would not admit them to Sannyasa. The people of Madras even now occupy the principal seats of religion. It was in the South that when people of North India were hiding themselves in woods and forests, giving up their treasures, their household deities, and wives and children, before the triumphant war-cry of Mohammedan invaders — the suzerainty of the King of Vidyânagar was established firm as ever. In the South, again, was born the wonderful Sâyanâchârya — the strength of whose arms, vanquishing the Mohammedans, kept King Bukka on his throne, whose wise counsels gave stability to the Vidyanagar Kingdom, whose state-policy established lasting peace and prosperity in the Deccan, whose superhuman genius and extraordinary industry produced the commentaries on the whole Vedas — and the product of whose wonderful sacrifice, renunciation, and researches was the Vedanta treatise named Panchadashi — that Sannyasin Vidyâranya Muni or Sayana (According to some, Sayana, the commentator of the Vedas, was the brother of Vidyaranya Muni.) was born in this land. The Madras Presidency is the habitat of that Tamil race whose civilisation was the most ancient, and a branch of whom, called the Sumerians, spread a vast civilisation on the banks of the Euphrates in very ancient times; whose astrology, religious lore, morals, rites, etc., furnished the foundation for the Assyrian and Babylonian civilisations; and whose mythology was the source of the Christian Bible. Another branch of these Tamils spread from the Malabar coast and gave rise to the wonderful Egyptian civilisation, and the Aryans also are indebted to this race in many respects. Their colossal temples in the South proclaim the triumph of the Veera Shaiva and Veera Vaishnava sects. The great Vaishnava religion of India has also sprung from a Tamil Pariah — Shathakopa — "who was a dealer in winnowing-fans but was a Yogin all the while". And the Tamil Alwars or devotees still command the respect of the whole Vaishnava sect. Even now the study of the Dvaita, Vishishtâdvaita and Advaita systems of Vedanta is cultivated more in South India than anywhere else. Even now the thirst for religion is stronger here than in any other place.

In the night of the 24th June, our ship reached Madras. Getting up from bed in the morning, I found that we were within the enclosed space of the Madras harbour. Within the harbour the water was still, but without, towering waves were roaring, which occasionally dashing against the harbour-wall were shooting up fifteen or twenty feet high into the air and breaking in a mass of foam. In front lay the well-known Strand Road of Madras. Two European Police Inspectors, a Jamadar of Madras and a dozen Constables boarded our ship and told me with great courtesy that "natives" were not allowed to land on the shore, but the Europeans were. A "native", whoever he might be, was of such dirty habits that there was every chance of his carrying plague germs about; but the Madrasis had asked for a special permit for me, which they might obtain. By degrees the friends of Madras began to come near our vessel on boats in small groups. As all contact was strictly forbidden, we could only speak from the ship, keeping some space between. I found all my friends — Alasinga, Biligiri, Narasimachary, Dr. Nanjunda Rao, Kidi, and others on the boats. Basketfuls of mangoes, plantains, cocoanuts, cooked rice-and-curd, and heaps of sweet and salt delicacies, etc. began to come in. Gradually the crowd thickened — men, women, and children in boats everywhere. I found also Mr. Chamier, my English friend who had come out to Madras as a barrister-at-law. Ramakrishnananda and Nirbhayananda made some trips near to the ship. They insisted on staying on the boat the whole day in the hot sun, and I had to remonstrate with them, when they gave up the idea. And as the news of my not being permitted to land got abroad, the crowd of boats began to increase still more. I, too, began to feel exhaustion from leaning against the railings too long. Then I bade farewell to my Madrasi friends and entered my cabin. Alasinga got no opportunity to consult me about the Brahmavadin and the Madras work; so he was going to accompany me to Colombo. The ship left the harbour in the evening, when I heard a great shout, and peeping through the cabin-window, I found that about a thousand men, women, and children of Madras who had been sitting on the harbour-walls, gave this farewell shout when the ship started. On a joyous occasion the people of Madras also, like the Bengalis, make the peculiar sound with the tongue known as the Hulu.

It took us four days to go from Madras to Ceylon. That rising and heaving of waves which had commenced from the mouth of the Ganga began to increase as we advanced, and after we had left Madras it increased still more. The ship began to roll heavily, and the passengers felt terribly sea-sick, and so did the two Bengali boys. One of them was certain he was going to die, and we had to console him with great difficulty, assuring him that there was nothing to be afraid of, as it was quite a common experience and nobody ever died of it. The second class, again, was right over the screw of the ship. The two

Bengali lads, being natives, were put into a cabin almost like a black-hole, where neither air nor light had any access. So the boys could not remain in the room, and on the deck the rolling was terrible. Again, when the prow of the ship settled into the hollow of a wave and the stern was pitched up, the screw rose clear out of the water and continued to wheel in the air, giving a tremendous jolting to the whole vessel. And the second class then shook as when a rat is seized by a cat and shaken.

However, this was the monsoon season. The more the ship would proceed westwards, the more gale and wind she would have to encounter. The people of Madras had given plenty of fruits, the greater part of which, and the sweets, and rice-and-curd, etc., I gave to the boys. Alasinga had hurriedly bought a ticket and boarded the ship barefooted. He says he wears shoes now and then. Ways and manners differ in different countries. In Europe it is a great shame on the part of ladies to show their feet, but they feel no delicacy in exposing half their bust. In our country, the head must be covered by all means, no matter if the rest of the body is well covered or not. Alasinga, the editor of the Brahmavadin, who is a Mysore Brahmin of the Ramanuja sect, having a fondness for Rasam (Pungent and sour dal soup.) with shaven head and forehead overspread with the caste-mark of the Tengale sect, has brought with him with great care, as his provision for the voyage, two small bundles, in one of which there is fried flattened rice, and in another popped rice and fried peas! His idea is to live upon these during the voyage to Ceylon, so that his caste may remain intact. Alasinga had been to Ceylon once before, at which his caste-people tried to put him into some trouble, without success. That is a saving feature in the caste-system of India — if one's caste-people do not object, no one else has any right to say anything against him. And as for the South India castes — some consist of five hundred souls in all, some even hundred, or at most a thousand, and so circumscribed is their limit that for want of any other likely bride, one marries one's sister's daughter! When railways were first introduced in Mysore, the Brahmins who went from a distance to see the trains were outcasted! However, one rarely finds men like our Alasinga in this world — one so unselfish, so hard-working and devoted to his Guru, and such an obedient disciple is indeed very rare on earth. A South Indian by birth, with his head shaven so as to leave a tuft in the centre, bare-footed, and wearing the Dhoti, he got into the first class; he was strolling now and then on the deck and when hungry, was chewing some of the popped rice and peas! The ship's servants generally take all South Indians to be Chettis (merchants) and say that they have lots of money, but will not spend a bit of it on either dress or food! But the servants are of opinion that in our company Alasinga's purity as a Brahmin is getting contaminated. And it is true — for the South Indians lose much of their caste-rigours through contact with us.

Alasinga did not feel sea-sick. Brother T__ felt a little trouble at the beginning but is now all right. So the four days passed in various pleasant talks and gossip. In front of us is Colombo. Here we have Sinhal — Lanka. Shri Ramachandra crossed over to Lanka by building a bridge across and conquered Ravana, her King. Well, I have seen the bridge, and also, in the palace of the Setupati Maharaja of Ramnad, the stone slab on which Bhagavan Ramachandra installed his ancestor as Setupati for the first time. But the Buddhist Ceylonese of these sophisticated times will not admit this. They say that in their country there is not even a tradition to indicate it. But what matters their denial? Are not our "old books" authorities enough? Then again, they call their country Sinhal and will not term it Lanka (Means also "Chillies" in Bengal.) — and how should they? There is no piquancy either in their words, or in their work, or in their nature, or in their appearance! Wearing gowns, with plaited hair, and in that a big comb — quite a feminine appearance! Again, they have slim, short, and tender woman-like bodies. These — the descendants of Ravana and Kumbhakarna! Not a bit of it! Tradition says they have migrated from Bengal — and it was well done. That new type of people who are springing in Bengal — dressed like women, speaking in soft and delicate accents, walking with a timid, faltering gait, unable to look any one in the face and from their very birth given to writing love poems and suffering the pangs of separation from their beloved — well, why do they not go to Ceylon, where they will find their fellows! Are the Government asleep? The other day they created a great row trying to capture some people in Puri. Why, in the metropolis itself are many worth seizing and packing off!

There was a very naughty Bengali Prince, named Vijaya Sinha, who quarrelled with his father, and getting together a few more fellows like him set sail in a ship, and finally came upon the Island of Ceylon. That country was then inhabited by an aboriginal tribe whose descendants are now known as the Bedouins. The aboriginal king received him very cordially and gave him his daughter in marriage. There he remained quietly for some time, when one night, conspiring with his wife, with a number of fellows, he took the king and his nobles by surprise and massacred them. Then Vijaya Sinha ascended the throne of Ceylon. But his wickedness did not end here. After a time he got tired of his aboriginal queen, and got more men and more girls from India and himself married a girl named Anurâdhâ, discarding his first aboriginal wife. Then he began to extirpate the whole race of the aborigines, almost all of whom were killed, leaving only a small remnant who are still to be met with in the forests and jungles. In this way Lanka came to be called Sinhal and became, to start with, colony of Bengali ruffians!

In course of time, under the regime of Emperor Asoka, his son Mahinda and his daughter Sanghamittâ, who had taken the vow of Sannyasa, came to the Island of Ceylon as religious missionaries. Reaching there, they found the people had grown quite barbarous, and, devoting their whole lives, they brought them back to civilisation as far as possible; they framed good moral laws for them and converted them to Buddhism. Soon the Ceylonese grew very staunch Buddhists, and built a great city in the centre of the island and called it Anuradhapuram. The sight of the remains of this city strikes one dumb even today — huge stupas, and dilapidated stone building extending for miles and miles are standing to this day; and a great part of it is overgrown with jungles which have not yet been cleared. Shaven-headed monks and nuns, with the begging bowl in hand and clothed in yellow robes, spread all over Ceylon. In places colossal temples were reared containing huge figure of Buddha in meditation, of Buddha preaching the Law, and of Buddha in a reclining posture — entering into Nirvana. And the Ceylonese, out of mischief, painted on the walls of the temples the supposed state of things in Purgatory — some are being thrashed by ghosts, some are being sawed, some burnt, some fried in hot oil, and some being flayed — altogether a hideous spectacle! Who could know that in this religion, which preached "noninjury as the highest virtue", there would be room for such things! Such is the case in China, too, so also in Japan. While preaching non-killing so much in theory, they provide for such an array of punishments as curdles up one's blood to see. Once a thief broke into the house of a man of this non-killing type. The boys of the house caught hold of the thief and were giving him a sound beating. The master hearing a great row came out on the upper balcony and after making inquiries shouted out, "Cease from beating, my boys. Don't beat him. Non-injury is the highest virtue." The fraternity of junior non-killers stopped beating and asked the master what they were to do with the thief. The master ordered, "Put him in a bag, and throw him into water." The thief, much obliged at this humane dispensation, with folded hands said, "Oh! How great is the master's compassion!" I had heard that the Buddhists were very quiet people and equally tolerant of all religions. Buddhist preachers come to Calcutta and abuse us with choice epithets, although we offer them enough respect. Once I was preaching at Anuradhapuram among the Hindus — not Buddhists — and that in an open maidan, not on anybody's property — when a whole host of Buddhist monks and laymen, men and women, came out beating drums and cymbals and set up an awful uproar. The lecture had to stop, of course, and there was the imminent risk of bloodshed. With great difficulty I had to persuade the Hindus that we at any rate might practise a bit of non-injury, if they did not. Then the matter ended peacefully.

Gradually Tamilian Hindus from the north began slowly to migrate into Ceylon. The Buddhists, finding themselves in untoward circumstances, left their capital to establish a hill-station called Kandy, which, too, the Tamilians wrested from them in a short time and placed a Hindu king on the throne. Then came hordes of Europeans — the Spaniards, the Portuguese, and the Dutch. Lastly the English have made themselves kings. The royal family of Kandy have been sent to Tanjore, where they are living on pension and Mulagutanni Rasam.

In northern Ceylon there is a great majority of Hindus, while in the southern part, Buddhists and hybrid Eurasians of different types preponderate. The principal seat of the Buddhists is Colombo, the present capital, and that of the Hindus is Jaffna. The restrictions of caste are here much less than in India; the Buddhists have a few in marriage affairs, but none in matters of food, in which respect the Hindus observe some restrictions. All the butchers of Ceylon were formerly Buddhists; now the number is decreasing owing to the revival of Buddhism. Most of the Buddhists are now changing their anglicised titles for native ones. All the Hindu castes have mixed together and formed a single Hindu caste, in which, like the Punjabi Jats, one can marry a girl of any caste — even a European girl at that. The son goes into a temple, puts the sacred trilinear mark on the forehead, utters "Shiva, Shiva", and becomes a Hindu. The husband may be a Hindu, while the wife is a Christian. The Christian rubs some sacred ash on the forehead, utters "Namah Pârvatipataye" (salutation to Shiva), and she straightway becomes a Hindu. This is what has made the Christian missionaries so cross with you. Since your coming into Ceylon, many Christians, putting sacred ash on their head and repeating "Salutation to Shiva", have become Hindus and gone back to their caste. Advaitavâda and Vira-Shaivavâda are the prevailing religions here. In place of the word "Hindu" one has to say "Shiva". The religious dance and Sankirtana which Shri Chaitanya introduced into Bengal had their origin in the South, among the Tamil race. The Tamil of Ceylon is pure Tamil and the religion of Ceylon is equally pure Tamil religion. That ecstatic chant of a hundred thousand men, and their singing of devotional hymns to Shiva, the noise of a thousand Mridangas (A kind of Indian drum.) with the metallic sound of big cymbals, and the frenzied dance of these ash-covered, red-eyed athletic Tamilians with stout rosaries of Rudrâksha beads on their neck, looking just like the great devotee, Hanuman — you can form no idea of these, unless you personally see the phenomenon.

Our Colombo friends had procured a permit for our landing, so we landed and met our friends there. Sir Coomara Swami is the foremost man among the Hindus: his wife is an English lady, and his son is barefooted and wears the sacred ashes on his forehead. Mr. Arunachalam and other friends came to meet me. After a long time I partook of Mulagutanni and the king-cocoanut. They put some green cocoanuts into my cabin. I met Mrs. Higgins and visited her boarding school for Buddhist girls. I also visited the monastery and school of our old acquaintance, the Countess of Canovara. The Countess' house is more spacious and furnished than Mrs. Higgins's. The Countess has invested her own money, whereas Mrs. Higgins has collected the money by begging. The Countess herself wears a Gerua cloth after the mode of the Bengali Sari. The Ceylonese Buddhists have taken a great fancy to this fashion, I found. I noticed carriage after carriage of women, all wearing the same Bengali Sari.

The principal place of pilgrimage for the Buddhists is the Dalada Maligawa or Tooth-temple at Kandy, which contains a tooth of Lord Buddha. The Ceylonese say it was at first in the Jagannath Temple at Puri and after many vicissitudes reached Ceylon, where also there was no little trouble over it. Now it is lying safe. The Ceylonese have kept good historical records of themselves, not like those of ours — merely cock and bull stories. And the Buddhist scriptures also are well preserved here in the ancient Magadhi dialect. From here the Buddhist religion spread to Burma, Siam, and other countries. The Ceylonese Buddhists recognise only Shâkyamuni mentioned in their scriptures and try to follow his precepts. They do not, like the people of Nepal, Sikkim, Bhutan, Ladak, China, and Japan, worship Shiva and do not know the worship with mystical Mantras of such goddesses as Târâ Devi and so forth. But they believe in possession by spirits and things of that sort. The Buddhists have now split into two schools, the Northern and the Southern; the Northern school calls itself the Mahâyâna, and the Southern school, comprising the Ceylonese, Burmese, Siamese, etc., Hinayâna. The Mahâyâna branch worships Buddha in name only; their real worship is of Tara Devi and of Avalokiteshwara (whom the Japanese, Chinese and Koreans call Wanyin); and there is much use of various cryptic rites and Mantras. The Tibetans are the real demons of Shiva. They all worship Hindu gods, play the Damaru, (A tabor shaped like an hour-glass.) keep human skulls, blow horns made of the bones of dead monks, are much given to wine and meat, and are always exorcising evil spirits and curing diseases by means of mystical incantations. In China and Japan, on the walls of all the temples I have observed various monosyllabic Mantras written in big gilt letters, which approach the Bengali characters so much that you can easily make out the resemblance.

Alasinga returned to Madras from Colombo, and we also got on board our ship, with presents of some lemons from the orchard of Coomara Swami, some king-cocoanuts, and two bottles of syrup, etc. (The god Kârtikeya has various names, such as Subrahmanya, Kamâra Swâmi etc. In the South the worship of this god is much in vogue; they call Kartikeya an incarnation of the sacred formula "Om".)

The ship left Colombo on the morning of 25th June. Now we have to encounter full monsoon conditions. The more our ship is advancing, the more is the storm increasing and the louder is the wind howling — there is incessant rain, and enveloping darkness; huge waves are dashing on the ship's deck with a terrible noise, so that it is impossible to stay on the deck. The dining table has been divided into small squares by means of wood partitions, placed lengthwise and breadthwise, called fiddle, out of which the food articles are jumping up. The ship is creaking, as if it were going to break to pieces. The Captain says, "Well, this year's monsoon seems to be unusually rough". The Captain is a very interesting person who spent many years in the Chinese Sea and Indian Ocean; a very entertaining fellow, very clever in telling cock and bull stories. Numerous stories of pirates — how Chinese coolies used to kill ship's officers, loot the whole ship and escape — and other stories of that ilk he is narrating. And there is nothing else to do, for reading or writing is out of the question in such heavy rolling. It is extremely difficult to sit inside the cabin; the window has been shut for fear of the waves getting in. One day Brother T__ kept it slightly ajar and a fragment of a wave entered and flooded the whole cabin! And who can describe the heaving and tossing on the deck! Amid such conditions, you must remember, the work for your Udbodhan is going on to a certain extent.

There are two Christian missionary passengers on our ship, one of whom is an American, with a family — a very good man, named Bogesh. He has been married seven years, and his children number half-a-dozen. The servants call it God's special grace — though the children perhaps, feel differently. Spreading a shabby bed on the deck, Mrs. Bogesh makes all the children lie on it and goes away. They make themselves dirty and roll on the deck, crying aloud. The passengers on the deck are always nervous and cannot walk about on the deck, lest they might tread on any of Bogesh's children. Making the youngest baby lie in a square basket with high sides, Mr. and Mrs. Bogesh sit in a corner for four hours, huddled together. One finds it hard to appreciate your European civilisation. If we rinse our mouth or wash our teeth in public — they say it is barbarous, these things ought to be done in private. All right, but I put it to you, if it is not also decent to avoid such acts as the one above referred to, in public. And you run after this civilisation! However you cannot understand what good Protestantism has done to North Europe, unless you see the Protestant clergy. If then ten crores of English people die, and only the priests survive, in twenty years another ten crores will be raised!

Owing to the rolling of the ship most of the passengers are suffering from headache. A little girl named Tootle is accompanying her father; she has lost her mother. Our Nivedita has become a mother to Tootle and Bogesh's children. Tootle has been brought up in Mysore with her father who is a planter. I asked her, "Tootle, how are you?" She replied, "This Bungalow is not good and rolls very much, which makes me sick." To her every house is a bungalow. One sickly child of Bogesh suffers specially from want of care; the poor thing is rolling on the wooden deck the whole day. The old Captain now and then comes out of his cabin and feeds him with some soup with a spoon, and pointing to his slender legs says, "What a sickly child — how sadly neglected!"

Many desire eternal happiness. But if happiness were eternal, misery also would be eternal, just think of that. Could we in that case have ever reached Aden! Fortunately neither happiness nor misery is eternal; therefore in spite of our six days' journey being prolonged into fourteen days, and our buffeting terrible wind and rain night and day, we at last did reach Aden. The more we were ahead of Colombo, the more the storm and rain increased, the sky became a lake, and the wind and the waves grew fierce; and it was almost impossible for the ship to proceed, breasting such wind and wave, and her speed was halved. Near the island of Socotra, the monsoon was at its worst. The Captain remarked that this was the centre of the monsoon, and that if we could pass this, we should gradually reach calmer waters. And so we did. And this nightmare also ended.

On the evening of the 8th, we reached Aden. No one, white or black, is allowed to land, neither is any cargo allowed into the ship. And there are not many things worth seeing here. You have only barren stretches of sand, bearing some resemblance to Rajputana, and treeless, verdureless hills. In between the hills there are forts and on the top are the soldiers' barracks. In front are the hotels and shops arranged in the form of a crescent, which are discernible from the ship. Many ships are lying in anchor. One English, and one German man-of-war came in; the rest are either cargo or passenger ships. I had visited the town last time. Behind the hills are the native barracks and the bazar. A few miles from there, there are big pits dug into the sides of the hills, where the rain-water accumulates. Formerly that was the only source of water. Now by means of an apparatus they distil the sea water and get good fresh water, which, however, is very dear. Aden is just like an Indian town — with its large percentage of Indian civil and military population. There are a good many Parsee shopkeepers and Sindhi merchants. Aden is a very ancient place — the Roman Emperor Constantius sent a batch of missionaries here to preach Christianity. Then the Arabs rose and killed these Christians, whereupon the Roman Emperor asked the King of Abyssinia — long a Christian country — to punish them. The Abyssinian King sent an army and severely punished the Arabs of Aden. Afterwards Aden passed into the hands of the Samanidi Kings of Persia. It is they who are reputed to have first excavated those caves for the accumulation of water. Then, after the rise of Mohammedanism, Aden passed into the hands of the Arabs. After a certain time, a Portuguese general made ineffectual attempts to capture the place. Then the Sultan of Turkey made the place a naval base with the object of expelling the Portuguese from the Indian Ocean.

Again it passed into the possession of the neighbouring Arabian ruler. Afterwards, the English purchased it and they built the present town. Now the warships of all the powerful nations are cruising all over the world, and everyone wants to have a voice in every trouble that arises in any part of it. Every nation wants to safeguard its supremacy, political interest, and commerce. Hence they are in need of coal every now and then. As it would not be possible to get a supply of coal from an enemy country in times of war, every Power wants to have a coaling station of its own. The best sites have been already occupied by the English; the French have come in for the next best; and after them the other Powers of Europe have secured, and are securing, sites for themselves either by force or by purchase, or by friendly overture. The Suez Canal is now the link between Europe and Asia, and it is under the control of the French. Consequently the English have made their position very strong at Aden, and the other Powers also have each made a base for themselves along the Red Sea. Sometimes this rage for land brings disastrous consequences. Italy, trodden under foreign feet for seven centuries, stood on her legs after enormous difficulties. But immediately after doing this, she began to think a lot of herself and became ambitious of foreign conquest. In Europe no nation can seize a bit of land belonging to another; for all the Powers would unite to crush the usurper. In Asia also, the big Powers — the English, Russians, French, and Dutch — have left little space unoccupied. Now there remained only a few bits of Africa, and thither Italy directed her attention. First she tried in North Africa, where she met with opposition from the French and desisted. Then the English gave her a piece of land on the Red Sea, with the ulterior object that from that centre Italy might absorb the Abyssinian territory. Italy, too, came on with an army. But the Abyssinian King, Manalik, gave her such a beating that Italy found it difficult to save herself by fleeing from Africa. Besides, Russian and Abyssinian Christianity being, as is alleged, very much alike, the Russian Czar is an ally of the Abyssinians at bottom.

Well, our ship is now passing through the Red Sea. The missionary said, "This is the Red Sea, which the Jewish leader Moses crossed on foot with his followers. And the army which the Egyptian King Pharaoh sent for their capture was drowned in the sea, the wheels of their war-chariots having stuck in the mud" — like Karna's in the Mahâbhârata story. He further said that this could now be proved by modern scientific reasons. Nowadays in every country it has become a fashion to support the miracles of religion by scientific argument. My friend, if these phenomena were the outcome of natural forces, where then is there room for their intervention of your god "Yave"? A great dilemma! — If they are opposed to science, those miracles are mere myths, and your religion is false. And even if they are borne out by science, the glory of your god is superfluous, and they are just like any other natural phenomena. To this, Priest Bogesh replied, "I do not know all the issues involved in it, I simply believe." This is all right — one can tolerate that. But then there is a party of men, who are very clear in criticising others' views and bringing forward arguments against them, but where they themselves are concerned, they simply say, "I only believe, my mind testifies to their veracity." These are simply unbearable. Pooh! What weight has their intellect? Absolutely nothing! They are very quick to label the religious beliefs of others as superstitious, especially those which have been condemned by the Europeans, while in their own case they concoct some fantastic notions of Godhead and are beside themselves with emotions over them.

The ship is steadily sailing north. The borders of this Red Sea were a great centre of ancient civilisation. There, on the other side, are the deserts of Arabia, and on this — Egypt. This is that ancient Egypt. Thousands of years ago, these Egyptians starting from Punt (probably Malabar) crossed the Red Sea, and steadily extended their kingdom till they reached Egypt. Wonderful was the expansion of their power, their territory, and their civilisation. The Greeks were the disciples of these. The wonderful mausoleums of their kings, the Pyramids, with figures of the Sphinx, and even their dead bodies are preserved to this day. Here lived the ancient Egyptian peoples, with curling hair and ear-rings, and wearing snow-white dhotis without one end being tucked up behind. This is Egypt — the memorable stage where the Hyksos, the Pharaohs, the Persian Emperors, Alexander the Great, and the Ptolemies, and the Roman and Arab conquerors played their part. So many centuries ago, they left their history inscribed in great detail in hieroglyphic characters on papyrus paper, on stone slabs, and on the sides of earthen vessels.

This is the land where Isis was worshipped and Horus flourished. According to these ancient Egyptians, when a man dies, his subtle body moves about; but any injury done to the dead body affects the subtle body, and the destruction of the former means the total annihilation of the latter. Hence they took so much pains to preserve the corpse. Hence the pyramids of the kings and emperors. What devices, how much labour — alas, all in vain!

Lured by the treasures, robbers have dug into the pyramids, and penetrating the mysteries of the labyrinths, have stolen the royal bodies. Not now — it was the work of the ancient Egyptians themselves. Some five or six centuries ago, these desiccated mummies the Jewish and Arab physicians looked upon as possessing great medicinal virtues and prescribed them for patients all over Europe. To this day, perhaps, it is the genuine "Mumia" of Unani and Hakimi methods of treatment!

Emperor Asoka sent preachers to this Egypt during the reign of the Ptolemy dynasty. They used to preach religion, cure diseases, live on vegetable food, lead celibate lives, and make Sannyasin disciples. They came to found many sects — the Therapeutae, Essenes, Manichaeans, and the like; from which modern Christianity has sprung. It was Egypt that became, during the Ptolemaic rule, the nursery of all learning. Here was that city of Alexandria, famous all over the world for its university, its library, and its literati — that Alexandria which, falling into the hands of illiterate, bigoted, and vulgar Christians suffered destruction, with its library burnt to ashes and learning stamped out! Finally, the Christians killed the lady servant, Hypatia, subjected her dead body to all sorts of abominable insult, and dragged it through the streets, till every bit of flesh was removed from the bones!

And to the south lie the deserts of Arabia — the mother of heroes. Have you ever seen a Bedouin Arab, with a cloak on, and a big kerchief tied on his head with a bunch of woollen strings? — That gait, that pose of standing, and that look, you will find in no other country. From head to foot emanates the freedom of open unconfined desert air — there you have the Arab. When the bigotry of the Christians and the barbarity of the Goths extinguished the ancient Greek and Roman civilisation, when Persia was trying to hide her internal putrefaction by adding layer after layer of gold-leaf upon it, when, in India, the sun of splendour of Pataliputra and Ujjain had set, leaving some illiterate, tyrant kings to rule over her, and the corruptions of dreadful obscenities and the worship of lust festering within — when such was the state of the world, this insignificant, semi-brutal Arab race spread like lightning over its surface.

There you see a steamer coming from Mecca, with a cargo of pilgrims; behold — the Turk in European dress, the Egyptian in half-European costume, the Syrian Mussalman in Iranian attire, and the real Arab wearing a cloth reaching down the knee. Before the time of Mohammed, it was the custom to circumambulate round the Cabba temple in a state of nudity; since his time they have to wrap round a cloth. It is for this reason, that our Mohammedans unloose the strings of their trousers, and let their cloth hang down to the feet. Gone are those days for the Arabs. A continual influx of Kaffir, Sidi, and Abyssinian blood has changed their physique, energy, and all — the Arab of the desert is completely shorn of his former glory. Those that live in the north are peaceful citizens of the Turkish State. But the Christian subjects of the Sultan hate the Turks and love the Arabs. They say that the Arabs are amenable to education, become gentlemen, and are not so troublesome, while the real Turks oppress the Christians very much.

Though the desert is very hot, that heat is not enervating. There is no further trouble if you cover your body and head against it. Dry heat is not only not enervating, on the contrary it has a marked toning effect. The people of Rajputana, Arabia, and Africa are illustrations of this. In certain districts of Marwar, men, cattle, horses, and all are strong and of great stature. It is a joy to look at the Arabs and Sidis. Where the heat is moist, as in Bengal, the body is very much enervated, and every animal is weak.

The very name of the Red Sea strikes terror into the hearts of the passengers — it is so dreadfully hot, specially in summer, as it is now. Everyone is seated on the deck and recounts a story of some terrible accident, according to his knowledge. The Captain has outbidden them all. He says that a few days ago a Chinese man-of-war was passing through the Red Sea, and her Captain and eight sailors who worked in the coal-room died of heat.

Indeed, those who work in the coal-room have in

the first place to stand in a pit of fire, and then there is the terrible heat of the Red Sea. Sometimes they run mad, rush up to the deck, plunge into the sea, and are drowned; or sometimes they die of heat in the engine-room itself.

These stories were enough to throw us out of our wits, nearly. But fortunately we did not experience so much heat. The breeze, instead of being a south-wind, continued to blow from the north, and it was the cool breeze of the Mediterranean.

On the 14th of July the steamer cleared the Red Sea and reached Suez. In front is the Suez Canal. The steamer has cargo for Suez. Well, Egypt is now under a visitation of plague, and possibly we are also carrying its germs. So there is the risk of contagion on both sides. Compared with the precautions taken here against mutual contact, well, those of our country are as nothing. The goods have to be unloaded, but the coolie of Suez must not touch the ship. It meant a good deal of extra trouble for the ship's sailors. They have to serve as coolies, lift up the cargo by means of cranes and drop it, without touching, on the Suez boats which carry it ashore. The agent of the Company has come near the ship in a small launch, but he is not allowed to board her. From the launch he is talking with the Captain who is in his ship. You must know this is not India, where the white man is beyond the plague regulations and all — here is the beginning of Europe. And all this precaution is taken lest the rat-borne plague finds an entrance into this heaven. The incubation period of plague-germs is ten days; hence the quarantine for ten days. We have however passed that period, so the disaster has been averted for us. But we shall be quarantined for ten days more if we but touch any Egyptian. In that case no passengers will be landed either at Naples or at Marseilles. Therefore every kind of work is being done from a distance, free from contact. Consequently it will take them the whole day to unload the cargo in this slow process. The ship can easily cross the Canal in the night, if she be provided with a searchlight; but if that is to be fitted, the Suez people will have to touch the ship — there, you have ten days' quarantine. She is therefore not to start in the night, and

we must remain as we are in this Suez harbour for twenty-four hours! This is a very beautiful natural harbour, surrounded almost on three sides by sandy mounds and hillocks, and the water also is very deep. There are innumerable fish and sharks swimming in it. Nowhere else on earth are sharks in such plenty as in this port and in the port of Sydney, in Australia — they are ready to swallow men at the slightest opportunity! Nobody dares to descend into the water. Men, too, on their part are dead against the snakes and sharks and never let slip an opportunity to kill them.

In the morning, even before breakfast, we came to learn that big sharks were moving about behind the ship. I had never before an opportunity to see live sharks — the last time I came, the ship called at Suez for only a very short time, and that too, close to the town. As soon as we heard of the sharks, we hastened to the spot. The second class was at the stern of the ship, and from its deck, crowds of men, women and children were leaning over the railings to see the sharks. But our friends, the sharks, had moved off a little when we appeared on the spot, which damped our spirit very much. But we noticed that shoals of a kind of fish with bill-like heads were swimming in the water, and there was a species of very tiny fish in great abundance. Now and then a big fish, greatly resembling the hilsa, was flitting like an arrow hither and thither. I thought, he might be a young shark, but on inquiry I found it was not. Bonito was his name. Of course I had formerly read of him, and this also I had read that he was imported into Bengal from the Maldives as dried fish, on big-sized boats. It was also a matter of report that his meat was red and very tasteful. And we were now glad to see his energy and speed. Such a large fish was flitting through the water like an arrow, and in that glassy sea-water every movement of his body was noticeable. We were thus watching the bonito's circuits and the restless movements of the tiny fish for twenty minutes of half an hour. Half an hour — three quarters — we were almost tired of it, when somebody announced — there he was. About a dozen people shouted, "There he is coming!" Casting my eyes I found that at some distance a huge black thing was moving towards us, six or seven inches below the surface of the water. Gradually the thing approached nearer and nearer. The huge flat head was visible; now massive his movement, there was nothing of the bonito's flitting in it. But once he turned his head, a big circuit was made. A gigantic fish; on he comes in a solemn gait, while in front of him are one or two small fish, and a number of tiny ones are playing on his back and all about his body. Some of them are holding fast on to his neck. He is your shark with retinue and followers. The fish which are preceding him are called the pilot fish. Their duty is to show the shark his prey, and perhaps be favoured with crumbs of his meal. But as one looks at the terrible gaping jaws of the shark, one doubts whether they succeed much in this latter respect. The fish which are moving about the shark and climbing on his back, are the "suckers". About their chest there is a flat, round portion, nearly four by two inches, which is furrowed and grooved, like the rubber soles of many English shoes. That portion the fish applies to the shark's body and sticks to it; that makes them appear as if riding on the shark's body and back. They are supposed to live on the worms etc. that grow on the shark's body. The shark must always have his retinue of these two classes of fish. And he never injures them, considering them perhaps as his followers and companions. One of these fish was caught with a small hook and line. Someone slightly pressed the sole of his shoe against its chest and when he raised his foot, it too was found to adhere to it. In the same way it sticks to the body of the shark.

The second class passengers have got their mettle highly roused. One of them is a military man and his enthusiasm knows no bounds. Rummaging the ship they found out a terrible hook — it outvied the hooks that are used in Bengal for recovering water-pots that have accidentally dropped into wells. To this they tightly fastened about two pounds of meat with a strong cord, and a stout cable was tied to it. About six feet from it, a big piece of wood was attached to act as a float. Then the hook with the float was dropped in the water. Below the ship a police boat was keeping guard ever since we came, lest there might be any contact between us and the people ashore. On this boat there were two men comfortably asleep, which made them much despised in the eyes of the passengers. At this moment they turned out to be great friends. Roused by the tremendous shouts, our friend, the Arab, rubbed his eyes and stood up. He was preparing to tuck up his dress, imagining some trouble was at hand, when he came to understand that so much shouting was nothing more than a request to him to remove the beam that was meant as a float to catch the shark, along with the hook, to a short distance. Then he breathed a sigh of relief, and grinning from ear to ear he managed to push the float to some distance by means of a pole. While we in eagerness stood on tiptoe, leaning over the railing, and anxiously waited for the shark — "watching his advent with restless eyes"; (From Jayadeva, the famous Sanskrit Poet of Bengal.) and as is always the case with those for whom somebody may be waiting with suspense, we suffered a similar fate — in other words, "the Beloved did not turn up". But all miseries have an end, and suddenly about a hundred yards from the ship, something of the shape of a water-carrier's leather bag, but much larger, appeared above the surface of the water, and immediately there was the hue and cry, "There is the shark!" "Silence, you boys and girls! — the shark may run off". — "Hallo, you people there, why don't you doff your white hats for a while? — the shark may shy". — While shouts like these were reaching the ear, the shark, denizen of the salt sea, rushed close by, like a boat under canvas, with a view to doing justice to the lump of pork attached to the hook. Seven or eight feet more and the shark's jaws would touch the bait. But that massive tail moved a little, and the straight course was transformed into a curve. Alas, the shark has made off! Again the tail slightly moved, and the gigantic body turned and faced the hook. Again he is rushing on — gaping, there, he is about to snap at the bait! Again the cursed tail moved, and the shark wheeled his body off to a distance. Again he is taking a circuit and coming on, he is gaping again; look now, he has put the bait into his jaws, there, he is tilting on his side; yes, he has swallowed the bait — pull, pull, forty or fifty pull together, pull on with all your might! What tremendous strength the fish has, what struggles he makes, how widely he gapes! Pull, pull! He is about to come above the surface, there he is turning in the water, and again turning on his side, pull, pull! Alas, he has extricated himself from the bait! The shark has fled. Indeed, what fussy people you all are! You could not wait to give him some time to swallow the bait! And you were impatient enough to pull so soon as he turned on his side! However, it is no use crying over spilt milk. The shark was rid of the hook and made a clean run ahead. Whether he taught the pilot fish a good lesson, we have got no information, but the fact was that the shark was clean off. And he was tiger-like, having black stripes over his body like a tiger. However, the "Tiger", with a view to avoiding the dangerous vicinity of the hook, disappeared, with his retinue of pilots and suckers.

But there is no need of giving up hopes altogether, for there, just by the side of the retreating "Tiger" is coming on another, a huge flat-headed creature! Alas, sharks have no language! Otherwise "Tiger" would surely have made an open breast of his secret to the newcomer and thus warned him. He would certainly have said, "Hallo, my friend, beware there is a new creature come over there, whose flesh is very tasteful and savoury, but what hard bones! Well, I have been born and brought up as a shark these many years and have devoured lots of animals — living, dead, and half-dead, and filled my stomach with lots of bones, bricks, and stones, and wooden stuff; but compared with these bones they are as butter, I tell you. Look, what has become of my teeth and jaws". And along with this he would certainly have shown to the new-comer those gaping jaws reaching almost to half his body. And the other too, with characteristic experience of maturer years, would have prescribed for him one or other of such infallible marine remedies as the bile of one fish, the spleen of another, the cooling broth of oysters, and so forth. But since nothing of the kind took place, we must conclude that either the sharks are sadly in want of a language, or that they may have one, but it is impossible to talk under water; therefore un-

til some characters fit for the sharks are discovered, it is impossible to use that language. Or it may be that "Tiger", mixing too much in human company, has imbibed a bit of human disposition too, and therefore, instead of giving out the real truth, asked "Flat-head", with a smile, if he was doing well, and bade him good-bye: "Shall I alone be befooled?"

Then Bengali poem has it, "First goes Bhagiratha blowing his conch, then comes Ganga bringing up the rear" etc. Well, of course, no blowing of the conch is heard, but first are going the pilot fish, and behind them comes "Flat-head", moving his massive body, while round about him dance the suckers. Ah, who can resist such a tempting bait? For a space of five yards on all sides, the surface of the sea is glossy with a film of fat, and it is for "Flat-head" himself to say how far the fragrance thereof has spread. Besides, what a spectacle it is! White, and red, and yellow — all in one place! It was real English pork, tied round a huge black hook, heaving under water most temptingly!

Silence now, every one — don't move about, and see that you don't be too hasty. But take care to keep close to the cable. There, he is moving near the hook, and examining the bait, putting it in his jaws! Let him do so. Hush — now he has turned on his side — look, he is swallowing it whole, silence — give him time to do it. Then, as "Flat-head", turning on his side, had leisurely swallowed the bait, and was about to depart, immediately there was the pull behind! " Flat-head", astonished, jerked his head and wanted to throw the bait off, but it made matters worse! The hook pierced him, and from above, men, young and old, began to pull violently at the cable. Look, the head of the shark is above water — pull, brothers, pull! There, about half the shark's body is above water! Oh, what jaws! It is all jaws and throat, it seems! Pull on! Ah, the whole of it is clear of water. There, the hook has pierced his jaws through and through — pull on! Wait, wait! — Hallo, you Arab Police boatman, will you tie a string round his tail? — He is such a huge monster that it is difficult to haul him up otherwise. Take care, brother, a blow from that tail is enough to fracture a horse's leg! Pull on — Oh, how very heavy! Good God, what have we here! Indeed, what is it that hangs down from under the shark's belly? Are they not the entrails! His own weight has forced them out! All right, cut them off, and let them drop into the sea, that will make the weight lighter. Pull on, brothers! Oh, it is a fountain of blood! No, there is no use trying to save the clothes. Pull, he is almost within reach. Now, set him on the deck; take care, brother, be very careful, if he but charges on anybody, he will bite off a whole arm! And beware of that tail! Now, slacken the rope — thud! Lord! What a big shark! And with what a thud he fell on board the ship! Well, one cannot be too careful — strike his head with that beam — hallo, military man, you are a soldier, you are the man to do it. — "Quite so". The military passenger, with body and clothes splashed with blood, raised the beam and began to land heavy blows on the shark's head. And the women went on shrieking, "Oh dear! How cruel! Don't kill him!" and so forth, but never stopped seeing the spectacle. Let that gruesome scene end here. How the shark's belly was ripped open, how a torrent of blood flowed, how the monster continued to shake and move for a long time even after his entrails and heart had been taken off and his body dismembered, how from his stomach a heap of bones, skin, flesh, and wood, etc. came out — let all these topics go. Suffice it to say, that I had my meal almost spoilt that day — everything smelt of that shark.

This Suez Canal is a triumph of canal engineering. It was dug by a French engineer, Ferdinand de Lesseps. By connecting the Mediterranean with the Red Sea, it has greatly facilitated the commerce between Europe and India.

Of all the causes which have worked for the present state of human civilisation from the ancient times, the commerce of India is perhaps the most important. From time immemorial India has beaten all other countries in point of fertility and commercial industries. Up till a century ago, the whole of the world's demand for cotton cloth, cotton, jute, indigo, lac, rice, diamonds, and pearls, etc. used to be supplied from India. Moreover, no other country could produce such excellent silk and woollen fabrics, like the kincob etc. as India. Again, India has been the land of various spices such as cloves, cardamom, pepper, nutmeg, and mace. Naturally, therefore, from very ancient times, whatever country became civilised at any particular epoch, depended upon India for those commodities. This trade used to follow two main routes — one was through land, via Afghanistan and Persia, and the other was by sea — through the Red Sea. After his conquest of Persia, Alexander the Great despatched a general named Niarchus to explore a sea-route, passing by the mouth of the Indus, across the ocean, and through the Red Sea. Most people are ignorant of the extent to which the opulence of ancient countries like Babylon, Persia, Greece, and Rome depended on Indian commerce. After the downfall of Rome, Baghdad in Mohammedan territory, and Venice and Genoa in Italy, became the chief Western marts of Indian commerce. And when the Turks made themselves masters of the Roman Empire and closed the trade-route to India for the Italians, then Christopher Columbus (Christobal Colon), a Spaniard or Genoese, tried to explore a new route to India across the Atlantic, which resulted in the discovery of the American continent. Even after reaching America, Columbus could not get rid of the delusion that it was India. It is therefore that the aborigines of America are to this day designated as Indians. In the Vedas we find both names, "Sindhu" and "Indu", for the Indus; the Persians transformed them into "Hindu", and the Greeks into "Indus", whence we derived the words "India" and "Indian". With the rise of Mohammedanism the word "Hindu" became degraded and meant "a dark-skinned fellow", as is the case with the word "native" now.

The Portuguese, in the meantime, discovered a new route to India, doubling Africa. The fortune of India smiled on Portugal — then came the turn of the French, the Dutch, the Danes, and the English. Indian commerce, Indian revenue and all are now in the possession of the English; it is therefore that they are the foremost of all nations now. But now, Indian products are being grown in countries like America and elsewhere, even better than in India, and she has therefore lost something of her prestige. This the Europeans are unwilling to admit. That India, the India of "natives", is the chief means and resources of their wealth and civilisation, is a fact which they refuse to admit, or even understand. We too, on our part, must not cease to bring it home to them.

Just weigh the matter in your mind. Those uncared-for lower classes of India — the peasants and weavers and the rest, who have been conquered by foreigners and are looked down upon by their own people — it is they who from time immemorial have been working silently, without even getting the remuneration of their labours! But what great changes are taking place slowly, all over the world, in pursuance of nature's law! Countries, civilisations, and supremacy are undergoing revolutions. Ye labouring classes of India, as a result of your silent, constant labours Babylon, Persia, Alexandria, Greece, Rome, Venice, Genoa, Baghdad, Samarqand, Spain, Portugal, France, Denmark, Holland, and England have successively attained supremacy and eminence! And you? — Well, who cares to think of you! My dear Swami, your ancestors wrote a few philosophical works, penned a dozen or so epics, or built a number of temples — that is all, and you rend the skies with triumphal shouts; while those whose heart's blood has contributed to all the progress that has been made in the world — well, who cares to praise them? The world-conquering heroes of spirituality, war, and poetry are in the eyes of all, and they have received the homage of mankind. But where nobody looks, no one gives a word of encouragement, where everybody hates — that living amid such circumstances and displaying boundless patience, infinite love, and dauntless practicality, our proletariat are doing their duty in their homes day and night, without the slightest murmur — well, is there no heroism in this? Many turn out to be heroes when they have got some great task to perform. Even a coward easily gives up his life, and the most selfish man behaves disinterestedly, when there is a multitude to cheer them on; but blessed indeed is he who manifests the same unselfishness and devotion to duty in the smallest of acts, unnoticed by all — and it is you who are actually doing this ye ever-trampled labouring classes of India! I bow to you.

This Suez Canal is also a thing of remote antiquity. During the reign of the Pharaohs in Egypt, a number of lagoons were connected with one another by a channel and formed a canal touching both seas. During the rule of the Roman Empire in Egypt also, attempts were made now and then to keep that channel open. Then the Mohammedan General Amru, after his conquest of Egypt, dug out the sand and changed certain features of it, so that it became almost transformed.

After that nobody paid much attention to it. The present canal was excavated by Khedive Ismail of Egypt, the Viceroy of the Sultan of Turkey, according to the advice of the French, and mostly through French capital. The difficulty with this canal is that owing to its running through a desert, it again and again becomes filled with sand. Only one good-sized merchant-ship can pass through it at a time, and it is said that very big men-of-war or merchantmen can never pass through it. Now, with a view to preventing incoming and outgoing ships from colliding against each other, the whole canal has been divided into a number of sections, and at both ends of each section there are open spaces broad enough for two or three ships to lie at anchor together. The Head Office is at the entrance to the Mediterranean, and there are stations in every section like railway stations. As soon as a ship enters the canal, messages are continually wired to this Head Office, where reports of how many ships are coming in and how many are going out, with their position at particular moments are telegraphed, and are marked on a big map. To prevent one ship confronting another, no ship is allowed to leave any station without a line-clear.

The Suez Canal is in the hands of the French. Though the majority of shares of the Canal Company are now owned by the English, yet, by a political agreement, the entire management rests with the French.

Now comes the Mediterranean. There is no more memorable region than this, outside India. It marks the end of Asia, Africa, and of ancient civilisation.

One type of manners and customs and modes of living ends here and another type of features and temperament, food and dress, customs and habits begins — we enter Europe. Not only this, but here also is the great centre of that historical admixture of colours, races, civilisations, culture, and customs, which extending over many centuries has led to the birth of modern civilisation. That religion, and culture, and civilisation, and extraordinary prowess which today have encircled the globe were born here in the regions surrounding the Mediterranean. There, on the south, is the very, very ancient Egypt, the birthplace of sculpture — overflowing in wealth and food-stuffs; on the east is Asia Minor, the ancient arena of the Phoenician, Philistine, Jewish, valiant Babylonian, Assyrian, and Persian civilisations; and on the north, the land where the Greeks — wonders of the world — flourished in ancient times.

Well, Swami, you have had enough of countries, and rivers, and mountains, and seas — now listen to a little of ancient history. Most wonderful are these annals of ancient days; not fiction, but truth — the true history of the human race. These ancient countries were almost buried in oblivion for eternity — the little that people knew of them consisted almost exclusively of the curiously fictitious compositions of the ancient Greek historians, or the miraculous descriptions of the Jewish mythology called the Bible. Now the inscriptions on ancient stones, buildings, rooms, and tiles, and linguistic analysis are voluble in their narration of the history of those countries. This recounting has but just commenced, but even now it has unearthed most wonderful tales, and who knows what more it will do in future? Great scholars of all countries are puzzling their heads day and night over a bit of rock inscription or a broken utensil, a building or a tile, and discovering the tales of ancient days sunk in oblivion.

When the Mohammedan leader Osman occupied Constantinople, and the banner of Islam began to flutter triumphantly over the whole of eastern Europe, then those books and that learning and culture of the ancient Greeks which were kept hidden with their powerless descendants spread over western Europe in the wake of the retreating Greeks. Though subjected for a long time to the Roman rule, the Greeks were the teachers of the Romans in point of learning and culture. So much so that owing to the Greeks embracing Christianity and the Christian Bible being written in the Greek tongue, Christianity got a hold over the whole Roman Empire. But the ancient Greeks, whom we call the Yavanas, and who were the first teachers of European civilisation, attained the zenith of their culture long before the Christians. Ever since they became Christians, all their learning and culture was extinguished. But as some part of the culture of their ancestors is still preserved in the Hindu homes, so it was with the Christian Greeks; these books found their way all over Europe. This it was that gave the first impetus to civilisation among the English, German, French, and other nations. There was a craze for learning the Greek language and Greek arts. First of all, they swallowed everything that was in those books. Then, as their own intelligence began to brighten up, and sciences began to develop, they commenced researches as to the date, author, subject, and authenticity, etc. of those books. There was no restriction whatever in passing free opinions on all books of the non-Christian Greeks, barring only the scriptures of the Christians, and consequently there cropped up a new science — that of external and internal criticism.

Suppose, for instance, that it is written in a book that such and such an incident took place on such and such a date. But must a thing be accepted as authentic, simply because some one has been pleased to write something about it in a book? It was customary with people, specially of those times, to write many things from imagination; moreover, they had very scanty knowledge about nature, and even of this earth we live in. All these raised grave doubts as to the authenticity of the subject-matter of a book. Suppose, for instance, that a Greek historian has written that on such and such a date there was a king in India called Chandragupta. If now, the books of India, too, mention that king under that particular date, the matter is certainly proved to a great extent. If a few coins of Chandragupta's reign be found, or a building of his time which contains references to him, the veracity of the matter is then assured.

Suppose another book records a particular incident as taking place in the reign of Alexander the Great, but there is mention of one or two Roman Emperors in such a way that they cannot be taken as interpolations — then that book is proved not to belong to Alexander's time.

Or again, language. Every language undergoes some change through the lapse of time, and authors have also their own peculiar style. If in any book there is suddenly introduced a description which has no bearing on the subject, and is in a style quite different from the author's, it will readily be suspected as an interpolation. Thus a new science of ascertaining the truth about a book, by means of doubting and testing and proving in various ways, was discovered.

To add to this, modern science began, with rapid strides, to throw new light on things from all sides, with the results that any book that contained a reference to supernatural incidents came to be wholly disbelieved.

To crown all, there were the entrance of the tidal wave of Sanskrit into Europe and the deciphering of ancient lapidary inscriptions found in India, on the banks of the Euphrates, and in Egypt, as well as the discovery of temples etc., hidden for ages under the earth or on hill-sides, and the correct reading of their history.

I have already said that this new science of research set the Bible or the New Testament books quite apart. Now there are no longer the tortures of the Inquisition, there is only the fear of social obloquy; disregarding that, many scholars have subjected those books also to a stringent analysis. Let us hope that as they mercilessly hack the Hindu and other scriptures to pieces, they will in time show the same moral courage towards the Jewish and Christian scriptures also. Let me give an illustration to explain why I say this. Maspero, a great savant and a highly reputed author on Egyptology, has written a voluminous history of the Egyptians and Babylonians entitled Histoire Ancienne Orientale. A few years ago I read an English translation of the book by an English archaeologist. This time, on my asking a Librarian of the British Museum about certain books on Egypt and Babylon, Maspero's book was mentioned. And when he learnt that I had with me an English translation of the book, he said that it would not do, for the translator was a rather bigoted Christian, and wherever Maspero's researches hit Christianity in any way, he (the translator) had managed to twist and torture those passages! He recommended me to read the book in original French. And on reading I found it was just as he had said — a terrible problem indeed! You know very well what a queer thing religious bigotry is; it makes a mess of truth and untruth. Thenceforth my faith in the translations of those research works has been greatly shaken.

Another new science has developed — ethnology, that is, the classification of men from an examination of their colour, hair, physique, shape of the head, language, and so forth.

The Germans, though masters in all sciences, are specially expert in Sanskrit and ancient Assyrian culture; Benfey and other German scholars are illustrations of this. The French are skilled in Egyptology — scholars like Maspero are French. The Dutch are famous for their analysis of Jewish and ancient Christian religions — writers like Kuenen have attained a world-celebrity. The English inaugurate many sciences and then leave off.

Let me now tell you some of the opinions of these scholars. If you do not like their views, you may fight them; but pray, do not lay the blame on me. According to the Hindus, Jews, ancient Babylonians, Egyptians, and other ancient races, all mankind have descended from the same primaeval parents. People do not much believe in this now.

Have you ever seen jet-black, flat-nosed, thick-lipped, curly-haired Kaffirs with receding foreheads? And have you seen the Santals, and Andamanese, and Bhils with about the same features, but of shorter stature, and with hair less curly? The first class are called Negroes; these live in Africa. The second class are called Negritos (little Negroes); in ancient times these used to inhabit certain parts of Arabia, portions of the banks of the Euphrates, the southern part of Persia, the whole of India, the Andamans, and other islands, even as far as Australia. In modern times they are to be met with in certain forests and jungles of India, in the Andamans, and in Australia.

Have you seen the Lepchas, Bhutias, and Chinese — white or yellow in colour, and with straight black hair? They have dark eyes — but these are set so as to form an angle — scanty beard and moustache, a flat face, and very prominent malar bones. Have you seen the Nepalese, Burmese, Siamese, Malays, and Japanese? They have the same shape, but have shorter stature.

The two species of this type are called Mongols and Mongoloids (little Mongols). The Mongolians have now occupied the greater part of Asia. It is they who, divided into many branches such as the Mongols, Kalmucks, Huns, Chinese, Tartars, Turks, Manchus, Kirghiz, etc. lead a nomadic life, carrying tents, and tending sheep, goats, cattle, and horses, and whenever an opportunity occurs, sweep like a swarm of locusts and unhinge the world. These Chinese and Tibetans alone are an exception to this. They are also known by the name of Turanians. It is the Turan which you find in the popular phrase, "Iran and Turan."

A race of a dark colour but with straight hair, straight nose and straight dark eyes, used to inhabit ancient Egypt and ancient Babylonia and now live all over India, specially in the southern portion; in Europe also one finds traces of them in rare places. They form one race, and have the technical name of Dravidians.

Another race has white colour, straight eyes, but ears and noses curved and thick towards the tip, receding foreheads, and thick lips — as, for instance, the people of north Arabia, the modern Jews and the ancient Babylonians, Assyrians, Phoenicians, etc.; their languages also have a common stock; these are called the Semitic race.

And those who speak a language allied to Sanskrit, who have straight noses, mouths, and eyes, a white complexion, black or brown hair, dark or blue eyes, are called Aryans.

All the modern races have sprung from an admixture of these races. A country which has a preponderance of one or other of these races, has also its language and physiognomy mostly like those of that particular race.

It is not a generally accepted theory in the West that a warm country produces dark complexion and a cold country white complexion. Many are of opinion that the existing shades between black and white have been the outcome of a fusion of races.

According to scholars, the civilisations of Egypt and ancient Babylonia are the oldest. Houses and remains of buildings are to be met with in these countries dating 6,000 B.C. or even earlier. In India the oldest building that may have been discovered date back to Chandragupta's time at the most; that is, only 300 B.C. Houses of greater antiquity have not yet been discovered. (The ancient remains at Harappa, Mohenjo-daro etc., in the Indus Valley in North-west India, which prove the existence of an advanced city civilisation in India dating back to more than 3000 B.C., were not dug out before 1922. — Ed.) But there are books, etc., of a far earlier date, which one cannot find in any other country. Pandit Bal Gangadhar Tilak has brought evidence to show that the Vedas of the Hindus existed in the present form at least five thousand years before the Christian era.

The borders of this Mediterranean were the birthplace of that European civilisation which has now conquered the world. On these shores the Semitic races such as the Egyptians, Babylonians, Phoenicians, and Jews, and the Aryan races such as the Persians, Greeks, and Romans, fused together — to form the modern European civilisation.

A big stone slab with inscriptions on it, called the Rosetta Stone, was discovered in Egypt. On this there are inscriptions in hieroglyphics, below which there is another kind of writing, and below them all there are inscriptions resembling Greek characters. A scholar conjectured that those three sets of inscriptions presented the same thing, and he deciphered these ancient Egyptian inscriptions with the help of Coptic characters — the Copts being the Christian race who yet inhabit Egypt and who are known as the descendants of the ancient Egyptians. Similarly the cuneiform characters inscribed on the bricks and tiles of the Babylonians were also gradually deciphered. Meanwhile certain Indian inscriptions in plough-shaped characters were discovered as belonging to the time of Emperor Asoka. No earlier inscriptions than these have been discovered in India. (The Indus script is now known to be contemporary with Sumerian and Egyptian. — Ed.) The hieroglyphics inscribed on various kinds of temples, columns, and sarcophagi all over Egypt are being gradually deciphered and making Egyptian antiquity more lucid.

The Egyptians entered into Egypt from a southern country called Punt, across the seas. Some say that that Punt is the modern Malabar, and that the Egyptians and Dravidians belong to the same race. Their first king was named Menes, and their ancient religion too resembles in some parts our mythological tales. The god Shibu was enveloped by the goddess Nui; later on another god Shu came and forcibly removed Nui. Nui's body became the sky, and her two hands and two legs became the four pillars of that sky. And Shibu became the earth. Osiris and Isis, the son and daughter of Nui, are the chief god and goddess in Egypt, and their son Horus is the object of universal worship. These three used to be worshipped in a group. Isis, again, is worshipped in the form of the cow.

Like the Nile on earth there is another Nile in the sky, of which the terrestrial Nile is only a part. According to the Egyptians, the Sun travels round the earth in a boat; now and then a serpent called Ahi devours him, then an eclipse takes place. The Moon is periodically attacked by a boar and torn to pieces, from which he takes fifteen days to recover. The deities of Egypt are some of them jackal-faced, some hawk-faced, others cow-faced, and so on.

Simultaneously with this, another civilisation had its rise on the banks of the Euphrates. Baal, Moloch, Istarte, and Damuzi were the chief of deities here. Istarte fell in love with a shepherd named Damuzi. A boar killed the latter and Istarte went to Hades, below the earth, in search of him. There she was subjected to various tortures by the terrible goddess Alat. At last Istarte declared that she would no more return to earth unless she got Damuzi back. This was a great difficulty; she was the goddess of sex-impulse, and unless she went back, neither men, nor animals, nor vegetables would multiply. Then the gods made a compromise that every year Damuzi was to reside in Hades for four months and live on earth during the remaining eight months. Then Istarte returned, there was the advent of spring and a good harvest followed.

Thus Damuzi again is known under the name of Adunoi or Adonis! The religion of all the Semitic races, with slight minor variations, was almost the same. The Babylonians, Jews, Phoenicians, and Arabs of a later date used the same form of worship. Almost every god was called Moloch — the word which persists to this day in the Bengali language as Mâlik (ruler), Mulluk (kingdom) and so forth — or Baal; but of course there were minor differences. According to some, the god called Alat afterwards turned into Allah of the Arab.

The worship of these gods also included certain terrible and abominable rites. Before Moloch or Baal children used to be burnt alive. In the temple of Istarte the natural and unnatural satisfaction of lust was the principal feature.

The history of the Jewish race is much more recent than that of Babylon. According to scholars the scripture known as the Bible was composed from 500 B.C. to several years after the Christian era. Many portions of the Bible which are generally supposed to be of earlier origin belong to a much later date. The main topics of the Bible concern the Babylonians. The Babylonian cosmology and description of the Deluge have in many parts been incorporated wholesale into the Bible. Over and above this, during the rule of the Persian Emperors in Asia Minor, many Persian doctrines found acceptance among the Jews. According to the Old Testament, this world is all; there is neither soul nor an after-life. In the New Testament there is mention of the Parsee doctrines of an after-life and resurrection of the dead, while the theory of Satan exclusively belongs to the Parsis.

The principal feature of the Jewish religion is the worship of Yave-Moloch. But this name does not belong to the Jewish language; according to some it is an Egyptian word. But nobody knows whence it came. There are descriptions in the Bible that the Israelites lived confined in Egypt for a long time, but all this is seldom accepted now, and the patriarchs such as Abraham, and Isaac, and Joseph are proved to be mere allegories.

The Jews would not utter the name "Yave", in place of which they used to say "Adunoi". When the Jews became divided into two branches, Israel and Ephraim, two principal temples were constructed in the two countries. In the temple that was built by the Israelites in Jerusalem, an image of Yave, consisting of a male and female figure united, was preserved in a coffer (ark), and there was a big phallic column at the door. In Ephraim, Yave used to be worshipped in the form of a gold-covered Bull.

In both places it was the practice to consign the eldest son alive to the flames before the god, and a band of women used to live in both the temples, within the very precincts of which they used to lead most immoral lives and their earnings were utilised for temple expenditure.

In course of time there appeared among the Jews a class of men who used to invoke the presence of deities in their person by means of music or dance. They were called Prophets. Many of these, through association with the Persians, set themselves against image-worship, sacrifice of sons, immorality, prostitution, and such other practices. By degrees, circumcision took the place of human sacrifice; and prostitution and image-worship etc. gradually disappeared. In course of time from among these Prophets Christianity had its rise.

There is a great dispute as to whether there ever was born a man with the name of Jesus. Of the four books comprising the New Testament, the Book of St. John has been rejected by some as spurious. As to the remaining three, the verdict is that they have been copied from some ancient book; and that, too, long after the date ascribed to Jesus Christ.

Moreover, about the time that Jesus is believed to have been born among the Jews themselves, there were born two historians, Josephus and Philo. They have mentioned even petty sects among the Jews, but not made the least reference to Jesus or the Christians, or that the Roman Judge sentenced him to death on the cross. Josephus' book had a single line about it, which has now been proved to be an interpolation. The Romans used to rule over the Jews at that time, and the Greeks taught all sciences and arts. They have all written a good many things about the Jews, but made no mention of either Jesus or the Christians.

Another difficulty is that the sayings, precepts, or doctrines which the New Testament preaches were already in existence among the Jews before the Christian era, having come from different quarters, and were being preached by Rabbis like Hillel and others. These are what scholars say; but they cannot, with safety to their reputation, give oracular verdicts off-hand on their own religion, as they are wont to do with regard to alien religions. So they proceed slowly. This is what is called Higher Criticism.

The Western scholars are thus studying the religions, customs, races, etc., of different and far-off countries. But we have nothing of the kind in Bengali! And how is it possible? If a man after ten years of hard labour translates a book of this kind, well, what will he himself live upon, and where will he get the funds to publish his book?

In the first place, our country is very poor, and in the second place, there is practically no cultivation of learning. Shall such a day dawn for our country when we shall be cultivating various kinds of arts and sciences? — "She whose grace makes the dumb eloquent and the lame to scale mountains" — She, the Divine Mother, only knows!

The ship touched Naples — we reached Italy. The capital of Italy is Rome — Rome, the capital of that ancient, most powerful Roman Empire, whose politics, military science, art of colonisation, and foreign conquest are to this day the model for the whole world!

After leaving Naples the ship called at Marseilles, and thence straight at London.

You have already heard a good deal about Europe — what they eat, how they dress, what are their manners and customs, and so forth — so I need not write on this. But about European civilisation, its origin, its relation to us, and the extent to which we should adopt it — about such things I shall have much to say in future. The body is no respecter of persons, dear brother, so I shall try to speak about them some other time. Or what is the use? Well, who on earth can vie with us (specially the Bengalis) as regards talking and discussing? Show it in action if you can. Let your work proclaim, and let the tongue rest. But let me mention one thing in passing, viz. that Europe began to advance from the date that learning and power began to flow in among the poor lower classes. Lots of suffering poor people of other countries, cast off like refuse as it were, find a house and shelter in America, and these are the very backbone of America! It matters little whether rich men and scholars listen to you, understand you, and praise or blame you — they are merely the ornaments, the decorations of the country! — It is the millions of poor lower class people who are its life. Numbers do not count, nor does wealth or poverty; a handful of men can throw the world off its hinges, provided they are united in thought, word, and deed — never forget this conviction. The more opposition there is, the better. Does a river acquire velocity unless there is resistence? The newer and better a thing is, the more opposition it will meet with at the outset. It is opposition which foretells success. Where there is no opposition there is no success either. Good-bye!

II

We have an adage among us that one that has a disc-like pattern on the soles of his feet becomes a vagabond. I fear, I have my soles inscribed all over with them. And there is not much room for probability, either. I have tried my best to discover them by scrutinising the soles, but all to no purpose — the feet have been dreadfully cracked through the severity of cold, and no discs or anything of the kind could be traced. However, when there is the tradition, I take it for granted that my soles are full of those signs. But the results are quite patent — it was my cherished desire to remain in Paris for some time and study the French language and civilisation; I left my old friends and acquaintances and put up with a new friend, a Frenchman of ordinary means, who knew no English, and my French — well, it was something quite extraordinary! I had this in mind that the inability to live like a dumb man would naturally force me to talk French, and I would attain fluency in that language in no time — but on the contrary I am now on a tour through Vienna, Turkey, Greece, Egypt, and Jerusalem! Well, who can stem the course of the inevitable! — And this letter I am writing to you from the last remaining capital of Mohammedan supremacy — from Constantinople!

I have three travelling companions — two of them French and the third an American. The American is Miss MacLeod whom you know very well; the French male companion is Monsieur Jules Bois, a famous philosopher and litterateur of France; and the French lady friend is the world-renowned singer, Mademoiselle Calvé. "Mister" is "Monsieur" in the French language, and "Miss" is "Mademoiselle" — with a Z-sound. Mademoiselle Calvé is the foremost singer — opera singer — of the present day. Her musical performances are so highly appreciated that she has an annual income of three to four lakhs of rupees, solely from singing. I had previously been acquainted with her. The foremost actress in the West, Madame Sarah Bernhardt, and the foremost singer, Calvé, are both of them of French extraction, and both totally ignorant of English, but they visit England and America occasionally and earn millions of dollars by acting and singing. French is the language of the civilised world, the mark of gentility in the West, and everybody knows it; consequently these two ladies have neither the leisure nor the inclination to learn English. Madame Bernhardt is an aged lady; but when she steps on the stage after dressing, her imitation of the age and sex of the role she plays is perfect! A girl or a boy — whatever part you want her to play, she is an exact representation of that. And that wonderful voice! People here say her voice has the ring of silver strings! Madame Bernhardt has a special regard for India; she tells me again and again that our country is "trés ancien, tres civilisé" — very ancient and very civilised. One year she performed a drama touching on India, in which she set up a whole Indian street-scene on the stage — men, women, and children, Sadhus and Nagas, and everything — an exact picture of India! After the performance she told me that for about a month she had visited every museum and made herself acquainted with the men and women and their dress, the streets and bathing ghats and everything relating to India. Madame Bernhardt has a very strong desire to visit India. — "C'est mon rave! — It is the dream of my life", she says. Again, the Prince of Wales (His late Majesty King Edward VII, the then Prince of Wales.) has promised to take her over to a tiger and elephant hunting excursion. But then she said she must spend some two lakhs of rupees if she went to India! She is of course in no want of money. "La divine Sarah" — the divine Sarah — is her name; how can she want money, she who never travels but by a special train! That pomp and luxury many a prince of Europe cannot afford to indulge in! One can only secure a seat for her performance by paying double the fees, and that a month in advance! Well, she is not going to suffer want of money! But Sarah Bernhardt is given to spending lavishly. Her travel to India is therefore put off for the present.

Mademoiselle Calve will not sing this winter, she will take a rest and is going to temperate climates like Egypt etc. I am going as her guest. Calve has not devoted herself to music alone, she is sufficiently learned and has a great love for philosophical and religious literature. She was born amidst very poor circumstances; gradually, through her own genius and undergoing great labour and much hardship, she has now amassed a large fortune and has become the object of adoration of kings and potentates!

There are famous lady singers, such as Madame Melba, Madame Emma Ames, and others; and very distinguished singers, such as Jean de Reszke, Plancon, and the rest — all of whom earn two or three lakhs of rupees a year! But with Calvé's art is coupled a unique genius. Extraordinary beauty, youth, genius, and a celestial voice — all these have conspired to raise Calvé to the forefront of all singers. But there is no better teacher than pain and poverty! That extreme penury and pain and hardship of childhood, a constant struggle against which has won for Calvé this victory, have engendered a remarkable sympathy and a profound seriousness in her life. Again, in the West, there are ample opportunities along with the enterprising spirit. But in our country, there is a sad dearth of opportunities, even if the spirit of enterprise be not absent. The Bengali woman may be keen after acquiring education, but it comes to nought for want of opportunities. And what is there to learn from in the Bengali language? At best some poor novels and dramas! Then again, learning is confined at present to a foreign tongue or to Sanskrit and is only for the chosen few. In these Western countries there are innumerable books in the mother-tongue; over and above that, whenever something new comes out in a foreign tongue, it is at once translated and placed before the public.

Monsieur Jules Bois is a famous writer; he is particularly an adept in the discovery of historical truths in the different religions and superstitions. He has written a famous book putting into historical form the devil-worship, sorcery, necromancy, incantation, and such other rites that were in vogue in Mediaeval Europe, and the traces of those that obtain to this day. He is a good poet, and is an advocate of the Indian Vedantic ideas that have crept into the great French poets, such as Victor Hugo and Lamartine and others, and the great German poets, such as Goethe, Schiller, and the rest. The influence of Vedanta on European poetry and philosophy is very great. Every good poet is a Vedantin, I find; and whoever writes some philosophical treatise has to draw upon Vedanta in some shape or other. Only some of them do not care to admit this indebtedness, and want to establish their complete originality, as Herbert Spencer and others, for instance. But the majority do openly acknowledge. And how can they help it — in these days of telegraphs and railways and newspapers? M. Jules Bois is very modest and gentle, and though a man of ordinary means, he very cordially received me as a guest into his house in Paris. Now he is accompanying us for travel.

We have two other companions on the journey as far as Constantinople — Père Hyacinthe and his wife. Père, i.e. Father Hyacinthe was a monk of a strict ascetic section of the Roman Catholic Church. His scholarship, extraordinary eloquence, and great austerities won for him a high reputation in France and in the whole Catholic Order. The great poet, Victor Hugo, used to praise the French style of two men — one of these was Père Hyacinthe. At forty years of age Père Hyacinthe fell in love with an American woman and eventually married her. This created a great sensation, and of course the Catholic Order immediately gave him up. Discarding his ascetic garb of bare feet and loose-fitting cloak, Père Hyacinthe took up the hat, coat, and boots of the householder and became — Monsieur Loyson. I, however, call him by his former name. It is an old, old tale, and the matter was the talk of the whole continent. The Protestants received him with honour, but the Catholics began to hate him. The Pope, in consideration of his attainments, was unwilling to part with him and asked him to remain a Greek Catholic priest, and not abandon the Roman Church. (The priests of the Greek Catholic section are allowed to marry but once, but do not get any high position). Mrs. Loyson, however, forcibly dragged him out of the Pope's fold. In course of time they had children and grandchildren; now the very aged Loyson is going to Jerusalem to try to establish cordial relations among the Christians and Mussulmans. His wife had perhaps seen many visions that Loyson might possibly turn out to be a second Martin Luther and overthrow the Pope's throne — into the Mediterranean. But nothing of the kind took place; and the only result was, as the French say, that he was placed between two stools. But Madame Loyson still cherishes her curious day-dreams! Old Loyson is very affable in speech, modest, and of a distinctly devotional turn of mind. Whenever he meets me, he holds pretty long talks about various religions and creeds. But being of a devotional temperament, he is a little afraid of the Advaita. Madame Loyson's attitude towards me is, I fear, rather unfavourable. When I discuss with the old man such topics as renunciation and monasticism etc., all those long-cherished sentiments wake up in his aged breast, and his wife most probably smarts all the while. Besides, all French people, of both sexes, lay the whole blame on the wife; they say, "That woman has spoilt one of our great ascetic monks!" Madame Loyson is really in a sorry predicament — specially as they live in Paris, in a Catholic country. They hate the very sight of a married priest; no Catholic would ever tolerate the preaching of religion by a man with family. And Madame Loyson has a bit of animus also. Once she expressed her dislike of an actress, saying, "It is very bad of you to live with Mr. So-and-so without marrying him". The actress immediately retorted, "I am a thousand times better than you. I live with a common man; it may be, I have not legally married him; whereas you are a great sinner — you have made such a great monk break his religious vows! If you were so desperately in love with the monk, why, you might as well live as his attending maid; but why did you bring ruin on him by marrying him and thus converting him into a householder?"

However I hear all and keep silent. But old Père Hyacinthe is a really sweet-natured and peaceful man, he is happy with his wife and family — and what can the whole French people have to say against this? I think, everything would be settled if but his wife climbed down a bit. But one thing I notice, viz. that men and women, in every country, have different ways of understanding and judging things. Men have one angle of vision, women another; men argue from one standpoint, women from another. Men extenuate women and lay the blame on men; while women exonerate men and heap all the blame on women.

One special benefit I get from the company of these ladies and gentlemen is that, except the one

American lady, no one knows English; talking in English is wholly eschewed, (It is not etiquette in the West to talk in company any language but one known to all party.) and consequently somehow or other I have to talk as well as hear French.

From Paris our friend Maxim has supplied me with letters of introduction to various places, so that the countries may be properly seen. Maxim is the inventor of the famous Maxim gun — the gun that sends off a continuous round of balls and is loaded and discharged automatically without intermission. Maxim is by birth an American; now he has settled in England, where he has his gun-factories etc. Maxim is vexed if anybody alludes too frequently to his guns in his presence and says, "My friend, have I done nothing else except invent that engine of destruction?" Maxim is an admirer of China and India and is a good writer on religion and philosophy etc. Having read my works long since, he holds me in great — I should say, excessive — admiration. He supplies guns to all kings and rulers and is well known in every country, though his particular friend is Li Hung Chang, his special regard is for China and his devotion, for Confucianism. He is in the habit of writing occasionally in the newspapers, under Chinese pseudonyms, against the Christians — about what takes them to China, their real motive, and so forth. He cannot at all bear the Christian missionaries preaching their religion in China! His wife also is just like her husband in her regard for China and hatred of Christianity! Maxim has no issue; he is an old man, and immensely rich.

The tour programme was as follows — from Paris to Vienna, and thence to Constantinople, by rail; then by steamer to Athens and Greece, then across the Mediterranean to Egypt, then Asia Minor, Jerusalem, and so on. The "Oriental Express" runs daily from Paris to Constantinople, and is provided with sleeping, sitting, and dining accommodations after the American model. Though not perfect like the American cars, they are fairly well furnished. I am to leave Paris by that train on October 24 (1900).

Today is the 23rd October; tomorrow evening I am to take leave of Paris. This year Paris is a centre of the civilised world, for it is the year of the Paris Exhibition, and there has been an assemblage of eminent men and women from all quarters of the globe. The master-minds of all countries have met today in Paris to spread the glory of their respective countries by means of their genius. The fortunate man whose name the bells of this great centre will ring today will at the same time crown his country also with glory, before the world. And where art thou, my Motherland, Bengal, in the great capital city swarming with German, French, English, Italian, and other scholars? Who is there to utter thy name? Who is there to proclaim thy existence? From among that white galaxy of geniuses there stepped forth one distinguished youthful hero to proclaim the name of our Motherland, Bengal — it was the world-renowned scientist, Dr. (Later, Sir.) J. C. Bose! Alone, the youthful Bengali physicist, with galvanic quickness, charmed the Western audience today with his splendid genius; that electric charge infused pulsations of new life into the half-dead body of the Motherland! At the top of all physicists today is — Jagadish Chandra Bose, an Indian, a Bengali! Well done, hero! Whichever countries, Dr. Bose and his accomplished, ideal wife may visit, everywhere they glorify India — add fresh laurels to the crown of Bengal. Blessed pair!

And the daily reunion of numbers of distinguished men and women which Mr. Leggett brought about at an enormous expense in his Parisian mansion, by inviting them to at-homes — that too ends today.

All types of distinguished personages — poets, philosophers, scientists, moralists, politicians, singers, professors, painters, artists, sculptors, musicians, and so on, of both sexes — used to be assembled in Mr. Leggett's residence, attracted by his hospitality and kindness. That incessant outflow of words, clear and limpid like a mountainfall, that expression of sentiments emanating from all sides like sparks of fire, bewitching music, the magic current of thoughts from master minds coming into conflict with one another — which used to hold all spellbound, making them forgetful of time and place — these too shall end.

Everything on earth has an end. Once again I took a round over the Paris Exhibition today — this accumulated mass of dazzling ideas, like lightning held steady as it were, this unique assemblage of celestial panorama on earth!

It has been raining in Paris for the last two or three days. During all this time the sun who is ever kind to France has held back his accustomed grace. Perhaps his face has been darkened over with clouds in disgust to witness the secretly flowing current of sensuality behind this assemblage of arts and artists, learning and learned folk, or perhaps he has hid his face under a pall of cloud in grief over the impending destruction of this illusive heaven of particoloured wood and canvas.

We too shall be happy to escape. The breaking up of the Exhibition is a big affair; the streets of this heaven on earth, the Eden-like Paris, will be filled with knee-deep mud and mortar. With the exception of one or two main buildings, all the houses and their parts are but a display of wood and rags and whitewashing — just as the whole world is! And when they are demolished, the lime-dust flies about and is suffocating; rags and sand etc. make the streets exceedingly dirty; and, if it rains in addition, it is an awful mess.

In the evening of October 24 the train left Paris. The night was dark and nothing could be seen. Monsieur Bois and myself occupied one compartment — and early went to bed. On awakening from sleep we found we had crossed the French frontier and entered German territory. I had already seen Germany thoroughly; but Germany, after France, produces quite a jarring effect. "On the one hand the moon is setting" (यात्येकतोऽस्तशिखरं पतिरोषधीनां — From Kalidasa's Shakuntalâ.) — the world-encompassing France is slowly consuming herself in the fire of contemplated retribution — while on the other hand, centralised, young, and mighty Germany has begun her upward march above the horizon with rapid strides. On one side is the artistic workmanship of the dark-haired, comparatively short-statured, luxurious, highly civilised French people, to whom art means life; and on the other, the clumsy daubing, the unskilful manipulation, of tawny-haired, tall, gigantic German. After Paris there is no other city in the Western world; everywhere it is an imitation of Paris — or at least an attempt at it. But in France that art is full of grace and ethereal beauty, while in Germany, England, and America the imitation is coarse and clumsy. Even the application of force on the part of the French is beautiful, as it were, whereas the attempt of the Germans to display beauty even is terrible. The countenance of French genius, even when frowning in anger, is beautiful; that of German genius, even when beaming with smiles, appears frightful, as it were. French civilisation is full of nerve, like camphor or musk — it volatilises and pervades the room in a moment; while German civilisation is full of muscle, heavy like lead or mercury — it remains motionless and inert wherever it lies. The German muscle can go on striking small blows untiringly, till death; the French have tender, feminine bodies, but when they do concentrate and strike, it is a sledge-hammer blow and is irresistible.

The Germans are constructing after the French fashion big houses and mansions, and placing big statues, equestrian figures, etc. on top of them, but on seeing a double-storeyed German building one is tempted to ask — is it a dwelling-house for men, or a stable for elephants and camels, while one mistakes a five-storeyed French stable for elephants and horses as a habitation for fairies.

America is inspired by German ideals; hundreds of thousand Germans are in every town. The language is of course English, but nevertheless America is being slowly Germanised. Germany is fast multiplying her population and is exceptionally hardy. Today Germany is the dictator to all Europe, her place is above all! Long before all other nations, Germany has given man and woman compulsory education, making illiteracy punishable by law, and today she is enjoying the fruits of that tree. The German army is the foremost in reputation, and Germany has vowed to become foremost in her navy also. German manufacture of commodities has beaten even England! German merchandise and the Germans themselves are slowly obtaining a monopoly even in the English colonies. At the behest of the German Emperor all the nations have ungrudgingly submitted to the lead of the German Generalissimo in the battle-fields of China!

The whole day the train rushed through Germany, till in the afternoon it reached the frontiers of Austria, the ancient sphere of German supremacy, but now an alien territory. There are certain troubles in travelling through Europe. In every country enormous duties are levied upon certain things, or some articles of merchandise are the monopoly of the Government, as for instance, tobacco. Again, in Russia and Turkey, you are totally forbidden to enter without a royal passport; a passport you must always have. Besides, in Russia and Turkey, all your books and papers will be seized; and when on perusal the authorities are satisfied that there is nothing in them against the Russian or Turkish Government and religion, then only they will be returned, otherwise they will all be confiscated. In other countries your tobacco is a source of great trouble. You must open your chest, and trunk and packages for inspection whether they contain tobacco etc. or not. And to come to Constantinople one has to pass through two big States — Germany and Austria, and many petty ones; the latter had formerly been districts of Turkey, but later on the independent Christian kings made a common cause and wrested as many of these Christian districts from Mohammedan hands as they could. The bite of these tiny ants is much worse than even that of the bigger ones.

In the evening of October 25 the train reached Vienna, the capital of Austria. The members of the royal family in Austria and Russia are styled Archdukes and Archduchesses. Two Archdukes are to get down at Vienna by this train; and until they have done so the other passengers are not allowed to get down. So we had to wait. A few officers in laced uniform and some soldiers with feathered caps were waiting for the Archdukes, who got down surrounded by them. We too felt relieved and made haste to get down and have our luggage passed. There were few passengers, and it did not take us much time to show our luggage and have it passed. A hotel had already been arranged for, and a man from the hotel was waiting for us with a carriage. We reached the hotel duly. It was out of the question to go out for sight-seeing during the night; so the next morning we started to see the town. In all hotels, and almost in all the countries of Europe except England and Germany, the French fashion prevails. They eat twice a day like the Hindus; in the morning by twelve o'clock, and in the evening by eight. Early in the morning, that is, about eight or nine, they take a little coffee. Tea is very little in vogue except in England and Russia. The morning meal is called in French déjeuner — that is, breakfast, and the evening meal dîner — that is, dinner. Tea is very much in use in Russia — it is too cold, and China is near enough. Chinese tea is excellent, and most of it goes to Russia. The Russian mode of drinking tea is also analogous to the Chinese, that is, without mixing milk. Tea or coffee becomes injurious like poison if you mix milk with it. The real tea-drinking races, the Chinese, Japanese, Russians, and the inhabitants of Central Asia, take tea without milk. Similarly, the original coffee-drinking races, such as the Turks, drink coffee without milk. Only in Russia they put a slice of lemon and a lump of sugar into the tea. The poor people place a lump of sugar in the mouth and drink tea over it, and when one has finished drinking, one passes that lump on to another, who repeats the process.

Vienna is a small city after the model of Paris. But the Austrians are German by race. The Austrian Emperor was hitherto the Emperor of almost the whole of Germany. In the present times, owing to the far-sightedness of King Wilhelm of Prussia, the wonderful diplomacy of his able minister, Bismark, and the military genius of General Von Moltke, the King of Prussia is the Emperor of the whole of Germany barring Austria. Austria, shorn of her glory and robbed of her power, is somehow maintaining her ancient name and prestige. The Austrian royal line — the Hapsburg Dynasty — is the oldest and most aristocratic dynasty in Europe. It was this Austrian dynasty which hitherto rules Germany as Emperors — Germany whose princes are seated on the thrones of almost all the countries of Europe, and whose petty feudatory chiefs even occupy the thrones of such powerful empires as England and Russia. The desire for that honour and prestige Austria still cherishes in full, only she lacks the power. Turkey is called "the sick man" of Europe; then

Austria should be called "the sick dame". Austria belongs to the Catholic sect, and until recently the Austrian Empire used to be called "the Holy Roman Empire". Modern Germany has a preponderance of Protestants. The Austrian Emperor has always been the right-hand man of the Pope, his faithful follower, and the leader of the Roman Catholic sect. Now the Austrian Emperor is the only Catholic Ruler in Europe; France, the eldest daughter of the Catholic Church, is now a Republic, while Spain and Portugal are downfallen! Italy has given only room enough for the Papal throne to be established, robbing the Pope's entire splendour and dominion; between the King of Italy and the Pope of Rome there is no love lost, they cannot bear each other's sight. Rome, the capital of the Pope, is now the capital of Italy. The King lives in the Pope's ancient palace which he has seized, and the ancient Italian kingdom of the Pope is now confined within the precincts of the Vatican. But the Pope has still great influence in religious matters — and the chief supporter of this is Austria. As a result of the struggle against Austria — against the age-long thraldom of Austria, the ally of the Pope — up rose modern Italy. Consequently Austria is against Italy — against, because she lost her. Unfortunately, however, young Italy, under England's misdirection, set herself to create a powerful army and navy. But where was the money? So, involved in debt, Italy is on the way to ruin; and to her misfortune, she brought on herself a fresh trouble by proceeding to extend her empire in Africa. Defeated by the Abyssinian monarch, she has sunk down, bereft of glory and prestige. Prussia in the meantime defeated Austria in a great war and thrust her off to a great distance. Austria is slowly dying, while Italy has similarly fettered herself by the misuse of her new life.

The Austrian royal line is still the proudest of all European royal families. It boasts of being a very ancient and very aristocratic dynasty. The marriages and other connections of this line are contracted with the greatest circumspection, and no such relationship can be established with families that are not Roman Catholic. It was the glamour of a connection with this line that led to the fall of Napoleon the Great. Quaintly enough, he took it into his head to marry a daughter of some noble royal family and found a great dynasty through a succession of descendents. The hero who, questioned as to his pedigree, had replied, "I owe the title to my nobility to none — I am to be the founder of a great dynasty" — that is to say, that he would originate a powerful dynasty, and that he was not born to glorify himself with the borrowed plumes of some ancestor — that hero fell into this abyss of family prestige.

The divorce of the Empress Josephine, the defeat of the Austrian Emperor in battle and taking his daughter to wife, the marriage of Bonaparte in great pomp with Marie Louise, the Princess of Austria, the birth of a son, the installation of the new-born babe as the King of Rome, the fall of Napoleon, the enmity of his father-in-law, Leipsic, Waterloo, St. Helena, Empress Marie Louise living in her father's house with her child, the marriage of Napoleon's royal consort with an ordinary soldier, the death of his only son, the King of Rome, in the house of his maternal grandfather — all these are well-known incidents of history.

Fallen in a comparatively weakened condition, France is now ruminating on her past glory — nowadays there are very many books on Napoleon. Dramatists like Sardou are writing many dramas on Napoleon dead and gone; and actresses like Madame Bernhardt and Réjane are performing those plays every night before bumper houses. Recently Madame Bernhardt has created a great attraction in Paris by playing a drama entitled L'aiglon (the Young Eagle).

The young Eagle is the only son of Napoleon, practically interned in his maternal grandfather's residence, the Palace of Vienna. The Austrian Emperor's minister, the Machiavellian Metternich, is always careful not to allow the tales of heroism of his father to enter into the boy's mind. But a few of Bonaparte's veterans contrived to get themselves admitted into the boy's service in the Schönbrunn Palace, incognito; their idea was to somehow take the boy over to France and found the Bonaparte line by driving out the Bourbons reinstated by the combined European potentates. The child was the son of a great hero, and very soon that latent heroism woke up in him to hear the glorious tales of battle of his father. One day the boy fled from the Schönbrunn Palace accompanied by the conspirators. But Metternich's keen intellect had already scented the matter, and he cut off the journey. The son of Bonaparte was carried back to the Schönbrunn Palace and the Young Eagle, with his wings tied, as it were, very soon died of a broken heart!

This Schönbrunn Palace is an ordinary palace. Of course, the rooms etc. are lavishly decorated; in one of them perhaps one meets with only Chinese workmanship, in another only works of Hindu art, in a third the productions of some other country, and so on; and the garden attached to the Palace is very charming indeed. But all the people that now go to visit this Palace go there with the object of seeing the room where Bonaparte's son used to lie, or his study, or the room in which he died, and so forth. Many thoughtless French men and women are interrogating the guard, which room belonged to "L'aiglon", which bed did "L'aiglon" use to occupy, and so on. What silly questions, these! The Austrians only know that he was the son of Bonaparte, and the relation was established by forcibly taking their girl in marriage; that hatred they have not yet forgotten. The Prince was a grandchild of the Emperor, and homeless, so they could not help giving him a shelter, but they could give him no such title as "King of Rome"; only, being the grandson of the Austrian Emperor, he was an Archduke, that was all. It may be that you French people have now written a book on him, making him the Young Eagle, and the addition of imaginary settings and the genius of Madame Bernhardt have created a great interest in the story, but how should an Austrian guard know that name? Besides, it has been written in that book that the Austrian Emperor, following the advice of his minister Metternich, in a way killed Napoleon's son!

Hearing the name "L'aiglon", the guard put on a long face and went on showing the rooms and other things thoroughly disgusted at heart; what else could he do? — it was too much for him to give up the tips. Moreover, in countries like Austria etc., the military department is too poorly paid, they have to live almost on a bare pittance; of course they are allowed to go back home after a few years' service. The guard's countenance darkened as an expression of his patriotism, but the hand instinctively moved towards the tip. The French visitors put some silver pieces into the guard's hand and returned home talking of "L'aiglon" and abusing Metternich, while the guard shut the doors with a long salute. In his heart he must have given sweet names to the ancestors of the whole French people.

The thing most worth seeing in Vienna is the Museum, specially the Scientific Museum, an institution of great benefit to the student. There is a fine collection of the skeletons of various species of ancient extinct animals. In the Art Gallery, paintings by Dutch artists form the major portion. In the Dutch school, there is very little attempt at suggestiveness; this school is famous for its exact copy of natural objects and creatures. One artist has spent years over the drawing of a basketful of fish, or a lump of flesh, or a tumbler of water — and that fish, or flesh, or water in the tumbler is wonderful. But the female figures of the Dutch school look just like athletes.

There is of course German scholarship and German intellectuality in Vienna, but the causes which helped the gradual decay of Turkey are at work here also — that is to say, the mixture of various races and languages. The population of Austria proper speaks German; the people of Hungary belong to the Tartar stock, and have a different language; while there are some who are Greek-speaking and are Christians belonging to the Greek Church. Austria has not the power to fuse together so many different sects. Hence she has fallen.

In the present times a huge wave of nationalism is sweeping over Europe, where people speaking the same tongue, professing the same religion, and belonging to the same race want to unite together. Wherever such union is being effectively accomplished, there is great power being manifested; and where this is impossible, death is inevitable. After the death of the present Austrian Emperor, (Francis Joseph II died in 1916) Germany will surely try to absorb the German-speaking portion of the Austrian Empire — and Russia and others are sure to oppose her; so there is the possibility of a dreadful war. The present Emperor being very old, that catastrophe may take place very early. The German Emperor is nowadays an ally of the Sultan of Turkey; and when Germany will attempt to seize Austrian territory, Turkey, which is Russia's enemy, will certainly offer some resistance to Russia; so the German Emperor is very friendly towards Turkey.

Three days in Vienna were sufficient to tire me. To visit Europe after Paris is like tasting an inferior preparation after a sumptuous feast — that dress, and style of eating, that same fashion everywhere; throughout the land you meet with that same black suit, and the same queer hat — disgusting! Besides, you have clouds above, and this swarm of people with black hats and black coats below — one feels suffocated, as it were. All Europe is gradually taking up that same style of dress, and that same mode of living! It is a law of nature that such are the symptoms of death! By hundreds of years of drill, our ancestors have so fashioned us that we all clean our teeth, wash our face, eat our meals, and do everything in the same way, and the result is that we have gradually become mere automata; the life has gone out, and we are moving about, simply like so many machines! Machines never say "yea" or "nay", never trouble their heads about anything, they move on "in the way their forefathers have gone", and then rot and die. The Europeans too will share the same fate! "The course of time is ever changing! If all people take to the same dress, same food, same manner of talking, and same everything, gradually they will become like so many machines, will gradually tread the path their forefathers have trod", and as an inevitable consequence of that — they will rot and die!

On the 28th October, at 9 p.m., we again took that Orient Express train, which reached Constantinople on the 30th. These two nights and one day the train ran through Hungary, Serbia, and Bulgaria. The people of Hungary are subjects of the Austrian Emperor, whose title, however, is "Emperor of Austria and King of Hungary". The Hungarians and Turks are of the same race, akin to the Tibetans. The Hungarians entered Europe along the north of the Caspian Sea, while the Turks slowly occupied Europe through the western borders of Persia and through Asia Minor. The people of Hungary are Christians, and the Turks are Mohammedans, but the martial spirit characteristic of Tartar blood is noticeable in both. The Hungarians have fought again and again for separation from Austria and are now but nominally united. The Austrian Emperor is King of Hungary in name only. Their capital, Budapest, is a very neat and beautiful city. The Hungarians are a pleasure-loving race and fond of music, and you will find Hungarian bands all over Paris.

Serbia, Bulgaria, and the rest were districts of Turkey and have become practically independent after the Russo-Turkish War; but the Sultan of Turkey is yet their Emperor; and Serbia and Bulgaria have no right regarding foreign affairs. There are three civilised nations in Europe — the French, the Germans, and the English. The rest are almost as badly off as we are, and the majority of them are so uncivilised that you can find no race in Asia so degraded. Throughout Serbia and Bulgaria you find the same mud houses, and people dressed in tattered rags, and heaps of filth — and I was almost inclined to think I was back to India! Again, as they are Christians, they must have a number of hogs; and a single hog will make a place more dirty than two hundred barbarous men will be able to do. Living in a mud house with mud roof, with tattered rags on his person, and surrounded by hogs — there you have your Serb or Bulgarian! After much bloodshed and many wars, they have thrown off the yoke of Turkey; but along with this they have got a serious disadvantage — they must construct their army after the European model, otherwise the existence of not one of them is safe for a day. Of course, sooner or later they will all one day be absorbed by Russia; but even this two days' existence is impossible without an army. So they must have conscription.

In an evil hour, did France suffer defeat from Germany. Through anger and fear she made every citizen a soldier. Every man must serve for some time in the army and learn the military science;

there is no exemption for anybody. He must have to live in the barracks for three years and learn to fight, shouldering his gun, be he a millionaire by birth. The government will provide for his food and clothing, and the salary will be a centime (one pice) a day. After this he must be always ready for active service for two years at his home; and another fifteen years he must be ready to present himself for service at the first call. Germany set a lion to fury, so she too had to be ready. In other countries also conscription has been introduced in mutual dread of one another — so throughout Europe, excepting only England. England, being an island, is continually strengthening her navy, but who knows if the lessons of the Boer War will not force her to introduce conscription. Russia has the largest population of all, so she can amass the biggest army in Europe. Now, the titular states, like Serbia and Bulgaria, which the European Powers are creating by dismembering Turkey — they, too, as soon as they are born, must have up-to-date trained and well-equipped armies and guns etc. But ultimately who is to supply the funds? Consequently the peasants have had to put on tattered rags — while in the towns you will find soldiers dressed in gorgeous uniforms. Throughout Europe there is a craze for soldiers — soldiers everywhere. Still, liberty is one thing and slavery another; even best work loses its charm if one is forced to do it by another. Without the idea of personal responsibility, no one can achieve anything great. Freedom with but one meal a day and tattered rags on is a million times better than slavery in gold chains. A slave suffers the miseries of hell both here and hereafter. The people of Europe joke about the Serbs and Bulgarians etc., and taunt them with their mistakes and shortcomings. But can they attain proficiency all in a day, after so many years of servitude? Mistakes they are bound to commit — ay, by the hundreds — but they will learn through these mistakes and set them right when they have learnt. Give him responsibility and the weakest man will become strong, and the ignorant man sagacious.

The train is traversing Hungary, Rumania, and other countries. Among the races that inhabit the moribund Austrian Empire, the Hungarians yet possess vitality. All the races of Europe, except one or two small ones, belong to the great stock which European scholars term the Indo-European or Aryan race. The Hungarians are among the few races which do not speak a Sanskritic language. The Hungarians and Turks, as already stated, belong to the same race. In comparatively modern times this very powerful race established their sovereignty in Asia and Europe. The country now called Turkistan, lying to the north of the Western Himalayas and the Hindukush range, was the original home of the Turks. The Turkish name for that country is Chagwoi. The Mogul dynasty of Delhi, the present Persian royal line, the dynasty of the Turkish Sultan of Constantinople, and the Hungarians have all gradually extended their dominion from that country, beginning with India, and pushing right up to Europe, and even today these dynasties style themselves as Chagwois and speak a common language. Of course these Turks were uncivilised ages ago, and used to roam with herds of sheep, horses, and cattle, taking their wives and children and every earthly possession with them, and encamp for some time wherever they could find enough pasture for their beasts. And when grass and water ran short there, they used to remove somewhere else. Even now many families of this race lead nomadic lives in this way in Central Asia. They have got a perfect similarity with the races of Central Asia as regards language, but some difference in point of physiognomy. The Turk's face resembles that of the Mongolian in the shape of the head and in the prominence of the cheek-bone, but the Turk's nose is not flat, but rather long, and the eyes are straight and large, though the space between the eyes of comparatively wide, as with the Mongolians. It appears that from a long time past Aryan and Semitic blood has found its way into this Turkish race. From time immemorial the Turks have been exceedingly fond of war. And the mixture with them of Sanskrit-speaking races and the people of Kandahar and Persia has produced the war-loving races such as the Afghans, Khiljis, Hazaras, Barakhais, Usufjais, etc., to whom war is a passion and who have frequently oppressed

India.

In very ancient times this Turkish race repeatedly conquered the western provinces of India and founded extensive kingdoms. They were Buddhists, or would turn Buddhists after occupying Indian territory. In the ancient history of Kashmir there is mention of these famous Turkish Emperors, Hushka, Yushka, and Kanishka. It was this Kanishka who founded the Northern school of Buddhism called the Mahâyâna. Long after, the majority of them took to Mohammedanism and completely devastated the chief Buddhistic seats of Central Asia such as Kandahar and Kabul. Before their conversion to Mohammedanism they used to imbibe the learning and culture of the countries they conquered, and by assimilating the culture of other countries would try to propagate civilisation. But ever since they became Mohammedans, they have only the instinct for war left in them; they have not got the least vestige of learning and culture; on the contrary, the countries that come under their sway gradually have their civilisation extinguished. In many places of modern Afghanistan and Kandahar etc., there yet exist wonderful Stupas, monasteries, temples and gigantic statues built by their Buddhistic ancestors. As a result of Turkish admixture and their conversion to Mohammedanism, those temples etc. are almost in ruins, and the present Afghans and allied races have grown so uncivilised and illiterate that far from imitating those ancient works of architecture, they believe them to be the creation of supernatural spirits like the Jinn etc., and are firmly convinced that such great undertakings are beyond the power of man to accomplish. The principal cause of the present degradation of Persia is that the royal line belongs to the powerful, uncivilised Turkish stock, whereas the subjects are the descendants of the highly civilised ancient Persians, who were Aryans. In this way the Empire of Constantinople — the last political arena of the Greeks and Romans, the descendants of civilised Aryans — has been ruined under the blasting feet of powerful, barbarous Turkey. The Mogul Emperors of India were the only exceptions to this rule; perhaps that was due to an admixture of Hindu ideas and Hindu blood. In the chronicles of Rajput bards and minstrels all the Mohammedan dynasties who conquered India are styled as Turks. This is a very correct appellation, for, or whatever races the conquering Mohammedan armies might be made up, the leadership was always vested in the Turks alone.

What is called the Mohammedan invasion, conquest, or colonisation of India means only this that, under the leadership of Mohammedan Turks who were renegades from Buddhism, those sections of the Hindu race who continued in the faith of their ancestors were repeatedly conquered by the other section of that very race who also were renegades from Buddhism or the Vedic religion and served under the Turks, having been forcibly converted to Mohammedanism by their superior strength. Of course, the language of the Turks has, like their physiognomy, been considerably mixed up; specially those sections that have gone farthest from their native place. Chagwoi have got the most hybrid form of language. This year the Shah of Persia visited the Paris Exhibition and returned to his country by rail via Constantinople. Despite the immense difference in time and place, the Sultan and the Shah talked with each other in their ancient Turkish mother tongue. But the Sultan's Turkish was mixed up with Persian, Arabic, and a few Greek words, while that of the Shah was comparatively pure.

In ancient times these Chagwoi Turks were divided into two sections; one was called the "white sheep", and the other, "black sheep". But these sections started from their birthplace on the north of Kashmir, tending their flocks of sheep and ravaging countries, till they reached the shore of the Caspian Sea. The "white sheep" penetrated into Europe along the north of the Caspian Sea and founded the Kingdom of Hungary, seizing a fragment of the Roman Empire then almost in ruins, while the "black sheep", advancing along the south of the Caspian Sea, gradually occupied the western portion of Persia and, crossing the Caucasus, by degrees made themselves masters of Arabian territory such as Asia Minor and so forth; gradually they seized the throne of the Caliph, and bit by bit annexed the small remnant of the western Roman Empire. In very remote ages these Turks were great snake-worshippers. Most probably it was these dynasties whom the ancient Hindus used to designate as Nagas and Takshakas. Later on they became Buddhists; and afterwards they very often used to embrace the religion of any particular country they might conquer at any particular time. In comparatively recent times, of the two sections we are speaking about, the "white sheep" conquered the Christians and became converts to Christianity, while the "black sheep" conquered the Mohammedans and adopted their religion. But in their Christianity or Mohammedanism one may even now trace on research the strata of serpent-worship and of Buddhism.

The Hungarians, though Turks by race and language, are Christians — Roman Catholics — in religion. In the past, religious fanaticism had no respect for any tie — neither the tie of language, nor that of blood, nor that of country. The Hungarians are ever the deadly enemies of Turkey; and but for the Hungarians' aid Christian states, such as Austria etc., would not have been able to maintain their existence on many an occasion. In modern times, owing to the spread of education and the discovery of Linguistics and Ethnology, people are being more attracted to the kinship of language and blood, while religious solidarity is gradually slackening. So, among the educated Hungarians and Turks, there is growing up a feeling of racial unity. Though a part of the Austrian Empire, Hungary has repeatedly tried to cut off from her. The result of many revolutions and rebellions has been that Hungary is now only nominally a province of the Austrian Empire, but practically independent in all respects. The Austrian Emperor is styled "the Emperor of Austria and King of Hungary". Hungary manages all her internal affairs independently of Austria and in these the subjects have full power. The Austrian Emperor continues to be a titular leader here, but even this bit of relation, it appears, will not last long. Skill in war, magnanimity and other characteristic virtues of the Turkish race are sufficiently present in the Hungarian also. Besides, not being converted to Mohammedanism they do not consider such heavenly arts as music etc. as the devil's snare, and consequently the Hungarians are great adepts in music and are renowned for this all over Europe.

Formerly I had the notion that people of cold climates did not take hot chillies, which was merely a bad habit of warm climate people. But the habit of taking chillies, which we observed to begin with Hungary and which reached its climax in Rumania and Bulgaria etc., appeared to me to beat even your South Indians.

ADDENDA

These interesting jottings were found among Swamiji's papers — Ed.

The first view of Constantinople we had from the train. It is an ancient city, with big drains running across the walls, narrow and crooked lanes full of dirt, and wooden houses, etc., but in them there is a certain beauty owing to their novelty. At the station we had great trouble over our books. Mademoiselle Calvé and Jules Bois tried much, in French, to reason with the octroi officers, which gradually led to a quarrel between the parties. The head of the officers was a Turk, and his dinner was ready; so the quarrel ended without further complications. They returned all the books with the exception of two which they held back. They promised to send them to the hotel immediately, which they never did. We went round the town and bazar of Stamboul or Constantinople. Beyond the Pont or creek is the Pera or foreigners' quarters, hotels, etc., whence we got into a carriage, saw the town, and then took some rest. In the evening we went to visit Woods Pasha, and the next day started on an excursion along the Bosphorus in a boat. It was extremely cold and there was a strong wind. So I and Miss MacLeod got down at the first station. It was decided that we would cross over to Scutari and see Pére Hyacinthe. Not knowing the language we engaged a boat by signs merely, crossed over, and hired a carriage. On the way we saw the seat of a Sufi Fakir. These Fakirs cure people's diseases, which they do in the following manner. First they read a portion of their scriptures, moving their body backward and forward; then they begin to dance and gradually get a sort of inspiration, after which they heal the disease by treading on the patient's body.

We had a long talk with Père Hyacinthe about the American Colleges, after which we went to an Arab shop where we met a Turkish student. Then we returned from Scutari. — We had found out a boat, but it failed to reach its exact destination. However, we took a tram from the place where we were landed and returned to our quarters at the hotel at Stamboul. The Museum at Stamboul is situated where the ancient harem of the Greek Emperors once stood. We saw some remarkable sarcophagi and other things, and had a charming view of the city from above Topkhana. I enjoyed taking fried chick peas here after such a long time, and had spiced rice and some other dishes, prepared in the Turkish fashion. After visiting the cemetery of Scutari we went to see the ancient walls. Within the walls was the prison — a dreadful place. Next we met Woods Pasha and started for the Bosphorus. We had our dinner with the French chargé d'affaires and met a Greek Pasha and an Albanian gentleman. The Police have prohibited Père Hyacinthe's lectures; so I too cannot lecture. We saw Mr. Devanmall and Chobeji — a Gujarâti Brahmin. There are a good many Indians here — Hindustanis, Mussalmans, etc. We had a talk on Turkish Philosophy and heard of Noor Bey, whose gradfather was a Frenchman. They say he is as handsome as a Kashmari. The women here have got no purdah system and are very free. Prostitution is chiefly a Mohammedan practice. We heard of Kurd Pasha and the massacre of Armenians. The Armenians have really no country of their own, and those countries which they inhabit have generally a preponderating Mohammedan population. A particular tract called Armenia is unknown. The present Sultan is constructing a Hamidian cavalry out of the Kurds who will be trained in the manner of the Cossacks and they will be exempted from conscription.

The Sultan called the Armenian and Greek Patriarchs and proposed to them conscription as an alternative for payment of taxes. They might thus serve to protect their motherland. They replied that if they went as soldiers to fight and died by the side of the Mohammedans, there would be some confusion about the interment of Christian soldiers. The Sultan's rejoinder to this was that it might be remedied by providing for both Mohammedan and Christian priests in each regiment, who would conduct the funeral service together when in the exigencies of battle the dead bodies of Christian and Mohammedan soldiers would have to be buried in a heap all together, and there could possibly be no harm if the souls of men of one religion heard in addition the funeral services meant for those of the other religion. But the Christians did not agree — so they continue to pay taxes. The surest reason of their not acquiescing in the proposal was their fear lest by living with the Mohammedans they might turn Mohammedan wholesale. The present Sultan of Stamboul is a very hard-working man and he personally supervises everything, including even the arrangement of amusements, such as theatrical performances etc., in the palace. His predecessor, Murad, was really a most unfit man, but the present Sultan is very intelligent. The amount of improvement he has made in the condition of the State in which he found it at his accession is simply wonderful. The Parliamentary system will not be successful in this country.

At 10 in the morning we left Constantinople, passing a night and a day on the sea, which was perfectly placid. By degrees we reached the Golden Horn and the Sea of Marmora. In one of the islands of the Marmora we saw a monastery of the Greek religion. Formerly there was ample opportunity for religious education here, for it was situated between Asia on one side and Europe on the other. While out in the morning on a visit of the Mediterranean Archipelago we came across Professor Liper, whose acquaintance I had already made in the Pachiappa College at Madras. In one of the islands we came upon the ruins of a temple, which had probably been dedicated to Neptune, judging from its position on the sea-shore. In the evening we reached Athens, and after passing a whole night under quarantine we obtained permission for landing in the morning. Port Peiraeus is a small town, but very beautiful, having a European air about it in all respects, except that one meets now and then with one or two Greeks dressed in gowns. From there we drove five miles to have a look at the ancient walls of Athens which used to connect the city with the port. Then we went through the town; the Acropolis, the hotels, houses, and streets, and all were very neat and clean. The palace is a small one. The same day, again, we climbed the hillock and had a view of the Acropolis, the temple of the Wingless Victory, and the Parthenon, etc. The temple is made of white marble. Some standing remains of columns also we saw. The next day we again went to see these with Mademoiselle Melcarvi, who explained to us various historical facts relating thereto. On the second day we visited the temple of Olympian Zeus, Theatre Dionysius etc., as far as the sea-shore. The third day we set out for Eleusis, which was the chief religious seat of the Greeks. Here it was that the famous Eleusinian Mysteries used to be played. The ancient theatre of this place has been built anew by a rich Greek. The Olympian games too have been revived in the present times. They are held at a place near Sparta, the Americans carrying off the palm in them in many respects. But the Greeks won in the race from that place to this theatre of Athens. This year they gave undisputed proof of this trait of theirs in a competition with the Turks also. At 10 a.m. on the fourth day we got on board the Russian steamer, Czar, bound for Egypt. After reaching the dock we came to learn that the steamer was to start at 4 a.m. — perhaps we were too early or there would be some extra delay in loading the cargo. So, having no other alternative, we went round and made a cursory acquaintance with the sculpture of Ageladas and his three pupils, Phidias, Myron, and Polycletus, who had flourished between 576 B.C. and 486 B.C. Even here we began to feel the great heat. In a Russian ship the first class is over the screw, and the rest is only deck — full of passengers, and cattle, and sheep. Besides, no ice was available in this steamer.

From a visit to the Louvre Museum in Paris I came to understand the three stages of Greek art. First, there was the Mycenoean art, then Greek art proper. The Achaean kingdom had spread its sway over the neighbouring islands and also mastered all the arts that flourished there, being imported from Asia. Thus did art first make its appearance in Greece. From the prehistoric times up to 776 B.C. was the age of the Mycenoean art. This art principally engaged itself in merely copying Asiatic art. Then from 776 B.C. to 146 B.C. was the age of Hellenic or true Greek art. After the destruction of the Achaean Empire by the Dorian race, the Greeks living on the continent and in the Archipelago founded many colonies in Asia. This led to a close conflict between them and Babylon and Egypt, which first gave rise to Greek art. This art in course of time gave up its Asiatic tinge and applied itself to an exact imitation of nature. The difference between Greek art and the art of other countries consists in this, that the former faithfully delineates the living phenomena of natural life.

From 776 B.C. to 475 B.C. is the age of Archaic Greek art. The figures are yet stiff — not lifelike. The lips are slightly parted, as if always in smiles. In this respect they resemble the works of Egyptian artists. All the statues stand erect on their legs — quite stiff. The hair and beard etc. and all carved in regular lines and the clothes in the statues are all wrapped close round the body, in a jumble — not like flowing dress.

Next to Archaic Greek art comes the age of Classic Greek art — from 475 B.C. to 323 B.C., that is to say, from the hegemony of Athens up to the death of Alexander the Great. Peloponnesus and Attica were the states where the art of this period flourished most. Athens was the chief city of Attica. A learned French art critic has written, "(Classic) Greek art at its highest development freed itself completely from the fetters of all established canons and became independent. It then recognised the art regulations of no country, nor guided itself according to them. The more we study the fifth century B.C., so brilliant in its art development — during which period all the perfect specimens of sculpture were turned out — the more is the idea brought home to our mind that Greek art owed its life and vigour to its cutting loose from the pale of stereotyped rules". This Classic Greek art had two schools

— first, the Attic, and second, the Peloponnesian. In the Attic school, again, there were two different types — the first was the outcome of the genius of the gifted sculptor, Phidias, which a French scholar has described in the following terms: "A marvel of perfection in beauty and a glorious specimen of pure and sublime ideas, which will never lose their hold upon the human mind". The masters in the second type of the Attic school were Scopas and Praxiteles. The work of this school was to completely divorce art from religion and keep it restricted to the delineation of merely human life.

The chief exponents of the second or Peloponnesian school of Classic Greek art were Polycletus and Lysippus. One of these was born in the fifth century B.C., and the other in the fourth century B.C. They chiefly aimed at laying down the rule that the proportion of the human body must be faithfully reproduced in art.

From 323 B.C. to 146 B.C., that is, from the death of Alexander to the conquest of Attica by the Romans, is the period of decadence in Greek art. One notices in the Greek art of this period an undue attention to gorgeous embellishments, and an attempt to make the statues unusually large in bulk. Then at the time of the Roman occupation of Greece, Greek art contented itself merely by copying the works of previous artists of that country; and the only novelty there was, consisted in reproducing exactly the face of some particular individual.

NOTES OF CLASS TALKS AND LECTURES

ON ART

In art, interest must be centred on the principal theme. Drama is the most difficult of all arts. In it two things are to be satisfied — first, the ears, and second, the eyes. To paint a scene, if one thing be painted, it is easy enough; but to paint different things and yet to keep up the central interest is very difficult. Another difficult thing is stage-management, that is, combining different things in such a manner as to keep the central interest intact.

ON MUSIC

There is science in Dhrupad, Kheyal, etc., but it is in Kirtana, i.e. in Mathura and Viraha and other like compositions that there is real music — for there is feeling. Feeling is the soul, the secret of everything. There is more music in common people's songs, and they should be collected together. The science of Dhrupad etc., applied to the music of Kirtana will produce the perfect music.

ON MANTRA AND MANTRA-CHAITANYA

The Mantra-shastris (upholders of the Mantra theory) believe that some words have been handed down through a succession of teachers and disciples, and the mere utterance of them will lead to some form of realisation. There are two different meanings of the word Mantra-chaitanya. According to some, if you practise the repetition of a certain Mantra, you will see the Ishta-devata who is the object or deity of that Mantra. But according to others, the word means that if you practise the repetition of a certain Mantra received from a Guru not competent, you will have to perform certain ceremonials by which that Mantra will become Chetana or living, and then its repetition will be successful. Different Mantras, when they are thus "living", show different signs, but the general sign is that one will be able to repeat it for a long time without feeling any strain and that his mind will very soon be concentrated. This is about the Tantrika Mantras.

From the time of the Vedas, two different opinions have been held about Mantras. Yaska and others say that the Vedas have meanings, but the ancient Mantra-shastris say that they have no meaning, and that their use consists only in uttering them in connection with certain sacrifices, when they will surely produce effect in the form of various material enjoyments or spiritual knowledge. The latter arises from the utterance of the Upanishads.

ON CONCEPTIONS OF GODHEAD

Man's inner hankering is to find some one who is free, that is, beyond the laws of nature. The Vedantins believe in such an Eternal Ishvara, while the Buddhists and the Sankhyas believe only a Janyeshvara (created God), that is, a God who was a man before, but has become God through spiritual practice. The Puranas reconcile these two positions by the doctrine of Incarna-tion. That is, they say that the Janyeshvara is nothing but the Nitya (Eternal) Ishvara, taking by Maya the form of a Janyeshvara. The argument of the Sankhyas against the doctrine of Eternal Ishvara, viz "how a liberated soul can create the universe", is based on false grounds. For you cannot dictate anything to a liberated soul. He is free, that is, he may do whatever he likes. According to the Vedanta, the Janyeshvaras cannot create, preserve, or destroy the universe.

ON FOOD

You preach to others to be men but cannot give them good food. I have been thinking over this problem for the last four years. I wish to make an experiment whether something of the nature of flattened rice can be made out of wheat. Then we can get a different food every day. About drinking water, I searched for a filter which would suit our country. I found one pan-like porcelain vessel through which water was made to pass, and all the bacilli remained in the porcelain pan. But gradually that filter would itself become the hotbed of all germs. This is the danger of all filters. After continued searching I found one method by which water was distilled and then oxygen was passed into it. After this the water became so pure that great improvement of health was sure to result from its use.

ON SANNYASA AND FAMILY LIFE

Talking of the respective duties of a monk and a householder, Swamiji said:

A Sannyasin should avoid the food, bedding, etc., which have been touched or used by householders, in order to save himself — not from hatred towards them — so long as he has not risen to the highest grade, that is, become a Paramahamsa. A householder should salute him with "Namo Narayanaya", and a Sannyasin should bless the former.

मेरुसर्षपयोर्यद्यत् सूर्यखद्योतयोरवि।
सरित्सागरयोर्यद्यत् तथा भक्तिपुगृहस्थयो:॥

— Like the difference between the biggest mountain and a mustard-seed, between the sun and a glow-worm, between the ocean and a streamlet, is the wide gulf between a Sannyasin and a householder.

Swami Vivekananda made everyone utter this and, chanting some Vedanta stanzas, said, "You should always repeat to yourselves these Shlokas. 'Shravana' not only means hearing from the Guru, but also repetition to our own selves. आवृत्ततरिसकृदुपदेशात्— scriptural truth should be often repeated for such has been repeatedly enjoined'— in this Sutra of Vedanta, Vyasa lays stress on repetition."

ON QUESTIONING THE COMPETENCY OF THE GURU

In the course of a conversation Swamiji spiritedly remarked, "Leave off your commercial calculating ideas. If you can get rid of your attachment to a single thing, you are on the way to liberation. Do not see a public woman, or sinner, or Sadhu. That vile woman also is the Divine Mother. A Sannyasin says once, twice, that she is Mother; then he gets deluded again and says, 'Hence, O vile, unchaste woman!' At a moment all your ignorance may vanish. It is foolish talk that ignorance disperses gradually. There are disciples who have been devoted to the Guru even when he has fallen from the ideal. I have seen in Rajputana one whose spiritual teacher had turned a Christian, but who nevertheless went on giving him his regular dues. Give up your Western ideas. Once you have pledged your faith to a particular teacher, stick to him with all force. It is children who say that there is no morality in the Vedanta. Yes, they are right. Vedanta is above morality. Talk of high things, as you have become Sannyasins."

SHRI RAMAKRISHNA: THE SIGNIFICANCE OF HIS LIFE AND TEACHINGS

In a narrow society there is depth and intensity of spirituality. The narrow stream is very rapid. In a catholic society, along with the breadth of vision we find a proportionate loss in depth and intensity. But the life of Sri Ramakrishna upsets all records of history. It is a remarkable phenomenon that in Sri Ramakrishna there has been an assemblage of ideas deeper than the sea and vaster than the skies.

We must interpret the Vedas in the light of the experience of Sri Ramakrishna. Shankaracharya and all other commentators made the tremendous mistake to think that the whole of the Vedas spoke the same truth. Therefore they were guilty of torturing those of the apparently conflicting Vedic texts which go against their own doctrines, into the meaning of their particular schools. As, in the olden times, it was the Lord alone, the deliverer of the Gita, who partially harmonised these apparently conflicting statements, so with a view to completely settling this dispute, immensely magnified in the process of time, He Himself has come as Sri Ramakrishna. Therefore no one can truly understand the Vedas and Vedanta, unless one studies them in the light of the utterance of Sri Ramakrishna who first exemplified in his life and taught that these scriptural statements which appear to the cursory view as contradictory, are meant for different grades of aspirants and are arranged in the order of evolution. The whole world will undoubtedly forget its fights and disputes and be united in a fraternal tie in religious and other matters as a consequence of these teachings.

If there is anything which Sri Ramakrishna has urged us to give up as carefully as lust and wealth, it is the limiting of the infinitude of God by circumscribing it within narrow bounds. Whoever, therefore, will try to limit the infinite ideals of Sri Ramakrishna in that way, will go against him and be his enemy.

One of his own utterances is that those who have seen the chameleon only once, know only one colour of the animal, but those who have lived under the tree, know all the colours that it puts on. For this reason, no saying of Sri Ramakrishna can be accepted as authentic, unless it is verified by those who constantly lived with him and whom he brought up to fulfil his life's mission.

Such a unique personality, such a synthesis of the utmost of Jnana, Yoga, Bhakti and Karma, has never before appeared among mankind. The life of Sri Ramakrishna proves that the greatest breadth, the highest catholicity and the utmost intensity can exist side by side in the same individual, and that society also can be constructed like that, for society is nothing but an aggregate of individuals.

He is the true disciple and follower of Sri Ramakrishna, whose character is perfect and all-sided like this. The formation of such a perfect character is the ideal of this age, and everyone should strive for that alone.

ON SHRI RAMAKRISHNA AND HIS VIEWS

By force, think of one thing at least as Brahman. Of course it is easier to think of Ramakrishna as God, but the danger is that we cannot form Ishvara-buddhi (vision of Divinity) in others. God is eternal, without any form, omnipresent. To think of Him as possessing any form is blasphemy. But the secret of image-worship is that you are trying to develop your vision of Divinity in one thing.

Shri Ramakrishna used to consider himself as an Incarnation in the ordinary sense of the term, though I could not understand it. I used to say that he was Brahman in the Vedantic sense; but just before his passing away, when he was suffering from the characteristic difficulty in breathing, he said to me as I was cogitating in my mind whether he could even in that pain say that he was an Incarnation, "He who was Rama and Krishna has now actually become Ramakrishna — but not in your Vedantic sense!" He used to love me intensely, which made many quite jealous of me. He knew one's character by sight, and never changed his opinion. He could perceive, as it were, supersensual things, while we try to know one's character by reason, with the result that our judgments are often fallacious. He called some persons his Antarangas or 'belonging to the inner circle', and he used to teach them the secrets of his own nature and those of Yoga. To the outsiders or Bahirangas he taught those parables now known as "Sayings". He used to prepare those young men (the former class) for his work, and though many complained to him about them, he paid no heed. I may have perhaps a better opinion of a Bahiranga than an Antaranga through his actions, but I have a superstitious regard for the latter. "Love me, love my dog", as they say. I love that Brahmin priest intensely, and therefore, love whatever he used to love, whatever he used to regard! He was afraid about me that I might create a sect, if left to myself.

He used to say to some, "You will not attain spirituality in this life." He sensed everything, and this will explain his apparent partiality to some. He, as a scientist, used to see that different people required different treatment. None except those of the "inner circle" were allowed to sleep in his room. It is not true that those who have not seen him will not attain salvation; neither is it true that a man who has seen him thrice will attain Mukti (liberation).

Devotion as taught by Narada, he used to preach to the masses, those who were incapable of any higher training.

He used generally to teach dualism. As a rule, he never taught Advaitism. But he taught it to me. I had been a dualist before.

SHRI RAMAKRISHNA: THE NATION'S IDEAL

In order that a nation may rise, it must have a high ideal. Now, that ideal is, of course, the abstract Brahman. But as you all cannot be inspired by an abstract ideal, you must have a personal ideal. You have got that, in the person of Shri Ramakrishna. The reason why other personages cannot be our ideal now is, that their days are gone; and in order that Vedanta may come to everyone, there must be a person who is in sympathy with the present generation. This is fulfilled in Shri Ramakrishna. So now you should place him before everyone. Whether one accepts him as a Sadhu or an Avatara does not matter.

He said he would come once more with us. Then, I think, he will embrace Videha-mukti (Absolute Emancipation). If you wish to work, you must have such an Ishta-devata, or Guardian Angel, as the Christian nations call it. I sometimes imagine that different nations have different Ishta-devatas, and these are each trying for supremacy. Sometimes I fancy, such an Ishta-devata becomes powerless to do service to a nation.

NOTES OF LECTURES MERCENARIES IN RELIGION

Delivered in Minneapolis on November 26, 1893: Reported in the Minneapolis Journal.

The Unitarian church was crowded yesterday morning by an audience anxious to learn something of eastern religious thought as outlined by Swami Vivekananda, a Brahmin priest, who was prominent in the Parliament of Religions at Chicago last summer. The distinguished representative of the Brahmin faith was brought to Minneapolis by the Peripatetic Club, and he addressed that body last Friday evening. He was induced to remain until this week, in order that he might deliver the address yesterday. . . . Dr. H.M. Simmons, the pastor, . . . read from Paul's lesson of faith, hope and charity, and "the greatest of these is charity", supplementing that reading by a selection from the Brahmin scripture which teaches the same lesson, and also a selection from the Moslem faith, and poems from the Hindu literature, all of which are in harmony with Paul's utterances.

After a second hymn Swami Vivekandi [sic] was introduced. He stepped to the edge of the platform and at once had his audience interested by the recital of a Hindu story. He said in excellent English: "I will tell you a story of five blind men. There was a procession in a village in India, and all the people turned out to see the procession, and specially the gaily caparisoned elephant. The people were delighted, and as the five blind men could not see, they determined to touch the elephant that they might acquaint themselves with its form. They were given the privilege, and after the pro-cession had passed, they returned home together with the people, and they began to talk about the elephant. 'It was just like a wall,' said one. 'No it wasn't,' said another, 'it was like a piece of rope.' 'You are mistaken,' said a third, 'I felt him and it was just a serpent.' The discussion grew excited, and the fourth declared the elephant was like a pillow. The argument soon broke into more angry expressions, and the five blind men took to fighting. Along came a man with two eyes, and he said, 'My friends, what is the matter?' The disputation was explained, whereupon the new-comer said, 'Men, you are all right: the trouble is you touched the elephant at different points. The wall was the side, the rope was the tail, the serpent was the trunk, and the toes were the pillow. Stop your quarrelling; you are all right, only you have been viewing the elephant from different standpoints."

Religion, he said, had become involved in such a quarrel. The people of the West thought they had the only religion of God, and the people of the East held the same prejudice. Both were wrong; God was in every religion.

There were many bright criticisms on Western thought. The Christians were characterised as having a "shopkeeping religion". They were always begging of God —"O God, give me this and give me that; O God, do this and do that." The Hindu couldn't understand this. He thought it wrong to be begging of God. Instead of begging, the religious man should give. The Hindu believed in giving to God, to his fellows, instead of asking God to give to them. He had observed that the people of the West, very many of them, thought a great deal of God, so long as they got along all right, but when the reverse came, then God was forgotten: not so with the Hindu, who had come to look upon God as a being of love. The Hindu faith recognised the motherhood of God as well as the fatherhood, because the former was a better fulfilment of the idea of love. The Western Christian would work all the week for the dollar, and when he succeeded he would pray, "O God, we thank thee for giving us this benefit", and then he would put all the money into his pocket; the Hindu would make the money and then give it to God by helping the poor and the less fortunate. And so comparisons were made between the ideas of the West and the ideas of the East. In speaking of God, Vivekanandi said in substance: "You people of the West think you have God. What is it to have God? If you have Him, why is it that so much criminality exists, that nine out of ten people are hypocrites? Hypocrisy cannot exist where God is. You have your palaces for the worship of God, and you attend them in part for a time once a week, but how few go to worship God. It is the fashion in the West to attend church, and many of you attend for no other reason. Have you then, you people of the West, any right to lay exclusive claim to the possession of God?"

Here the speaker was interrupted by spontaneous applause. He proceeded: "We of the Hindu faith believe in worshipping God for love's sake, not for what He gives us, but because God is love, and no nation, no people, no religion has God until it is willing to worship Him for love's sake. You of the West are practical in business, practical in great inventions, but we of the East are practical in religion. You make commerce your business; we make religion our business. If you will come to India and talk with the workman in the field, you will find he has no opinion on politics. He knows nothing of politics. But you talk to him of religion, and the humblest knows about monotheism, deism, and all the isms of religion. You ask: "What government do you live under?' and he will reply: 'I don't know. I pay my taxes, and that's all I know about it.' I have talked with your labourers, your farmers, and I find that in politics they are all posted. They are either Democrat or Republican, and they know whether they prefer free silver or a gold standard. But you talk to them of religion; they are like the Indian farmer, they don't know, they attend such a church, but they don't know what it believes; they just pay their pew rent, and that's all they know about it — or God."

The superstitions of India were admitted, "but what nation doesn't have them?" he asked. In summing up, he held that the nations had been looking at God as a monopoly. All nations had God, and any impulse for good was God. The Western people, as well as the Eastern people, must learn to "want God", and this "want" was compared to the man under water, struggling for air; he wanted it, he couldn't live without it. When the people of the West "wanted" God in that manner, then they would be welcome in India, because the missionaries would then come to them with God, not with the idea that India knows not God, but with love in their hearts and not dogma.

THE DESTINY OF MAN

Delivered in Memphis on January 17, 1894: Reported in Appeal-Avalanche.

The audience was moderately large, and was made up of the best literary and musical talent of the city, including some of the most distinguished members of the legal fraternity and financial institutions.

The speaker differs in one respect in particular from some American orators. He advances his ideas with as much deliberation as a professor of mathematics demon-strates an example in algebra to his students. Kananda[1] speaks with perfect faith in his own powers and ability to hold successfully his position against all argument. He advances no ideas, nor make assertions that he does not follow up to a logical conclusion. Much of his lecture is something on the order of Ingersoll's philosophy. He does not believe in future punishment nor in God as Christians believe in Him. He does not believe the mind is immortal, from the fact that it is dependent, and nothing can be immortal except it is independent of all things. He says: "God is not a king sitting away in one corner of the universe to deal out punishment or rewards according to a man's deeds here on earth, and the time will come when man will know the truth, and stand up and say, 'I am God,' am life of His life. Why teach that God is far away when our real nature, our immortal principle is God? "Be not deluded by your religion teaching original sin, for the same religion teaches original purity. When Adam fell, he fell from purity. (Applause) Purity is our real nature, and to regain that is the object of all religion. All men are pure; all men are good. Some objections can be raised to them, and you ask why some men are brutes? That man you call a brute is like the diamond in the dirt and dust — brush the dust off and it is a diamond, just as pure as if the dust had never been on it, and we must admit that every soul is a big diamond. "Nothing is baser than calling our brother a sinner. A lioness once fell upon a flock of sheep and killed a lamb. A sheep found a very young lion, and it followed her, and he gave it suck, and it grew up with the sheep and learned to eat grass like a sheep. One day an old lion saw the sheep lion and tried to get it away from the sheep, but it ran away as he approached. The big lion waited till he caught the sheep lion alone, and he seized it and carried it to a clear pool of water and said, 'You are not a sheep, but a lion; look at your picture in the water.' The sheep lion, seeing its picture reflected from the water, said, 'I am a lion and not a sheep.' Let us not think we are sheep, but be lions, and don't bleat and eat grass like a sheep. "For four months I have been in America. In Massachusetts I visited a reformatory prison. The jailor at that prison never knows for what crimes the prisoners are incarcerated. The mantle of charity is thrown around them. In another city there were three newspapers, edited by very learned men, trying to prove that severe punishment was a necessity, while one other paper contended that mercy was better than punishment. The editor of one paper proved by statistics that only fifty per cent of criminals who received severe punishment returned to honest lives, while ninety per cent of those who received light punishment returned to useful pursuits in life. "Religion is not the outcome of the weakness of human nature; religion is not here because we fear a tyrant; religion is love, unfolding, expanding, growing. Take the watch — within the little case is machinery and a spring. The spring, when wound up, tries to regain its natural state. You are like the spring in the watch, and it is not necessary that all watches have the same kind of a spring, and it is not necessary that we all have the same religion. And why should we quarrel? If we all had the same ideas the world would be dead. External motion we call action; internal motion is

---

1. In those days Swamiji was generally referred to by American press as Vive Kananda.

human thought. The stone falls to the earth. You say it is caused by the law of gravitation. The horse draws the cart and God draws the horse. That is the law of motion. Whirlpools show the strength of the current; stop the current and stag-nation ensues. Motion is life. We must have unity and variety. The rose would smell as sweet by any other name, and it does not matter what your religion is called. "Six blind men lived in a village. They could not see the elephant, but they went out and felt of him. One put his hand on the elephant's tail, one of them on his side, one on his tongue[trunk], one on his ear. They began to describe the elephant. One said he was like a rope; one said he was like a great wall; one said he was like a boa constrictor, and another said he was like a fan. They finally came to blows and went to pummelling each other. A man who could see came along and inquired the trouble, and the blind men said they had seen the elephant and disagreed because one accused the other of lying. 'Well,' said the man, 'you have all lied; you are blind, and neither of you have seen it.' That is what is the matter with our religion. We let the blind see the elephant. (Applause). "A monk of India said, 'I would believe you if you were to say that I could press the sands of the desert and get oil, or that I could pluck the tooth from the mouth of the crocodile without being bitten, but I cannot believe you when you say a bigot can be changed.' You ask why is there so much variance in religions? The answer is this: The little streams that ripple down a thousand mountain sides are destined to come at last to the mighty ocean. So with the different religions. They are destined at last to bring us to the bosom of God. For 1,900 years you have been trying to crush the Jews. Why could you not crush them? Echo answers: Ignorance and bigotry can never crush truth."

The speaker continued in this strain of reasoning for nearly two hours, and concluded by saying: "Let us help, and not destroy."

REINCARNATION

Delivered in Memphis on January 19, 1894: Reported in Appeal-Avalanche.

Swami Vive Kananda, the beturbaned and yellow-robed monk, lectured again last night to a fair-sized and appreciative audience at the La Salette Academy on Third street.

The subject was "Transmigration of the Soul, or "metempsychosis". Possibly Vive Kananda never appeared to greater advantage than in this role, so to speak. Metempsychosis is one of the most widely-accepted beliefs among the Eastern races, and one that they are ever ready to defend, at home or abroad. As Kananda said: "Many of you do not know that it is one of the oldest religious doctrines of all the old religions. It was known among the Pharisees, among the Jews, among the first fathers of the Christian Church, and was a common belief among the Arabs. And it lingers still with the Hindus and the Buddhists. "This state of things went on until the days of science which is merely a contemplation of energies. Now, you Western people believe this doctrine to be subversive of morality. In order to have a full survey of the argument, its logical and metaphysical features, we will have to go over all the ground. All of us believe in a moral governor of this universe; yet nature reveals to us instead of justice, injustice. One man is born under the best of circumstances. Throughout his entire life circumstances come ready made to his hands — all conducive to happiness and a higher order of things. Another is born, and at every point his life is at variance with that of his neighbour. He dies in depravity, exiled from society. Why so much impartiality [partiality] in the distribution of happiness? "The theory of metempsychosis reconciles this dis -

harmonious chord in your common beliefs. Instead of making us immoral, this theory give us the idea of justice. Some of you say: 'It is God's will.' This is no answer. It is unscientific. Everything has a cause. The sole cause and whole theory of causation being left with God, makes Him a most immoral creature. But materialism is as much illogical as the other. So far as we go, perception [causation?] involves all things. Therefore, this doctrine of the transmigration of the soul is necessary on these grounds. Here we are all born. Is this the first creation? Is creation something coming out of nothing? Analysed completely, this sentence is nonsense. It is not creation, but manifestation. "A something cannot be the effect of a cause that is not. If I put my finger in the fire, the burn is a simultaneous effect, and I know that the cause of the burn was the action of my placing my finger in contact with the fire. And as in the case of nature, there never was a time when nature did not exist, because the cause has always existed. But for argument['s] sake, admit that there was a time when there was no existence. Where was all this mass of matter? To create something new would be the introduction of so much more energy into the universe. This is impossible. Old things can be re-created, but there can be no addition to the universe. "No mathematical demonstration could be made that would have this theory of metempsychosis. According to logic, hypothesis and theory must not be believed. But my contention is that no better hypothesis has been forwarded by the human intellect to explain the phenomena of life. "I met with a peculiar incident while on a train leaving the city of Minneapolis. There was a cowboy on the train. He was a rough sort of a fellow and a Presbyterian of the blue nose type. He walked up and asked me where I was from. I told him India. 'What are you?' he said. 'Hindu', I replied. 'Then you must go to hell', he remarked. I told him of this theory, and after [my] explaining it, he said he had always believed in it because he said that one day when he was chopping a log, his little sister came out in her clothes and said that she used to be a man. That is why he believed in the transmigration of souls. The whole basis of the theory is this: If a man's actions be good, he must be a higher being, and vice versa. "There is another beauty in this theory — the moral motor [motive] it supplies. What is done is done. It says, 'Ah, that it were done better.' Do not put your finger in the fire again. Every moment is a new chance."

Vive Kananda spoke in this strain for some time, and he was frequently applauded.

Swami Vive Kananda will lecture again this afternoon at 4 o'clock at La Salette Academy on "The Manners and Customs of India."

COMPARATIVE THEOLOGY

Delivered in Memphis on January 21, 1894: Reported in Appeal-Avalanche.

"Comparative Theology" was the subject of a discourse last night by Swami Vive Kananda at the Young Men's Hebrew Association Hall. It was the blue-ribbon lecture of the series, and no doubt increased the general admiration the people of this city entertain for the learned gentleman.

Heretofore Vive Kananda has lectured for the benefit of one charity-worthy object or another, and it can be safely said that he has rendered them material aid. Last night, however, he lectured for his own benefit. The lecture was planned and sustained by Mr. Hu L. Brinkley, one of Vive Kananda's warmest friends and most ardent admirers. In the neighbourhood of two hundred gathered at the hall last night to hear the eminent Easterner for the last time in this city.

The first question the speaker asserted in connection with the subject was: "Can there be such a distinction between religions as their creeds would imply?"

He asserted that no differences existed now, and he retraced the line of progress made by all religions and brought it back to the present day. He showed that such variance of opinion must of necessity have existed with primitive man in regard to the idea of God, but that as the world advanced step by step in a moral and intellectual way, the distinctions became more and more indistinct, until finally it had faded away entirely, and now there was one all-prevalent doctrine — that of an absolute existence. "No savage", said the speaker, "can be found who does not believe in some kind of a god." "Modern science does not say whether it looks upon this as a revelation or not. Love among savage nations is not very strong. They live in terror. To their superstitious imaginations is pictured some malignant spirit, before the thought of which they quake in fear and terror. Whatever he likes he thinks will please the evil spirit. What will pacify him he thinks will appease the wrath of the spirit. To this end he labours even against his fellow-savage."

The speaker went on to show by historical facts that the savage man went from ancestral worship to the worship of elephants, and later to gods, such as the God of Thunder and Storms. Then the religion of the world was polytheism. "The beauty of the sunrise, the grandeur of the sunset, the mystifying appearance of the star-bedecked skies, and the weirdness of thunder and lightning[nature] impressed primitive man with a force that he could not explain, and suggested the idea of a higher and more powerful being controlling the infinities that flocked before his gaze," said Vive Kananda.

Then came another period — the period of monotheism. All the gods disappeared and blended into one, the God of Gods, the ruler of the universe. Then the speaker traced the Aryan race up to that period, where they said: "We live and move in God. He is motion." Then there came another period known to metaphysics as the "period of Pantheism". This race rejected Polytheism and Monotheism, and the idea that God was the universe, and said "the soul of my soul is the only true existence. My nature is my existence and will expand to me."

Vive Kananda then took up Buddhism. He said that they neither asserted nor denied the existence of a God. Buddha would simply say, when his counsel was sought: "You see misery. Then try to lessen it." To a Buddhist misery is ever present, and society measures the scope of his existence. Mohammedans, he said, believed in the Old Testament of the Hindu [Hebrew] and the New Testament of the Christian. They do not like the Christians, for they say they are heretics and teach man-worship. Mohammed ever forbade his followers having a picture of himself. "The next question that arises," said he, "are these religions true or are some of them true and some of them false? They have all reached one conclusion, that of an absolute and infinite existence. Unity is the object of religion. The multiple of phenomena that is seen at every hand is only the infinite variety of unity. an analysis of religion shows that man does not travel from fallacy to truth, but from a lower truth to a higher truth. "A man brings in a coat to a lot of people. Some say the coat does not fit them. Well, you get out; you can't have a coat. Ask one Christian minister what is the matter with all the other sects that are opposed to his doctrines and dogmas, and he will answer: 'Oh, they're not Christians.' But we have better instruction than these. Our own natures, love, and science — they teach us better. Like the eddies to a river, take them away and stagnation follows. Kill the difference in opinions, and it is the death of thought. Motion is necessity. Thought is the motion of the mind, and when that ceases death begins. "If you put a simple molecule of air in the bottom of a glass of water it at once begins a struggle to join the infinite atmosphere above. So it is with the soul. It is struggling to regain its pure nature and to free itself from this material body. It wants to regain its own infinite expansion. This is everywhere the same. Among Christians, Buddhists, Mohammedans, agnostic, or priest, the soul is struggling. A river flows a thousand miles down the circuitous mountain side to where it joins the seas, and a man is standing there to tell it to go back and start anew and assume a more direct course! That man is a fool. You are a river that flows from the heights of Zion. I flow from the lofty peaks of the Himalayas. I don't say to you, go back and come down as I did, you're wrong. That is more wrong than foolish. Stick to your beliefs. The truth is never lost. Books may perish, nations may go down in a crash, but the truth is preserved and is taken up by some man and handed back to society, which proves a grand and continuous revelation of God."

THE SCIENCE OF YOGA[1]

Delivered at Tucker Hall, Alameda, California, on April 13, 1900.

The old Sanskrit word Yoga is defined as [Chittavrittinirodha]. It means that Yoga is the science that teaches us to bring the Chitta under control from the state of change. The Chitta is the stuff from which our minds are made and which is being constantly churned into waves by external and internal influences. Yoga teaches us how to control the mind so that it is not thrown out of balance into wave forms....

What does this mean? To the student of religion almost ninety-nine per cent of the books and thoughts of religion are mere speculations. One man thinks religion is this and another, that. If one man is more clever than the others, he overthrows their speculations and starts a new one. Men have been studying new religious systems for the last two thousand, four thousand, years — how long exactly nobody knows.... When they could not reason them out, they said, "Believe!" If they were powerful, they forced their beliefs. This is going on even now.

But there are a set of people who are not entirely satisfied with this sort of thing. "Is there no way out?" they ask. You do not speculate that way in physics, chemistry, and mathematics. Why cannot the science of religion be like any other science? They proposed this way: If such a thing as the soul of man really exists, if it is immortal, if God really exists as the ruler of this universe — he must be [known] here; and all that must be [realised] in [your own] consciousness.

The mind cannot be analysed by any external machine. Supposing you could look into my brain while I am thinking, you would only see certain molecules interchanged. You could not see thought, consciousness, ideas, images. You would simply see the mass of vibrations — chemical and physical changes. From this example we see that this sort of analysis would not do.

[1]. Fragmentary notes of a lecture recorded by Ida Ansell and reprinted from Vedanta and the West, July-August, 1957.

Is there any other method by which the mind can be analysed as mind? If there is, then the real science of religion is possible. The science of Raja-yoga claims there is such a possibility. We can all attempt it and succeed to a certain degree. There is this great difficulty: In external sciences the object is [comparatively easy to observe]. The instruments of analysis are rigid; and both are external. But in the analysis of the mind the object and the instruments of analysis are the same thing.... The subject and the object become one....

External analysis will go to the brain and find physical and chemical changes. It would never succeed [in answering the questions]: What is the consciousness? What is your imagination? Where does this vast mass of ideas you have come from, and where do they go? We cannot deny them. They are facts. I never saw my own brain. I have to take for granted I have one. But man can never deny his own conscious imagination....

The great problem is ourselves. Am I the long chain I do not see — one piece following the other in rapid succession but quite unconnected? Am I such a state of consciousness [for ever in a flux]? Or am I something more than that — a substance, an entity, what we call the soul? In other words, has man a soul or not? Is he a bundle of states of consciousness without any connection, or is he a unified substance? That is the great controversy. If we are merely bundles of consciousness, ... such a question as immortality would be merely delusion. ... On the other hand, if there is something in me which is a unit, a substance, then of course I am immortal. The unit cannot be destroyed or broken into pieces. Only compounds can be broken up....

All religions except Buddhism believe and struggle in some way or other to reach such a substance. Buddhism denies the substance and is quite satisfied with that. It says, this business about God, the soul, immortality, and all that — do not vex yourselves with such questions. But all the other religions of the world cling to this substance. They all believe that the soul is the substance in man in spite of all the changes, that God is the substance which is in the universe. They all believe in the immortality of the soul. These are speculations. Who is to decide the controversy between the Buddhists and the Christians? Christianity says there is a substance that will live for ever. The Christian says, "My Bible says so." The Buddhist says, "I do not believe in your book."...

The question is: Are we the substance [the soul] or this subtle matter, the changing, billowing mind? ... Our minds are constantly changing. Where is the substance within? We do not find it. I am now this and now that. I will believe in the substance if for a moment you can stop these changes....

Of course all the beliefs in God and heaven are little beliefs of organised religions. Any scientific religion never proposes such things.

Yoga is the science that teaches us to stop the Chitta [the mind-stuff] from getting into these changes. Suppose you succeed in leading the mind to a perfect state of Yoga. That moment you have solved the problem. You have known what you are. You have mastered all the changes. After that you may let the mind run about, but it is not the same mind any more. It is perfectly under your control. No more like wild horses that dash you down.... You have seen God. This is no longer a matter of speculation. There is no more Mr. So-and-so, ... no more books or Vedas, or controversy of preachers, or anything. You have been yourself: I am the substance beyond all these changes. I am not the changes; if I were, I could not stop them. I can stop the changes, and therefore I can never be the changes. This is the proposition of the science of Yoga....

We do not like these changes. We do not like changes at all. Every change is being forced upon us.... In our country bullocks carry a yoke on their shoulders [which is connected by a pole with an oil press]. From the yoke projects a piece of wood [to which is tied a bundle of grass] just far enough to tempt the bullock, but he cannot reach it. He wants to eat the grass and goes a little farther [thereby turning the oil press].... We are like these bullocks, always trying to eat the grass and stretching our necks to reach it. We go round and round this way. Nobody likes these changes. Certainly not! ...

All these changes are forced upon us.... We cannot help it. Once we have put ourselves in the machine, we must go on and on. The moment we stop, there is greater evil than if we continued forward....

Of course misery comes to us. It is all misery because it is all unwilling. It is all forced. Nature orders us and we obey, but there is not much love lost between us and nature. All our work is an attempt to escape nature. We say we are enjoying nature. If we analyse ourselves, we find that we are trying to escape everything and invent ways to enjoy this and that.... [Nature is] like the Frenchman who had invited an English friend and told him of his old wines in the cellar. He called for a bottle of old wine. It was so beautiful, and the light sparkled inside like a piece of gold. His butler poured out a glass, and the Englishman quietly drank it. The butler had brought in a bottle of castor oil! We are drinking castor oil all the time; we cannot help it.... [People in general] ... are so reduced to machinery they do not ... even think. Just like cats, dogs and other animals, they are also driven with the whip by nature. They never disobey, never think of it. But even they have some experience of life.... [Some, however,] begin to question: What is this? What are all these experiences for? What is the Self? Is there any escape? Any meaning to life? ...

The good will die. The wicked will die. Kings will die, and beggars will die. The great misery is death. ... All the time we are trying to avoid it. And if we die in a comfortable religion, we think we will see Johns and Jacks afterwards and have a good time.

In your country they bring Johns and Jacks down to show you [in Seances]. I saw such people numbers of times and shook hands with them. Many of you may have seen them. They bang the piano and sing "Beulah Land": America is a vast land. My home is on the other side of the world. I do not know where Beulah Land is. You will not find it in any geography. See our good comfortable religion! The old, old moth-eaten belief!

Those people cannot think. What can be done for them? They have been eaten up by the world. There is nothing in them to think. Their bones have become hollow, their brains are like cheese.... I sympathise with them. Let them have their comfort! Some people are evidently very much comforted by seeing their ancestors from Beulah Land.

One of these mediums offered to bring my ancestors down to me. I said, "Stop there. Do anything you like, but if you bring my ancestors, I don't know if I can restrain myself." The medium was very kind and stopped.

In our country, when we begin to get worried by things, we pay something to the priests and make a bargain with God.... For the time being we feel comforted, otherwise we will not pay the priests. A little comfort comes, but [it turns] into reaction shortly.... So again misery comes. The same misery is here all the time. Your people in our country says, "If you believe in our doctrine you are safe." Our people among the lower classes believe in your doctrines. The only change is that they become beggars. ... But is that religion? It is politics — not religion. You may call it religion, dragging the word religion down to that sense. But it is not spiritual.

Among thousands of men and women a few are inclined to something higher than this life. The others are like sheep.... Some among thousands try to understand things, to find a way out. The question is: Is there a way out? If there is a way out, it is in the soul and nowhere else. The ways out from other sources have been tried enough, and all [have been found wanting]. People do not find satisfaction. The very fact that those myriads of theories and sects exist show that people do not find satisfaction.

The science of Yoga proposes this, that the one way out is through ourselves. We have to individualise ourselves. If there is any truth, we can [realise it as our very essence].... We will cease being driven about by nature from place to place....

The phenomenal world is always changing: [to reach the Changeless] that is our goal. We want to be That, to realise that Absolute, the [changeless] Reality. What is preventing us from realising that Reality? It is the fact of creation. The creative mind is creating all the time and gets mixed up with its own creation. [But we must also remember that] it is creation that discovered God. It is creation that discovered the Absolute in every individual soul....

Going back to our definition: Yoga is stopping the Chitta, the mind-stuff, from getting into these changes. When all this creation has been stopped — if it is possible to stop it — then we shall see for ourselves what we are in reality.... The Uncreated, the One that creates, manifests itself.

The methods of Yoga are various. Some of them are very difficult; it takes long training to succeed. Some are easy. Those who have the perseverance and strength to follow it through attain to great results. Those who do not may take a simpler method and get some benefit out of it.

As to the proper analysis of the mind, we see at once how difficult it is to grapple with the mind itself. We have become bodies. That we are souls we have forgotten entirely. When we think of ourselves, it is the body that comes into our imagination. We behave as bodies. We talk as bodies. We are all body. From this body we have to separate the soul. Therefore the training begins with the body itself, [until ultimately] the spirit manifests itself.... The central idea in all this training is to attain to that power of concentration, the power of meditation.

EPISTLES-THIRD SERIES

Before leaving for the USA, Swamiji used to change his name very often. In earlier years he signed as Narendra or Naren; then for some time as Vividishananda or Sachchidananda. But for the convenience of the readers, these volumes use the more familiar name Vivekananda.

—PUBLISHER

I — SHRI BALARAM BOSE

Translated from Bengali

Glory to Ramakrishna!

BAIDYANATH,
25th December, 1889.

DEAR SIR (Shri Balaram Bose),

I have been staying for the last few days at Baidyanath in Purna Babu's Lodge. It is not so cold, and my health too is indifferent. I am suffering from indigestion, probably due to excess of iron in the water. I have found nothing agreeable here — neither the place, nor the season, nor the company. I leave for Varanasi tomorrow. Achyutananda stopped at Govinda Chaudhury's place at Deoghar, and the latter, as soon as he got news of us, earnestly insisted on our becoming his guests. Finally, he met us once again and prevailed on us to accede to his request. The man is a great worker, but has a number of women with him — old women most of them, of the ordinary Vaishnava type. . . . His clerks too revere us much; some of them are very much ill-disposed towards him, and they spoke of his misdeeds. Incidentally, I raised the topic of __. You have many wrong ideas or doubts about her; hence I write all this after particular investigation. Even the aged clerks of this establishment highly respect and revere her. She came to stop with __ while she was a mere child, and ever lived as his wife. . . . Everyone admits in one voice that her character is spotless. She was all along a perfectly chaste woman and never behaved with __ in any relation but that of wife to husband, and she was absolutely faithful. She came at too early an age to have incurred any moral taint. After she had separated from __, she wrote to him to say that she had never treated him as anything but her husband, but that it was impossible for her to live with a man with a loose character. His old office-bearers too believe him to be satanic in character; but they consider __ a Devi (angel), and remark that it was following her departure that __ lost all sense of shame.

My object in writing all this is that formerly I was not a believer in the tale of the lady's early life. The idea that there might be such purity in the midst of a relation which society does not recognise, I used to consider as romance. But after thorough investigation I have come to know that it is all right. She is very pure, pure from her infancy — I have not the least doubt about it. For entertaining those doubts, you and I and everyone are guilty to her; I make repeated salutations to her, and ask her pardon for my guilt. She is not a liar.

I take this opportunity to record that such courage is impossible in a lying and unchaste woman. I have also been told that she had a lifelong ardent faith in religion also.

Well, your disease is not yet improving! I don't think this is a place for patients unless one is ready to spend a good deal of money. Please think out some judicious course. Here every article will have to be procured from elsewhere.

Yours affectionately,
Vivekananda.

II — SHRI BALARAM BOSE

Translated from Bengali

Glory to Ramakrishna!

ALLAHABAD,
30th December, 1889.

DEAR SIR (Shri Balaram Bose),

Gupta left a slip when coming and the next day a letter from Yogananda gave me all the news and I immediately started for Allahabad which I reached the day after, to find that Yogananda had completely recovered. He had chicken-pox (with one or two smallpox rashes also). The doctor is a noble soul, and they have got a brotherhood, who are all great pious men and highly devoted to the service of Sâdhus. They are particularly anxious that I pass the month of Mâgh here, but I am leaving for Varanasi. . . . How are you? I pray to God for the welfare of yourself and your family. Please convey my compliments to Tulasiram, Chuni Babu, and the rest.

Yours affectionately,
Vivekananda.

III — SHRI BALARAM BOSE

Translated from Bengali

GHAZIPUR,
30th January, 1890.

REVERED SIR (Shri Balaram Bose),

I am now stopping with Satish Babu at Ghazipur. Of the few places I have recently visited, this is the healthiest. The water of Baidyanath is very bad — it leads to indigestion. Allahabad is very congested. The few days I passed at Varanasi, I suffered from fever day and night — the place is so malarious! Ghazipur has a very salubrious climate — specially the quarter I am living in. I have visited Pavhari Baba's house — there are high walls all round, and it is fashioned like an English bungalow. There is a garden inside and big rooms and chimneys, etc. He allows nobody to enter. If he is so inclined, he comes up to the door and speaks from inside — that is all. One day I went and waited and waited in the cold and had to return. I shall go to Varanasi on Sunday next. If the meeting with the Babaji takes place in the meantime, all right, otherwise I bid him good-bye. About Pramada Babu's place I shall write definitely from Varanasi. If Kali Bhattacharya is determined to come, let him do so after I leave for Varanasi on Sunday, but he should rather not. After a few days' stay at Varanasi, I shall start for Hrishikesh. Pramada Babu may accompany me. Please accept all of you my cordial greetings — and blessing to Fakir, Ram, Krishnamayi, etc.

Yours affectionately,
Vivekananda.

PS. In my opinion, it will do you much good if you come and stay for some time at Ghazipur. Here Satish will be able to secure a bungalow for you, and there is a gentleman, Gagan Chandra Ray by name, who is the head of the Opium Office and is exceedingly courteous, philanthropic, and social — they will arrange for everything. The house-rent is fifteen to twenty rupees; rice is dear, and milk sells at sixteen to twenty seers a rupee; all other things are very cheap. Besides, under the care of these gentlemen, there is no chance of any difficulty. But it is slightly expensive — it will cost over forty to fifty rupees. Varanasi is horribly malarious. I have never lived in Pramada Babu's garden. He likes to have me always in his company. The garden is indeed very beautiful, richly laid out, spacious, and open. This time when I go, I shall live there and report to you.

IV — SHRI BALARAM BOSE

Translated from Bengali

Salutation to Bhagavan Ramakrishna!

C/O Satish Mukherji,
GORABAZAR, GHAZIPUR.
14th February, 1890.

REVERED SIR (Shri Balaram Bose),

I am in receipt of your letter of contrition. I am not leaving this place soon — it is impossible to avoid the Babaji's request. You have expressed remorse at not having reaped any appreciable results by serving the Sadhus. It is true, and yet not true; it is true if you look towards ideal bliss; but if you look behind to the place from which you started, you will find that before you were an animal, now you are a man, and will be a god or God Himself in future. Moreover, that sort of regret and dissatisfaction is very good; it is the prelude to improvement. Without this none can rise. He who puts on a turban and immediately sees the Lord, progresses thus far and no farther. You are blessed indeed to have that constant dissatisfaction preying upon your mind — rest assured that there is no danger for you. . . . You are a keenly intelligent man, and know full well that patience is the best means of success. In this respect I have no doubt that we light-headed boys have much to learn from you. . . . You are a considerate man, and I need not add anything. Man has two ears but one mouth. You specially are given to plain-speaking and are chary of making large promises — things that sometimes make me cross with you, but upon reflection I find that it is you who have acted with discretion. "Slow but sure." "What is lost in power is gained in speed." However, in this world everything depends upon one's words. To get an insight behind the words (specially, with your economical spirit masking all) is not given to all, and one must associate long with a man to be able to understand him. . . . Religion is not in sects, nor in making a fuss — why do you forget these teachings of our revered Master? Please help as far as it lies in you, but to judge what came of it, whether it was turned to good or evil account, is perhaps beyond our jurisdiction. . . . Considering the great shock which Girish Babu has received, it will give him immense peace to serve Mother at this moment. He is a very keen-witted person. And our beloved Master had perfect confidence in you, used to dine nowhere else except at your place, and, I have heard, Mother too has the fullest confidence in you. In view of these, you will please bear and forbear all shortcomings of us fickle boys, treating them as if they were done by your own boy. This is all I have got to say. Please let me know by return of post when the Anniversary is to take place. A pain in the loins is giving me much trouble. In a few days the place will look exceedingly beautiful, with miles and miles of rose-banks all in flower. Satish says he will then send some fresh roses and cuttings for the Festival. . . . May the Lord ordain that your son becomes a man, and never a coward!

Yours affectionately,
Vivekananda.

PS. If Mother has come, please convey to her my countless salutations, and ask her to bless me that I may have unflinching perseverance. Or, if that be impossible in this body, may it fall off soon!

V — GUPTA

Translated from Bengali

GHAZIPUR,
14th Feb.,1890.

MY DEAR GUPTA (Swami Sadananda),

I hope you are doing well. Do your own spiritual exercises, and knowing yourself to be the humblest servant of all, serve them. Those with whom you are staying are such that even I am not worthy to call myself their humblest servant and take the dust of their feet. Knowing this, serve them and have devotion for them. Don't be angry even if they abuse or even hurt you grievously. Never mix with women. Try to be hardy little by little, and gradually accustom yourself to maintaining the body out of the proceeds of begging. Whoever takes the name of Ramakrishna, know him to be your Guru. Everyone can play the role of a master, but it is very difficult to be a servant. Specially you should follow Shashi. Know it for certain that without steady devotion for the Guru and unflinching patience and perseverance, nothing is to be achieved. You must have strict morality. Deviate an inch from this, and you are gone forever.

Yours affectionately,
Vivekananda.

VI — SHRI BALARAM BOSE

Translated from Bengali

Glory to Ramakrishna!

GHAZIPUR,
15th March, 1890.

REVERED SIR (Shri Balaram Bose),

Received your kind note yesterday. I am very sorry to learn that Suresh Babu's illness is extremely serious. What is destined will surely happen. It is a matter of great regret that you too have fallen ill. So long as egoism lasts, any shortcoming in adopting remedial measures is to be considered as idleness — it is a fault and a guilt. For one who has not that egoistic idea, the best course is to forbear. The dwelling-place of the Jivâtman, this body, is a veritable means of work, and he who converts this into an infernal den is guilty, and he who neglects it is also to blame. Please act according to circumstances as they present themselves, without the least hesitation.

— "The highest duty consists in doing the little that lies in one's power, seeking neither death nor life, and biding one's time like a servant ready to do any behest."

There is a dreadful outbreak of influenza at Varanasi and Pramada Babu has gone to Allahabad. Baburam has suddenly come here. He has got fever; he was wrong to start under such circumstances.... I am leaving this place tomorrow.... My countless salutations to Mother. You all bless me that I may have sameness of vision, that after avoiding the bondages which one is heir to by one's very birth, I may not again get stuck in self-imposed bondages. If there be any Doer of good and if He have the power and the opportunity, may He vouchsafe the highest blessings unto you all — this is my constant prayer.

Yours affectionately,
Vivekananda.

VII — ATUL BABU

Translated from Bengali

GHAZIPUR,
15th March, 1890.

DEAR ATUL BABU (Atul Chandra Ghosh.),

I am extremely sorry to hear that you are passing through mental afflictions. Please do only what is agreeable to you.

— "While there is birth there is death, and again entering the mother's womb. This is the manifest evil of transmigration. How, O man, dost thou want satisfaction in such a world!"

Yours affectionately,
Vivekananda.

PS. I am leaving this place tomorrow. Let me see which way destiny leads!

VIII — ADHYAPAKJI

SALEM (U.S.A.),
30th Aug., 1893.

DEAR ADHYAPAKJI (HONOURABLE PROFESSOR) (Prof. John Henry Wright),

I am going off from here today. I hope you have received some reply from Chicago. I have received an invitation with full directions from Mr. Sanborn. So I am going to Saratoga on Monday. My respects to your wife. And my love to Austin and all the children. You are a real Mahâtmâ (a great soul) and Mrs. Wright is nonpareil.

Yours affectionately,
Vivekananda.

IX — ADHYAPAKJI

SALEM,
Saturday, 4th Sept., 1893.

DEAR ADHYAPAKJI (Prof. John Henry Wright),

I hasten to tender my heartfelt gratitude to you for your letters of introduction. I have received a letter from Mr. Theles of Chicago giving me the names of some of the delegates and other things about the Congress.

Your professor of Sanskrit in his note to Miss Sanborn mistakes me for Purushottama Joshi and states that there is a Sanskrit library in Boston the like of which can scarcely be met with in India. I would be so happy to see it.

Mr. Sanborn has written to me to come over to Saratoga on Monday and I am going accordingly. I would stop then at a boarding house called Sanatorium. If any news come from Chicago in the meanwhile I hope you will kindly send it over to the Sanatorium, Saratoga.

You and your noble wife and sweet children have made an impression in my brain which is simply indelible, and I thought myself so much nearer to heaven when living with you. May He, the giver of all gifts, shower on your head His choicest blessings.

Here are a few lines written as an attempt at poetry. Hoping your love will pardon this infliction.

Ever your friend,
Vivekananda.

O'er hill and dale and mountain range,
In temple, church, and mosque,
In Vedas, Bible, Al Koran
I had searched for Thee in vain.
Like a child in the wildest forest lost
I have cried and cried alone,
"Where art Thou gone, my God, my love?"
The echo answered, "gone."

And days and nights and years then passed —
A fire was in the brain;
I knew not when day changed in night,
The heart seemed rent in twain.
I laid me down on Gangâ's shore,
Exposed to sun and rain;
With burning tears I laid the dust
And wailed with waters' roar.

I called on all the holy names
Of every clime and creed,
"Show me the way, in mercy, ye
Great ones who have reached the goal".

Years then passed in bitter cry,
Each moment seemed an age,
Till one day midst my cries and groans
Some one seemed calling me.

A gentle soft and soothing voice
That said "my son", "my son",
That seemed to thrill in unison
With all the chords of my soul.

I stood on my feet and tried to find
The place the voice came from;
I searched and searched and turned to see
Round me, before, behind.
Again, again it seemed to speak —
The voice divine to me.
In rapture all my soul was hushed,
Entranced, enthralled in bliss.

A flash illumined all my soul;
The heart of my heart opened wide.
O joy, O bliss, what do I find!
My love, my love, you are here,
And you are here, my love, my all!

And I was searching thee!
From all eternity you were there
Enthroned in majesty!

From that day forth, where'er I roam,
I feel Him standing by
O'er hill and dale, high mount and vale,
Far far away and high.

The moon's soft light, the stars so bright,
The glorious orb of day,
He shines in them; His beauty — might —
Reflected lights are they.
The majestic morn, the melting eve,
The boundless billowy sea,
In nature's beauty, songs of birds,
I see through them — it is He.

When dire calamity seizes me,
The heart seems weak and faint,
All nature seems to crush me down,
With laws that never bend.

Meseems I hear Thee whispering sweet
My love, "I am near", "I am near".
My heart gets strong. With Thee, my love,
A thousand deaths no fear.
Thou speakest in the mother's lay
That shuts the baby's eye;
When innocent children laugh and play
I see Thee standing by.

When holy friendship shakes the hand,
He stands between them too;
He pours the nectar in mother's kiss
And the baby's sweet "mama".
Thou wert my God with prophets old;

All creeds do come from Thee;
The Vedas, Bible, and Koran bold
Sing Thee in harmony.

"Thou art", "Thou art" the Soul of souls
In the rushing stream of life.
"Om tat Sat om." (Tat Sat means that only real existence. [Swamiji's note].) Thou art my God.
My love, I am thine, I am thine.

X — ADHYAPAKJI

CHICAGO,
2nd October, 1893.

DEAR ADHYAPAKJI (Prof. John Henry Wright),

I do not know what you are thinking of my long silence. In the first place I dropped in on the Congress in the eleventh hour, and quite unprepared; and that kept me very very busy for some time. Secondly, I was speaking almost every day in the Congress and had no time to write; and last and greatest of all — my kind friend, I owe so much to you that it would have been an insult to your ahetuka (unselfish) friendship to have written you business-like letters in a hurry. The Congress is now over.

Dear brother, I was so so afraid to stand before that great assembly of fine speakers and thinkers from all over the world and speak; but the Lord gave me strength, and I almost every day heroically (?) faced the platform and the audience. If I have done well, He gave me the strength for it; if I have miserably failed — I knew that beforehand — for I am hopelessly ignorant.

Your friend Prof. Bradley was very kind to me and he always cheered me on. And oh! everybody is so kind here to me who am nothing — that it is beyond my power of expression. Glory unto Him in the highest in whose sight the poor ignorant monk from India is the same as the learned divines of this mighty land. And how the Lord is helping me every day of my life, brother — I sometimes wish for a life of [a] million million ages to serve Him through the work, dressed in rags and fed by charity.

Oh, how I wished that you were here to see some of our sweet ones from India — the tender-hearted Buddhist Dharmapala, the orator Mazoomdar — and realise that in that far-off and poor India there are hearts that beat in sympathy to yours, born and brought up in this mighty and great country.

My eternal respects to your holy wife; and to your sweet children my eternal love and blessings.

Col. Higginson, a very broad man, told me that your daughter had written to his daughter about me; and he was very sympathetic to me. I am going to Evanston tomorrow and hope to see Prof. Bradley there.

May He make us all more and more pure and holy so that we may live a perfect spiritual life even before throwing off this earthly body.

Vivekananda.

[The letter continues on a separate sheet of paper:]

I am now going to be reconciled to my life here. All my life I have been taking every circumstance as coming from Him and calmly adapting myself to it. At first in America I was almost out of my water. I was afraid I would have to give up the accustomed way of being guided by the Lord and cater for myself — and what a horrid piece of mischief and ingratitude was that. I now clearly see that He who was guiding me on the snow tops of the Himalayas and the burning plains of India is here to help me and guide me. Glory unto Him in the highest. So I have calmly fallen into my old ways. Somebody or other gives me a shelter and food, somebody or other comes to ask me to speak about Him, and I know He sends them and mine is to obey. And then He is supplying my necessities, and His will be done!

"He who rests [in] Me and gives up all other self-assertion and struggles I carry to him whatever he needs" (Gitâ).

So it is in Asia. So in Europe. So in America. So in the deserts of India. So in the rush of business in America. For is He not here also? And if He does not, I only would take for granted that He wants that I should lay aside this three minutes' body of clay — and hope to lay it down gladly.

We may or may not meet, brother. He knows. You are great, learned, and holy. I dare not preach to you or your wife; but to your children I quote these passages from the Vedas —

"The four Vedas, sciences, languages, philosophy, and all other learnings are only ornamental. The real learning, the true knowledge is that which enables us to reach Him who is unchangeable in His love."

"How real, how tangible, how visible is He through whom the skin touches, the eyes see, and the world gets its reality!"

"Hearing Him nothing remains to be heard,

Seeing Him nothing remains to be seen,

Attaining Him nothing remains to be attained."

"He is the eye of our eyes, the ear of our ears, the Soul of our souls."

He is nearer to you, my dears, than even your father and mother. You are innocent and pure as flowers. Remain so, and He will reveal Himself unto you. Dear Austin, when you are playing, there is another playmate playing with you who loves you more than anybody else; and Oh, He is so full of fun. He is always playing — sometimes with great big balls which we call the sun and earth, sometimes with little children like you and laughing and playing with you. How funny it would be to see Him and play with Him! My dear, think of it.

Dear Adhyapakji, I am moving about just now. Only when I come to Chicago, I always go to see Mr. and Mrs. Lyons, one of the noblest couples I have seen here. If you would be kind enough to write to me, kindly address it to the care of Mr. John B. Lyon, 262 Michigan Ave., Chicago.

"He who gets hold of the One in this world of many — the one constant existence in a world of flitting shadows — the one life in a world of death — he alone crosses this sea of misery and struggle. None else, none else" (Vedas).

"He who is the Brahman of the Vedântins, Ishvara of the Naiyâyikas, Purusha of the Sânkhyas, cause of the Mimâmsakas, law of the Buddhists, absolute zero of the Atheists, and love infinite unto those that love, may [He] take us all under His merciful protection": Udayanâchârya — a great philosopher of the Nyâya or Dualistic school. And this is the Benediction pronounced at the very beginning of his wonderful book Kusumânjali (A handful of flowers), in which he attempts to establish the existence of a personal creator and moral ruler of infinite love independently of revelation.

Your ever grateful friend,
Vivekananda.

XI — MRS. TANNATT WOODS

CHICAGO,
10th October, 1893.

DEAR MRS. TANNATT WOODS,

I received your letter yesterday. Just now I am lecturing about Chicago — and am doing as I think very well; it is ranging from 30 to 80 dollars a lecture, and just now I have been so well advertised in Chicago gratis by the Parliament of Religions that it is not advisable to give up this field now. To which I am sure you will agree. However I may come soon to Boston, but when I cannot say. Yesterday I returned from Streator where I got 87 dollars for a lecture. I have engagements every day this week. And hope more will come by the end of the week. My love to Mr. Woods and compliments to all our friends.

Yours truly,
Vivekananda.

XII — ADHYAPAKJI

C/O J. LYON,
262 MICHIGAN AVENUE, CHICAGO,
26th October, 1893.

DEAR ADHYAPAKJI (Prof. John Henry Wright),

You would be glad to know that I am doing well here and that almost everybody has been very kind to me, except of course the very orthodox. Many of the men brought together here from far-off lands have got projects and ideas and missions to carry out, and America is the only place where there is a chance of success for everything. But I thought better and have given up speaking about my project entirely — because I am sure now — the heathen draws more than his project. So I want to go to work earnestly for my own project only keeping the project in the background and working like any other lecturer.

He who has brought me hither and has not left me yet will not leave me ever I am here. You will be glad to know that I am doing well and expect to do very well in the way of getting money. Of course I am too green in the business but would soon learn my trade. I am very popular in Chicago. So I want to stay here a little more and get money.

Tomorrow I am going to lecture on Buddhism at the ladies' fortnightly club — which is the most influential in this city. How to thank you my kind friend or Him who brought you to me; for now I think the success of my project probable, and it is you who have made it so.

May blessings and happiness attend every step of your progress in this world.

My love and blessings to your children.

Yours affectionately ever,
Vivekananda.

XIII — MRS. WOODS

541 DEARBORN AVENUE, CHICAGO,
19th November, 1893.

DEAR MRS. WOODS,

Excuse my delay in answering your letter. I do not know when I will be able to see you again. I am starting tomorrow for Madison and Minneapolis.

The English gentleman you speak of is Dr. Momerie of London. He is a well-known worker amongst the poor of London and is a very sweet man. You perhaps do not know that the English church was the only religious denomination in the world who did not send to us a representative, and Dr. Momerie came to the Parliament in spite of the Archbishop of Canterbury's denouncing of the Parliament of Religions.

My love for you, my kind friend, and your noble son is all the same whether I write pretty often or not.

Can you express my books and the cover-all to the care of Mr. Hale? I am in need of them. The express will be paid here.

The blessings of the Lord on you and yours.

Ever your friend,
Vivekananda.

PS. If you have the occasion to write to Miss Sanborn and others of our friends in the east, kindly give them my deepest respects.

XIV — SISTER

DETROIT,
17th March, 1894.

DEAR SISTER (Miss Harriet McKindley of Chicago),

Got your package yesterday. Sorry that you send those stockings — I could have got some myself here. Glad that it shows your love. After all, the satchel has become more than a thoroughly stuffed sausage. I do not know how to carry it along.

I have returned today to Mrs. Bagley's as she was sorry that I would remain so long with Mr. Palmer. Of course in Palmer's house there was real "good time". He is a real jovial heartwhole fellow, and likes "good time" a little too much and his "hot Scotch". But he is right along innocent and childlike in his simplicity.

He was very sorry that I came away, but I could not help. Here is a beautiful young girl. I saw her twice, I do not remember her name. So brainy, so beautiful, so spiritual, so unworldly! Lord bless her! She came this morning with Mrs. M'cDuvel and talked so beautifully and deep and spiritually — that I was quite astounded. She knows everything about the Yogis and is herself much advanced in practice!!

"Thy ways are beyond searching out." Lord bless her — so innocent, holy, and pure! This is the grandest recompense in my terribly toilsome, miserable life — the finding of holy happy faces like you from time to time. The great Buddhist prayer is, "I bow down to all holy men on earth". I feel the real meaning of this prayer whenever I see a face upon which the finger of the Lord has written in unmistakable letters "mine". May you all be happy, blessed, good and pure as you are for ever and ever. May your feet never touch the mud and dirt of this terrible world. May you live and pass away like flowers as you are born — is the constant prayer of your brother.

Vivekananda.

XV — BROTHER

DETROIT,
29th March, 1894.

DEAR BROTHER,

Your letter just reached me here. I am in a hurry, so excuse a few points which I would take the liberty of correcting you in.

In the first place, I have not one word to say against any religion or founder of religion in the world — whatever you may think of our religion. All religions are sacred to me. Secondly, it is a misstatement that I said that missionaries do not learn our vernaculars. I still stick to my statement that few, if any, of them pay any attention to Sanskrit; nor is it true that I said anything against any religious body — except that I do insist on my statement that India can never be converted to Christianity, and further I deny that the conditions of the lower classes are made any better by Christianity, and add that the majority of southern Indian Christians are not only Catholics, but what they call themselves, caste Christians, that is, they stick close to their castes, and I am thoroughly persuaded that if the Hindu society gives up its exclusive policy, ninety per cent of them would rush back to Hinduism with all its defects.

Lastly, I thank you from the bottom of my heart for calling me your fellow-countryman. This is the first time any European foreigner, born in India though he be, has dared to call a detested native by that name — missionary or no missionary. Would you dare call me the same in India? Ask your missionaries, born in India, to do the same — and those not born, to treat them as fellow human beings. As to the rest, you yourself would call me a fool if I admit that my religion or society submits to be judged by strolling globe-trotters or story-writers' narratives.

My brother — excuse me — what do you know of my society or religion, though born in India? It is absolutely impossible — the society is so closed; and over and above, everyone judges from his preconceived standard of race and religion, does he not? Lord bless you for calling me a fellow-countryman. There may still come a brotherly love and fellowship between the East and West.

Yours fraternally,
Vivekananda.

XVI — PROFESSOR

NEW YORK,
25th April, 1894.

DEAR PROFESSOR (Prof. John Henry Wright),

I am very very grateful for your invitation. And will come on May 7th. As for the bed — my friend, your love and noble heart can convert the stone into down.

I am sorry I am not going to the authors' breakfast at Salem.

I am coming home by May 7th.

Yours truly,
Vivekananda.

XVII — SISTER

NEW YORK,
26th April, 1894.

DEAR SISTER (Miss Isabelle McKindley.),

Your letter reached me yesterday. You were perfectly right — I enjoyed the fun of the lunatic Interior, (Chicago Interior, a Presbyterian newspaper which opposed Swamiji. — Ed.) but the mail you sent yesterday from India was really, as Mother Church says in her letter, a good news after a long interval. There is a beautiful letter from Dewanji. The old man — Lord bless him — offers as usual to help me. Then there was a little pamphlet published in Calcutta about me — revealing that once at least in my life the prophet has been honoured in his own country. There are extracts from American and Indian papers and magazines about me. The extracts printed from Calcutta papers were especially gratifying, although the strain is so fulsome that I refuse to send the pamphlet over to you. They call me illustrious, wonderful, and all sorts of nonsense, but they forward me the gratitude of the whole nation. Now I do not care what they even of my own people say about me — except for one thing. I have an old mother. She has suffered much all her life and in the midst of all she could bear to give me up for the service of God and man; but to have given up the most beloved of her children — her hope — to live a beastly immoral life in a far distant country, as Mazoomdar was telling in Calcutta, would have simply killed her. But the Lord is great, none can injure His children.

The cat is out of the bag — without my seeking at all. And who do you think is the editor of one of our leading papers which praise me so much and thank God that I came to America to represent Hinduism? Mazoomdar's cousin!! — Poor Mazoomdar — he has injured his cause by telling lies through jealousy. Lord knows I never attempted any defence.

I read the article of Mr. Gandhi in the Forum before this.

If you have got the Review of Reviews of last month — read to mother the testimony about the Hindus in connection with the opium question in India by one of the highest officials of the English in India. He compares the English with the Hindus and lauds the Hindu to the skies. Sir Lepel Griffin was one of the bitterest enemies of our race. What made this change of front?

I had a very good time in Boston at Mrs. Breed's — and saw Prof. Wright. I am going to Boston again. The tailor is making my new gown. I am going to speak at Cambridge University [Harvard] and would be the guest of Prof. Wright there. They write grand welcomes to me in the Boston papers.

I am tired of all this nonsense. Towards the latter part of May I will come back to Chicago, and after a few day's stay would come back to the East again.

I spoke last night at the Waldorf hotel. Mrs. Smith sold tickets at $2 each. I had a full hall which by the way was a small one. I have not seen anything of the money yet. Hope to see in the course of the day.

I made a hundred dollars at Lynn which I do not send because I have to make my new gown and other nonsense.

Do not expect to make any money at Boston. Still I must touch the brain of America and stir it up if I can.

Your loving brother,
Vivekananda.

XVIII — SISTER

NEW YORK,
2nd [actually 1st] May, 1894.

DEAR SISTER (Miss Isabelle McKindley.),

I am afraid I cannot send you the pamphlet just now. But I got a little bit of a newspaper cutting from India yesterday which I send you up. After you have read it kindly send it over to Mrs. Bagley. The editor of this paper is a relative of Mr. Mazoomdar. I am now sorry for poor Mazoomdar!! (The last two sentences were written crosswise on the left margin.)

I could not find the exact orange colour of my coat here, so I have been obliged to satisfy myself with the next best — a cardinal red with more of yellow.

The coat will be ready in a few days.

Got about $70 the other day by lecturing at Waldorf. And hope to get some more by tomorrow's lecture.

From 7th to 19th there are engagements in Boston, but they pay very little.

Yesterday I bought a pipe for $13 — meerschaum do not tell it to father Pope. The coat will cost $30. I am all right getting food . . . and money enough. Hope very soon to put something in the bank after the coming lecture.

. . . in the evening I am going to speak in a vegetarian dinner! Well, I am a vegetarian . . ., because I prefer it when I can get it. I have another invitation to lunch with Lyman Abbott day after tomorrow. After all, I am having very nice time and hope to have very nice time in Boston — only that nasty nasty lecturing — disgusting. However as soon as 19th is over — one leap from Boston . . . to Chicago

... and then I will have a long long breath and rest, rest for two three weeks. I will simply sit down and talk — talk and smoke.

By the by, your New York people are very good — only more money than brains.

I am going to speak to the students of the Harvard University. Three lectures at Boston, three at Harvard — all arranged by Mrs. Breed. They are arranging something here too, so that I will, on my way to Chicago, come to New York once more — give them a few hard raps and pocket the boodle and fly to Chicago.

If you want anything from New York or Boston which cannot be had at Chicago — write sharp. I have plenty of dollars now. I will send you over anything you want in a minute. Don't think it would be indelicate anyway — no humbug about me. If I am a brother so I am. I hate only one thing in the world — hypocrisy.

Your affectionate brother,
Vivekananda.

XIX — ADHYAPAKJI

NEW YORK,
4th May, 1894.

DEAR ADHYAPAKJI (Prof. John Henry Wright),

I have received your kind note just now. And it is unnecessary for me to say that I will be very happy to do as you say.

I have also received Col. Higginson's letter. I will reply to him.

I will be in Boston on Sunday [May 6]. On Monday I lecture at the Women's Club of Mrs. Howe.

Yours ever truly,
Vivekananda.

XX — ADHYAPAKJI

17 BEACON STREET, BOSTON,
May, 1894.

DEAR ADHYAPAKJI (Prof. John Henry Wright),

By this time you have got the pamphlet and the letters. If you like, I would send you over from Chicago some letters from Indian Princes and ministers — one of these ministers was one of the Commissioners of the late opium commission that sat under Royal Commission in India. If you like, I will have them write to you to convince you of my not being a cheat. But, my brother, our ideal of life is to hide, to suppress, and to deny.

We are to give up and not to take. Had I not the "Fad" in my head, I would never have come over here. And it was with a hope that it would help my cause that I joined the Parliament of Religions — having always refused it when our people wanted to send me for it. I came over telling them — "that I may or may not join that assembly — and you may send me over if you like". They sent me over leaving me quite free.

You did the rest.

I am morally bound to afford you every satisfaction, my kind friend; but for the rest of the world I do not care what they say — the Sannyasin must not have self-defence. So I beg of you not to publish or show anybody anything in that pamphlet or the letters. I do not care for the attempts of the old missionary; but the fever of jealousy which attacked Mazoomdar gave me a terrible shock, and I pray that he would know better — for he is a great and good man who has tried all his life to do good. But this proves one of my Master's sayings, "Living in a room covered with black soot — however careful you may be — some spots must stick to your clothes." So, however one may try to be good and holy, so long he is in the world, some part of his nature must gravitate downwards.

The way to God is the opposite to that of the world. And to few, very few, are given to have God and mammon at the same time.

I was never a missionary, nor ever would be one — my place is in the Himalayas. I have satisfied myself so far that I can with a full conscience say, "My God, I saw terrible misery amongst my brethren; I searched and discovered the way out of it, tried my best to apply the remedy, but failed. So Thy will be done."

May his blessings be on you and yours for ever and ever.

Yours affectionately,
Vivekananda.

541 DEARBORN AVE., CHICAGO
I go to Chicago tomorrow or day after.

XXI — ADHYAPAKJI

541 DEARBORN AVE.,
CHICAGO,
24th May, 1894.

DEAR ADHYAPAKJI (Prof. John Henry Wright),

Herewith I forward to you a letter from one of our ruling princes of Rajputana, His Highness the Maharaja of Khetri, and another from the opium commissioner, late minister of Junagad, one of the largest states in India, and a man who is called the Gladstone of India. These I hope would convince you of my being no fraud.

One thing I forgot to tell you. I never identified myself anyway with Mr. Mazoomdar's party chief. (Evidently, Keshab Chandra Sen.) If he says so, he does not speak the truth.

I hope, after your perusal, you will kindly send the letters over to me, except the pamphlet which I do not care for.

I am bound, my dear friend, to give you every satisfaction of my being a genuine Sannyasin, but to you alone. I do not care what the rabbles say or think about me.

"Some would call you a saint, some a chandala; some a lunatic, others a demon. Go on then straight to thy work without heeding either" — thus saith one of our great Sannyasins, an old emperor of India, King Bhartrihari, who joined the order in old times.

May the Lord bless you for ever and ever. My love to all your children and my respects to your noble wife.

I remain ever your friend,
Vivekananda.

PS. — I had connection with Pundit Shiva Nath Shastri's party — but only on points of social reform. Mazoomdar and Chandra Sen — I always considered as not sincere, and I have no reason to change my opinion even now. Of course in religious matters even with my friend Punditji I differed much, the chief being, I thinking Sannyasa or (giving up the world) the highest ideal, and he, a sin. So the Brahmo Samajists consider becoming a monk a sin!!

The Brahmo Samaj, like Christian Science in your country, spread in Calcutta for a certain time and then died out. I am not sorry, neither glad that it died. It has done its work — viz social reform. Its religion was not worth a cent, and so it must die out. If Mazoomdar thinks I was one of the causes of its death, he errs. I am even now a great sympathiser of its reforms; but the "booby" religion could not hold its own against the old "Vedanta". What shall I do? Is that my fault? Mazoomdar has become childish in his old age and takes to tactics not a whit better than some of your Christian missionaries. Lord bless him and show him better ways.

When are you going to Annisquam? My love to Austin and Bime. My respects to your wife; and for you my love and gratitude is too deep for expression.

XXII — ADHYAPAKJI

541 DEARBORN AVENUE,
18th June, 1894.

DEAR ADHYAPAKJI (Prof. John Henry Wright),

Excuse my delay in sending the other letters; I could not find them earlier. I am going to New York in a week.

I do not know whether I will come to Annisquam or not. The letters need not be sent over to me until I write you again. Mrs. Bagley seems to be unsettled by that article in the Boston paper against me. She sent me over a copy from Detroit and has ceased correspondence with me. Lord bless her. She has been very kind to me.

Stout hearts like yours are not common, my brother. This is a queer place — this world of ours. On the whole I am very very thankful to the Lord for the amount of kindness I have received at the hands of the people of this country — I, a complete stranger here without even "credentials". Everything works for the best.

Yours ever in gratitude,
Vivekananda.

PS. The East India stamps are for your children if they like.

XXIII — MR. BHATTACHARYA

Translated from Bengali

U.S.A.
5th September, 1894.

DEAR MR. BHATTACHARYA (Mr. Manmatha Nath Bhattacharya),

I was much pleased to read your affectionate letter. I shall make inquiries about the weaving machine as soon as I can, and let you know. Now I am resting at Annisquam, a village on the seacoast; soon I shall go to the city and attend to the matter of the machine. These seaside places are filled with people during the summer; some come to bathe in the sea, some to take rest, and some to catch husbands.

There is a strong sense of decorum in this country.

You have to keep yourself always covered from neck to foot in the presence of women. You cannot so much as mention the normal functions of the body: nobody knows when anyone goes to the toilet — one has to live so circumspectly. In this country, you can blow your nose a thousand times into your handkerchief — there is no harm in that; but it is highly uncivilised to belch. Women sometimes are not embarrassed to expose their bodies above the waist — you must have seen the kind of low-cut gown they wear — but they say that to go bare-foot is as bad as being naked. Just as we always dwell on the soul, so they take care of the body, and there is no end to the cleaning and embellishing of it. One who fails to do this has no place in society.

Our method of cooking with cow-dung fuel and eating on the floor they consider eating like pigs: they say that the Hindus have no sense of disgust and that, like pigs, they eat cow-dung. The word "cow-dung" is taboo in English. On the other hand, numbers of people will drink water with the same glass without thinking of washing it, and they rarely observe the rule that things must be washed before cooking. But should the clothes of the cook be a little soiled, they will throw her out. The table-ware is all spick and span. They are the richest people on earth; their enjoyments and luxuries beggar description.

In Rajputana they imitate the Mohammedans in their mode of dining, which is, on the whole, good. They sit on a low seat and place their plate of rice on a low table. This is much better than spreading a banana leaf on the earthen floor plastered with cow-dung and filth. And how disastrous if the leaf gets torn! The Hindus did not know much about clothes or food. Moreover, whatever Hindu civilisation there was existed in the Punjab and the northwest provinces....

Our women lose caste if they put on shoes, but the Rajput women lose their caste if they don't put on shoes! Says Manu: "One shall always wear shoes". There is no denying that people should have a decent enough standard of living. I say they should be neat and clean even though not luxurious.... I say, why do we have to be Englishmen? It is enough for the present if we imitate our brothers of the western provinces. If group after group of Indians travel all over the world and back for some years, the face of India will be changed within twenty years by that alone; nothing else need be done. But how will anything happen if the people of one village do not visit the next? However, everything will take place by and by. By and by, the stubborn Bengali boys will awaken the country. But Manmatha Babu, you will have to stop this shameful business of marrying off nine-year-old girls. That is the root of all sins. It is a very great sin, my boy. Consider further what a terrible thing it was that when the government wanted to pass a law stopping early marriage, our worthless people raised a tremendous howl! If we don't stop it ourselves, the government will naturally intervene, and that is just what it wants to do. All the world cries fie upon us. You remain shut up in your homes, but the people outside spit upon you. How far can I quarrel with them? What a horror — even a father and mother allow their ten-year-old daughter to be given in marriage to a full-grown fat husband! O Lord, is there any punishment unless there has been a sin? It is all the fruit of Karma. If ours were not a terribly sinful nation, then why should it have been booted and beaten for seven hundred years?

Now, just as in our country the parents suffer a lot to have their daughter married, here in the same way the girls suffer — the parents only a little — it is the job of the girls to capture husbands. I am now closely associated with them in all their affairs; I am, as it were, a woman amongst women. Therefore, I have seen, and am seeing, all their play. To give dinners, to dance, to go to musical parties, go to the watering places — all that is all right. But all the while the young women are scheming within themselves how to capture husbands. They hang round the boys. The boys, on the other hand, are so cautious that, though they mingle with the girls and flirt with them all the time, when it is time to surrender they run away. The boys place the girls above themselves; they show them respect and slave for them; but the moment the girls stretch their hands to catch them, they run away beyond their reach. After many efforts of this kind, a girl succeeds in capturing a boy. If the girl has money, then many a boy dances attendance upon her, but the poor have great difficulty. If a poor girl is exceedingly beautiful, she can marry quickly; otherwise, she has to wait all her life. Just as in our country, so here, one marriage in a thousand takes place through love and courtship; the rest are based on money. After that, quarrel, and then, 'Get out!' — divorce. We do not have this; the only way out is to hang oneself. It is the same in all countries. Only, here the girls take matters into their own hands; and in our country, we get the help of the parents to give their married life a decent appearance. The result is the same in either case.

Nowadays, however, American girls don't want to marry. During the Civil War a large number of men were killed and women began to do all kinds of work. Since then, they have not wanted to give up the rights they have acquired. They earn their own living, and therefore they say, "There is no use in marrying. If we truly fall in love, then we shall marry; otherwise, we shall earn and meet our own expenses". Even if the father is a millionaire, the son has to earn enough before he marries. One may not marry depending on an allowance from the father. The girls also want the same thing now. When a son marries he becomes like a stranger to his own family, but when a girl marries she brings her husband, as it were, into her parents' home. Men will visit their wives' parents ten times, but rarely go to their own parents. Yet they are very much afraid of having their mothers-in-law on their neck.

In this country, there are rivers of wealth and waves of beauty, and an abundance of knowledge everywhere. The country is very healthy; they know how to enjoy this earth.... When princes of Europe become poor they come to marry here. The average American doesn't like this; but some rich, beautiful women fall for the titles. Yet it is very difficult for American women to live in Europe. The husbands of this country are slaves of their wives; but the European wives are slaves to their husbands — this the American women don't like. In everything, the men here have to say, 'Yes dear'; otherwise the wives lose face before people.

The women in America are very sentimental and have a mania for romance. I am, however, a strange sort of animal who hasn't any romantic feeling, and therefore they could not sustain any such feeling toward me and they show me great respect. I make all of them call me "father" or "brother". I don't allow them to come near me with any other feeling, and gradually they have all been straightened out. . . .

The ministers in this country . . . are eager to throw sinners into hell. A few of them are very good, however. . . . I have a great reputation among the women in this country. I have not as yet seen a single unchaste girl among the unmarried. It is either a widow or a married woman who turn unchaste. The unmarried girls are exceedingly good, because their future is bright. . . .

Those emaciated Western women, looking like old dried-up fruit, whom you see in India, are English, and the English are an ugly race amongst the Europeans. In America, the best blood strains of Europe have been blended, and therefore, the American women are very beautiful. And how they take care of their beauty! Can a woman retain her beauty if she gives birth to children . . . every hour from her tenth year on? Damn nonsense! What a terrible sin! Even the most beautiful woman of our country will look like a black owl here. Yet it must be admitted that the women of the Punjab have very well-drawn features. Many of the American women are very well educated and put many a learned professor to shame; nor do they care for anyone's opinion. And as regards their virtues: what kindness, what noble thought and action! Just think, if a man of this country were to visit India, nobody would even touch him; yet here I am allowed to do as I please in the houses of the best families — like their own son! I am like a child; their women shop for me, run errands for me. For example: I have just written to a girl for information about the machine, which she will gather carefully and send to me. Again, a phonograph was sent to the Maharaj of Khetri: the girls managed the whole affair very well. Lord! Lord! It is the difference between heaven and hell! "They are the goddess Lakshmi in beauty and the goddess Saraswati in talents and accomplishments." This cannot be achieved through the study of books. I say, can you send out some men and women to see the world? Only then will the country wake up — not through the reading of books. The men here are very clever in earning wealth. Where others do not see even dust, there they see gold. Whoever will leave India and visit another country will earn great merit.

Keeping aloof from the community of nations is the only cause for the downfall of India. Since the English came, they have been forcing you back into communion with other nations, and you are visibly rising again. Everyone that comes out of the country confers a benefit on the whole nation; for it is by doing that alone that your horizon will expand. And as women cannot avail themselves of this advantage, they have made almost no progress in India. There is no station of rest; either you progress upwards or you go back and die out. The only sign of life is going outward and forward and expansion. Contraction is death. Why should you do good to others? Because that is the only condition of life; thereby you expand beyond your little self; you live and grow. All narrowness, all contraction, all selfishness is simply slow suicide, and when a nation commits the fatal mistake of contracting itself and of thus cutting off all expansion and life, it must die. Women similarly must go forward or become idiots and soulless tools in the hands of their tyrannical lords. The children are the result of the combination of the tyrant and the idiot, and they are slaves. And this is the whole history of modern India. Oh, who would break this horrible crystallisation of death? Lord help us! (This paragraph was written in English.)

Gradually all this will come about: "One should

cross a road slowly and cautiously; one should patch a quilt carefully and cautiously; so should one be slow and cautious in crossing a mountain".

The papers have arrived duly and in good shape; there has not been any difficulty about that. The enemy has been silenced. Consider this: They have allowed me, an unknown young man, to live among their grown-up young daughters, and when my own countryman, Mazoomdar, says I am a rogue, they don't pay any attention! How noble they are, and how kind! I shall not be able to repay this debt even in a hundred lives, I am like a foster son to the American women; they are really my mother. If they don't flourish in every way, who would?

A while back several hundred intellectual men and women were gathered in a place called Greenacre, and I was there for nearly two months. Every day I would sit in our Hindu fashion under a tree, and my followers and disciples would sit on the grass all around me. Every morning I would instruct them, and how earnest they were!

The whole country now knows me. The ministers are very angry; but, naturally, not all of them. There are many followers of mine amongst the learned ministers of this country. The ignorant and the stubborn amongst them don't understand anything but only make trouble, and thereby they only hurt themselves. But abusing me, Mazoomdar has lost three-fourths of what little popularity he had in this country. I have been adopted by them. When anyone abuses me he is condemned everywhere by the women.

I cannot say when I shall return to India, possibly next winter. There I shall have to wander, and here also I do the same.

There is nothing more to add. Please don't make this letter public. You understand, I have to be careful about every word I say — I am now a public man. Everybody is watching, particularly the clergy.

Yours faithfully,
Vivekananda.

XXIV — KALI

Translated from Bengali

U.S.A.
(November ?) 1894.

DEAR KALI [ABHEDANANDA],

Thanks for all that I come to know from your letter. I had no news of the telegram in question having appeared in the Tribune. It is six months since I left Chicago, and I have not been yet free to return. So I could not keep myself well posted. You have taken great pains indeed! And for this how can I thank you adequately? You have all evinced a wonderful capacity for work. And how can Shri Ramakrishna's words prove false? — You have got wonderful spirit in you. About Shashi Sanyal, I have already written. Nothing remains undetected, through the grace of Shri Ramakrishna. But let him found a sect or whatever he will, what harm? "— May blessings attend your path!" Secondly, I could not catch the drift of your letter. I shall collect my own funds to build a monastery for ourselves, and if people criticise me for it, I see nothing in this to affect us either way. You have your minds pitched high and steady, it will do you no harm. May you have exceeding love for one another among yourselves, and it would be enough to have an attitude of indifference towards public criticisms. Kalikrishna Babu has deep love for the cause and is a great man. Please convey my special love to him. So long as there is no feeling of disunion amongst you, through the grace of the Lord, I assure you, there is no danger for you, " mountains". "— All noble undertakings are fraught with obstacles". It is quite in the nature of things. Keep up the deepest mental poise. Take not even the slightest notice of what puerile creatures may be saying against you. Indifference, indifference, indifference! I have already written to Shashi (Ramakrishnananda) in detail. Please do not send newspapers and tracts any more. "Take the husking hammer to heaven, and there it will do its husking", as the Bengali saying goes. The same trudging about here as it was in India, only with the carrying of others' loads added! How can I procure customers for people's books in this land? I am only one amongst the many here and nothing more. Whatever the papers and things of that sort in this country write about me, I make an offering of to the Fire-God. You also do the same. That is the proper course.

A bit of public demonstration was necessary for Guru Maharaja's work. It is done, and so far so good. Now you must on no account pay any heed to what the rabble may be prattling about us. Whether I make my pile or do whatever else I am reported to, shall the opinions of the riff-raff stand in the way of His work? My dear brother, you are yet a boy, while I am growing grey. What regard I have for the pronouncements and opinions of such people, you should guess from this. So long as you gird up your loins and rally behind me, there is no fear even if the whole world combine against us. This much I understand that I shall have to take up a very lofty attitude, I should not, I think, write to anyone except to you. By the by, where is Gunanidhi? Try to find him out and bring him to the Math with all kindness. He is a very sincere man and highly learned. You must try your best to secure two plots of land, let people say what they will. Let anyone write anything for or against me in the papers; you shouldn't take the slightest notice. And my dear brother, I beseech you repeatedly not to send me any more newspapers by the basketful. How can you talk of rest now? We shall have rest awhile only when we give up this body. Just do once get up the celebration, brother, in that spirit, so that all the country around may burn with enthusiasm. Bravo! Capital indeed! The whole band of scoffers will be swept away by the tidal wave of love. You are elephants, forsooth, what do you fear from an ant-bite?

The address (The Address presented by the citizens of Calcutta who gathered at a meeting at the Town Hall on September 5, 1894, under the Presidentship of Raja Pyari Mohan Mookherjee.) you sent me reached me long ago and the reply to it has also been despatched to Pyari Babu (18 Nov. 1894).

Bear in mind — the eyes are two in number and so the ears, but the mouth is but one! Indifference, indifference, indifference! "— The doer of good deeds never comes to grief, my dear". Ah! To fear! and whom are we going to fear, brother? Here the missionaries and their ilk have howled themselves into silence — and the whole world will but do likewise.

— Whether people skilled in policy praise or blame, whether the Goddess of Fortune favours or goes her way, whether death befalls today or after hundreds of years — persons of steady mind never swerve from the path of righteousness" (Bhartrihari, Nitishataka)

You need not even mix with the humdrub people, nor beg of them either. The Lord is supplying everything and will do so in future. What fear, my brother? All great undertakings are achieved through mighty obstacles.

— You valiant one, put forth your manly efforts; wretched people under the grip of lust and gold deserve to be looked upon with indifference. Now I have got a firm footing in this country, and therefore need no assistance. But my one prayer to you all is that you should apply to the service of the Lord that active impulse of manliness which your eagerness to help me through brotherly love has brought out in you. Do not open out your mind, unless you feel it will be positively beneficial. Use agreeable and wholesome language towards even the greatest enemy. The desire for fame, for riches, for enjoyment is quite natural to every mortal, dear brother, and if that agrees well with serving both ways (i.e. serving both God and mammon), why, all men would exhibit great zeal! It is only the great saint who can work, making a mountain of an atom of virtue in others and cherishing no desire but that of the good of the world —"Bhartrihari, Nitishataka."

Therefore let dullards whose intellect is steeped in ignorance and who look upon the non-Self as all in all, play out their boyish pranks. They will of themselves leave off the moment they find it too hot. Let them try to spit upon the moon — it will but recoil upon themselves. — Godspeed to them! If they have got anything substantial in them, who can bar their success? But if it be only empty swagger due to jealousy, then all will be in vain. Haramohan has sent rosaries. All right. But you should know that religion of the type that obtains in our country does not go here. You must suit it to the taste of the people. If you ask them to become Hindus, they will all give you a wide berth and hate you, as we do the Christian missionaries. They like some of the ideas of the Hindu scriptures — that is all. Nothing more than that, you should know. The men, most of them, do not trouble about religion and all that. The women are a little interested — that is all, but no large doses of it! A few thousands of people have faith in the Advaita doctrine. But they will give you the go-by if you talk obscure mannerisms about sacred writings, caste, or women. Everything proceeds slowly, by degrees. Patience, purity, perseverance.

Yours etc.,
Vivekananda.

XXV — BROTHER SHIVANANDA

Translated from Bengali

U.S.A.,
1894.

DEAR BROTHER SHIVANANDA,

Your letter just reached me. Perhaps by this time you have received my other letters and learnt that it is not necessary to send anything to America any more. Too much of everything is bad. This newspaper booming has given me popularity no doubt, but its effect is more in India than here. Here, on the other hand, constant booming creates a distaste in the minds of the higher class people; so enough. Now try to organise yourselves in India on the lines of these meetings. You need not send anything more in this country. As to money, I have determined first to build some place for Mother, (Holy Mother, Shri Sarada Devi.) for women require it first.... I can send nearly Rs. 7,000 for a place for Mother. If the place is first secured, then I do not care for anything else. I hope to be able to get Rs. 1,600 a year from this country even when I am gone. That sum I will make over to the support of the Women's place, and then it will grow. I have written to you already to secure a place....

I would have, before this, returned to India, but India has no money. Thousands honour Ramakrishna Paramahamsa, but nobody will give a cent — that is India.... In the meanwhile live in harmony at any price. The world cares little for principles. They care for persons. They will hear with patience the words of a man they like, however nonsense, and will not listen to anyone they do not like. Think of this and modify your conduct accordingly. Everything will come all right. Be the servant if you will rule. That is the real secret. Your love will tell even if your words be harsh. Instinctively men feel the love clothed in whatever language. (These two paragraphs and the last half of the fourth were written in English.)

My dear brother, that Ramakrishna Paramahamsa was God incarnate, I have not the least doubt; but then you must let people find out for themselves what he used to teach — you cannot thrust these things upon them — this is my only objection.

Let people speak out their own opinions, why should we object? Without studying Ramakrishna Paramahamsa first, one can never understand the real import of the Vedas, the Vedanta, of the Bhâgavata and the other Purânas. His life is a searchlight of infinite power thrown upon the whole mass of Indian religious thought. He was the living commentary to the Vedas and to their aim. He had lived in one life the whole cycle of the national religious existence in India.

Whether Bhagavân Shri Krishna was born at all we are not sure; and Avataras like Buddha and Chaitanya are monotonous; Ramakrishna Paramahamsa is the latest and the most perfect — the concentrated embodiment of knowledge, love, renunciation, catholicity, and the desire to serve mankind. So where is anyone to compare with him? He must have been born in vain who cannot appreciate him! My supreme good fortune is that I am his servant through life after life. A single word of his is to me far weightier than the Vedas and the Vedanta. — Oh, I am the servant of the servants of his servants. But narrow bigotry militates against his principles, and this makes me cross. Rather let his name be drowned in oblivion, and his teachings bear fruit instead! Why, was he a slave to fame? Certain fishermen and illiterate people called Jesus Christ a God, but the literate people killed him. Buddha was honoured in his lifetime by a number of merchants and cowherds. But Ramakrishna has been worshipped in his lifetime — towards the end of this nineteenth century — by the demons and giants of the university as God incarnate.... Only a few things have been jotted down in the books about them (Krishna, Buddha, Christ, etc.). "One must be a wonderful housekeeper with whom we have never yet lived!" so the Bengali proverb goes. But here is a man in whose company we have been day and night and yet consider him to be a far greater personality than any of them. Can you understand this phenomenon?

You have not yet understood the wonderful significance of Mother's life — none of you. But gradually you will know. Without Shakti (Power) there is no regeneration for the world. Why is it that our country is the weakest and the most backward of all countries? — Because Shakti is held in dishonour there. Mother has been born to revive that wonderful Shakti in India; and making her the nucleus, once more will Gârgis and Maitreyis be born into the world. Dear brother, you understand little now, but by degrees you will come to know it all. Hence it is her Math that I want first.... Without the grace of Shakti nothing is to be accomplished. What do I find in America and Europe? — the worship of Shakti, the worship of Power. Yet they worship Her ignorantly through sense-gratification. Imagine, then, what a lot of good they will achieve who will worship Her with all purity, in a Sattvika spirit, looking upon Her as their mother! I am coming to understand things clearer every day, my insight is opening out more and more. Hence we must first build a Math for Mother. First Mother and Mother's daughters, then Father and Father's sons — can you understand this? ... To me, Mother's grace is a hundred thousand times more valuable than Father's. Mother's grace, Mother's blessings are all paramount to me.... Please pardon me. I am a little bigoted there, as regards Mother. If but Mother orders, her demons can work anything. Brother, before proceeding to America I wrote to Mother to bless me. Her blessings came, and at one bound I cleared the ocean. There, you see. In this terrible winter I am lecturing from place to place and fighting against odds, so that funds may be collected for Mother's Math. Baburam's mother must have lost her sense owing to old age and that is why she is about to worship Durga in the earthen image, ignoring the living one. (Viz. Holy Mother Shri Sarada Devi.) Brother, faith is very difficult to achieve. Brother, I shall show how to worship the living Durga and then only shall I be worthy of my name. I shall be relieved when you will have purchased a plot of land and established there the living Durga, the Mother. Till then I am not returning to my native land. As soon as you can do that, I shall have a sigh of relief after sending the money. Do you accomplish this festival of Durga of mine by making all the necessary arrangements. Girish Ghosh is adoring the Mother splendidly; blessed is he, and blessed are his followers. Brother, often enough, when I am reminded of the Mother, I ejaculate, "What after all is Rama?" Brother, that is where my fanaticism lies, I tell you. Of Ramakrishna, you may aver, my brother, that he was an Incarnation or whatever else you may like but fie on him who has no devotion for the Mother. Niranjan has a militant disposition, but he has great devotion for Mother and all his vagaries I can easily put up with. He is now doing the most marvellous work. I am keeping myself well posted. And you too have done excellently in co-operating with the Madrasis. Dear brother, I expect much from you, you should organise all for conjoint work. As soon as you have secured the land for Mother, I go to India straight. It must be a big plot; let there be a mud-house to begin with, in due course I shall erect a decent building, don't be afraid.

The chief cause of malaria lies in water. Why do you not construct two or three filters? If you first boil the water and then filter it, it will be harmless. .

. . Please buy two big Pasteur's bacteria-proof filters. Let the cooking be done in that water and use it for drinking purposes also, and you will never hear of malaria any more. . . . On and on, work, work, work, this is only the beginning.

Yours ever,
Vivekananda.

XXVI — BRAHMANANDA

Translated from Bengali

Salutation to Bhagavan Ramakrishna!

1894.

DEAR AND BELOVED (Swami Brahmananda.),

. . . Well, do you think there is any religion left in India! The paths of knowledge, devotion, and Yoga — all have gone, and now there remains only that of Don't touchism — "Don't touch me! Don't touch me!" The whole world is impure, and I alone am pure. Lucid Brahmajnâna! Bravo! Great God! Nowadays Brahman is neither in the recesses of the heart, nor in the highest heaven, nor in all beings — now He is in the cooking-pot. Formerly the characteristic of a noble-minded man was "— Pleasing the whole universe by one's numerous acts of service" but now it is — I am pure and the whole world is impure — go and get money and set it at my feet. . . . Tell the sapient sage who writes to me to finish my preaching work here and return home, . . . that this country is more my home. What is there in Hindusthan? Who appreciates religion? Who appreciates learning?

To return home! Where is the home! I do not care for liberation, or for devotion, I would rather go to a hundred thousand hells, " — this is my religion. I do not want to have any connection with lazy, hard-hearted, cruel and selfish men. He whose good fortune it is, may help in this great cause.

. . . Please convey to all my love, I want the help of everyone. Neither money pays, nor name, nor fame, nor learning; it is character that can cleave through adamantine walls of difficulties. Bear this in mind. . . .

Yours ever in love,
Vivekananda.

XXVII — ALASINGA

1895.

DEAR ALASINGA,

We have no organisation, nor want to build any. Each one is quite independent to teach, quite free to preach whatever he or she likes.

If you have the spirit within, you will never fail to attract others. Theosophists' method can never be ours, for the very simple reason that they are an organised sect, we are not.

Individuality is my motto. I have no ambition beyond training individuals up. I know very little; that little I teach without reserve; where I am ignorant, I confess it as such, and never am I so glad as when I find people being helped by Theosophists, Christians, Mohammedans, or anybody in the world. I am a Sannyasin; as such I consider myself as a servant, not as a master in the world. . . . If people love me, they are welcome, if they hate, they are also welcome.

Each one will have to save himself, each one to do his own work. I seek no help, I reject none. Nor have I any right in the world to be helped. Whosoever has helped me or will help, it will be their mercy to me, not my right, and as such I am eternally grateful.

When I became a Sannyasin, I consciously took the step, knowing that this body would have to die of starvation. What of that, I am a beggar. My friends are poor, I love the poor, I welcome poverty. I am glad that I sometimes have to starve. I ask help of none. What is the use? Truth will preach itself, it will not die for the want of the helping hands of me!

"Making happiness and misery the same, making success and failure the same, fight thou on" (Gita). It is that eternal love, unruffled equanimity under all circumstances, and perfect freedom from jealousy or animosity that will tell. That will tell, nothing else.

Yours,
Vivekananda.

XXVIII — BROTHER

54 W. 33 NEW YORK,
25th April, 1895.

DEAR BROTHER (To Dr. I. Janes),

I was away in the Catskill mountains and it was almost impossible to get a letter regularly posted from where I was — so accept my apology for the delay in offering you my most heartfelt thanks for your letter in the "Eagle".

It was so scholarly, truthful and noble and withal so permeated with your natural universal love for the good and true everywhere. It is a great work to bring this world into a spirit of sympathy with each other but it should be done no doubt when such brave souls as you still hold your own. Lord help you ever and ever my brother and may you live long to carry on the mighty work you and your society has undertaken.

With my gratitude and love to you and to the members of the Ethical Society.

I remain Yours ever truly,
Vivekananda.

XXIX — DEAR __

54 W. 33 NEW YORK,
May, 1895.

DEAR __,

Since writing to you my pupils have come round me with help, and the classes will go on nicely now no doubt.

I was so glad at it because teaching has become a part of my life, as necessary to my life as eating or breathing.

Yours,
Vivekananda.

PS. I saw a lot of things about __ in an English paper, the Borderland. __ is doing good work in India, making the Hindus, very much to appreciate their own religion. . . . I do not find any scholarship in __'s writing, . . . nor do I find any spirituality whatever. However Godspeed to anyone who wants to do good to the world.

How easily this world can be duped by humbugs and what a mass of fraud has gathered over the devoted head of poor humanity since the dawn of civilisation.

XXX — RAKHAL

Translated from Bengali

19 WEST 38th STREET, NEW YORK,
August, 1895.

BELOVED RAKHAL,

. . . I am now in New York City. The city is hot in summer, exactly like Calcutta. You perspire profusely, and there is not a breath of air. I made a tour in the north for a couple of months. Please answer this letter by return of post to England, for which I shall start before this will have reached you.

Yours affectionately,
Vivekananda.

XXXI — ALASINGA

U.S.A.
March, 1896.

DEAR ALASINGA,

Last week I wrote you about the Brahmavâdin. I forgot to write about the Bhakti lectures. They ought to be published in a book all together. A few hundreds may be sent to America to Goodyear in New York. Within twenty days I sail for England. I have other big books on Karma, Jnana, and Raja Yogas — the Karma is out already, the Raja will be a very big book and is already in the Press. The Jnana will have to be published, I think, in England.

A letter you published from Kripananda in the Brahmavadin was rather unfortunate. Kripananda is smarting under the blows the Christians have given him and that sort of letter is vulgar, pitching into everybody. It is not in accord with the tone of the Brahmavadin. So in future when Kripananda writes, tone down everything that is an attack upon any sect, however cranky or crude. Nothing which is against any sect, good or bad, should get into the Brahmavadin. Of course, we must not show active sympathy with frauds. Again let me remind you that the paper is too technical to find any subscriber here. The average Western neither knows nor cares to know all about jaw-breaking Sanskrit terms and technicalities. The paper is well fitted for India — that I see. Every word of special pleading should be eliminated from the Editorials, and you must always remember that you are addressing the whole world, not India alone, and that the same world is entirely ignorant of what you have got to tell them. Use the translation of every Sanskrit term carefully and make things as easy as possible.

Before this reaches you I will be in England. So address me c/o E. T. Sturdy, Esq., High View, Caversham, Eng.

Yours etc.,
Vivekananda.

XXXII — DEAR

Translated from Bengali

HIGH VIEW, CAVERSHAM, READING,
27th April, 1896.

DEAR (Members of the Alambazar Math),

... Let me write something for you all. It is not for gaining personal authority that I do this, but for your good and for fulfilling the purpose for which the Lord came. He gave me the charge of you all, and you shall contribute to the great well-being of the world — though most of you are not yet aware of it — this is the special reason of my writing to you. It will be a great pity if any feeling of jealousy or egotism gain ground amongst you. Is it possible for those to establish cordial relations on earth who cannot cordially live with one another for any length of time? No doubt it is an evil to be bound by laws, but it is necessary at the immature stage to be guided by rules; in other words, as the Master used to say that the sapling must be hedged round, and so on. Secondly, it is quite natural for idle minds to indulge in gossip, and faction-mongering, and so forth. Hence I jot down the following hints. If you follow them, you will undoubtedly prosper, but if you don't do so, then there is a danger of all our labours coming to naught.

First let me write about the management of the Math:

1. For the purposes of the Math please hire a commodious house or garden, where everyone may have a small room to himself. There must be a spacious hall where the books may be kept, and a smaller room for meeting the visitors. If possible, there should be another big hall in the house where study of the scriptures and religious discourses will be held every day for the public.

2. Anyone wishing to visit anybody in the Math should see him only and depart, without troubling others.

3. By turns someone should be present in the hall for a few hours every day for the public, so that they

may get satisfactory replies to what they come to ask.

4. Everyone must keep to his room and except on special business must not go to others' rooms. Anyone who wishes may go to the Library and read, but it should be strictly forbidden to smoke there or talk with others. The reading should be silent.

5. It shall be wholly forbidden to huddle together in a room and chat the whole day away, with any number of outsiders coming and joining in the hubbub.

6. Only those that are seekers after religion may come and peacefully wait in the Visitors' Hall and when they have seen the particular persons they want, they should depart. Or, if they have any general question to ask, they should refer to the person in charge of that function for the day and leave.

7. Tale-bearing, caballing, or reporting scandals about others should be altogether eschewed.

8. A small room should serve as the office. The Secretary should live in that room, which should contain paper, ink, and other materials for letter-writing. He should keep an account of the income and expenditure. All correspondence should come to him, and he should deliver all letters unopened to their addressees. Books and pamphlets should be sent to the Library.

9. There will be a small room for smoking, which should not be indulged in outside this room.

10. He who wants to indulge in invectives or show temper must do so outside the boundaries of the Math. This should not be deviated from even by an inch.

THE GOVERNING BODY

1. Every year a President should be elected by a majority of votes. The next year, another, and so on.

2. For this year make Brahmananda the President and likewise make another the Secretary, and elect a third man for superintending the worship etc., as well as the arrangement of food.

3. The Secretary shall have another function, viz to keep watch over the general health. Regarding this I have three instructions to give: (i) In every room for each man there shall be a Nair charpoy, mattress, etc. Everyone must keep his room clean. (ii) All arrangements must be made to provide clear and pure water for drinking and cooking purposes, for it is a deadly sin to cook sacramental food in impure or unclean water.

(iii) Give everyone two ochre cloaks of the type that you have made for Saradananda, and see that clothing is kept clean.

4. Anyone wishing to be a Sannyâsin should be admitted as a Brahmacharin first. He should live one year at the Math and one year outside, after which he may be initiated into Sannyâsa.

5. Make over charge of the worship to one of these Brahmacharins, and change them now and then.

DEPARTMENTS

There shall be the following departments in the Math:

I. Study. II. Propaganda. III. Religious Practice.

I. Study — The object of this department is to provide books and teachers for those who want to study. Every morning and evening the teachers should be ready for them.

II. Propaganda — Within the Math, and abroad. The preachers in the Math should teach the inquirers by reading out scriptures to them and by means of question-classes. The preachers abroad will preach from village to village and try to start Maths like the above in different places.

III. Religious Practice — This department will try to provide those who want to practise with the requisites for this. But it should not be allowed that because one has taken to religious practice he will prevent others from study or preaching. Any one infringing this rule shall be immediately asked to clear out, and this is imperative.

The preachers at home should give lessons on devotion, knowledge, Yoga, and work by turns; for this, the days and hours should be fixed, and the routine hung up at the door of the class-room. That is to say, a seeker after devotion may not present himself on the day fixed for knowledge and feel wounded thereby; and so on.

None of you are fit for the Vâmâchâra form of practice. Therefore this should on no account be practised at the Math. Anyone demurring to this must step out of this Order. This form of practice must never even be mentioned in the Math. Ruin shall seize the wicked man, both here and hereafter, who would introduce vile Vamachara into His fold!

SOME GENERAL REMARKS

1. If any woman comes to have a talk with a Sannyasin, she should do it in the Visitors' Hall. No woman shall be allowed to enter any other room — except the Worship-room.

2. No Sannyasin shall be allowed to reside in the Women's Math. Anyone refusing to obey this rule shall be expelled from the Math. "Better an empty fold than a wicked herd."

3. Men of evil character shall be rigorously kept out. On no pretence shall their shadow even cross the threshold of my room. If anyone amongst you become wicked, turn him out at once, whoever he be. We want no black sheep. The Lord will bring lots of good people.

4. Any woman can come to the class-room (or preaching hall) during class time or preaching hour, but must leave the place directly when that period is over.

5. Never show temper, or harbour jealousy, or backbite another in secret. It would be the height of cruelty and hard-heartedness to take note of others' shortcoming instead of rectifying one's own.

6. There should be fixed hours of meals. Everyone must have a seat and a low dining table. He will sit on the former and put his plate on the latter, as is the custom in Rajputana.

THE OFFICE-BEARERS

All the office-bearers you should elect by ballot, as was the mandate of Lord Buddha. That is to say, one should propose that such and such should be the President this year; and all should write on bits of paper 'yes' or 'no' and put them in a pitcher. If the 'yes' have a majority, he should be elected President, and so on. Though you should elect office-bearers in this way, yet I suggest that this year Brahmananda should be President, Nirmalananda, Secretary and Treasurer, Sadananda Librarian, and Ramakrishnananda, Abhedananda, Turiyananda, and Trigunatitananda should take charge of the teaching and preaching work by turns, and so on.

It is no doubt a good idea that Trigunatita has of starting a magazine. But I shall consent to it if only you can work jointly.

About doctrines and so forth I have to say only this, that if anyone accepts Paramahamsa Deva as Avatâra etc., it is all right; if he doesn't do so, it is just the same. The truth about it is that in point of character, Paramahamsa Deva beats all previous records; and as regards teaching, he was more liberal, more original, and more progressive than all his predecessors. In other words, the older Teachers were rather one-sided, while the teaching of this new Incarnation or Teacher is that the best point of Yoga, devotion, knowledge, and work must be combined now so as to form a new society.... The older ones were no doubt good, but this is the new religion of this age — the synthesis of Yoga, knowledge, devotion, and work — the propagation of knowledge and devotion to all, down to the very lowest, without distinction of age or sex. The previous Incarnations were all right, but they have been synthesised in the person of Ramakrishna. For the ordinary man and the beginner, steady devotion (Nishthâ) to an ideal is of paramount importance. That is to say, teach them that all great Personalities should be duly honoured, but homage should be paid now to Ramakrishna. There can be no vigour without steady devotion. Without it one cannot preach with the intensity of a Mahâvira (Hanumân). Besides, the previous ones have become rather old. Now we have a new India, with its new God, new religion, and new Vedas. When, O Lord, shall our land be free from this eternal dwelling upon the past? Well, a little bigotry also is a necessity. But we must harbour no antagonistic feelings towards others.

If you consider it wise to be guided by my ideas and if you follow these rules, then I shall supply on all necessary funds.... Moreover, please show this letter to Gour-Mâ, Yogin-Mâ, and others, and through them establish a Women's Math. Let Gour-Ma be the President there for one year, and so on. But none of you shall be allowed to visit the place. They will manage their own affairs. They will not have to work at your dictation. I shall supply all necessary expenses for that work also.

May the Lord guide you in the right direction! Two persons went to see the Lord Jagannatha. One of them beheld the Deity — while the other saw some trash that was haunting his mind! My friends, many have no doubt served the Master, but whenever anyone would be disposed to consider himself an extraordinary personage, he should think that although he was associated with Shri Ramakrishna, he has seen only the trash that was uppermost in his mind! Were it not so, he would manifest the results. The Master himself used to quote, "They would sing and dance in the name of the Lord but come to grief in the end." The root of that degeneration is egotism — to think that one is just as great as any other, indeed! "He used to love me too!" — one would plead. Alas, Nick Bottom, would you then be thus translated? Would such a man envy or quarrel with another and degrade himself? Bear in mind that through His grace lots of men will be turned out with the nobility of gods — ay, wherever His mercy would drop! . . . Obedience is the first duty. Well, just do with alacrity what I ask you to. Let me see how you carry out these few small things. Then gradually great things will come to pass.

Yours,
Vivekananda.

PS. Please read the contents of this letter to all, and let me know whether you consider the suggestions worth carrying out. Please tell Brahmananda that he who is the servant of all is their true master. He never becomes a leader in whose love there is a consideration of high or low. He whose love knows no end, and never stops to consider high or low, has the whole world lying at his feet.

XXXIII — SISTER

63 ST. GEORGE'S ROAD, LONDON,
May, 1896.

DEAR SISTER,

In London once more. The climate now in England is nice and cool. We have fire in the grate. We have a whole house to ourselves, you know, this time. It is small but convenient, and in London they do not cost so much as in America. Don't you know what I was thinking — about your mother! I just wrote her a letter and duly posted it to her, care of Monroe & Co., 7 Rue Scribe, Paris. Some old friends are here, and Miss MacLeod came over from the Continent. She is good as gold, and as kind as ever. We have a nice little family, in the house, with another monk from India. Poor man! — a typical Hindu with nothing of that pluck and go which I have, he is always dreamy and gentle and sweet! That won't do. I will try to put a little activity into him. I have had two classes already — they will go on for four or five months and after that to India I go. But it is to Amerique — there where the heart is. I love the Yankee land. I like to see new things. I do not care a fig to loaf about old ruins and mope a life out about old histories and keep sighing about the ancients. I have too much vigour in my blood for that. In America is the place, the people, the opportunity for everything. I have become horribly radical. I am just going to India to see what I can do in that awful mass of conservative jelly-fish, and start a new thing, entirely new — simple, strong, new and fresh as the first born baby. The eternal, the infinite, the omnipresent, the omniscient is a principle, not a person. You, I, and everyone are but embodiments of that principle, and the more of this infinite principle is embodied in a person, the greater is he, and all in the end will be the perfect embodiment of that and thus all will be one as they are now essentially. This is all there is of religion, and the practice is through this feeling of oneness that is love. All old fogy forms are mere old superstitions. Now, why struggle to keep them alive? Why give thirsty people ditch-water to drink whilst the river of life and truth flows by? This is only human selfishness, nothing else. Life is short — time is flying — that place and people where one's ideas work best should be the country and the people for everyone. Ay, for a dozen bold hearts, large, noble, and sincere!

I am very well indeed and enjoying life immensely.

Yours ever with love,
Vivekananda.

XXXIV — SHASHI

Translated from Bengali

C/O E. T. STURDY, ESQ.
HIGH VIEW, CAVERSHAM, READING,
May (?) 1896.

DEAR SHASHI (RAMAKRISHNANADA),

. . . This City of London is a sea of human heads — ten or fifteen Calcuttas put together. One is apt to be lost in the mazes unless he arranges for somebody to meet him on arrival. . . . However, let Kali start at once. If he be late in starting like Sharat, better let no one come. It won't do to loiter and procrastinate like that. It is a task that requires the height of Rajas (activity). . . . Our whole country is steeped in Tamas, and nothing but that. We want Rajas first, and Sattva will come afterwards — a thing far, far removed.

Yours affectionately,
Vivekananda.

XXXV — ADHYAPAKJI

63 ST. GEORGE'S ROAD,
LONDON, S.W.
16th May, 1896.

DEAR ADHYAPAKJI, (Prof. John Henry Wright. The letter was written on the death of his daughter, aged 16.)

Last mail brought the very very sad news of the blow that has fallen on you.

This is the world my brother — this illusion of Mâyâ — the Lord alone is true. The forms are evanescent; but the spirit, being in the Lord and of the Lord, is immortal and omnipresent. All that we ever had are round us this minute, for the spirit can neither come nor go, it only changes its plane of manifestation.

You are strong and pure and so is Mrs. Wright, and I am sure that the Divine in you has arisen and thrown away the lie and delusion that there can be death for anyone.

"He who sees in this world of manifoldness that one support of everything, in the midst of a world of unconsciousness that one eternal consciousness, in this evanescent world that one eternal and unchangeable, unto him belongs eternal peace."

May the peace of the Lord descend upon you and yours in abundance is the prayer of

Your ever loving friend,
Vivekananda.

XXXVI — MISS NOBLE

63 ST. GEORGE'S ROAD, LONDON,
7th June, 1896.

DEAR MISS NOBLE,

My ideal indeed can be put into a few words and that is: to preach unto mankind their divinity, and how to make it manifest in every movement of life.

This world is in chain of superstition. I pity the oppressed, whether man or woman, and I pity more the oppressors.

One idea that I see clear as daylight is that misery is caused by ignorance and nothing else. Who will give the world light? Sacrifice in the past has been the Law, it will be, alas, for ages to come. The earth's bravest and best will have to sacrifice themselves for the good of many, for the welfare of all. Buddhas by the hundred are necessary with eternal love and pity.

Religions of the world have become lifeless mockeries. What the world wants is character. The world is in need of those whose life is one burning love, selfless. That love will make every word tell like thunderbolt.

It is no superstition with you, I am sure, you have the making in you of a world-mover, and others will also come. Bold words and bolder deeds are what we want. Awake, awake, great ones! The world is burning with misery. Can you sleep? Let us call and call till the sleeping gods awake, till the god within answers to the call. What more is in life? What greater work? The details come to me as I go. I never make plans. Plans grow and work themselves. I only say, awake, awake!

May all blessings attend you for ever!

Yours affectionately,
Vivekananda.

XXXVII — FRIEND AND BROTHER

63 ST. GEORGE'S ROAD,
LONDON, S.W.
6th July, 1896.

DEAR FRIEND AND BROTHER, (To Dr. Lewis I. Janes)

Yours of the 25th June has duly reached and gave me great pleasure. I am so glad to see the noble work progressing. I had learnt with the greatest delight from Mrs. Bull of the work that is going to be done in Cambridge this winter and no better person could have been selected to direct it as yourself. May all power attend you. I will be only too glad to write for the magazine from time to time and my first instalment was to be in a few weeks, when I hope to get some leisure. Certainly it goes without saying that no one of the types we call religious ought to die — they like races require fresh infusion of blood in the form of ideas. It is wonderful to be able to sympathise with others from their standpoints of view.

By this time Goodwin and the other Swami must have reached America. They I trust will be of help to you in your noble work. Godspeed to all good work and infinite blessings on all workers for good.

Yours ever in the truth,
Vivekananda.

XXXVIII — SHARAT CHANDRA CHAKRAVARTI

Written to Sj. Sharat Chandra Chakravarti, B.A.

Translated from Sankrit

DARJEELING,
19th March, 1897.

Salutation to Bhagavan Ramakrishna!

May you prosper! May this letter conveying blessings and cordial embrace make you happy! Nowadays this fleshy tabernacle of mine is comparatively well. Meseems, the snow-capped peaks of the Himalayas, the Chief among mountains, bring even the moribund back to life. And the fatigue of the journeys also seems to have somewhat abated. I have already felt that yearning for Freedom — potent enough to put the heart into turmoil — which your letter suggests you are experiencing. It is this yearning that gradually brings on a concentration of the mind on the eternal Brahman. "There is no other way to go by." May this desire blaze up more and more in you, until all your past Karma and future tendencies are absolutely annihilated. Close upon the heels of that will follow, all on a sudden, the manifestation of Brahman, and with it the destruction of all craving for the sense-world. That this freedom-in-life is approaching for your welfare is easily to be inferred from the strength of your fervour. Now I pray to that world-teacher, Shri Ramakrishna, the Preacher of the gospel of universal synthesis, to manifest himself in the region of your heart, so that, having attained the consummation of your desires, you may with an undaunted heart try your best to deliver others from this dreadful ocean of infatuation. May you be ever possessed of valour! It is the hero alone, not the coward, who has liberation within his easy reach. Gird up your loins, ye heroes, for before you are your enemies — the dire army of infatuation. It is undoubtedly true that "all great achievements are fraught with numerous impediments"; still you should exert your utmost for your end. Behold, how men are already in the jaws of the shark of infatuation! Oh, listen to their piteous heart-rending wails. Advance, forward, O ye brave souls, to set free those that are in fetters, to lessen the burden of woe of the miserable, and to illumine the abysmal darkness of ignorant hearts! Look, how the Vedanta proclaims by beat of drums, "Be fearless!" May that solemn sound remove the heart's knot of all denizens of the earth.

Ever your well-wisher,
Vivekananda.

XXXIX — MRS. BULL

ALAMBAZAR MATH, CALCUTTA,
May 5th, 1897.

DEAR MRS. BULL,

I have been to Darjeeling for a month to recuperate my shattered health. I am very much better now. The disease disappeared altogether in Darjeeling. I am going tomorrow to Almora, another hill station, to perfect this improvement.

Things are looking not very hopeful here as I have already written you — though the whole nation has risen as one man to honour me and people went almost mad over me! The practical part cannot be had in India. Again, the price of the land has gone up very much near Calcutta. My idea at present is to start three centres at three capitals. These would be my normal schools, from thence I want to invade India.

India is already Ramakrishna's whether I live a few years more or not.

I have a very kind letter from Prof. Janes in which he points out my remarks about degraded Buddhism. You also write that Dharmapala is very wroth about it. Mr. Dharmapala is a good man, and I love him; but it would be entirely wrong for him to go into fits over things Indian.

I am perfectly convinced that what they call modern Hinduism with all its ugliness is only stranded Buddhism. Let the Hindus understand this clearly, and then it would be easier for them to reject it without murmur. As for the ancient form which the Buddha preached, I have the greatest respect for it, as well as for His person. And you well know that we Hindus worship Him as an Incarnation. Neither is the Buddhism of Ceylon any good. My visit to Ceylon has entirely disillusioned me, and the only living people there are the Hindus. The Buddhists are all much Europeanised — even Mr. Dharmapala and his father had European names, which they have since changed. The only respect the Buddhists pay to their great tenet of non-killing is by opening "butcher-stalls" in every place! And the priests encourage this. The real Buddhism, I once thought, would yet do much good. But I have given up the idea entirely, and I clearly see the reason why Buddhism was driven out of India, and we will only be too glad if the Ceylonese carry off the remnant of this religion with its hideous idols and licentious rites.

About the Theosophists, you must remember first that in India Theosophists and Buddhists are non-entities. They publish a few papers and make a lot of splash and try to catch Occidental ears. . .

I was one man in America and another here. Here the whole nation is looking upon me as their authority — there I was a much reviled preacher. Here Princes draw my carriage, there I would not be admitted to a decent hotel. My utterances here, therefore, must be for the good of the race, my people — however unpleasant they might appear to a few. Acceptance, love, toleration for everything sincere and honest — but never for hypocrisy. The Theosophists tried to fawn upon and flatter me as I am the authority now in India, and therefore it was necessary for me to stop my work giving any sanction to their humbugs, by a few bold, decisive words; and the thing is done. I am very glad. If my health had permitted, I would have cleared India by this time of these upstart humbugs, at least tried my best.... Let me tell you that India is already Ramakrishna's and for a purified Hinduism I have organised my work here a bit.

Yours,
Vivekananda.

XL — SHUDDHANANDA

ALMORA,
11th July, 1897,

MY DEAR SHUDDHANANDA,

I was very glad to receive your last report. I have very little criticism to make except that you ought to write a bit more legibly.

I am quite satisfied with the work done so far, but it must be pushed forward. I have not learnt as yet of the suggestion I made before as to getting a set of chemical and physical apparatus and starting classes in elementary and experimental Chemistry and Physics, especially in Physiology.

What about the other suggestion of buying sets of all the scientific books that have been translated into Bengali?

It now seems to me that there must at least be three Mahantas (heads) elected at a time — one to direct the business part, one the experimental, the other the intellectual part.

The difficulty is to get the director of education. Brahmananda and Turiyananda may well fill the other two. Of visitors I am sorry to learn that you are only getting Babus from Calcutta. They are no good. What we want are brave young men who will work, not tomfools.

Ask Brahmananda to write to both Abhedananda and Saradananda to send weekly reports to the Math without fail, also to send Bengali articles and notes for the would-be paper. Is G. C. Ghosh getting up things for the paper? Work on with a will and be ready.

Akhandananda is working wonderfully at Mahula, but the system is not good. It seems they are frittering away their energies in one little village and that only doling out rice. I do not hear that any preaching has been done along with this helping. All the wealth of the world cannot help one little Indian village if the people are not taught to help themselves. Our work should be mainly educational, both moral and intellectual. I have not learnt anything abut it — only so many beggars are helped! Ask Brahmananda to open centres in different districts so as to cover the largest space with our small means.

And then, so far it seems to have been ineffectual, for they have not succeeded in rousing the people of the place to start societies to educate the people, so that they may learn to be self-reliant, frugal, and not given to marrying, and thus save themselves from future famine. Charity opens the heart, but work on through that wedge.

The easiest way is to take a hut — make it a temple of Guru Maharaj! Let the poor come here to be helped, also to worship. Let there be Kathâ (Puranic recitals) morning and evening there — through that you may teach all you want to teach the people. By degrees the people will be interested. They will keep up the temple themselves; maybe the hut temple will evolve into a great institution in a few years. Let those that go to relief-work first select a central spot in each district and start such a hut-temple, from which all our little work is to proceed.

Even the greatest fool can accomplish a task if it be after his heart. But the intelligent man is he who can convert every work into one that suits his taste. No work is petty. Everything in this world is like a banyan-seed, which, though appearing tiny as a mustard-seed, has yet the gigantic banyan tree latent within it. He indeed is intelligent who notices this and succeeds in making all work truly great. *This paragraph only is translated from Bengali.*

Moreover, they have to see that cheats do not get the food of the deserving. India is full of lazy rogues, and curious, they never die of hunger, they always get something. Ask Brahmananda to write this to everyone in relief-work — they must not be allowed to spend money to no good. We want the greatest possible good work permanent from the least outlay.

Now you see you must try to think out original ideas — else, as soon as I die, the whole thing will tumble to pieces. For example, you hold a meeting to consider, "How we can reap the best permanent results out of the small means at our disposal." Let all have notice a few days before and let each suggest something and discuss all the suggestions, criticising them; and then send me a report.

Lastly, you must remember I expect more from my children than from my brethren. I want each one of my children to be a hundred times greater than I could ever be. Everyone of you must be a giant — must, that is my word. Obedience, readiness, and love for the cause — if you have these three, nothing can hold you back.

With love and blessings,
Vivekananda.

XLI — MISS NOBLE

ALMORA,
23rd July, 1897.

MY DEAR MISS NOBLE,

Excuse these few lines. I shall write more fully as soon as I reach some place. I am on my way from the hills to the plains.

I do not understand what you mean by frankness without familiarity — I for one will give anything to get rid of the last lingering bit of Oriental formality in me and speak out like a child of nature. Oh, to live even for a day in the full light of freedom, to breathe the free air of simplicity! Is not that the highest purity?

In this world we work through fear of others, we talk through fear, we think through fear, alas! we are born in a land of enemies. Who is there who has been able to get rid of this feeling of fear, as if everyone is a spy set specially to watch him? And woe unto the man who pushes himself forward! Will it ever be a land of friends? Who knows? We can only try.

The work has already begun and at present famine-relief is the thing next to hand. Several centres have been opened and the work goes on; famine-relief, preaching, and a little teaching. As yet of course it is very very insignificant, the boys in training are being taken out as opportunity is offering itself. The sphere of action at present is Madras and Calcutta. Mr. Goodwin working in Madras. Also one has gone to Colombo. From the next week a monthly report of the whole work will be forwarded to you if it has not already reached you. I am away from the centre of work, so things go a little slow, you see; but the work is satisfactory on the whole.

You can do more work for us from England than by coming here. Lord bless you for your great self-sacrifice for the poor Indians.

I entirely agree with you that the work in England will look up when I am there. But all the same it is not proper to leave India before the machine is moving at some rate and I am sure that there are many to guide it in my absence. That will be done in a few months. "God willing", as the Mussulmans say. One of my best workers is now in England, the Raja of Khetri. I expect him soon in India, and he will be of great service to me no doubt.

With everlasting love and blessings,

Yours,
Vivekananda.

XLII — MISS NOBLE

ALMORA,
29th July, 1897.

MY DEAR MISS NOBLE,

A letter from Sturdy reached me yesterday, informing me that you are determined to come to India and see things with your own eyes. I replied to that yesterday, but what I learnt from Miss Muller about your plans makes this further note necessary, and it is better that it should be direct.

Let me tell you frankly that I am now convinced that you have a great future in the work for India. What was wanted was not a man, but a woman — a real lioness — to work for the Indians, women specially.

India cannot yet produce great women, she must borrow them from other nations. Your education, sincerity, purity, immense love, determination, and above all, the Celtic blood make you just the woman wanted.

Yet the difficulties are many. You cannot form any idea of misery, the superstition, and the slavery that are here. You will be in the midst of a mass of half-naked men and women with quaint ideas of caste and isolation, shunning the white skin through fear or hatred and hated by them intensely. On the other hand, you will be looked upon by the white as a crank, and every one of your movements will be watched with suspicion.

Then the climate is fearfully hot; our winter in most places being like your summer, and in the south it is always blazing.

Not one European comfort is to be had in places out of the cities. If in spite of all this, you dare venture into the work, you are welcome, a hundred times welcome. As for me, I am nobody here as elsewhere, but what little influence I have shall be devoted to your service.

You must think well before you plunge in; and after work, if you fail in this or get disgusted, on my part I promise you, I will stand by you unto death whether you work for India or not, whether you give up Vedanta or remain in it. "The tusks of the elephant come out, but never go back"; so are the words of a man never retracted. I promise you that. Again, I must give you a bit of warning. You must stand on your own feet and not be under the wings of Miss Muller or anybody else. Miss Muller is a good lady in her own way, but unfortunately it got into her head, when she was a girl, that she was a born leader and that no other qualifications were necessary to move world but money! This idea is coming on the surface again and again in spite of herself, and you will find it impossible to pull on with her in a few days. She now intends to take a house in Calcutta for herself and yourself and other European or American friends who may come.

It is very kind and good of her, but her Lady Abbess plan will never be carried out for two reasons — her violent temper and overbearing conduct, and her awfully vacillating mind. Friendship with many is best at a distance, and everything goes well with the person who stands on his own feet.

Mrs. Sevier is a jewel of a lady — so good, so kind! The Seviers are the only English people who do not hate the natives, Sturdy not excepted. Mr. and Mrs. Sevier are the only persons who did not come to patronise us, but they have no fixed plans yet. When you come, you may get them to work with you, and that will be really helpful to them and to you. But after all it is absolutely necessary to stand on one's own feet.

I learn from America that two friends of mine, Mrs. Ole Bull of Boston and Miss MacLeod, are coming on a visit to India this autumn. Miss MacLeod you already know in London, that Paris-dressed young American lady; Mrs. Ole Bull is about fifty and has been a kind friend to me in America. I may suggest that your joining the party may while away the tedium of the journey, as they also are coming by way of Europe.

I am glad to receive a note at least from Sturdy after long. But it was so stiff and cold. It seems he is disappointed at the collapse of the London work.

With everlasting love,

Yours ever in the Lord,
Vivekananda.

XLIII — MADAM

Translated from Bengali

BELUR MATH,
16th April, 1899.

DEAR MADAM (Shrimati Sarala Ghosal, B. A.),

Very glad to receive your kind note. If by the sacrifice of some specially cherished object of either myself or my brother-disciples many pure and genuinely patriotic souls come forward to help our cause, rest assured, we will not hesitate in the least to make that sacrifice nor shed a tear-drop — you will see this verified in action. But up till now I have seen nobody coming forward to assist in this way. Only some have wished to put their own hobby in place of ours — that is all. If it really help our country or humanity — not to speak of giving up Guru-worship — believe me, we are prepared to commit any dire iniquity and suffer the eternal damnation of the Christians. But my hairs have turned grey since I began the study of man. This world is a most trying place, and it is long since I have taken to wandering with the lantern of the Grecian Philosopher in hand. A popular song my Master often used to sing comes to my mind:

"He who's a man after one's heart

Betrays himself by his very looks.

Rare indeed is such a one!

He's a man of aesthetic perceptions

Who treads a path contrary to others."

This much from my side. Please know that not one word of it is exaggerated — which you will find to be actually the case. But then I have some doubts about those patriotic souls who can join with us if only we give up the worship of the Guru. Well, if, as they pose, they are indeed panting and struggling so much — almost to the point of dissolution from their body — to serve the country, how can the single accident of Guru-worship stop everything!

This impetuous river with rolling waves which bade fair to sweep away whole hills and mountains — was a bit of Guru-worship sufficient to turn it back to the Himalayas! I put it to you, do you think anything great will come of such patriotism, or any substantial good proceed from such assistance? It is for you to say; I can make nothing out of it. For a thirsty man to weigh so much the merits of water, or for a man about to die of hunger to cogitate so much and turn up his nose at the food presented! Well, people have strange ways of thinking. I, for one, am inclined to think that those people were best in a glass-case; the more they keep away from actual work, the better.

"Love stops not for questions of birth.

Nor the hungry man for stale food."

This is what I know. But I may be wholly mistaken. Well, if this trifle of Guru-worship sticks in one's throat to choke one to death, we had better extricate him from this predicament.

However, I have a great longing to talk over these points with you in detail. For talking these things over, affliction and death have given me leave till now, and I hope they will do so yet.

May all your wishes be fulfilled in this New Year!

Yours sincerely,
Vivekananda.

XLIV — STURDY

C/O F. H. LEGGETT,
21 WEST THIRTY-FOURTH STREET
NEW YORK
Nov., 1899.

MY DEAR STURDY,

This is not to defend my conduct. Words cannot wipe off the evils I have done, nor any censor stop from working the good deeds, if any.

For the last few months I have been hearing so much of the luxuries I was given to enjoy by the people of the West — luxuries which the hypocrite myself has been enjoying, although preaching renunciation all the while: luxuries, the enjoyment of which has been the great stumbling-block in my way, in England at least. I nearly hypnotised myself into the belief that there has at least been a little oasis in the dreary desert of my life, a little spot of light in one whole life of misery and gloom; one moment of relaxation in a life of hard work and harder curses — even that oasis, that spot, that moment was only one of sense-enjoyment!!

I was glad, I blessed a hundred times a day those that had helped me to get it, when, lo, your last letter comes like a thunderclap, and the dream is vanished. I begin to disbelieve your criticisms — have little faith left in all this talk of luxuries and enjoyments and other visions memory calls up. These I state. Hope you will send it round to friends, if you think fit, and correct me where I am wrong.

I remember your place at Reading, where I was fed with boiled cabbage and potatoes and boiled rice and boiled lentils, three times a day, with your wife's curses for sauce all the time. I do not remember your giving me any cigar to smoke — shilling or penny ones. Nor do I remember myself as complaining of either the food or your wife's incessant curses, though I lived as a thief, shaking through fear all the time, and working every day for you.

The next memory is of the house on St. George's Road — you and Miss Muller at the head. My poor brother was ill there and Miss Müller drove him away. There too I don't remember to have had any luxuries as to food or drink or bed or even the room given to me.

The next was Miss Müller's place. Though she has been very kind to me, I was living on nuts and fruits. The next memory is that of the black hole of London where I had to work almost day and night and cook the meals oft-times for five or six, and most nights with a bite of bread and butter.

I remember Mrs. Sturdy giving me a dinner and a night's lodging in her place, and then the next day criticising the black savage — so dirty and smoking all over the house.

With the exception of Capt. and Mrs. Sevier, I do not remember even one piece of rag as big as a handkerchief I got from England. On the other hand, the incessant demand on my body and mind in England is the cause of my breakdown in health. This was all you English people gave me, whilst working me to death; and now I am cursed for the luxuries I lived in!! Whosoever of you have given me a coat? Whosoever a cigar? Whosoever a bit of fish or flesh? Whosoever of you dare say I asked food or drink or smoke or dress or money from you? Ask, Sturdy, ask for God's sake, ask your friends, and first ask your own "God within who never sleeps."

You have given me money for my work. Every penny of it is there. Before your eyes I sent my brother away, perhaps to his death; and I would not give him a farthing of the money which was not my private property.

On the other hand, I remember in England Capt. and Mrs. Sevier, who have clad me when I was cold, nursed me better than my own mother would have, borne with me in my weakness, my trials; and they have nothing but blessings for me. And that Mrs. Sevier, because she did not care for honours, has the worship of thousands today; and when she is dead millions will remember her as one of the great benefactresses of the poor Indians. And they never cursed me for my luxuries, though they are ready to give me luxuries, if I need or wish.

I need not tell you of Mrs. Bull, Miss MacLeod, Mr. and Mrs. Leggett. You know their love and kindness for me; and Mrs. Bull and Miss MacLeod have been to our country, moved and lived with us as no foreigner ever did, roughing it all, and they do not ever curse me and my luxuries either; they will be only too glad to have me eat well and smoke dollar cigars if I wish. And there Leggetts and Bulls were the people whose bread whose money bought my smokes and several times paid my rent, whilst I was killing myself for your people, when you were taking my pound of flesh for the dirty hole and starvation and reserving all this accusation of luxury.

"The clouds of autumn make great noise but send no rain; The clouds of the rainy season without a word flood the earth."

See Sturdy, those that have helped or are still

helping have no criticism, no curses: it is only those who do nothing, who only come to grind their own axes, that curse, that criticise. That such worthless, heartless, selfish, rubbish criticise, is the greatest blessing that can come to me. I want nothing so much in life as to be miles off from these extremely selfish axe-grinders.

Talking of luxuries! Take these critics up one after the other — It is all flesh, all flesh and no spirit anywhere. Thank God, they come out sooner or later in their true colours. And you advise me to regulate my conduct, my work, according to the desires of such heartless, selfish persons, and are at your wit's end because I do not!

As to my Gurubhais (brother-disciples), they do nothing but what I insist on their doing. If they have shown any selfishness anywhere, that is because of my ordering them, not what they would do themselves.

Would you like your children put into that dark hole you got for me in London, made to work to death, and almost starved all the time? Would Mrs. Sturdy like that? They are Sannyasins, and that means, no Sannyasin should unnecessarily throw away his life or undertake unnecessary hardship.

In undergoing all this hardship in the West we have been only breaking the rules of Sannyasa. They are my brothers, my children. I do not want them to die in holes for my sake. I don't, by all that is good and true I don't, want them starved and worked and cursed for all their pains.

A word more. I shall be very glad if you can point out to me where I have preached torturing the flesh. As for the Shâstras (scriptures), I shall be only too glad if a Shâstri (Pundit) dares oppose us with the rules of life laid down for Sannyasins and Paramahamsas.

Well, Sturdy, my heart aches. I understand it all. I know what you are in — you are in the clutches of people who want to use you. I don't mean your wife. She is too simple to be dangerous. But, my poor boy, you have got the flesh-smell — a little money — and vultures are around. Such is life.

You said a lot about ancient India. That India still lives, Sturdy, is not dead, and that living India dares even today to deliver her message without fear or favour of the rich, without fear of anybody's opinion, either in the land where her feet are in chains or in the very face of those who hold the end of the chain, her rulers. That India still lives, Sturdy, India of undying love, of everlasting faithfulness, the unchangeable, not only in manners and customs, but also in love, in faith, in friendship. And I, the least of that India's children, love you, Sturdy, with Indian love, and would any day give up a thousand bodies to help you out of this delusion.

Ever yours,
Vivekananda.

XLV — MRS. LEGGETT

CHICAGO,
26th Nov., 1899.

MY DEAR MRS. LEGGETT,

Many, many thanks for all your kindness and especially the kind note. I am going to start from Chicago on Thursday next, and got the ticket and berth ready for that day.

Miss Noble is doing very well here, and working her way out. I saw Alberta the other day. She is enjoying every minute of her stay here and is very happy. Miss Adams (Jane Adams), as ever is an angel.

I shall wire to Joe Joe before I start and read all night.

With all love to Mr. Leggett and yourself,

Ever yours affectionately,
Vivekananda.

XLVI — MOTHER

CHICAGO,
30th Nov., 1899.

MY DEAR MOTHER, (Mrs. Leggett.)

Nothing new — except Madame Calvé's visit. She is a great woman. I wish I saw more of her. It is a grand sight to see a giant pine struggling against a cyclone. Is it not?

I leave here tonight. These lines in haste as A__ is waiting. Mrs. Adams is kind as usual. Margot doing splendidly. Will write more from California.

With all love to Frankincense,

Ever your son,
Vivekananda.

XLVII — MARGOT

LOS ANGELES,
6th Dec., 1899.

DEAR MARGOT,

Your sixth has arrived, but with it yet no change in my fortune. Would change be any good, do you think? Some people are made that way, to love being miserable. If I did not break my heart over people I was born amongst, I would do it for somebody else. I am sure of that. This is the way of some, I am coming to see it. We are all after happiness, true, but that some are only happy in being unhappy — queer, is it not? There is no harm in it either, except that happiness and unhappiness are both infectious. Ingersoll said once that if he were God, he would make health catching, instead of disease, little dreaming that health is quite as catching as disease, if not more! That is the only danger. No harm in the world in my being happy, in being miserable, but others must not catch it. This is the great fact. No sooner a prophet feels miserable for the state of man than he sours his face, beats his breast, and calls upon everyone to drink tartaric acid, munch charcoal, sit upon a dung-heap covered with ashes, and speak only in groans and tears! — I find they all have been wanting. Yes, they have. If you are really ready to take the world's burden, take it by all means. But do not let us hear your groans and curses. Do not frighten us with your sufferings, so that we came to feel we were better off with our own burdens. The man who really takes the burden blesses the world and goes his own way. He has not a word of condemnation, a word of criticism, not because there was no evil but that he has taken it on his own shoulders willingly, voluntarily. It is the Saviour who should "go his way rejoicing, and not the saved".

This is the only light I have caught this morning. This is enough if it has come to live with me and permeate my life.

Come ye that are heavy laden and lay all your burden on me, and then do whatever you like and be happy and forget that I ever existed.

Ever with love,

Your father,
Vivekananda.

XLVIII — MOTHER

1719 TURK STREET,
SAN FRANCISCO,
17th March, 1900.

MY DEAR MOTHER (Mrs. Leggett.),

So glad to get your nice letter. Well, you may be sure I am keeping in touch with my friends. Yet a delay may sometimes cause nervousness.

Dr. and Mrs. Hiller returned to the city, much benefited, as they declare, by Mrs. Melton's rubbings. As for me, I have got several huge red patches on my chest. What materialises later on as to complete recovery, I will let you know. Of course, my case is such that it will take time to come round by itself.

So thankful to you and to Mrs. Adams for the kindness. I will surely go and call on them in Chicago.

How are things going on with you? I have been following the "Put up or shut up" plan here, and so far it has not proved bad. Mrs. Hansborough, the second of the three sisters, is here, and she is working, working, working — to help me. Lord bless their hearts. The three sisters are three angels, are they not? Seeing such souls here and there repays for all the nonsense of this life.

Well, all blessings to you for ever is my prayer. You are one of the angels also, say I.

With love to Miss Kate,

Ever your son,
Vivekananda.

PS. How is the "Mother's child"?

How is Miss Spencer? All love to her. You know already I am a very bad correspondent, but the heart never fails. Tell this to Miss Spencer.

IL — MOTHER

1719 TURK STREET,
SAN FRANCISCO,
17th March, 1900.

DEAR MOTHER (Mrs. Leggett.),

I had a letter from Joe asking me to send my signature on four slips of paper, so that Mr. Leggett may put my money in the bank for me. As I cannot possibly reach her in time, I send the slips to you.

I am getting better in health and doing financially something. I am quite satisfied. I am not at all sorry that more people did not respond to your call. I knew they would not. But I am eternally thankful to you for all your kindness. May all blessings follow you and yours for ever.

It is better that my mail be sent to 1231 Pine Street, C/o the Home of Truth. For though I be moving about, that place is a permanent establishment, and the people there are very kind to me.

I am so glad to learn that you are very well now. Mrs. Melton has left Los Angeles — I am informed by Mrs. Blodgett. Has she gone to New York? Dr. and Mrs. Hiller came back to San Francisco day before yesterday. They declare themselves very much helped by Mrs. Melton. Mrs. Hiller expects to get completely cured in a short time.

I had a number of lectures here already and in Oakland. The Oakland lectures paid well. The first week in San Francisco was not paying, this week is. Hope the next week will pay also. I am so glad to hear the nice arrangement made by Mr. Leggett for the Vedanta Society. He is so good.

With all love,

Yours,
Vivekananda.

PS. Do you know anything about Turiyananda? Has he got completely cured?

L — MOTHER

1719 TURK STREET,
SAN FRANCISCO,
7th April, 1900.

DEAR MOTHER (Mrs. Leggett.),

Accept my congratulations for the news of the cause of the wound being completely removed. I have no doubt of your being perfectly cured this time.

Your very kind note cheered me a good deal. I do not mind at all whether people come round to help me or not; I am becoming calm and less worried.

Kindly convey my best love to Mrs. Melton. I am sure to recover in the long run. My health has been improving in the main, though there are occasional relapses. Each relapse becoming less, both in tone and in time.

It is just like you to have Turiyananda and Siri treated. The Lord has blessed you for your great heart. May all blessings ever follow you and yours.

It is perfectly true that I should go to France and work on French. I hope to reach France in July or earlier. Mother knows. May all good ever follow you, is the constant prayer of

Your son,
Vivekananda.

LI — MR. LEGGETT

17th April, 1900.

MY DEAR MR. LEGGETT,

Herewith I send the executed Will to you. It has been executed as desired by her, and of course, as usual, I am requesting you for the trouble of taking charge of it.

You and yours have been so uniformly kind to me. But you know, dear friend, it is human nature to ask for more favours (now that they have come) where it gets from.

I am only a man, your child.

I am so sorry A__ has made disturbances. He does that now and then, at least used to. I do not venture to meddle, for fear of creating more trouble. You know how to manage him best. By the time you receive this letter, I will be off from San Francisco. Will you kindly send my Indian mail C/o Mrs. Hale, 10 Aster Street, Chicago, and to Margot in the same place? Margot writes very thankfully of your gift of a thousand dollars for her school.

May all blessings ever follow you and yours for your uniform kindness to me and mine, is the constant prayer of

Yours affectionately,
Vivekananda.

PS. I am so glad to learn that Mrs. Leggett has already recovered.

LII — AUNT ROXY

2nd May, 1900.

DEAR AUNT ROXY, (Mrs. Blodgett of Los Angeles),

Your very, very kind letter came. I am down again with nerves and fever, after six months of hard work. However, I found out that my kidneys and heart are as good as ever. I am going to take a few days' rest in the country and then start for Chicago.

I have just written to Mrs. Milward Adams and also have given an introduction to my daughter, Miss Noble, to go and call upon Mrs. Adams and give her all information she wants about the work.

Well, dear good mother, may all blessings attend you and peace. I just want a bit of peace badly — pray for me. With love to Kate,

Ever your son,
Vivekananda.

PS. Love to Miss Spencer — the Basaquisitz(?), Mrs. S__, and the other friends.

A heap of loving pats on the head to Tricks.

LIII — ALBERTA

PERROS GUIREC
BERTAGNE,
22nd September, 1900.

To Miss Alberta Sturges on her 23rd birthday

> The mother's heart, the hero's will,
> The softest flower's sweetest feel;
> The charm and force that ever sway
> The altar fire's flaming play;
> The strength that leads, in love obeys;
> Far-reaching dreams, and patient ways,
> Eternal faith in Self, in all
> The sight Divine in great in small;

All these, and more than I could see
Today may "Mother" grant to thee.

> Ever yours with love and blessings,
> Vivekananda.

DEAR ALBERTA,

This little poem is for your birthday. It is not good, but it has all my love. I am sure, therefore, you will like it.

Will you kindly send a copy each of the pamphlets there to madame Besnard, Clairoix, Bres Compiegne, Oise, and oblige?

> Your well-wisher,
> Vivekananda.

Discovery Publisher is a multimedia publisher whose mission is to inspire and support personal transformation, spiritual growth and awakening. We strive with every title to preserve the essential wisdom of the author, spiritual teacher, thinker, healer, and visionary artist.

www.ingramcontent.com/pod-product-compliance
Lightning Source LLC
Chambersburg PA
CBHW080241170426
43192CB00014BA/2526